*Recovering Ancestors in
Anthropological Traditions*

Histories of Anthropology Annual

Recovering Ancestors in Anthropological Traditions

Histories of Anthropology Annual, Volume 15

EDITED BY REGNA DARNELL
AND FREDERIC W. GLEACH

University of Nebraska Press | Lincoln

Chapter 9 was originally published in *Corpus, Archivos virtuales de la alteridad americana,* June 28, 2016.

Chapters 10–17 are used by permission of Grant Arndt.

The University of Nebraska Press is part of a land-grant institution with campuses and programs on the past, present, and future homelands of the Pawnee, Ponca, Otoe-Missouria, Omaha, Dakota, Lakota, Kaw, Cheyenne, and Arapaho Peoples, as well as those of the relocated Ho-Chunk, Sac and Fox, and Iowa Peoples.

∞

Publication of this work was assisted by the Murray-Hong Family Trust, to honor and sustain the distinguished legacy of Stephen O. Murray in the History of Anthropology at the University of Nebraska Press.

For customers in the EU with safety/GPSR concerns, contact:
gpsr@mare-nostrum.co.uk
Mare Nostrum Group BV
Mauritskade 21D
1091 GC Amsterdam
The Netherlands

Library of Congress Control Number: 2025004969

Set in Arno Pro by A. Shahan

CONTENTS

ILLUSTRATIONS

Figures

Table

Editors' Introduction

Each volume of *Histories of Anthropology Annual* presents a stand-alone collection of essays that reflect a theme or set of themes of concern to contemporary anthropologists, historians, and multiple disciplinary and community-based others. This is not a structured plan, but a consequence of scholarship in the moment: Rather than soliciting contributions around a set theme, we encourage and look for scholarship broadly and generally located in the realm of disciplinary history, and then we see what themes are found in the works submitted. The juxtapositions invite readers to compare perspectives and explore particular disciplinary and theoretical traditions. At the same time, we aspire to build a critical mass of scholarship in which each volume extends the definition of what anthropology's history might encompass and expands the audience for this body of work. The choice of *histories* in the plural is a self-conscious claim that history exists only when interpretations are imposed on primary data of various kinds.

Volume 15 in the series, *Recovering Ancestors in Anthropological Traditions*, brings together a collection of essays that individually focus on specific individuals and national developments, but together build toward an understanding of the discipline as a global, international set of approaches and methods, distinct yet interrelated. Much like the cultures that anthropologists study in the field, the discipline is messy, diverse, and sometimes internally contradictory, challenging if not impossible to grasp in its entirety. Each tradition articulates with others to create a network of practitioners, institutions, and interpretations, and historical investigations may take a variety of approaches and work at different levels of analysis. The archives and oral traditions of the discipline constitute the primary data to be organized and interpreted.

In chapter 1, Dmitry V. Arzyutov takes the study of Arctic Samoyedic-language legends of underground-dwelling dwarfs as a case to examine the history of ethnographic interpretations and developing disciplines. Those narratives wove into both Indigenous and scholarly analytical schemas of Siberian—and Soviet—ethnogenesis. The study of these narratives is traced through the nineteenth and twentieth centuries, placed in chronological and evolutionary frameworks, and taken up in arguments of authenticity. These interpretations were in dialogue with North American and other scholarship on indigeneity in the Soviet era, particularly that of Franz Boas and Aleš Hrdlička, but the epistemic conceptualization of Indigenous authenticity proved quite stable even as political structures changed.

Anna Engelking expands our understanding of the interconnections of Polish and British academic traditions in chapter 2 by turning to local manifestations of British functionalism in the field. The first ethnography of a European village was carried out by Józef Obrębski, who studied with Malinowski during three years as a Rockefeller Foundation fellow in London. While preparing his PhD under Malinowski he carried out fieldwork in Macedonia, but his results never saw publication, which some attributed to his perfectionism. He left Poland after the war and since 1948 lived in the United States, where he published some of his more recent material in the 1960s, but his village fieldwork research remained in manuscript form when he died at the age of sixty-two. The unpublished materials are held at the University of Massachusetts–Amherst. Engelking argues persuasively for the need to bring these materials into contemporary focus on issues of importance to Obrębski and allow anthropologists to consider his work as part of an ongoing process.

In chapter 3, John David Smith and Sylvia Angelica Smith turn to another neglected ancestor, German ethnologist Felix von Luschan, who conducted research on Black Americans and race with his wife, Emma von Hochstetter. In consultation with Booker T. Washington and W. E. B. Du Bois, the couple studied and measured hundreds of families over a few months in early 1915, publishing the results later that year. The methods deployed were already becoming obsolete, and even though their work was written with the intent to correct biases, it exhibited outmoded and sometimes condescending ethnocentrism and judgment. Nevertheless, the project can be seen as part of the antiracist movement.

Patrícia Ferraz de Matos, in the first of her essays included here (chapter 4), describes the institutional context for the development of the discipline of academic anthropology at the University of Coimbra. Anthropology emerged in Portugal in the nineteenth century, and by the early twentieth century the museum and laboratory at Coimbra were active. Institutionalization included both university programs and research-focused societies. A museological and educational dimension was central in much of this development, and there was also a public health dimension, albeit framed through eugenics. In her second essay (chapter 5), she examines the career of a key figure in this institutional history, Mendes Correia, using the case of a specific individual to clarify how the general patterns explored in her first essay worked on the ground, with motive and aspiration as driving forces in that development. Correia had broad interests in science and history, and he saw anthropology (including archaeology) as a practical field that could help educate and guide action in many areas. Relatedly, he also worked in politics, seeking to put into practice his understandings, particularly for the benefit of underprivileged classes—although he must be seen as a nationalist as well. We rarely include two chapters by the same author in a single volume, but these are closely interrelated, taking different focuses to better understand the development and nature of anthropology in Portugal.

In chapter 6, Leila Monaghan draws in linguistic anthropology in its North American quadratic subdisciplinarity, expanding our sense structure of the forgotten principals of the debates about the nature and origin of American Indian languages. Focusing on John Wesley Powell and John DeWitt Clinton Atkins, Monaghan considers their writing on Native American language in the historical and political contexts of the late nineteenth century. Both were influenced by their locations, by working in the U.S. federal government, and by the dominance of evolutionary frameworks, all of which shaped their studies of language to include significance in such realms as citizenship and nation status, individualism, and social organization. This is in contrast to Franz Boas's later, more "purely" linguistic *Handbook of American Indian Languages*. Sadly, Professor Monaghan passed away while this volume was in preparation, and we thank her husband, Robert McGovern, for allowing us to keep this contribution in the book.

James M. Nyce looks at the literary and poetic output of anthropologist and linguist Edward Sapir between 1917 and 1922 in chapter 7, examining these works in relation to Sapir's ethnography rather than solely to separate genres. Taking the poem and prose pieces about Tom, Sapir's Nootka informant, in conversation with Sapir's 1917 paper on literary technique, Nyce argues that Sapir was exploring a set of issues using different tools in different ways. The "writing culture" movement took up one set of issues around representation, but Nyce questions what more can and should be done: Can text-based representational strategies be overcome? Can we reduce the divide between the logical, intelligible, lifelike, and the real?

Continuing a focus on Edward Sapir in chapter 8, Richard J. Preston examines his late-career collaborations with psychiatrist Harry Stack Sullivan and political scientist Harold Lasswell. Sapir was a multifaceted thinker, and followers have often focused on just one strand in characterizing his work and imagining what he might have produced had he lived longer. These collaborations highlight Sapir's long-term interest in the interplay of the individual/personality/psychiatric and the collective/culture/sociological, suggesting that this large-scale structure may yet be unattainable but nevertheless remains important and of interest.

In chapter 9, Sandra Tolosa and Lena Dávila consider the development of the Museum of Ethnography in Argentina in the early twentieth century and the human remains accessioned and studied there. Founded to encompass ethnographic, archaeological, and physical anthropological approaches to documenting humankind, the museum sought human skeletal remains as exemplars. The nation's military expansion through Indigenous territories in the late nineteenth and early twentieth centuries provided a potential source, creating an alliance between the museum and the military forces, whose repressive action focused on the removal of communities that the museum was committed to study. This case resonates clearly with others that have been documented in the United States and elsewhere, calling for engagement with today's communities and the return of ancestral human remains.

The remainder of this volume is a special section focusing on the legacy of Nancy Oestreich Lurie, particularly in the domain of applied anthropology. Chapter 10, Larry Nesper's introduction to the essays he edited with Grant Arndt, offers an overview of this collection, which goes beyond the scope or focus of individual contributors as each approaches Lurie's life and work from a different angle. The absence of a published synthesis of her work has muted its visibility for contemporary readers, and the many facets of Nancy Lurie emerge here from a variety of intersecting positions. Her prominence ranged from the global, as the president of the American Anthropological Association, to the local, as the curator of anthropology at the Milwaukee Public Museum for twenty years. Nesper explains how Ada Deer, also a complex border crosser, as chair of American Indian studies, encouraged him to seek an honorary doctorate for Lurie. Among the "watershed historic moments" of her career, Lurie honored and celebrated "the differences between the tribal cultures of the state," the particular needs of the Menominee Tribe, and the Ho-Chunk Tribe's reorganization.

In chapter 11, Judy Daubenmier explores the working relationships between Lurie and Sol Tax, and Grant Arndt considers her work with the Ho-Chunk through tribal reorganization in the context of Tax's action anthropology in chapter 12. Patrick J. Jung examines Lurie's documentary research in chapter 13, and Alice B. Kehoe and Dawn Scher Thomae focus on her museum exhibits and the importance of "hanging out with Indian people" in chapter 14. Chapter 15 is an introduction by Joshua Smith to Lurie's hitherto unpublished memorandum on applied anthropology, which is included as chapter 16. This is a manifesto to anthropology as she understood it, highlighting the importance of bringing implicit synthesis back to the attention of contemporary readers. Finally, in chapter 17, Patrick Jung provides the most complete bibliography of Nancy Oestreich Lurie to date, a meticulously prepared resource for contemporary researchers. It is a living document that users are encouraged to supplement by adding materials from their particular points of intersection with Lurie's life and work.

Histories of Anthropology Annual owes much to the legacy of our late friend and colleague Stephen O. Murray, who served on the editorial board from the inception of the series in 2004. He was also coeditor of the University of Nebraska's Critical Studies in the History of Anthropology, from the planning stages preceding the first publication to his death in August 2019. Steve personified the ethos underlying the history of anthropology as a prominent cluster of University of Nebraska PRESS publications, which also includes the Franz Boas Papers series. His career developed at the institutional margins of several academic disciplines and activist discourses, but his distinctive voice has long been and will remain at the center of anthropology's history. Long-term sustainability of the series is supported by an endowment from the Murray-Hong Family Trust, which continues to be administered by Keelung Hong in accordance with Steve's wishes. We also want to acknowledge the editorial contributions of Nathan Dawthorne, who helped with preparing the manuscript and keeping us organized through professional transitions and pandemic upheaval.

REGNA DARNELL

FREDERIC W. GLEACH

*Recovering Ancestors in
Anthropological Traditions*

1

Rooting in the Subterranean

Underground Dwellers in Northern Indigenous Narratives
and Metropolitan Anthropological Theories

DMITRY V. ARZYUTOV

> A detective investigates everything that stands out on the crime scene
> as a revelatory sign of the criminal's voluntary or involuntary work,
> the hunter follows the trace of the game that reflects the activity and
> the path taken by the animals he is tracking, the historian discovers
> ancient civilizations on the horizons of our world from vestiges of their
> existence. Everything lines up in order in a world where each thing
> reveals the other or is revealed with regards to it.
>
> —Emmanuel Lévinas, *Humanism of the Other*

To what extent do Indigenous narratives from Siberia recorded by anthropologists move beyond the borders of national disciplines and engage in a more transnational conversation?[1] To answer this question, I explore how Indigenous narratives and material artifacts intersect with academic ideologies and frameworks, resulting in the emergence of the concept of Indigenous ethnohistory. For this purpose, I focus on discussions in Russian/Soviet ethnography regarding Indigenous origins, also known as ethnogenesis (*étnogenez*), ethnic history (*étnicheskaia istoriia*), or sometimes paleoethnology (*paleoétnologiia*).[2]

While critically examining Soviet circumpolar ethnography today, scholars may notice two distinct directions in its development. On one hand, Soviet ethnographers assisted the state in its aim to construct the "new [Soviet] way of living" and delineate ethnic borders in the North, thereby discrediting Indigenous groups as peoples without history. On the other hand, they demonstrated a profound interest in the relatively understudied history of Indigenous peoples (see Anderson 2000, 81–90). On closer examination, however, these appear surprisingly intertwined, shaping complex epistemologies that I attempt to elucidate in this chapter. One such "invisible" connection between Soviet ethnography and Arctic Indigenous peoples was the subterranean world: narratives about underground dwellers—humanlike creatures known by different names—that many Indigenous communities share, and the way those stories (and the material artifacts assigned to them) have affected the development of anthropological theories, in particular the Soviet theory of ethnogenesis.

I argue that the narratives, in their vernacular forms and academic "translations," led to the construction of a peculiar concept of Indigeneity that dealt with the stories about underground dwellers. Ethnographers' guides and interlocutors in the field shared narratives about people who used to inhabit their lands, and who continued to be present in their lives through both abandoned material (archaeological) artifacts and the stories of encounters with them, while scholars trained in the evolutionistic paradigm searched for the most ancient groups in Siberia, whose material traces might reveal the deeper history of the region. This idea of origin caused them to collaborate and conduct interdisciplinary studies where research objects of different natures might coalesce and be at the center of academic reflections. The intersection of these two approaches constituted the epistemic core of ethnogenesis as a dominant theoretical framework in Siberian ethnography. As I show in this chapter, local people and visiting scholars grew their roots in the subterranean, or in other words, they made the subterranean landscapes the "most" Indigenous on the northern Indigenous land.

One could argue that Siberian ethnogenesis, as a theoretical construct, bore similarities to that in North America (for critics of the Soviet notion of ethnogenesis, see Slezkine 1996; Anderson 2007). Despite the known entanglements of Boasian and early Soviet anthropology in the field of peopling the Americas (see Arzyutov 2020, 77–79; Arzyutov et al., forthcoming), these two anthropological traditions always remained quite distant, although they encountered each other many times throughout the twentieth century. The historical interest of the North American tradition lay in the identities formed through "a creative adaptation to a general history of violent changes . . . imposed during the historical expansion of colonial and national states in the Americas" (Hill 1996, 1). This made American ethnohistory a polyphonic field with diverse ways of narrating and writing about Indigenous historicities in relation to the history of colonization.

For Soviet ethnographers, research into ethnogenesis served as a means to construct rather paternalistic genealogies for defined ethnic groups. Simultaneously, this concept facilitated the crossing of boundaries between these groups and even countries to reconstruct their migration histories (see Arzyutov and Lukin 2023).[3] In this chapter, I demonstrate how, thanks to this controversial intersection, Soviet ethnographers employed fragments of Indigenous narratives, material artifacts, and partly environmental histories. This approach, to a certain extent, mirrored that of their field interlocutors, who recounted their past through folklore heroes, human-landscape interactions, and the value of surrounding material objects (see Nabokov 2002). However, unlike Soviet scholars, they tended not to narrate a comprehensive and unilinear history of the region. In other words, academic and Indigenous narratives were not separated and read independently; in fact, they still hold a mutual epistemic dependence produced under colonial inequalities. This brings me to the famous and provocative statement of Eric Wolf (1923–99): "The more ethnohistory we know, the more clearly 'their' history and 'our' history emerge as part of the same history" (1982, 19). Ironically, Soviet ethnographers in the 1920s suggested the same idea. Eurakhim (Iuriĭ) A. Kreinovich (1906–85) wrote in a letter to his supervisor, Karl Ia. Luks (1888–1932), in 1928, "We are not doing ethnography in the old sense of the word. All words that end in '-logy' or '-graphy' are bound up in that process or activity, call it what you like, that divides subject from object, 'us' (the scholar or researcher) from 'them' (the studied, our wards), who in the best instance we 'feel for.' We want to *erase* this line between subject and object, between us and them. . . . The objects of study must become subjects" (Grant 1995, 77).

Despite the similarity between Wolf's approach to historical entanglements and Kreinovich's idea of ethnopolitical object/subject unity, as well as their attempts to conceptualize the coproduction of knowledge in anthropology and history, these notions did not necessarily hold a uniform meaning for all groups of Siberian anthropologists across the seventy-year span of the Soviet era. Historical anthropologist of Central Asia Sergei Abashin has recently indicated that relations between the "center" and "periphery" in knowledge production was rather unusual for other impe-rial situations. Those "informal relationships between 'masters and natives', personal exchanges of skills and administrative support, and the creation of informal disciplinary and area studies coalitions with their own cor-porate interests . . . enabled Soviet ethnographic knowledge produced in Moscow and Leningrad to engage in constant dialogue with the inhabit-ants of, and experts from, the Soviet periphery, taking into account their interpretations and interests" (2024, 22). Accepting this, I nevertheless aim to show in my discussion of the history of anthropology from the field the way Russian anthropology relied on the Indigenous narratives, which not only legitimized the academic theories but also were the major actors in transnational and transdisciplinary dialogues of scholars.

In this chapter, I reflect on the role of the Samoyedic-language legends (Tundra Nenets *waql°* ~ *wal°* [Tapani Salminen 1998, 81, 525]) about dwarfs who retreated underground once Nenetses, a Samoyedic Indigenous group, came and occupied areas in the Russian Arctic, where they still reside.[4] I examine the epistemic effects these legends have produced. These dwarfs are known in various Tundra Nenets dialects as *Sʲix̌irtʲa* (eastern dialects) or *Sᷓrtʲa* (western and central dialects).[5] According to Tundra Nenets beliefs, the dwarfs have neither entirely disappeared nor died; instead, they continue to inhabit their subterranean landscapes and have become a certain Indigenous people among the Indigenous people. Occasionally, they make their presence known to reindeer herders through material traces left on the tundra ground, unexpected encounters with humanlike ghosts, and other means. One way Nenetses jest about their relationships with Sʲix̌irtʲa is by searching for family resemblances to those enigmatic dwarfs in their human neighbors' physical features.

Many generations of Arctic anthropologists who have worked among Nenetses, including myself, have heard these stories and documented them in field notes and publications (e.g., Khomich 1970; Vasil'ev 1970, 1979, 48). They usually tell us about a quite stable set of identifiers asso-ciated with Sʲix̌irtʲa: harnessing mammoths (Arzyutov 2019, 144; Lukin 2020; AMAĖ RAN 2/1/65, 113–14); producing and wearing metal knives or other metal items (AMAĖ RAN 2/1/65, 111–12); and most important, the subterranean way of living (Anderson 2019; see a detailed analysis of Nenets folklore in Lukin 2011, 170–94).

Linguistically speaking, the term sʲiχirtʲa also signifies this group's strong link with the surrounding landscape and spiritual entities. The word sʲiχirtʲa contains the syllable sʲi-, which means "hole." It is likely associated with the folkloric underground dwellings, which have a small hole at the top through which Sʲiχirtʲa enter. Moreover, the word also corresponds with the neighboring Samoyedic Enets S'ixi'o (Gracheva 1990) and Nganasan S'igi'ə, both referring to a kind of evil spirit or even a cannibal (Valentin Gusev, pers. comm., December 5, 2017).[6] In Soviet ethnography, some of these linguistic and material elements appear as historical arguments in ethnohistorical reflections of archaeologists and anthropologists working in the Arctic and Siberia. Following are two examples of Sʲiχirtʲa narratives. The first was recorded by Soviet ethnographer Grigoriĭ D. Verbov (1909–42) in Yamal on July 2, 1936: "Under the ground, there are seven more lands. On the first of them live *Sirti* [Sʲiχirtʲa], for whom our earth serves as their sky. Our sun and moon are one [for them? – D.A.]. They shine for *Sirti* through the water and our land. There are other *Sirti* whose traces are found. They live on our earth, within its depths (R. *tolshcha*), and [they] are afraid of sunlight" (AMAĖ RAN 2/1/65, 3rev).

The nuanced multiplicity of Sʲiχirtʲa, however, was later simplified into a singular representation in the notes of Verbov's student Liudmila V. Khomich (1921–2011) in the Nyda settlement, also in Yamal, in 1962. This shift may have stemmed from her field interlocutors, who were influenced by the Soviet education system, or from her own interpretations as an ethnogenesis scholar. Khomich recorded the following story:

A Nenets lived with his mother near a large lake, where they raised reindeer. One day, while grazing the reindeer near a hill, the son spotted a girl sitting and sewing. She possessed a beautiful gilded knife (referred to by the narrator as the *sikhirtia khar* [Sʲiχirtʲah χør° – D.A.], meaning the *sikhirtia* [Sʲiχirtʲa – D.A.] knife).[7] Intrigued by the knife, he attempted to approach it stealthily, but the girl vanished before his eyes. The same incident occurred the next time he encountered her. Some time later, the Nenets, feeling weary, rested near a *chum*, sat upon a hillock, and drifted off to sleep.[8] He was awakened by someone and saw a young man who tended to mammoths (in Nenets, mammoths are referred to as *ia khora* [jah χora – D.A.], meaning earthly reindeer male individuals) instead of reindeer.[9] The young man called out to him, and they walked toward the hill, entering a cave [sic] where an old man, an old woman, and the girl were seated. The old man instructed to feed the guest. The old man then brought forth a huge fish and skillfully filleted it using the beautiful knife (or a similar one). The Nenets couldn't take his eyes off the knife. Afterward, he departed. The following day, he returned to the spot where he had seen the girl and found the knife lying there, so he kept it. The elders witnessed this event.[10] (1970, 61)

These narratives, recorded by Soviet field ethnographers (see the detailed overview of other recordings of Sʲix̌irtʲa narratives in Laptander 2019) a quarter of a century apart, can be situated within broader historical and epistemic contexts, which I discuss in this chapter. For this purpose, I transition from the conceptualizations of Indigeneity in the Russian Empire, intertwined with stories about underground Sʲix̌irtʲa, to the emergence of geological discourse in presenting Indigenous ethnohistories, and then to the early Soviet notions of Indigenous ethnogenesis, which placed Sʲix̌irtʲa in a historical perspective. As a result of these transformations, Sʲix̌irtʲa and the archaeological artifacts assigned to them became the holy grail of circumpolar studies (Fitzhugh 1997), aiding Arctic archaeologists and anthropologists in reimagining transnational Indigenous histories. In other words, the verbal and material traces of Sʲix̌irtʲa, to some extent, charted their own course through the ocean of Indigenous ontologies and academic theories. These narratives and artifacts shape the academic understanding of Indigenous peoples' past and signify the Indigenous sense of belonging to the land.

LOOKING FROM THE WEST

While traveling to Archangelsk and Murmansk in 1837, Alexander von Schrenk (1816–76), a Russian naturalist of Baltic German origin, was astonished by the legends about the Chud' among Russians and Pomors and about Sʲix̌irtʲa among Tundra Nenets. According to known legends, the Chud' lived underground and shared many similar features with Sʲix̌irtʲa (Drannikova 2008). This comparative approach allowed Schrenk to assert that these two folkloric tribes are likely branches of the same legend (A. Shrenk 1855, 325). In his interpretations, Schrenk followed his predecessor, naturalist and traveler Ivan I. Lepekhin (1740–1802), who drew a similar conclusion after his travels across Nenets-Russian lands in the North (1805, 203). How deeply rooted in history these two vernacular narratives about underground inhabitants are remains unclear because of a lack of written evidence. However, Schrenk's observations correspond to those in the earlier sporadic notes of eighteenth-century travelers and naturalists who sought the origins of Russians and Siberian Indigenous peoples (Vermeulen 2015, 29–30, 52–54, 66, 164–65). The links between the Chud' and Sʲixirtʲa were among the most intriguing aspects in the history of academic and vernacular conceptualizations of Indigenous histories.[11] This section provides an overview of these Sʲixirtʲa/Chud' connections.

In the *Rus' Primary Chronicle* (also known as *The Tale of Bygone Years*), dating back to the early eleventh century, the list of ethnic groups decorated with Old Testament genealogies includes the Chud' (Adrianova-Peretts 1950, 10), which remained an enigmatic tribe for many. The Chud' is listed among those tribes colonized by Rus' Varangian chieftains. Russian imperial and Soviet historians, guided by genealogical concepts regarding the history of local and Indigenous groups, endeavored to integrate the Chud' into their ethnogenetic narratives. The presence of the name in Russia's earliest historical documents, along with the existence of the word *chud'* as a toponym across the territory of today's Russia, enabled them to construct a chronologically expansive reconstruction of ethnic histories and to incorporate local and Indigenous narratives into the official narratives of Russian sovereignty.[12]

Despite being associated with Russian ethnic genealogy, *chud'* appears to belong to the cluster of words closely associated with the concept of the "other." Historical linguists remind us that the word *chud'* was derived from Proto-Germanic *þeudō*, meaning "people" (Anikin 2000; Fasmer 1987, 378). Over the development of the Russian language, this term acquired new connotations, indicating the "other," which today encompasses Russian words such as *chuzhoĭ* (meaning "alien" or "foreign"), *chudak* (meaning an "odd person"), and *chudo* (meaning a "miracle" or "wonder"). Moreover, historically, it can be noted that the Old Russian word *kudo*, from which the word *kudesnik* (meaning a "sorcerer" or "wizard") was derived, has the same origin (*ch ~ k*). This linguistic prehistory allows us to consider the concept of Chud' as one of the earliest articulations of Indigeneity in

Russia and possibly in Eastern Europe (see also Lashuk 1969). Moreover, the intellectual history of Chud' in Russia was closely linked to the Tundra Nenets Sʲixirtʲa discussed in this chapter.[13] Because of the scarcity of written sources, the extent of coexistence of the Chud' and Sʲixirtʲa or mutual influences between them remain rather unclear.

Since the eighteenth century, the legends and artifacts associated with the Chud' have been significant evidence in academic models of Indigenous ethnohistories. This significance was likely prompted by the mass delivery of random Siberian archaeological artifacts to the imperial capital, Saint Petersburg, shaping the collection known as the Siberian Collection of Peter the Great (see Rudenko 1962). But Siberian "dark archaeologists" (*bugrovschiki*) searched not only for those archaeological remains but also for resources like metal ore, crucial for further colonizing Siberia and the circumpolar North in general.[14] These mines were widely known among Russian settler colonizers as *chudskie kopi*, literally, "the mines of Chud'" (Ėĭkhval'd 1856). Precolonial (or pre-Russian) human activities, beyond what is documented in Russian written sources, were attributed to the enigmatic Chud'. As early as the nineteenth century, metropolitan scholars crafted a Siberian cartography of the Chud' in their descriptions of mines, extending beyond metropolitan narratives. The Urals and Altai emerged as focal points on this amalgamated geological and ethnohistorical map (Spasskiĭ 1819). Additionally, the historical presence of Chud' was evidenced by early modern archaeological surveys of ancient mounds in the Urals and South Siberia (particularly in Altai), known locally among Russian inhabitants as *chudskie mogily*, literally, "the graves of Chud'" (N. Popov 1876). These (quasi-)archaeological sites illustrate the extent to which vernacular and academic conceptualizations of Indigeneity were rooted in the subterranean.

The abandoned ancient dwellings, mines, and burials, as archaeological traces of the Chud', did not remain devoid of stories and material artifacts. On the contrary, encounters with the narratives about Chud' and Sʲixirtʲa, along with the material remains assigned to them, formed a local understanding of northern subterranean Indigeneity through a peculiar "ethno-ethnohistory," as Raymond D. Fogelson (1974) termed it, or Indigenous history conceptualized in Indigenous terms.

The ethnographic comprehension of this complexity began to take shape in the mid-nineteenth century. Motivated by Finnish nationalist ideologies, and employing comparative linguistic and folkloristic methodologies influenced by biblical narratives, renowned Finnish linguist and ethnographer Matthias A. Castrén (1813–52) embarked on a quest to trace the Eastern origin of Finns (see Branch 1973; Siikala 2006). Between 1838 and 1849 he journeyed across the Eurasian circumpolar North and Siberia (Castrén 2017). Upon his return to Finland, he synthesized his own notes and the insights of Lepekhin, Schrenk, and other travelers into a relatively cohesive theory aiming to historically and linguistically link various Indigenous groups and their languages, from the Ural to the Altai Mountains.

Historical linguists remind us that "Castrén consciously placed Samoyedic at the center of his Siberian studies" (Janhunen 2009, 484). This decision was influenced by the geographic proximity of these languages, which were in contact with Finno-Ugrian languages in the West, Tungusic in the East, and Turkic in the South. Castrén believed that the small Samoyed-speaking groups in South Siberia—such as the Kalmazh (Kamasins), Karagasses, and Motors—living among Turkic-language communities were remnants of the original Samoyed (and Finnish) cultures. These groups were perceived as the most Indigenous in West Siberia, possessing the ability to convey the "unwritten" history of Siberia and the North. Thus, Indigenous narratives about underground dwellers and metropolitan conceptualizations of Indigeneity were brought closer together.

In Castrén's notes (2017, 83; 2019, 1:645), the enigmatic *Siirtje* or *Sihrtieh* (Sʲiχirtʲa) have been firmly associated with the equally enigmatic Chud', whose territory stretches from Karelia in the West to Altai and Khakassia in the East.[15] Interestingly, in his classifications of languages, Castrén groups Finnish and Samoyedic languages under the common name of Chudic, implicitly supporting the Chud'/Sʲiχirtʲa connectivity.[16] These theoretical ideas appeared in his lectures and writings, primarily published posthumously, and influenced the imagination of Nordic and Russian archaeologists, anthropologists, and linguists, bringing them together under the umbrella of the Ural-Altai Hypothesis. By the beginning of the twentieth century, however, this hypothesis had already come under criticism in Finland and other parts of the world (Timo Salminen 2006; see Shirokogoroff

1931). Since then, however, Sⁱiχirtⁱa has entered academic discourse and quietly assisted scholars in the "objective" organization of ethnic, cultural, and historical landscapes of the "illiterate" North and Siberia. Castrén's ideas followed a certain German-Swedish-Finnish tradition of historical linguistics and later, in cooperation with the American project of historical anthropology, contributed to the development of the Soviet epistemology of linearly reconstructing ethnogenesis and ethnic histories. According to that perspective, all ethnic groups from the past were expected to have a place of origin, and their genealogies were required to coherently lead to one of today's ethnic or language groups.

The names of numerous ethnic groups among the Russian Arctic and Siberian Indigenous peoples are derived from Chud', reflecting the broad expansion of the Sⁱiχirtⁱa/Chud' world. Descriptions of the mysterious Chuchunaa in East Siberia by Soviet ethnographers served as evidence of a historical encounter with people who arrived by the sea (Gurvich 1975).[17] Linguistically, however, it reflects a convergence of Chud' legends with local narratives of Evenkis and Sakha/Yakuts regarding enigmatic tundra dwellers (Anikin 1999). Although the term *chud'* disappeared in the Far East, similar legends persisted. Farther east, ethnographers documented comparable tales about mysterious inhabitants on Arctic islands, such as Onkilons (from the Chukchi *aŋqaɬʔət*), popularized by the 1968 novel *Sannikov's Land* by Soviet geologist and geographer Vladimir A. Obruchev (1863–1956) (see also Tugolukov 1986). The roster of such subterranean dwellers in the circumpolar region extends beyond those mentioned, as numerous variants of these legends exist across the circumpolar region and beyond (see also Krech 1999, 30).

LOOKING FROM THE EAST

On the other end of the continent, Alexander von Schrenk's brother, Leopold von Schrenk (1826–94), who was the director of the Museum of Anthropology and Ethnography (Kunstkamera) in Saint Petersburg, added a Far Eastern component to this picture. This contribution became important in the development of evolutionistic and even geological conceptualizations of Sⁱiχirtⁱa. These conceptualizations not only aided the first Russian ethnographers but also influenced the "founder of American anthropology," Franz Boas (1858–1942), and some of his students in shaping the historical profile of the emerging field of Arctic anthropology (Arzyutov et al., forthcoming).

Leopold von Schrenk was dispatched to the Amur borderlands and Sakhalin Island of the Russian Empire for a detailed natural science and ethnographic survey of the region, which he conducted in 1853–57. In his ethnographically rich book on the Indigenous peoples of the Amur basin, Schrenk employed then-fashionable geological language to describe Indigenous ethnohistories. As noted by historian of science Chris Manias, "Models derived from geological thought frequently influenced ideas of human development, yet humans themselves were largely absent from geological debates" (2013, 277). Therefore, it is not surprising that the nineteenth-century geological and ethnographic vocabulary, partly inherited from European nationalisms, can be readily found in the works of travelers and naturalists, including Schrenk. In this section, I reflect on the role of geological language in conceptualizing Indigenous ethnohistory and its subsequent contribution to interpreting Sⁱiχirtⁱa.

While conducting field research, Schrenk aimed, among other things, to collect data for classifying Indigenous languages, aspiring to achieve a significance akin to that attained by paleontologists and geologists through the collection of fossils or rocks. He identified a number of "language isolates," which significantly influenced his understanding of the historical development of Indigenous peoples in the Far East. By introducing geographic and geological dimensions, he posited that all these isolates were situated along the "edges of the continents or generally vast geographical and ethnographic areas." Schrenk categorized all such languages and peoples under the umbrella term *paleoasiatic*, or Palæ-Asiats, clarifying that they represented "only the remnants of the former, more numerous, widespread, and ramified tribes, so to speak, *outcrops of the layers* of the more ancient ethnographic formation, over which new formations, due to their repeatedly recurrent influxes, were deposited" (L. Shrenk 1883, 256; italics added).

In his geological interpretation, Schrenk juxtaposed the stratigraphic representation of the past with its colonial geographic distribution, thus bridging the vertical and horizontal axes of historical imagination (see Simonetti 2013). The "outcrops" on the imperial outskirts became a valuable source for metropolitan historical reconstructions and further governance of the Indigenous past in this region and beyond. Languages, narratives, and particularly material culture were objectified through chronological ordering. Palæ-Asiats, as extant Asians, became a benchmark for all subsequent evolutionistic reconstructions of Siberian and North American Indigenous histories, where discovered survivals became cultural traces.

Being published in German, Schrenk's book *Die Völker des Amur-Landes* (The peoples of the Amur region) profoundly influenced young Franz Boas, who stated in one of his reports that this research was "of fundamental importance" (Stocking 1989, 110) for designing the research plan of the renowned Jesup North Pacific Expedition (1897–1902), funded by Morris Jesup, president of the American Museum of Natural History. Schrenk's Palæ-Asiats and the intellectual milieu of Eskimo studies in Europe and North America (Krupnik 2016, 3–7; see also Kendall and Krupnik 2003) were the main sources for Boas's historical imagination. As historians of American anthropology remind us, the Jesup expedition also aimed to reconstruct the directions of ancient Indigenous migrations across the Bering Strait, which would help many anthropologists answer the question of the peopling of America and reconstruct the general "circumpolar culture" (see Boas 1940, 344–55). Boas asserts that Indigenous history preceded anthropological theories themselves, stating, "We must, so far as we can, reconstruct the actual history of mankind, before we can hope to discover the laws underlying that history" (Stocking 1989, 108). The question of the peopling of the Americas not only epistemically shaped American anthropology but also held political significance, notably as a reaction to the colonial expansion of the United States to the west and encounters with various Indigenous groups whose historical situatedness remained unclear (Burba 2006).

The expansion of the Russian Empire to the East also necessitated knowledge about the people on the country's periphery. This knowledge was derived not solely from state-sponsored expeditions like those led by the Schrenk brothers but also from projects that Russian Empire administrators viewed with skepticism. Thus upon returning from their fieldwork, the Russian participants of the Jesup expedition, Vladimir G. Bogoraz (Waldemar Bogoras; 1865–1936) and Vladimir I. Iokhel'son (Waldemar Jochelson; 1855–1937), who were former revolutionary exiles, attempted to conceptualize their field data using existing schemes proposed by Schrenk and Castrén.

In his 1902 folklore report on what was hypothesized as the "Eskimo wedge," Bogoras wrote about a potential "connection . . . on the Arctic shore between the Eskimo and Chukchee and the tribes farther to the west—the Yenisey Samoyeds, the Yenisey Ostiaks, and the European Samoyeds" (1902, 670; see also Shternberg 1999, 31–38). Jochelson, on the other hand, focused on underground dwellings, which were already a significant aspect in studies of Sʲiχirtʲa and Chud' and would gain further prominence in Soviet academia (see Jochelson 1907, 1920). These captivating legends, coupled with somewhat amateurish theoretical frameworks, contributed to an imagined geology where layers of human traces from the distant past melded with "real" geology, fostering new theoretical developments in anthropology and yielding academically substantiated histories for "illiterate" peoples. This somewhat parallels modern theoretical constructs of historians and anthropologists discussing "deep time" and the new human-centered geological epoch known as the Anthropocene (Irvine 2020; Chakrabarty 2021).

Politically, all these constructions nonetheless assisted scholars in building theoretical connections between Europe, Asia, and America, thereby invisibly linking the Indigenous past, as they perceived it, with the present. This connection also extended to the scholars themselves. The scientifically validated arguments supported the emergence of the "Americanoid theory," which positioned Siberia as a revered "cradle" of American Indians.[18] This marked the inception of the Soviet theories of ethnogenesis, which influenced identity politics and shaped the theoretical frameworks of Soviet ethnographers.

LOOKING FROM METROPOLITAN OFFICES

Brief field notes of travelers and grand "armchair" theories largely determined the development of anthropology in the early Soviet era. Castrén, Leopold von Schrenk, and later Boas became influential figures who shaped new ethnogenetic thinking in Soviet academia. Regarding Boas's contribution to Soviet ethnography, the leading Soviet anthropologist of the North, Waldemar Bogoras, asserts, "In this area [the 'Eskimo problem'] we, Soviet ethnographers, are the disciples and successors of Boas" (Bogoraz-Tan 1933, 190).[19] The ethnographic work and imagination of these scholars also delineated the geographic boundaries of such knowledge, prompting new field researchers and their mentors in the metropolis to take an interest in the Siberian Arctic as a benchmark for reconstructing Indigenous ethnohistories. Moreover, the intellectual framework of these projects inherited and developed the ideas of searching for the earliest Indigenous peoples who settled in Siberia, whose traces could still be visible and even audible through narratives and "unusual" words and language constructions. In this section, I illustrate the interwoven ideas of Castrén and Leopold von Schrenk and the role of Sⁱiχirtⁱa in shaping them in the early Soviet period.

Danish anthropologist Kaj Birket-Smith (1893–1977), a member of the renowned Fifth Thule Expedition (1921–24), asked Bogoras this question in a letter dated January 23, 1936: "Which problems concerning Arctic ethnology [do] you consider most urgent at present?" (SPF ARAN 250/4/31, 5). After a lengthy correspondence, Birket-Smith formulated the scientific geography of Indigenous ethnohistory that Bogoras had proposed. Here is what Birket-Smith stated before the members of the Committee for International Research in Arctic Ethnology in May 1936: "In the vast regions of Siberia, the problems are still more numerous than in the American Arctic. According to the information from Professor Bogoras, the government of the USSR has taken up several investigations of unusual interest, and expeditions are now being organized for going to Chukchi Peninsula, the Amur Region, and the Samoyed area[s]. Ethnologically these parts are exactly the most important, and all students of Arctic culture will look forward to the results with eagerness" (SPF ARAN 250/4/31, 13; see also APS, Boas Papers, Birket-Smith to Boas, May 4, 1936).

This geography reflects the discussions and theoretical constructions in anthropology described in the previous sections: the Bering Strait theory and the peopling of the Americas, Leopold von Schrenk's Palæ-Asiats, and the stories about Sⁱiχirtⁱa. To grasp why and how Bogoras, representing all Soviet Arctic anthropologists, integrated these ideas to conceptualize the origins of Siberian Indigenous peoples, it is necessary to delve into the events of the 1920s.

During that decade extensive discussions took place among Soviet Siberian and Arctic anthropologists, archaeologists, and linguists, with Castrén emerging as a central figure. He was recognized for his ability to establish historical connections among various ethnic groups across the Eurasian continent. Bogoras, in his 1927 article published in a Leningrad newspaper, remarked, "Despite his Finnish origin, Castrén is the Russian glory" (SPF ARAN 250/1/210, 1). In homage to Castrén, the Soviet Academy of Sciences organized a special conference dedicated to him and his ideas on May 7, 1927 (Bogoraz 1927b). This conference, along with numerous publications based on Castrén's cartography of Indigenous histories in the North and Siberia, served as the guiding thread for future models of ethnogenesis.[20] His insights into the origins of Finno-Ugric, Samoyedic, Tungus, and Turkic peoples in Siberia and beyond facilitated the organization of diverse ethnographic maps of the region. Bogoras not only acknowledged Castrén's theory of the Altai origin of Indigenous peoples in Siberia and the Arctic but also observed its replication by Americanists, "with the only difference that they [Indigenous peoples] came to Altai not from the West but from the East" (Bogoraz-Tan 1928a, 238). This could also be interpreted as a direct reference to Leopold von Schrenk and, consequently, Boas.

A year before the Castrén conference, Bogoras published his renowned article on the migrations of peoples in Eurasia and North America in Russian, partially translated into English (Bogoraz 1927a; Bogoras 1928a, 1928b, 1930). He crafted this paper for the International Congress of Americanists, a convergence point for Americanists and Arctic scholars during that era. These texts were intended for publication and also served as lectures for his students in Leningrad (AMAĖ RAN K-I/1/29; SPF ARAN 849/5/587). In essence, all these publications and articles from the late 1920s aimed to equip the first generation of Soviet ethnographers, particularly those focusing on the North, with theories to effectively integrate elements of Indigenous languages, material artifacts, and the diverse environment they would document in the field. Bogoras's lectures and comprehensive conceptualization of Siberian anthropology and archaeology were a logical extension of the ideas of the Jesup expedition (see also Arzyutov and Kan 2017), intertwined with concepts and metaphors from Castrén and Schrenk (Bogoraz-Tan 1928b). It comes as no surprise that the updated version of Siberian Indigenous ethnogenesis was reinforced with data from ancient animal migrations and glaciation history, concepts that Bogoras advocated in his ethnogenetic research (Sushkin 1925; see also Sushkin 1928; see American interdisciplinary research at that time, Fewkes et al. 1912). In the 1920s Bogoras wrote:

They [Indigenous peoples of the North] dwelt amidst the snow, as fragments of past ages, Neolithic and paleolithic, as living evidence of that glacial epoch which has retreated thousand years ago with its flora and fauna, with mosses and Arctic foxes and seals, and polar bears, from the south to the north, drawing along the hunter and the fishermen.... The Russian scientists studying the Americanoid tribes of Asia are considered to form a special eastern branch of the Americanist lore. In the last years, however, the name of Americanoids is being replaced by another name of more general meaning, Proto-Asiatics [Schrenk's Palæ-Asiats – D.A.]. All the primitive tribes of Siberia are included under that term. (SPF ARAN 250/1/25, 1, 9)

The geological features of Beringia and Angaraland became intertwined with the social and cultural histories of Siberian natives (see Bogoras 1928b, 191; Zolotarev 1938; see also Krech 1999, 29–43 and Demuth 2019) and were legitimated by the metaphors employed by Schrenk. It's interesting to observe how some of Bogoras's students in the 1920s adjusted their field descriptions of Nenets narratives about Sʲiχirtʲa according to geological trends in the Leningrad Academy of Sciences, imbuing them with a sense of scientific significance and integrating them into a broader historical perspective. For instance, a passage from Verbov's 1936 field notes concerning multiple Sʲiχirtʲas, quoted in the introduction to this chapter, received a distinctive interpretation from his colleague Ekaterina D. Prokof'eva. In her article, drafted before the Second World War but published afterward, the Sʲiχirtʲa's "lands" (*zemli*) were referred to as "layers" (*sloi*) (Prokof'eva 1953, 203), lending an academic geological context to the Nenets stories.

As Bogoras, who was criticized at that time for not being sufficiently Marxist (ARAN 358/2/177), noted, "Upon further examination of the economic (*khoziaĭstvennye*) forms of Arctic culture, we see that they are arranged in successive tiers (*iarusy*)" (Bogoraz 1927a, 46). The geological perspective was supplemented with evolutionary and diffusionistic ideas akin to the two-volume work of Friedrich Ratzel (1844–1904), *Anthropogeographie* (1882, 1891). In another work, Bogoras pointed out that "[the] polar culture originated in the Arctic region and was adopted and assimilated by peoples migrating from the south. Whether it had one or multiple centers of origin is unknown; however, it is natural to assume that this culture originated in one area and subsequently spread throughout the polar world" (Bogoras 1928b, 189).[21] Soviet ethnographers embraced this volumetric topology of layers and cradles as they endeavored to uncover the elusive Indigenous past and place it within the universal timeline. It's worth noting that the geological metaphors were widely accepted by scholars across various disciplines at that time, becoming part of the "common sense." For instance, there were visionary theories such as the biosphere theory of Vladimir I. Vernadskiĭ (1863–1945) and the "palaeontology of speech" of Nikolaĭ Ya. Marr (1864–1934), both emerging from the same intellectual and social milieu in postrevolutionary Petrograd. The theory of ethnogenesis that was emerging at that time was internally complex and somewhat contradictory, stemming from a few theoretical sources with the aim of constructing a coherent history of Siberian natives. Bogoras was the figure who managed to merge these ideas and cartographies, with the assistance of his students conducting research in Siberia.

FINDING THE "MISSING LINK"

Beginning in the early 1920s, numerous students of Shternberg and Bogoras were dispatched to Siberia to uncover traces of Palæ-Asiatic cultures. Among them were Georgiĭ N. Prokof'ev and Ekaterina D. Prokof'eva, Valeriĭ N. Chernetsov, and Natalia A. Kotovshchikova. They collected folklore and linguistic and material artifacts from Nenets and other Samoyedic groups, which they brought back to Leningrad, thereby bolstering the ideas of their academic mentors. But their objective extended beyond mere artifact collection: They sought to identify the "true" Indigenous peoples, the most ancient inhabitants of the North, whose culture might offer insights into the unwritten history of the region. Their diaries and often contentious correspondence with their supervisors abound with reflections on Indigenous origins and references to the works of Castrén and other pioneers of ethnogenesis discourse previously discussed. In this section, I recount the story of how Soviet field ethnographers encountered the legends and "artifacts" of Sⁱiχirtⁱa and interpreted them within the frameworks described earlier.

The Prokof'evs

With a preliminary theoretical framework in place, the students hoped to bolster the theories with new "facts" gathered from the field. The ethnography and linguistics couple of Georgiĭ Prokof'ev (1897–1942) and Ekaterina Prokof'eva (1902–78) made significant efforts to reconstruct the ethnohistory of Samoyedic peoples (Nenetses, Selkups, Nganasans, and Enetses) through folklore and language analysis. Their field research aimed to study the "real Samoyeds," as they referred in their field notes and publication to Selkups, among whom the couple had lived for three years between 1925 and 1928 (SPF ARAN 804/2/621; for more on the Prokof'evs, see Kazakevich 2010).[22]

Influenced by Marr's historical linguistics and Castrén's and Bogoras's theories, as well as the newly emerged but still incompletely understood Soviet Marxism (AMAĖ RAN 36/1/100, 19), Georgiĭ Prokof'ev proposed that an Indigenous origin could be reconstructed through analysis of the progressive development of economic "types," from primitive hunting and gathering to reindeer herding.[23] Of particular significance was his emphasis on underground dwellings among the Selkups, which would soon become one of the key arguments in the academic construction of Sⁱiχirtⁱa (Prokof'ev 1928, 101). Prokof'ev wrote, "The cultural tie between these two groups—the Ostyak-Samoyed and the Keto [Kets or Yeniseian Ostyaks in Russian colonial documents. – D.A.]—proves intimate contact in the past, which according to all indications must have occurred in their common ancestral home, southern Siberia" (Prokofjew 1933, 131).

While Sⁱiχirtⁱa remained enshrouded in legends and certain elements of the material culture of contemporary Tundra Nenets, Selkups were depicted as one of the ancient surviving Siberian Indigenous groups, as asserted by Bogoras as early as 1902 (Bogoras 1902, 670). Among other aspects of their field research, the Prokof'evs focused on Selkup folklore. Later they undertook a similar endeavor in documenting the historical folklore of Nenetses to reconstruct the history of the Indigenous North and Siberia. The stories they heard and recorded in the field served to prove the theoretical ideas they had encountered during their student years in Leningrad.

Upon their return from Siberia to Leningrad, Georgiĭ Prokof'ev commenced work on his "habilitation" dissertation (*doktorskaia dissertatsiia*) with the goal of integrating theoretical constructs with extensive ethnographic materials. In numerous unpublished manuscripts (OR RNB 324/1147; SPF ARAN 282/1/169) as well as his final article (1940), Prokof'ev indicated the connections between Selkups and Sⁱiχirtⁱa. While he had only briefly mentioned the underground dwellings of Selkups, in his later works these subterranean architectural constructions became a significant component of his arguments. These works were attributed to the reconstructed "ancient aboriginal population," in his case Sⁱiχirtⁱa, which, as he pointed out, could also be referred to as Chud' (Prokof'ev 1940, 70–71). In other texts, he further reinforced this notion with one of the variants of the ethnonym for Selkups as şeļ qup, meaning "an earthy man," and legends among Enetses and Tundra Nenetses referring to Selkups as *bayka* and *boggo* (Prokof'ev's transliteration), signifying "pit people" (SPF ARAN 282/1/169, 8).

After Georgiĭ Prokof'ev's tragic death during the siege of Leningrad, his widow and colleague, Ekaterina Prokof'eva, continued to write about Selkups' underground dwellings and their ethnogenetic significance, following the path charted by her husband (Prokof'eva 1947).

In summary, the Prokof'evs' conceptual framework integrated Castrén's Chud' and Schrenk's and Bogoras's Palæ-Asiats through a narrative of ancient migrations.[24] As these groups migrated from the South (Altai or Sayan) to the North, the Samoyedic groups split into two distinct groups influenced by the environment (from taiga to tundra): a northeastern group (Nenetses, Enetses, and Nganasans) and a northwestern group (Selkups). Over the course of "ethnic development," the northeastern group interacted with various Indigenous communities likely of Palæ-Asiatic origin. This concept later became known as the "bi-componential" origin of Nenets and was attributed exclusively to Georgiĭ Prokof'ev.

An episode from the book of Soviet propaganda journalist Viktorin A. Popov (1900–1949) about Bol'shezemel'skaia (or Bol'shaia Zemlia) tundra (1932) is helpful to understand the Prokof'evs' perspective on ethnogenesis. During his trip in early spring of 1930, Popov encountered Prokof'ev (with no mention of Ekaterina), who was there as a representative of the

Soviet authorities and a scholar conducting linguistic and ethnographic research—a classic early Soviet academic career strategy (for more on the politics of early Soviet ethnography, see Hirsch 2005).

> We were warming up our cold legs and hands. The local lore student (*kraeved*) Prokof'ev sitting on his *sovik* [a Nenets fur or felt overcoat. – D.A.] in the relaxed way and telling me about Nenets. . . . More recently—Prokof'ev said—the remains of the Samoyed tribes have lived on the Sayan Mountains, but Sayan Samoyed denationalized, dissolved among the Turkic peoples and lost their language and culture. Only the existence of reindeer among Sayan Karagases proves the Samoyedic past of [this] Turkic tribe. It is possible to listen to many things in shamanistic songs that allow us to speculate on the direct but very old relationship between Karagases and Samoyeds. And Bol'shaia Zemlia Samoyeds have lost face, mingling with Komi-Izhemts population. Only this eastern region of Bol'shaia Zemlia has retained a relative purity of culture. That's why I came here.[25] (V. Popov 1932, 49–50)

In this brief story, Prokof'ev probably explained his (and his wife's) vision of the Samoyeds' "southern" origin and their farther northward migrations in the clearest way. Although he did not mention Sʲiχirtʲa, Prokof'ev believed they were in the North where the Samoyeds arrived.

Natalia A. Kotovshchikova, Valeriĭ N. Chernetsov, and Konstantin Ia. Ratner

Simultaneously with the Prokof'evs, a group of young archaeologists, ethnographers, and linguists—Valeriĭ N. Chernetsov (1905–70); Natalia A. Kotovshchikova (1906–29), who was the actual head of the expedition; and Konstantin Ya. Ratner (1907–42)—commenced the ethnoarchaeological research of Sʲiχirtʲa in Yamal. Inspired by the quest for traces of the past within living Arctic cultures, especially the possible historical Nenets-Inuit/Eskimo contacts suggested by Bogoras, they embarked on their journey to Yamal in 1928. Drawing on various archival documents, including the private archive of her father, Tat'iana Sotnikova-Ratner (2017) writes that from its inception, the expedition aimed to excavate the burials of Sʲiχirtʲa, which they believed were on the northern edge of the peninsula near one of the Nenets sacred sites.

Chernetsov and his colleagues, as well as the Prokof'evs, were excited about the Palæ-Asiatic cultures that Bogoras had vividly described to them. Consequently, all their findings were promptly attributed to that "layer," which Chernetsov extensively mapped from Scandinavia to Far Eastern Asia and North America (1935, 109). It represented a cartographic amalgamation of the ideas presented by Castrén, Leopold von Schrenk, Bogoras, and the notion of Chud'.

The promising archaeological research was halted following the tragic death of the expedition's twenty-four-year-old leader, Natalia Kotovsh-chikova, in August 1929 (see Pika 1989). Natalia V. Fëdorova (1949-2024), a leading figure in modern Yamal archaeology, provides insight into the excavations of Sʲixirtʲa, explaining that Chernetsov had only ten or eleven days for an early-summer Arctic archaeological survey and, in reality, did not discover any Eskimo-like underground dwellings as he had envisioned while in Leningrad (Fëdorova 2002; see also SPF ARAN 250/3/158, 55–66). However, he was able to claim that he had indeed found Sʲixirtʲa because of the revised epistemology of Sʲixirtʲa that he proposed. He juxtaposed Nenets legends, kinship diagrams drawn in the field (while staying in the tent of the *Wen ꭓa* family [*Wɘnoŋɘ* in his transliteration, *Vengo* in translit-eration from Russian]), and his rather rapid archaeological findings at the Tiuteĭ-Sale site on the western shore of Yamal (Chernetsov 1935). All this lent a sense of social and material reality to Sʲixirtʲa, while still maintain-ing its elusive nature. "It should be noted that the term *S´irt´s´i* [Sʲixirtʲa] is hardly to be understood as the name of a single ethnic group," Cher-netsov wrote. "Most likely like the word *chud'*, it did not have sufficiently clear boundaries and was probably applied for various tribes" (1935, 127).

Through these reconstructions, Chernetsov asserted that the pre-Nenets populations in Yamal were sea mammal hunters (1935, 109) and that later—no earlier than the seventeenth century—Samoyeds introduced large-scale reindeer herding. His concept garnered full acceptance from most of his colleagues and later gained support from a younger generation of anthropologists (see Krupnik 1976). A year before the publication of Chernetsov's first summary article on the excavation (1935), his colleague Vasiliĭ S. Adrianov (1904–36), from the nearby Zoological Museum in Leningrad, was also dispatched to Yamal to locate a mammoth corpse. However, he altered his route and conducted an archaeological survey near modern Salekhard, with his findings aligning with the Chernetsov hypothesis (Adrianov 1934; Reshetov 2000). Already in May 1936, in his official report on Arctic ethnology, Kaj Birket-Smith stated:

> Going further west along the Arctic shores of Siberia we find, on the Yamal Peninsula, the remains of a remarkable, præ-Samoyedic (?) coast culture recently described by Chernetsov. While the house sites show some resemblances to the Eskimo whalebone house, probably still more features connect this ancient civilization with the comb-ceramic culture of northern Europe and the culture of the Coast Lapps on the Kola Peninsula and in the northern Scandinavia, Further excavations are necessary to elucidate the exact relations of the Yamal culture, which involves questions of far more than local interest.[26] (APS, Boas Papers, Birket-Smith to Boas, May 4, 1936)

The archaeological discoveries from Yamal coincided with the debates of the 1920s and 1930s regarding the origin of reindeer husbandry. Since this theory had been discussed by some participants of the Jesup expedition, it was revitalized within the new Soviet context. The case of Sʲixirtʲa appeared to offer a potential answer to the question of how and where reindeer domestication originated. On one hand, it provided an opportunity to engage with and critique "bourgeois" scholars, aligning with the ideology of the Soviet state. On the other hand, it aligned with the Marxist agenda, particularly in terms of classifications of economic forms and, consequently, with the class differentiation elements present in the works of Prokof'ev and Chernetsov.

One of the key theorists of reindeer domestication during that period was Berthold Laufer (1874–1934), who proposed a model of reindeer domestication as a historical event occurring on the borderland between the boreal forest and the steppes of Central Asia, specifically near Lake Baikal (Laufer 1917, 123; see also Bogoraz-Tan 1928b, 63). His assertion drew on a variety of published works, including those of Castrén and others who discussed the South Siberian origin of the Samoyeds (see the theory proposed by the Prokof'evs). These ideas aligned well with the concepts promoted by Bogoras, who embraced and popularized this notion (Bogoraz-Tan 1928a, 240), while collaborating with the genetic laboratory of the renowned geneticist Nikolaĭ I. Vavilov (1887–1943). Today Sʲix̌irtʲa and the archaeological findings from the 1930s continue to capture the imagination of scholars who endeavor to address the highly complex and significant question of animal domestication practices (see Anderson, Harrault, et al. 2019; Nomokonova et al. 2018).

The anthropological and archaeological imagination, folklore, and material artifacts intertwined to form new theoretical models, which, thanks to Nikolaĭ Marr, became known as *étnogoniia* (ethnogony), later referred to as *étnogenez* (ethnogenesis). By the 1930s the first models of ethnogenesis had already made their way into Bogoras's lectures on ethnography, where the theory aimed to "describe how tribes and peoples of our Union [had] formed" (AMAĖ RAN K-I/1/77, 106). On the eve of the Second World War, this theory was weaponized in the ideological campaign against Nazi race policy and Indo-European theories. In 1939 the Presidium of the Soviet Academy of Sciences established the Commission on Ethnogenesis (Komissiia po étnogenezu) (ARAN 2/1(1939)/84, 3; see also Shnirel'man 1993), which, among other objectives, was to map ethnic groups on the wartime borderlands of the country (Alymov 2019). This newly constituted agency organized only one meeting about the ethnogenesis of the peoples of Siberia before the outbreak of war (Bibikov 1941; ARAN 457/1(1940)/38, 39, 40). Archaeologists and ethnographers of Siberia and the North presented their papers, based on long-term field research and literature reviews, at the 1940 ethnogenesis conference. They formulated the concept of ethnogenesis as an all-encompassing approach to writing history for Indigenous ("illiterate") peoples or about the "illiterate" ancestors of modern peoples. This internal colonial approach also shaped the methodologies and data used by scholars, including material artifacts, folklore, language etymologies, human somatic features, and any written evidence, viewed from a diachronic perspective. These synthetic entities were placed on modernistic timelines and were meant to sequentially lead to the present-day peoples. Sʲix̌irtʲa, mentioned at this meeting, illustrated the tangible and intangible Indigenous past from which Samoyedic ethnohistory might originate. Simultaneously, the newly found artifacts, along with Indigenous and academic narratives, brought Sʲix̌irtʲa to the global stage.

In the early stages of Soviet ethnography, Bogoras and Shternberg, leaders in ethnographic education in Petrograd/Leningrad, introduced a course on the study of the origins of Indigenous peoples. They positioned this course alongside efforts in socialist development in villages, nomadic camps, Jewish shtetls, and other communities. This research and educational program was driven not only by the Soviet nationality policy but also by an established network with American and European scholars, whose works were actively discussed and translated. As early as 1923 Bogoras initiated the publication of a book by the renowned British anthropologist Alfred Haddon (1855–1940), *The Wanderings of Peoples* (Haddon 1911; Geddon 1923), to support the ideas he discussed with his students and that formed the basis of his emerging notion of Palæ-Asiatic peoples. Haddon, along with some naturalists and travelers, followed Castrén in their writings and tended to view Chudes (Chud') as a distinct race (often described as a "blond race"; see also Robinson 2016) in South Siberia, particularly near Baikal (Haddon 1911, 16), coinciding with the region where Laufer located the "cradle" of reindeer domestication.

The sincere interest of numerous world anthropologists in migrations and the origins of peoples, coupled with the ethnographic achievements of Prokof'ev and Chernetsov, enabled Bogoras to showcase the scope of the newly emerged Soviet ethnography in the Arctic to his overseas colleagues. He took great pride in uncovering the "missing links" in the transnational history of Indigenous migrations across continents, which allowed him to reconcile a wide range of theories. However, the 1930s in the Soviet Union were not the most conducive period for international collaboration.

Bogoras's correspondence with Soviet academic leaders and American anthropologist Aleš Hrdlička reveals his ambiguous position within academic diplomacy. In a letter to the head of the human sciences in the Soviet Academy of Sciences, Sergeĭ F. Ol'denburg (1863–1934), dated December 12, 1926, he advocated for the "closing" of the Soviet Arctic, stating, "The Soviet Union cannot allow the expansion of foreign initiative and the strengthening of foreign influence on the Russian coast of the Bering Sea, neither in the field of economy, nor in the field of science. . . .

This corresponds to the world significance of the USSR and the proportion of Russian scientific work in the field of ethnology of the Bering Sea and the ancient migrations and ties of Eurasia with America" (SPF ARAN 2/1(after 1917)/15, 93).

Ironically, just a few years later, Bogoras and Hrdlička negotiated a collaborative archaeological survey on the Aleutian Islands (AMNH, Hrdlička/14; see also SPF ARAN 250/1/224, 11–12). Consequently, following the 1928 Congress of Americanists, they initiated academic and student exchanges between the United States and USSR (SPF ARAN 142/1(1928)/7, 8–11). After the 1928 congress, Boas planned to visit Leningrad to collaborate with the newly delivered museum collections of the Arctic. He believed that his visit might help resolve many questions related to North American anthropology, as conveyed in a letter to Bogoras on November 24, 1928 (APS, Boas Papers). Boas also attempted to launch a highly transnational project on Arctic anthropology, aiming to involve scholars not only from the United States and USSR but also from Canada, Denmark, and Norway (APS, Boas Papers, Boas to Bogoras, December 22, 1927). However, this project was never realized.[27]

In his report, most likely intended for Soviet administrators, Bogoras emphasized the significance of Sⱼiχirtⱼa and Chernetsov's excavations in Yamal for "resolving the question of the migration of peoples from Asia to America across the Bering Bridge, particularly concerning the routes of Eskimo colonization" (SPF ARAN 250/1/224, 12). This theme of Sⱼiχirtⱼa was also prominent in Bogoras's American correspondence, in which he eagerly shared updates about the field research in Yamal, sparking curiosity from the American side. He wrote to Hrdlička on July 8, 1935:

Perhaps it [the Samoyed lands] is even more interesting than any part of Northern Siberia. In 1929, a party of young students of Leningrad University spent a year on the peninsula of Yamil [Yamal]. . . . They found some underground houses mostly ancient ruins, the details of material culture had a curious Eskimo-like appearance. . . . You see that both expeditions [to Amur River and Yamal Peninsula] promise a heap of interesting materials. But we do not know yet which of them will do first in 1936 and which will follow in 1937. (AMNH, Hrdlička/14, 15)

Hrdlička enthusiastically responded to Bogoras on August 30, 1935: *"Northern Siberia holds, too, the final word as to the origin of the Eskimo.* There must be many extinct sites there with contents of great value both scientifically and for museum purposes. Your note about archaeological work on the Yamil [Yamal] Peninsula with the discovery there of underground houses interested me very much" (AMNH, Hrdlička/14, 17; italics added).

After the Jesup expedition, Russian and American anthropologies appear to have shared a newfound common interest, despite escalating tensions between Boas and Bogoras (Kan 2008) and Bogoras's somewhat ambiguous efforts to appease both the Soviet authorities and his American colleagues. However, Bogoras passed away in May 1936 without witnessing the outcomes of his controversial collaborations. In a private letter to Kaj Birket-Smith dated August 4, 1936, Franz Boas wrote, "I do not need to say that I shall do everything in my power to maintain the relations between American and Russian ethnologists. The death of Bogoras was a great shock to me because our relations were not only scientific but of a very personal character" (APS, Boas Papers).

The continuation of these relations was managed by Hrdlička, who not only succeeded in assuming the role of diplomat between Soviet and American anthropology but also was permitted to conduct the final American archaeological survey in the Soviet Aleutian Islands from 1936 to 1938, following in the footsteps of Jochelson (see ASCCL UAA 360/5/77).[28] In June 1939 Hrdlička made his last visit to Leningrad, where he met with Soviet ethnographers and delivered a lecture at the Institute of Ethnography. Some eyewitnesses recalled that Prokof'ev and Chernetsov, who were present in the room, actively supported Hrdlička's arguments and, along with other colleagues, proposed organizing a Russian-American expedition to the Russian Far East (Okladnikov 1980, 170). Interestingly, during discussions of early Arctic history at the meeting, participants shared narratives about underground dwellings recorded in various locations in the North, including Yamal (AMAĖ RAN K-I/3/13, 33–34).

Amid widespread rumors about unique discoveries in Yamal, archaeologist Adrianov, shortly after his 1936 expedition there, was contacted by American anthropologist Henry Field, who offered to collaborate (Reshetov 2000, 244). Accused of Trotskyism, Adrianov was murdered later that year. His death, coupled with the rise of Stalinism in Soviet academia, rendered collaboration with the Chicago Field Museum of Natural History impossible. Nonetheless, Field and Eugene V. Prostov (1906–?) made significant efforts to introduce Soviet archaeological findings to American and broader Western audiences through regular overviews published in *American Anthropologist* and *Antiquity* from 1936 to 1946. These publications included descriptions of archaeological data from North Siberia, which "testified to both a higher culture than that of the modern inhabitants, the Nentsi [Nenetses] (Samoyeds) and the Khanta [Khants], as well as to a different type of climate" (Field and Prostov 1937, 487; see also Collins 1937, 320).

The updates from Siberia continued to captivate American archaeologists and anthropologists, sparking their interest not only in organizing expeditions to the remote reaches of the Soviet Union but also in initiating museum exchange projects. Eugene A. Golomshtok (1897–1950), a Russian émigré in the United States and a student of Alfred L. Kroeber (1876–1960), launched the Russian Project at the Penn Museum in Philadelphia. Motivated by the notion of discovering traces of a "blond race" in Chud' burials in South Siberia, he aimed to conduct archaeological research in the same area (Golomshtok 1932, 1933b; see also Kupina 2004). Additionally, according to his research program titled "A Survey of the Archaeology and Ethnography of Siberia," which he sent to Franz Boas (APS, Boas Papers, Golomshtok to Boas, December 9, 1938), he intended to compile a survey of all archaeological and ethnographic data from Siberia available in Russian, French, German, and English. He wrote, "The tremendous territory of Siberia is considered by most scientists as the cradle, or the place of origin, for those early groups of people, which some ten thousand years ago crossed over into the New World, and spread throughout North and South America." However, this ambitious historiographical project ultimately faltered, likely due to the political circumstances of the time. Golomshtok had to revise his initial plan and redirect his efforts to the Crimea instead.

The search for Sʲiχirtʲa and the discovery of the Siberian Neolithic rendered Siberia a promising location for American-Soviet anthropological collaborations (see Michael 1958; Tolstoy 1958), aspirations that Golomshtok had envisioned and articulated (1933a, 302). Furthermore, in both Russian and American publications, the material remnants of Sʲiχirtʲa and the Neolithic discoveries in South Siberia had significantly impacts on the understanding of the Paleo-Eskimo past (see Field and Prostov 1942, 400; Collins 1943; see also PMA 0069/1-c).

* * *

In this chapter, I have narrated the story of how the subterranean world and its inhabitants in the Arctic and Siberia have influenced not only local perceptions of the past but also the trajectory of academic disciplines. Tracing the life history of Sʲiχirtʲa reveals how academic and vernacular understandings of Indigeneity intersected and subsequently shaped an epistemic realm that remained relatively consistent despite shifts in political regimes and intellectual paradigms. Premodern conceptions of Indigeneity merged with evolutionistic geological metaphors, influencing the epistemologies of Soviet ethnogenesis. The search for "true" Indigenous peoples served as a unifying force for anthropologists, linguists, and archaeologists, enabling them to transcend the confines of identity politics in which they played a central role. The central figure of this narrative—Sʲiχirtʲa—both revealed the vibrant subterranean landscapes and also subtly guided all those who encountered them to reconsider the North and Indigeneity.

NOTES

1. This chapter is adapted from the author's book project *The Northern Book of Origin: Siberian Indigenous Narratives and Metropolitan Ethnogenesis Theories* (under contract with the University of Nebraska Press). The research is sponsored by the GRETPOL ERC and RSF projects (18-18-00309). The final phase of research has been supported by the SEEDARC at University of Oulu, Finland.

2. In the writings of Soviet ethnographers, the distinction between ethnogenesis and ethnic history was typically delineated by the process of Russian colonization. Ethnogenesis pertained to the early history of various ethnic groups, whereas ethnic history was informed by Russian colonial documents (see Khomich 1974). The concept of ethnogenesis as both a Soviet and post-Soviet scientific and political project has been extensively explored in the following works, among others, with a specific emphasis on Central Asia: Gullette (2008); Laruelle (2008); Abashin (2014, 2024).

3. They preferred to use the term *étnos*, which was a rather controversial concept in defining ethnicity (see Anderson, Arzyutov, and Alymov 2019; Anderson and Arzyutov 2019).

4. The symbol ° in Tapani Salminen's 1998 transcription refers to the deep vowel reduction in the phoneme, which holds a special meaning for Tundra Nenets dialects. The symbol *q*, also in Salminen's transcription, indicates the voiceless consonant glottal stop (also known as ' in Tereshchenko's 1965 transcription). *S^{j}iχirt^{j}a* also could be written as *Syix°rtya* in Salminen's transcription (1998, 235, 513). It is worth noting that *S^{j}iχirt^{j}a* is used as a countable noun in Nenets, Russian, and English.

5. *S^{j}irt^{j}a* could also be written as *Syi°rtya* in Tapani Salminen's transcription (1998, 235).

6. The Soviet ethnographer of the North, Boris O. Dolgikh (1904–71), mentions that according to his field notes, Nganasans believed that *S 'ixi ʔo/ S 'igi ʔə* "live only among Nenets and do not come here [Taymyr]" (1960, 73). A colleague of Dolgikh's, Ekaterina D. Prokof'eva (1902–78), in her overview of Enets religious practices (1953, 203), points out that *S 'ixi ʔo/ S 'igi ʔə* were of different kinds and inhabited various underground "layers" of the Enets universe.

7. The symbol *h* in Salminen's transcription refers to the voiced consonant glottal stop (also known as ' in Tereshchenko's 1965 transcription).

8. *Chum* is a Komi/Russian loan word for a Nenets conical dwelling, which the Nenets called *myaq*.

9. For more on this folklore episode, see Lukin (2020).

10. The translation has been done from the Russian text published by Khomich (1970), which most likely was edited before publication.

11. It is also notable how these narratives are spatially depicted, portraying the Chud' and S^{j}iχirt^{j}a as inhabitants of various landscapes, such as the aforementioned underground worlds, islands like Novaya Zemlya (Nosilov 1903, 28; Chernetsov 1935, based on La Martinière 1671, chaps. 26–29, 38), or the taiga (Pimenov 1965; with the Chud' considered ancestors of the modern Veps). However, their remoteness or subterranean existence did not imply isolation; instead, it conveyed a sense of proximity—they were always nearby and recent. The Nenets frequented Novaya Zemlya, an Arctic archipelago, seasonally for hunting and fishing to sustain themselves in the face of potential shortages on the mainland, while the subterranean landscapes lay just beneath their feet.

12. We can assume that the spread of Chud' toponyms and legends in Siberia was related to the movement of the first generation of Russian colonizers, many of whom originated from the territory of Northwest Russia. Soviet historians have agreed that the Chud' was a Finno-Ugric tribe whose ancestors can be traced to various modern Finno-Ugric groups in Europe. The

name Chud' later sparked debates among historians about the tribe's association with the Veps, a less numerous Finno-Ugric group residing in the Russian North forest. The cultural distinctiveness of the Veps, among other Finno-Ugric and Russian neighbors, along with the fact that their history appeared deep and murky, made them an enigmatic group. The first field ethnographers substantiated historical observations and textual criticism with documented firsthand accounts from the Russian North, where some Veps people referred to themselves as Chud'. The intersection of these "historical" and "ethnographic" descriptions of the Chud' eventually merged into a coherent ethnogenetic genealogy (Bubrikh [2005] 1947; Pimenov 1965, 117–70; see also Siragusa 2017, 29, 66, 104).

13. In the European context, it bears some similarities to the Victorian narratives drawn from Scandinavian folklore about dwarfs as "savage" and "secret" people (Silver 1999, 120–29; see also the Russian historical narratives regarding the relations between Chud' and Scandinavians in Lomonosov 1952, 196–203).

14. The word *bugrovschiki* has its root in *bugor*, meaning "hillock," which refers to archaeological objects visible on the earth's surface. It was these objects that Russian settlers in Siberia frequently attributed to the Chud'.

15. In his field notes written in Swedish, Castrén defined *Siirtje* (in that context, he used *Siirát*) as "the spirit of a deceased" (2019, 2:1273). This note harks back to the liminal position of Sʲiχirtʲa in early Russian ethnography.

16. The name Chudic was also used by Elias Lönnrot (1802–84), author of *The Kalevala*, in his dissertation on Veps titled "Om det nord-tschudiska språket," which he defended in 1853.

17. It is noteworthy that some of the examples cited were employed to bolster the research pursuits of Soviet cryptozoology, led by Boris F. Porshnev (1905–72) (see Il'ina 2015; Roeder and Afinogenov 2018). Consequently, creatures like Chuchunaa among the Sakha/Yakuts or Almases among various groups in South Siberia and Central Asia were regarded as possible surviving hominids, sometimes even integrated into European Yeti lineages. In contrast, Sʲiχirtʲa primarily retained its place within ethnohistorical modeling.

18. To shed light on discussions outside the major metropolitan centers, I refer to the works of regional researchers and colleagues who collaborated with pioneers of Soviet ethnography such as Lev Ya. Shternberg (1861–1927) and Bogoras, continuing the development of established Palæ-Asiatic ideas. Two anthropologists who conducted fieldwork in the same regions as Leopold von Schrenk during the late imperial and early Soviet

eras, the "white" émigré in China Sergei M. Shirokogoroff [史祿國] (1887–1939) and the Russian/Soviet military ethnographer Vladimir K. Arsen'ev (1872–1930), actively applied these ideas not only in their written works (see Shirokogoroff's concept of "ethnic amalgamation," 1925, 67–90) but also in their private discussions with colleagues. In a letter dated June 15, 1927, Shirokogoroff outlined his research method for writing Tungus ethnohistory: "[If we] peel these layers of borrowing one by one, [we] can reach the core that is further 'indivisible'" (BN PAU i PAN 4600/6, 52). Similarly, on December 7, 1928, Arsen'ev expressed his conviction: "I am convinced that we have Paleo-Asiatic elements . . . [that] exhibit many Manchu traits. Over the past two years, I have been searching for these elements (Paleo-Asian) among the Udekhe and have found evidence not only in ethnographic remnants but also in the language" (AMAĖ RAN 8/1/477, 14rev).

19. As Nikolai Vakhtin has noted, the definitive Siberian research program of the Jesup expedition was deliberated and formulated in the autumn of 1899, when Boas, Jochelson, and Bogoras convened in New York (2005, 268). It would also be accurate to assert that the theory of ethnogenesis in its Siberian/Far Eastern manifestation, later championed in Soviet ethnography of the North by Bogoras, first arose as a theoretical concept at that very juncture and location.

20. During the significant 1929 conference of ethnographers from Moscow and Leningrad, held after the October coup, Soviet ethnographers made numerous references to Castrén (Arzyutov et al. 2014, 48).

21. The "polar culture" was likely adapted from the Boasian "circumpolar culture."

22. The Prokof'evs actively advocated for the adoption of a new ethnic designation for Selkups, moving away from the colonial term Ostyak-Samoyeds. Instead, they proposed a combination of two authentic Selkup words: *söl kup/səļ qup* and *şəļ qup*, meaning "a forest man" and "an earthy man," respectively (Prokof'ev's transliteration). For insights into the politics of renaming Siberian Indigenous groups, see Anderson and Arzyutov (2016, 194–95).

23. While in the field, Prokof'ev compared his notes with Castrén's publications (SPF ARAN 282/2/242, 1–3).

24. It is interesting to observe how these ideas were reflected in the field notes of ethnographers during that period. Grigoriĭ D. Verbov, while documenting Nenets folklore narratives and riddles in the Malozemel'skaia (Malaia zemlia) tundra in 1930, included this comment in his field notes: "There is

another quite curious element: a set of shiny whale ribs, [which] represent the poles of the lodge. I wonder if this gives [us] a hint to longstanding Palæ-Asiatic elements. [This is] another feather (*eshche odna kaplia na mel'nitsu*) in Vladimir Germanovich's [Bogoras's] cap" (AMAĖ RAN 2/1/15, 51).

25. The history of this field research has been published in Arzyutov (2016). See also the documentary shot by the Prokof'evs at https://www.youtube .com/watch?v=A48p9hY1adI, which I edited. It depicts to some extent the research questions the Prokof'evs discussed and visually applied to their field.

26. Even local interests significantly influenced Eurasian archaeology. The achievements of Chernetsov, the Prokof'evs, and Adrianov inspired future Soviet archaeology leader Alekseĭ P. Okladnikov (1908–81) in his archaeo-logical surveys in the Cis-Baikal region, guided by Bogoras. He rediscov-ered Neolithic cultures in the basin of the Angara River (Okladnikov 1938; see also Petri 1916), aligning his findings with the visionary map proposed by Bogoras in the 1920s. Okladnikov aimed to substantiate this map with tangible archaeological evidence from the past (see Korsun 2015, 302, 337–38; see also Michael 1958). Intriguingly, Bogoras also proposed that Roy F. Barton (1883–1947), an American anthropologist specializing in the Philippines and working at the Museum of Anthropology and Eth-nography in Leningrad, spend two years in the Amur region. In a letter to Boas dated July 11, 1930, Barton wrote, "I would have gone to the Far East with the commissioner in charge of the work amongst the primitive folk of Northern Siberia. . . . It would have been a long trip and I would have had a few days with perhaps twenty tribes. However, I shall probably be able to take the trip with him next summer. . . . Professor Bogoras thinks I ought to spend about two years with one of the Amur River tribes" (APS, Boas Papers, Barton to Boas, July 11, 1930). A month later he wrote, "I should then like to go to Siberia with the fellowship we spoke of. I believe that I could most profitably make a cultural study of the Goldi or Oroki of the lower Amur region and at the same time look for Malay influ-ence, which is supposed to have reached into Korea, on the lower Amur" (APS, Boas Papers, Barton to Boas, August 26, 1930). Bogoras intended to secure funding from the Guggenheim Foundation through Boas for these endeavors (APS, Boas Papers, Bogoras to Boas, February 26, 1931). These exchanges suggest ongoing intellectual collaborations between Bogoras and Boas following the Jesup expedition.

27. The destiny of this project bears similarities to the initiative proposed by Fridtjof Nansen (1861–1930) in collaboration with Boas and Bogoras dur-

ing the same period. Nansen's concept involved orchestrating an international expedition to the Kola Peninsula, with plans to extend field research farther eastward (see Lönngren 2019). Arzyutov and Sergei Kan are currently researching and drafting an article on the history of this project.

28. Two of his previous fieldworks in Russia were in 1909 and 1912 (see SPF ARAN 282/2/81, 3–4). In the islands, Hrdlička is still remembered by the ironic nickname "Hard Liquor" (Veltre 2008).

REFERENCES

Manuscripts and Archives

AMAÉ RAN. Archive of Peter the Great Museum of Anthropology and Ethnography (Kunstkamera) of the Russian Academy of Sciences, Saint Petersburg, Russia.

AMNH. American Museum of Natural History. Division of Anthropology, New York.

APS. Boas, Franz. Papers. MSS.B. B.61. American Philosophical Society, Philadelphia.

ARAN. Archive of the Russian Academy of Sciences, Moscow, Russia.

ASCCL UAA. Archives and Special Collections, Consortium Library, University of Alaska Anchorage.

BN PAU i PAN. Scientific Library of the Polish Academy of Skills and the Polish Academy of Sciences, Kraków, Poland.

OR RNB. The Department of Manuscripts at the Russian National Library, Saint Petersburg.

PMA. Penn Museum Archives. University of Pennsylvania, Philadelphia.

SPF ARAN. Saint Petersburg Branch of the Archive of Russian Academy of Sciences, Saint Petersburg, Russia.

Published Works

Abashin, Sergei N. 2014. "Ethnogenesis and Historiography: Historical Narratives for Central Asia in the 1940s and 1950s." In *An Empire of Others: Creating Ethnographic Knowledge in Imperial Russia and the USSR*, edited by Roland Cvetkovski and Alexis Hofmeister, 145–68. Budapest: Central European University Press.

———. 2024. "Ethnogenesis Through the Lens of Soviet Ethnography: Academic Research in the Service of Nation-Building and Socialist Modernity." In *The Central Asian World*, edited by Jeanne Féaux de la Croix and Madeleine Reeves, 21–38. New York: Routledge.

Adrianov, Vasiliĭ S. 1934. "Otchet o komandirovke v Sale-Khard v 1932 g." *Problemy istorii dokapitalisticheskikh obshchestv* 7–8:173–76.

Adrianova-Peretts, Varvara P., ed. 1950. *Povest' vremennykh let*. Vol. 10/1. Literaturnye Pamiatniki. Moscow: Izdatel'stvo AN SSSR.

Alymov, Sergei S. 2019. "World War II and the Cold War as a Context for Discipline Formation: The Case of Soviet Ethnography, 1940s–1960s." In *In Search of Other Worlds: Essays Towards a Cross-Regional History of Area Studies*, edited by Katja Naumann, Torsten Loschke, Steffi Marung, and Matthias Middell, 23–50. Leipzig: Leipziger Universitätsvlg.

Anderson, David G. 2000. *Identity and Ecology in Arctic Siberia: The Number One Reindeer Brigade*. Oxford: Oxford University Press.

———. 2007. "Ethnohistory and Ethnic History: A Comparative Analysis of English and Russian Language Traditions of Writing the History of Indigenous People." In *Ėtnoistoriia i arkheologiia Severnoĭ Evrazii: Teoriia, metodologiia i praktika issledovaniia*, 581–83. Irkutsk.

———. 2019. "Environmentalism, Cultural Resilience and Submerged Societies in Northern Eurasia" Paper presented at the 11th International Convention of Asia Scholars (ICAS), Leiden, Netherlands, July 15–19, 2019.

Anderson, David G., and Dmitry V. Arzyutov. 2016. "The Construction of Soviet Ethnography and 'The Peoples of Siberia.'" *History and Anthropology* 27 (2): 183–209.

———. 2019. "The *Etnos* Archipelago: Sergei M. Shirokogoroff and the Life History of a Controversial Anthropological Concept." *Current Anthropology* 60 (6): 741–73.

Anderson, David G., Dmitry V. Arzyutov, and Sergei S. Alymov, eds. 2019. *Life Histories of Etnos Theory in Russia and Beyond*. Cambridge, UK: Open Book.

Anderson, David G., Loïc Harrault, Karen B. Milek, Bruce C. Forbes, Mari Kuoppamaa, and Andreĭ V. Plekhanov. 2019. "Animal Domestication in the High Arctic: Hunting and Holding Reindeer on the IAmal Peninsula, Northwest Siberia." *Journal of Anthropological Archaeology* 55 (September): 101079.

Anikin, Aleksandr E. 1999. "O iakutskikh nazvaniiakh dikikh liudeĭ." In *IAzyki i fol'klor korennykh narodov Sibiri*, vol. 5, edited by Natal'ia N. Shirobokova, 214–20. Novosibirsk: Sibirskiĭ khronograf.

———. 2000. *Ėtimologicheskiĭ slovar' russkikh dialektov Sibiri: Zaimstvovaniia iz ural'skikh, altaĭskikh i paleoaziatskikh iazykov*. 2nd ed. Moscow: Nauka.

Arzyutov, Dmitry V. 2016. "Samoyedic Diary: Early Years of Visual Anthropology in the Soviet Arctic." *Visual Anthropology* 29 (4–5): 331–59.

———. 2019. "Environmental Encounters: Woolly Mammoth, Indigenous Communities and Metropolitan Scientists in the Soviet Arctic." *Polar Record* 55 (3): 142–53.

———. 2020. "'American Dreams' of Early Soviet Ethnography: Some Reflections on Bogoras's Legacy." *Ab Imperio* 1:75–89.

Arzyutov, Dmitry V., Sergei S. Alymov, and David G. Anderson, eds. 2014. *Ot klassikov k marksizmu: Soveshchanie ėtnografov Moskvy i Leningrada (5–11 aprelia 1929 g.).* Vol. 7. Saint Petersburg: AMAĖ RAN.

Arzyutov, Dmitry V., and Sergei A. Kan. 2017. "The Concept of the 'Field' in Early Soviet Ethnography: A Northern Perspective." *Sibirica: Interdisciplinary Journal of Siberian Studies* 16 (1): 31–74.

Arzyutov, Dmitry V., Sergei A. Kan, Laura Siragusa, and Alexander Pershai, eds. Forthcoming. *Paper Bridges Between Franz Boas and Russian Anthropology.* Franz Boas Papers. 2 vols. Lincoln: University of Nebraska Press.

Arzyutov, Dmitry, and Karina Lukin. 2023. "Introduction to 'Entangled Indigenous Historicities from the Eurasian North.'" *Suomen Antropologi: Journal of the Finnish Anthropological Society* 47 (3): 9–17.

Bibikov, Sergeĭ N., ed. 1941. *Kratkie soobshcheniia Instituta istorii material'noĭ kul'tury.* Vol. 9. Moscow: Izdatel'stvo AN SSSR.

Boas, Franz. 1940. *Race, Language, and Culture.* New York: Macmillan.

Bogoras, Waldemar [Vladimir G. Bogoraz]. 1902. "The Folklore of Northeastern Asia, as Compared with That of Northwestern America." *American Anthropologist* 4 (4): 577–683.

———. 1928a. "Ethnographic Problems of the Eurasian Arctic." In *Problems of Polar Research,* vol. 7, edited by W. L. G. Joerg, 189–207. American Geographic Society Special Publications. New York: American Geographical Society.

———. 1928b. "Paleoasiatic Tribes of South Siberia." In *Atti del XXII Congresso internazionale degli americanisti, Roma, settembre 1926,* 249–72. Roma: R. Garroni.

———. 1930. "New Data on the Types and Distribution of Reindeer Breeding in Northern Eurasia." In *Proceedings of the Twenty-Third International Congress of Americanists, September 17–22, 1928,* 403–10. Lancaster PA: Science Press.

Bogoraz, Vladimir G. 1927a. "Drevnie pereseleniia narodov v Severnoĭ Evrazii i Amerike." *Sbornik Muzeia antropologii i ėtnografii Akademii nauk SSSR* 6:37–62.

———, ed. 1927b. *Pamiati M.A. Kastrena: k 75-letiiu so dnia smerti.* Vol. 2. Ocherki po istorii znaniĭ. Leningrad: Izdatel'stvo AN SSSR.

Bogoraz-Tan, Vladimir G. 1928a. "Novye dannye k voprosu o proto-aziatakh."
Izvestiia Leningradskogo gosudarstvennogo universiteta 1:235–43.

———. 1928b. *Rasprostranenie kul'tury na Zemle: Osnovy étnogeografii*. Moscow:
Gosudarstvennoe izdatel'stvo.

———. 1933. "Zamechaniia k stat'e Frantsa Boaza." *Sovetskaia étnografiia*
3–4:189–93.

Branch, Michael. 1973. *A. J. Sjögren: Studies of the North*. Helsinki: Suomalais-
ugrilainen Seura.

Bubrikh, Dmitriĭ V. (2005) 1947. "Proiskhozhdenie karel'skogo naroda: Povest'
o soiuznike i druge russkogo naroda na Severe." In *Pribaltiĭsko-finskoe
iazykoznanie. Izbrannye raboty*, by Dmitriĭ V. Bubrikh, 347–79. Saint Petersburg: Filologicheskiĭ fakul'tet SPbGU.

Burba, Juliet M. 2006. "'Whence Came the American Indians?' American
Anthropologists and the Origins Question, 1880–1935." PhD diss., University of Minnesota–Minneapolis.

Castrén, Matthias Alexander. 2017. *Archaeologica et Historica. Universita-
ria*. Edited by Timo Salminen. Vol. 1. Manuscripta Castreniana. Helsinki:
Finno-Ugrian Society.

———. 2019. *Itineraria*. Edited by Timo Salminen. 2 vols. Manuscripta Castreniana. Helsinki: Finno-Ugrian Society.

Chakrabarty, Dipesh. 2021. *The Climate of History in a Planetary Age*. Chicago:
University of Chicago Press.

Chernetsov, Valeriĭ N. 1935. "Drevniaia primorskaia kul'tura na poluostrove IA-
Mal." *Sovetskaia étnografiia* 4–5:109–33.

Collins, Henry B. 1937. *Archeology of St. Lawrence Island, Alaska*. Smithsonian
Miscellaneous Collections 96 (1). Washington DC: Smithsonian Institution.

———. 1943. "Eskimo Archaeology and Its Bearing on the Problem of Man's
Antiquity in America." *Proceedings of the American Philosophical Society* 86
(2): 220–35.

Demuth, Bathsheba. 2019. *Floating Coast: An Environmental History of the Bering Strait*. New York: W. W. Norton.

Dolgikh, Boris O. 1960. "Prinesenie v zhertvu oleneĭ u nganasan i éntsev." In
Kratkie soobshcheniia Instituta étnografii im. N. N. Miklukho-Maklaia AN SSSR,
33:72–81. Moscow: Izdatel'stvo AN SSSR.

Drannikova, Natal'ia V., ed. 2008. *Chud' v ustnoĭ traditsii Arkhangel'skogo Severa*.
Arkhangel'sk: Pomorskiĭ universitet.

Ëĭkhval'd, Ėduard I. 1856. *O chudskikh kopiakh*. Saint Petersburg: Tipografiia
Ėkspeditsii zagotovleniia gosudarstvennykh bumag.

Fasmer, Maks. 1987. *Ėtimologicheskiĭ slovar' russkogo iazyka*. Vol. 4. Moscow: Progress.

Fëdorova, Nataliia V. 2002. "Prizraki i real'nosti iamal'skoĭ arkheologii." *Rossiĭskaia arkheologiia* 4:99–110.

Fewkes, J. Walter, Aleš Hrdlička, William H. Dall, James W. Gidley, Austin Hobart Clark, William H Holmes, Alice C. Fletcher, et al. 1912. "The Problems of the Unity or Plurality and the Probable Place of Origin of the American Aborigines." *American Anthropologist* 14 (1): 1–59.

Field, Henry, and Eugene Prostov. 1937. "Archaeology in the Soviet Union." *American Anthropologist* 39 (3): 457–90.

———. 1942. "Results of Soviet Investigations in Siberia, 1940–1941." *American Anthropologist* 44 (3): 388–406.

Fitzhugh, William. 1997. "Searching for the Grail: Virtual Archaeology in Yamal and Circumpolar Theory." In *Fifty Years of Arctic Research: Anthropological Studies From Greenland to Siberia*, edited by Rolf Gilberg and H. C. Gulløv, 99–118. Publications of the National Museum, Ethnographical Series, vol. 18,. Copenhagen: National Museum of Denmark.

Fogelson, Raymond D. 1974. "On the Varieties of Indian History: Sequoyah and Traveller Bird." *Journal of Ethnic Studies* 2 (1): 105–12.

Geddon, Al'fred [Alfred Haddon]. 1923. *Pereselenie narodov*. Petrograd: Kniga.

Golomshtok, Eugene A. 1932. "The Russian Project." *University Museum Bulletin* 3 (3–4): 82–91.

———. 1933a. "Anthropological Activities in Soviet Russia." *American Anthropologist* 35 (2): 301–27.

———. 1933b. "Traces of a Blond Race in Siberia." *University Museum Bulletin* 4 (2): 40–45.

Gracheva, Galina N. 1990. "Paleoėtnograficheskie issledovaniia v Arktike." In *Dvesti let arkticheskoĭ arkheologii*, vol. 200, 21–26. Kratkie soobshcheniia Instituta arkheologii AN SSSR. Moscow: Nauka.

Grant, Bruce. 1995. *In the Soviet House of Culture: A Century of Perestroikas*. Princeton NJ: Princeton University Press.

Gullette, David. 2008. "A State of Passion: The Use of Ethnogenesis in Kyrgyzstan." *Inner Asia* 10 (2): 261–79.

Gurvich, Il'ia S. 1975. *Tainstvennyĭ chuchuna (istoriia odnogo ėtnograficheskogo poiska)*. Moscow: Mysl'.

Haddon, Alfred C. 1911. *The Wanderings of Peoples*. Cambridge: Cambridge University Press.

Hill, Jonathan D., ed. 1996. *History, Power, and Identity: Ethnogenesis in the Americas, 1492–1992*. Iowa City: University of Iowa Press.

Hirsch, Francine. 2005. *Empire of Nations: Ethnographic Knowledge and the Making of the Soviet Union*. Ithaca NY: Cornell University Press.

Il'ina, Irina N. 2015. "Dokumenty arkhiva RAN ob izuchenii 'snezhnogo cheloveka' v kontse 1950-kh gg." *Otechestvennye arkhivy* 3:37–43.

Irvine, Richard. 2020. *An Anthropology of Deep Time: Geological Temporality and Social Life*. Cambridge: Cambridge University Press.

Janhunen, Juha. 2009. "Language and the Search for Identity. M. A. Castrén and the Rise of the Uralic Concept, 1800–1880." In *Defining Self. Essays on Emergent Identities in Russia Seventeenth to Nineteenth Centuries*, edited by Michael Branch, 482–96. Studia Fennica, Ethnologica, vol. 10. Helsinki: Finnish Literature Society.

Jochelson, Waldemar [Vladimir I. Iokhel'son]. 1907. "Past and Present Subterranean Dwellings of the Tribes of North Eastern Asia and North Western America." In *Congrès International Des Américanistes: XVe Session*, vol. 2, 115–28. Québec: Dussault & Proulx.

———. 1920. "The Semisubterranean Houses of the Koryak of Northeastern Siberia." In *Source Book in Anthropology*, edited by Alfred L. Kroeber and Thomas T. Waterman, 278–85. Berkeley: University of California Press.

Kan, Sergei. 2008. "'My Old Friend in a Dead-End of Empiricism and Skepticism': Bogoras, Boas, and the Politics of Soviet Anthropology of the Late 1920s–Early 1930s." *Histories of Anthropology Annual* 2: 33–68.

Kazakevich, Olga A. 2010. "Arkhiv G. N. i E. D. Prokof'evykh: Samodiiskie iazykovye materialy." *Finnisch-Ugrische Mitteilungen* 32/33:257–78.

Kendall, Laurel, and Igor Krupnik, eds. 2003. *Constructing Cultures Then and Now: Celebrating Franz Boas and the Jesup North Pacific Expedition*. Contributions to Circumpolar Anthropology, vol. 4. Washington DC: Arctic Studies Center, NMNH, Smithsonian Institution.

Khomich, Liudmila V. 1970. "Nenetskie predaniia o sikhirtia." In *Fol'klor i ètnografiia*, edited by Boris N. Putilov, 59–72. Leningrad: Nauka.

———. 1974. "Sootnoshenie poniatiĭ ètnogenez i ètnicheskaia istoriia (na primere formirovaniia nenetskoĭ narodnosti)." In *Kratkoe soderzhanie dokladov godichnoĭ nauchnoĭ sessii instituta ètnografii AN SSSR. 1972–1973*, 61–65. Leningrad: Nauka.

Korsun, Sergeĭ A. 2015. *Amerikanistika v Kunstkamere (1714–2014)*. Saint Petersburg: AMAÈ RAN.

Krech, Shepard III. 1999. *The Ecological Indian: Myth and History*. New York: W. W. Norton.

Krupnik, Igor. 1976. "Stanovlenie krupnotabunnogo olenevodstva u tundrovykh nentsev." *Sovetskaia ètnografiia* 2:57–69.

————, ed. 2016. *Early Inuit Studies: Themes and Transitions, 1850s–1980s*. Washington DC: Smithsonian Institution.

Kupina, IUliia A. 2004. "Utraty ili priobreteniia? (istoriia kollektsionnykh obmenov MAÈ RAN s amerikanskimi muzeiami)." *Kur'er Petrovskoĭ Kunstkamery* 10–11:52–85.

La Martinière, P. Martin de. 1671. *Voyage des pays Septentrionaux: Dans lequel se void les moeurs, maniere de vivre, et superstitions des Norweguiens, Lappons, Kiloppes, Borandiens, Syberiens, Samojedes, Zembliens, et Islandois, enrichi de plusieurs figures*. Paris: Chez Louis Vendosme.

Laptander, Roza I. 2019. "Vodnye, podzemnye i nebesnye oleni sikhirtia." In *Lingvistika i drugie vazhnye veshchi*, edited by Evgenii V. Golovko, Aleksandr M. Pevnov, Maria Yu. Pupynina, Arzhaana A. Syuryun, and Anna Yu. Urmancheva, 184–227. Saint Petersburg: ILI RAN.

Laruelle, Marlène. 2008. "The Concept of Ethnogenesis in Central Asia: Political Context and Institutional Mediators (1940–50)." *Kritika: Explorations in Russian and Eurasian History* 9 (1): 169–88.

Lashuk, Leonid P. 1969. "Chud' istoricheskaia i chud' legendarnaia." *Voprosy istorii* 10:208–16.

Laufer, Berthold. 1917. *The Reindeer and Its Domestication*. Lancaster PA: American Anthropological Association.

Lepekhin, Ivan I. 1805. *Puteshestviia Akademika Ivana Lepekhina*. Vol. 4. Saint Petersburg: Imperatorskaia akademiia nauk.

Lévinas, Emmanuel. 2003. *Humanism of the Other*. Translated by Nidra Poller. Urbana: University of Illinois Press.

Lomonosov, Mikhail V. 1952. *Polnoe sobranie sochineniĭ*. Vol. 6. *Trudy po russkoĭ istorii, obshchestvenno-èkonomicheskim voprosam i geografii, 1747–1765*. Moscow: Izdatel'stvo AN SSSR.

Lönngren, Tamara. 2019. "'. . . otkladyvaetsia do bolee blagopriiatnogo vremeni': O Kol'skoĭ èkspeditsii Frit'ofa Nansena." *Scando-Slavica* 65 (2): 146–69.

Lukin, Karina. 2011. "Elämän ja entisyyden maisemat: Kolgujev nenetsien arjesssa, muistelussa ja kerronnassa." PhD thesis, Suomalaisen Kirjallisuuden Seura, Helsinki.

————. 2020. "Domesticated Mammoths: Mythic and Material in Nenets Verbal Tradition on Ya' Xora." *Multilingua* 40 (4): 511–36.

Manias, Chris. 2013. *Race, Science, and the Nation: Reconstructing the Ancient Past in Britain, France and Germany*. New York: Routledge.

Michael, Henry N. 1958. "The Neolithic Age in Eastern Siberia." *Transactions of the American Philosophical Society* 48 (2): 1–108.

Nabokov, Peter. 2002. *A Forest of Time: American Indian Ways of History*. Cambridge: Cambridge University Press.

Nomokonova, Tatiana, Robert J. Losey, Andreĭ V. Plekhanov, and Heather J. McIntyre. 2018. "Iarte VI and Late Holocene Reindeer Remains from the Iamal Peninsula of Arctic Siberia." *Arctic Anthropology* 55 (2): 56–75.

Nosilov, Konstantin D. 1903. *Na Novoĭ Zemle: ocherki i nabroski*. Saint Petersburg: Izdanie A.S. Suvorina.

Obruchev, Vladimir A. 1968. *Sannikov's Land*. Edited by Peter H. Collin. London: Harrap.

Okladnikov, Alekseĭ P. 1938. "Arkheologicheskie dannye o drevneĭsheĭ istorii Pribaĭkal'ia." *Vestnik drevneĭ istorii* 1 (2): 244–60.

———. 1980. "Khrdlichka ishchet pervykh amerikantsev." *Sibirskie ogni* 7: 162–73.

Petri, Berngard Ė. 1916. "Neoliticheskie nakhodki na beregu Baĭkala. Predvaritel'noe soobshchenie o raskopkakh stoianki Ulan-Khada." *Sbornik Muzeia antropologii i ėtnografii* 3:113–32.

Pika, Aleksandr I. 1989. "Novye materialy k istorii pervoĭ sovetskoĭ ėtnograficheskoĭ ėkspeditsii na poluostrov IAmal (1928–1929 gg.)." *Sovetskaia ėtnografiia* 6:100–108.

Pimenov, Vladimir V. 1965. *Vepsy: ocherk ėtnicheskoĭ istorii i genezisa kul'tury*. Moscow: Nauka.

Popov, Nikolaĭ. 1876. "O chudskikh mogilakh Minusinskogo kraia [I]." *Izvestiia Sibirskogo Otdela Imperatorskogo Russkogo Geograficheskogo Obshchestva* 7 (2–3): 69–78.

Popov, Viktorin. 1932. *Liudi Bol'shoĭ Zemli*. Moscow: Federatsiia.

Prokof'ev, Georgiĭ N. 1928. "Ostiako-samoedy Turukhanskogo kraia." *Ėtnografiia* 6 (2): 96–103.

———. 1940. "Ėtnogoniia narodnosteĭ Ob'-Eniseĭskogo basseĭna (nentsev, nganasanov, ėntsev, sel'kupov, ketov, khantov i mansov)." *Sovetskaia ėtnografiia* 3:67–76.

Prokof'eva, Ekaterina D. 1947. "Drevnie zhilishcha na rekakh Tym' i Ket." *Sovetskaia ėtnografiia* 2:199–202.

———. 1953. "Materialy po religioznym predstavleniiam ėntsev." *Sbornik Muzeia antropologii i ėtnografii AN SSSR* 14:194–230.

Prokofjew, Georgii N. [Georgiĭ N. Prokof'ev]. 1933. "Proto-Asiatic Elements in Ostyak-Samoyed Culture." *American Anthropologist*, n.s., 35 (1): 131–33.

Reshetov, Alexandr M. 2000. "Sovetskiĭ arkheolog i ėtnograf Vasiliĭ Stepanovich Adrianov: Zhizn', prervannaia na vzlete." In *Drevnosti IAmala*, vol. 1, edited by Andreĭ V. Golovnëv, 238–47. Ekaterinburg: UrO RAN.

Robinson, Michael F. 2016. *The Lost White Tribe: Explorers, Scientists, and the Theory That Changed a Continent*. Oxford: Oxford University Press.

Roeder, Carolin F., and Gregory Afinogenov. 2018. "Cold War Creatures: Soviet Science and the Problem of the Abominable Snowman." In *Frost, Ice, and Snow: Cold Climate in Russian History*, edited by Julia Herzberg, Christian Kehrt, and Franziska Torma, 236–53. New York: Berghahn.

Rudenko, Sergeĭ I. 1962. *Sibirskaia kollektsiia Petra I*. Vol. D3–9. Svod arkheologicheskikh istochnikov. Moscow: Iskusstvo.

Salminen, Tapani. 1998. *A Morphological Dictionary of Tundra Nenets*. Vol. 26. Helsinki: Lexica Societatis Fenno-Ugricae.

Salminen, Timo. 2006. "Searching for the Finnish Roots: Archaeological Cultures and Ethnic Groups in Works of Aspelin and Tallgren." In *People, Material Culture and Environment in the North. Proceedings of the 22 Nordic Archaeology Conference, University of Oulu, 18–23 August 2004*, edited by Vesa-Pekka Herva, 27–32. Studia Humaniora Ouluensia, vol. 1. Oulu: Gummerus Kirjapaino Oy.

Shirokogoroff, Sergei M. 1925. *Anthropology of Eastern China and Kwangtung Province*. Shanghai: Commercial Press.

———. 1931. *Ethnological and Linguistic Aspects of the Ural-Altaic Hypothesis*. Peiping: Commercial Press.

Shnirel'man, Viktor A. 1993. "Zlokliucheniia odnoĭ nauki: ėtnogeneticheskie issledovaniia i stalinskaia natsional'naia politika." *Etnographicheskoe obozrenie* 3:52–68.

Shrenk, Aleksandr I. [Alexander von Schrenk]. 1855. *Puteshestvie k severovostoku Evropeĭskoĭ Rossii cherez tundry samoedov k severnym Ural'skim goram*. Saint Petersburg: Tipografiia Grigoriia Trusova.

Shrenk, Leopol'd I. [Leopold von Schrenk]. 1883. *Ob inorodtsakh Amurskogo kraia*. Vol. 1. Saint Petersburg: Tipografiia Imperatorskoĭ Akademii nauk.

Shternberg, Lev. 1999. *The Social Organization of the Gilyak*. Edited by Bruce Grant. Anthropological Papers of the AMNH, vol. 82. New York: American Museum of Natural History.

Siikala, Jukka. 2006. "The Ethnography of Finland." *Annual Review of Anthropology* 35: 153–70.

Silver, Carole G. 1999. *Strange and Secret Peoples: Fairies and Victorian Consciousness*. Oxford: Oxford University Press.

Simonetti, Cristián. 2013. "Between the Vertical and the Horizontal: Time and Space in Archaeology." *History of the Human Sciences* 26 (1): 90–110.

Siragusa, Laura. 2017. *Promoting Heritage Language in Northwest Russia*. London: Routledge.

Slezkine, Yuri. 1996. "N. Ia. Marr and the National Origins of Soviet Ethnogenetics." *Slavic Review* 55 (4): 826–62.

Sotnikova-Ratner, Tat'iana. 2017. "Troe Na IAmale." *Zvezda* 3:107–40.

Spasskiĭ, Grigoriĭ I. 1819. "O chudskikh kopiakh v Sibiri." *Sibirskiĭ vestnik* 7:124–42.

Stocking, George W., Jr., ed. 1989. *A Franz Boas Reader: The Shaping of American Anthropology, 1883–1911*. Chicago: University of Chicago Press.

Sushkin, Petr. 1925. "Outlines of the History of the Recent Fauna of Palaearctic Asia." *Proceedings of the National Academy of Sciences of the United States of America* 11 (6): 299–302.

———. 1928. "Vysokogornye oblasti zemnogo shara i vopros o rodine pervobytnogo cheloveka." *Priroda* 3:249–78.

Tereshchenko, Natal'ia M. 1965. *Nenetsko-russkiĭ slovar'*. Moscow: Sovetskaia éntsiklopediia.

Tolstoy, Paul. 1958. "The Archaeology of the Lena Basin and Its New World Relationships, Part I." *American Antiquity* 23 (4): 397–418.

Tugolukov, Vladilen A. 1986. "Predaniia ob ukhode iukagirov na ostrova i 'za more.'" *Sovetskaia étnografiia* 6:94–100.

Vakhtin, Nikolaĭ B. 2005. "Tikhookeanskaia ėkspeditsiia Dzhesupa i eë russkie uchastniki." *Antropologicheskiĭ forum*, no. 2, 241–74.

Vasil'ev, Vladimir I. 1970. "Siirtia—legenda ili real'nost'?" *Sovetskaia étnografiia* 1:151–58.

———. 1979. *Problemy formirovaniia severo-samodiĭskikh narodnosteĭ*. Moscow: Nauka.

Veltre, Douglas W. 2008. "One of the Boys: Alan May's Three Seasons with Aleš Hrdlička in the Aleutian Islands." *Alaska Journal of Anthropology* 6 (1–2): 141–50.

Vermeulen, Han F. 2015. *Before Boas: The Genesis of Ethnography and Ethnology in the German Enlightenment*. Lincoln: University of Nebraska Press.

Wolf, Eric R. 1982. *Europe and the People Without History*. Berkeley: University of California Press.

Zolotarev, Alexander. 1938. "The Ancient Culture of North Asia." *American Anthropologist* 40 (1): 13–23.

2

Between Polish and British Academia and Macedonian Fieldwork

Józef Obrębski and the First Functionalist
Research of the European Village

ANNA ENGELKING

STUDENT OF MALINOWSKI

In 1932–33 a young Polish anthropologist, Józef Obrębski, conducted field-work among the farmer-shepherd highlanders in the Poreche region in Macedonia (then part of Yugoslavia).[1] This constituted the first ethnographic fieldwork of a European village carried out consistently, concerning both the theoretical framework and methodology, in the paradigm of functionalism. These highlanders lived, in the words of Obrębski, "farther than at the peripheries of civilization" (2022a, 56). They were a highly isolated group regarding communication, economy, society, and consciousness. The aim of the twenty-seven-year-old scholar was to provide a description of this society's "life, customs and institutions" (53), particularly family organization and the magico-religious system. "Simple and parsimonious, the folk culture of Poreche," he wrote, "constitutes a clear, concise, coherent system, with its proper logic, moderation and balance. Thus for a researcher whose interests are not confined to . . . apparent peculiarities of primitive culture, but who . . . aims at comprehending the complicated mechanism of primitive culture, at analysing its individual institutions and aspects, and at discovering the bonds fusing the life of the primeval group into a delineated and closed socio-cultural system, Poreche constitutes an ideal object of study" (Obrębski 2020, 13).

It is not difficult to see that Obrębski conceptualized his object of research by referring to the model supplied by Bronisław Malinowski's description of the sociocultural reality of the Trobriand Islands. It is beyond doubt that Malinowski's monographs of the Trobriand Islands were a theoretical and methodological inspiration for Obrębski's fieldwork.[2] He had read two of them—*Argonauts of the Western Pacific* (1922) and *The Sexual Life of Savages in North-Western Melanesia* (1929)—in the original English when he was still a student in Poland, long before he began his research. With *Coral Gardens and Their Magic* (1935), however, published two years after his return from Macedonia, he was acquainted from an unusual, practical side: He had worked on this book together with its author, accompanying Malinowski as his research assistant in Oberbozen and Tamaris in 1931–32.[3] Thus the lessons and inspiration he received from Malinowski and used in Poreche were not indirect.

Obrębski was part of a circle of Malinowski's close students (see Kuper 1987, 30–36). He participated in Malinowski's famous social anthropology seminar at the London School of Economics and Political Science and wrote a PhD under his supervision.[4] Direct contact between teacher and student lasted for three full years: from November 1930, when Obrębski came to London as a fellow of the Rockefeller Foundation, to January 1934, when he received a doctorate in social anthropology from the London School of Economics.[5] It is thus not surprising that his theoretical credo in the foreword to his monograph summing up his Macedonian fieldwork sounds as if uttered by Malinowski: "The ethnographic description must . . . make avail of the sociological method. It shows the types and variations of culture against the background of the collective life of primitive societies" (Obrębski 2022a, 53). In view of the background of Obrębski's work—a young academic conducting ethnography/ethnology in peripheral Poland, which was only beginning to be institutionalized—this sounded, if not revolutionary, then certainly innovative.

Whence did Józef Obrębski come, and who was he when he arrived in London to become first an adherent of the functionalist method and later its practitioner and exponent in Poland?[6] He obtained his education and master's degree from Jagiellonian University in Kraków, the same university from which Bronisław Malinowski had graduated and received his doctorate (1908) two decades earlier. Obrębski studied ethnography of Slavs and Slavic philology (1925–30) at an experimental institute founded at this university, the Slavic Study Center, which implemented the idea of integrated Slavic studies, comparable to the interdisciplinary Slavic studies of today (see Engelking 2019a). At the same time, from the beginning of his studies, Obrębski worked at the Slavic Study Center as an assistant, carrying out various subsidiary organizational and editorial tasks and teaching students.

As an ethnographer and ethnologist, he was a student of Kazimierz Moszyński, who was perhaps the greatest authority in Europe on the issues of ethnography of Slavs, and as a linguist, he was a student of the Slavist Kazimierz Nitsch. Nitsch in turn had studied linguistics under Lucjan Malinowski, Bronisław's father, and had worked as a tutor of the future anthropologist. During Malinowski's London years, it was Nitsch who was his main corresponding contact with Kraków and the university there. When the opportunity arose for Obrębski to go to London on a scholarship, both Moszyński and Nitsch supported this. They understood that studying under Malinowski would afford the young ethnologist, whom they saw as exceptionally talented, possibilities of further development that could not be provided by the university in Kraków regarding both the progress of his academic career and his potential future contribution to the advancement of Polish ethnology.

It was then that Obrębski's research, which had been focused on material culture (his master's thesis was an ethnogeographic-typological analysis of agricultural tools in the Balkan Peninsula), turned toward social anthropology, and he began to connect his academic future with studying the social organization of Eastern and Southern European peasants.[7] Even before the question of his going to London had been settled, he was planning, as he wrote to Malinowski, "fieldwork in the most primitive regions of White Russia" that "will be concerned to a great extent with aspects of sociology and will be founded on your methods, Professor, known to me through your works, which have done me v. much good" (LSE: Obrębski to Malinowski, May 31, 1930).

His ethnology teacher from Kraków, Kazimierz Moszyński, envisaged for Obrębski an academic career crowned by professorship at an ethnology department at one of the universities in Poland.[8] In a letter to John Van Sickle, the director of the Rockefeller Foundation's office in Paris, who was responsible for social science fellowships, Moszyński foresaw Obrębski as a future specialist "on the issue of social folk life of Slavs," emphasizing the fact that such a specialist "is not to be found today . . . neither in Poland nor in any other Slavic country." Obrębski had the predisposition to "study the primitive social life" in any of the Slavic countries, he wrote, which "he will carry out without difficulty, as he knows all of the Slavic languages." Moszyński saw Obrębski as an author of "critical studies" synthesizing the "extraordinarily plentiful, hitherto collected ethnographic material concerning the social folk life of Slavs," and at the same time an author "publishing his most important works in English, thus making the abundant Slavic ethnographic material available for the world at large" (IEiAKUJ: Moszyński to Van Sickle, n.d.).

Obrębski was thus beginning his studies under Malinowski as the hope of Polish ethnology.[9] His teacher in London quickly subscribed to this opinion. "Talented, agreeable, intelligent—he is liked by and large and popular with everybody who knows him," Malinowski wrote to Nitsch on June 10, 1931. "I believe Obrębski's future to be particularly promising" (Flis and Paluch 1985, 289). And to the Rockefeller Foundation, he wrote, "Personally, I have formed an extremely favourable opinion of the character, intelligence, and application of Obrebski, and if his health remains as good as it is . . . I am certain he will be able to take a front rank among the workers in Social Science" (LSE: Malinowski to Van Sickle, May 3, 1931).

THE "TROBRIAND" PROJECT OF THE MACEDONIAN MONOGRAPHS

Obrębski's Macedonian research project, a part and parcel of the program of his studies at the LSE, was supervised both by Malinowski and the Rockefeller Foundation and connected with the PhD thesis he worked on (see Engelking 2024). Obrębski carried out his fieldwork systematically for eight months, from August 1932 to March 1933, in a couple of villages in Upper Poreche. He was living at a farm in Volche, at the highest elevation of all the villages and difficult to reach in winter. His hosts—the widow Stefkoytsa and her adult sons Tsiro and Kolo, as well as their family, clan, and neighbors—constituted a microcosm in which the foreign ethnographer functioned on the basis of a "guest-friend" (the *gost-prijatel* category of Poreche, which encompasses relatives, godparents, kinsmen, and close friends).[10] He later told Moszyński:

I have spent nearly six months being almost a member of the zadruga, catching as if in flagrante and watching closely all those things which heretofore remained almost entirely unobserved: the private life of the southern Slavic family. . . . Apart from a number of [pieces of] useful information, I obtained the most important thing: thorough knowledge of this network of relationships exhibited by a (large) patriarchal family. . . . I have the feeling that when it comes to the subject of southern Slavic kinship, I am unparalleled, regarding the knowledge of the facts and the theoretical elaboration of this issue. (IEiAKUJ: Obrębski to Moszyński, April 4, 1933)

His ethnographic strategy consisted of observation, in which he was sensitive and reacted to turns of events; participation ("active participation in the life of the village"); and conversations with the people who surrounded him, which were mainly informal conversations and not formal interviews.[11] In the beginning, however, this was not easy; it took Obrębski a long time to move beyond conventional relationships with the villagers and overcome their initial distrust. Well aware of the fact that "beyond the outward respect for tradition, law and custom, staged for the stranger . . . there lies hidden a reality far different from the falsified appearances of the ideal," he endeavored to uncover "the underlying aspects of their social life, customary unwritten laws, and conscientiously hidden scandals and injustices" (Obrębski 2022b, 135, 153).

Following Malinowski's methodological instruction, he was alert to the "constant divergences between what people say, and what they do; what they really undertake and what they think" (Kuper 1987, 27). He was also very much aware of the fact that the reality under scrutiny often verifies the researcher's initial presuppositions.

Obrębski's aim in coming to Poreche was studying the local organization of family. However, he wrote,

empirical, ethnological research, the main tool of which is direct inperson observation . . . led to constant surprises. . . . The continuous stream of events and affairs of village life, taking place before my eyes and almost with my participation, broke open the rigorous and unrealistic frames in which I had wanted to contain my studies. Out of necessity, then, other issues and phenomena, going beyond the main subject of family life, had to be taken into account in my work. . . . One such incidental result of my research was the study of witchcraft, which proved particularly onerous because of the secrecy and furtiveness surrounding this area of life of the Porechians. It required highly intimate contacts with the locals and employment of methods far removed from questionnaire and interrogation. (Obrębski 2020, 13–14)

As a result, Obrębski collected far more diverse ethnographic material than he had initially planned. His fieldwork notes and studies based on them concern all the spheres of life of the society under scrutiny—the economy, annual and family rites, healing arts and magic, mythology and religion, marital relations, and the institution of family—in a broad sociocultural context. He wrote down a couple hundred short and long texts of folklore, including many spells; he also amassed rich photographic documentation, about 550 black-and-white photographs on glass plates.

He envisaged a series of monographs, a project that cannot be reconstructed today in its entirety. Over the following years, he worked on books and articles whose titles and outlines evolved over time, making it impossible to re-create their chronology and order of contents according to the author's final intentions.

Obrębski's work, preserved in the form of typescripts and manuscripts, unfinished and seemingly lacking an internal delimitation of its boundaries, on its own constitutes proof of the validity of the fundamental assumption of functionalism—that is, of the complex and multilayered character of social reality. The modern editor of Obrębski's writings, when trying to order, say, one of his descriptions of the social structure of the Poreche village for a monograph about the magico-religious system or witchcraft or about marriage and family, learns firsthand the great extent to which particular aspects of culture cannot be studied, perceived, and described in isolation.

We do not know if Obrębski's fieldwork and methodological materials have come down to us in their entirety. His monograph "Macedonian Faith and Rituals: A Sociological Account of the Beliefs and Magico-Religious Rituals of Poreche in Serbian Macedonia," on which he worked during the German occupation and which was ready for publication, was destroyed during the Warsaw Uprising in 1944. The legacy we have consists mainly of four unfinished monographs together with rich documentation from the field (Obrębski 2022a, 2022b). "The Giaours of Macedonia: An Account of the Magic and Religion of Shepherds in Poreche Against the Background of the Collective Life of Their Village" contains materials for the book that was destroyed. Another book manuscript, "The Witchcraft of Macedonian Poreche," was supposed to be published in English.[12] While working on this book in Warsaw in 1935, after having received a copy of the *Coral Gardens* from Malinowski, Obrębski wrote to him:

> "Witchcraft" was elaborated in the field and later, while my memories of my apprenticeship under you, Professor, were still fresh, and it stems from *Coral Gardens* both methodologically and theoretically. . . . I have taken up the work on "Witchcraft" only very recently and due to constant excurses into the field and my current research in Polesie, progress is made by very uneven and sporadic bursts.[13] . . . It is about this work that I wanted to ask you, Professor, if it were possible for you to write a foreword to this book—that is, of course, if you deem it worthy. I would be sincerely pleased if my first ethnological book was honored with such a distinction and this sign of school and method. I regret to say, however, that this as yet unfinished "Witchcraft" is far from not only *Coral Gardens*, which constituted for it an ideal [that was] unreachable and impossible to imitate, but even from *Sorcerers of Dobu*.[14] Although, as I hope, the field may be partially to blame for this. (LSE: Obrębski to Malinowski, January 24, 1935)

Another monograph, "Scandal in the Village," stemming from Obrębski's study of family organization, focuses on the institutions of bride wealth and marriage by elopement, as well as conjugal maladjustment.[15] And finally, the fourth, "Myth and Reality of Southern Slavs," is a study deconstructing myths common in ethnology that orientalized southern Slavic peasants (myths of selling wives, of killing the old, or of incest). Obrębski wrote of this project to Moszyński:

> [It is] work designed not as fieldwork but as a general theoretical work about the Balkans. . . . The theoretical thesis is that these myths are wrongly taken either as a tradition of a distant and lost culture . . . or . . . as a token of the national or state consciousness of Macedonian peas-

ants. . . . These myths function in the current social structure either as a way of sanctioning the present state of affairs or as a moral injunction in the system of social relations, inherent to the Balkan culture. The work therefore consists of two parts: a theoretical polemical part, where past ethnographic mistakes are dismantled, and a constructive part, where for each of the myths the appropriate social context is provided. This naturally includes an analysis of a number of spheres of life. (IEiAKUJ: Obrębski to Moszyński, April 4, 1933)

Among myths of this group analyzed by Obrębski was one from outside the Macedonian region, inscribed into the broader Slavic and Balkan context—the myth of man in labor, connected with "the structure of the family: its one way patrilineal filiation with its bilateral organization" (IEiAKUJ: Obrębski to Moszyński, April 4, 1933). The anthropological interpretation of this myth, put in the appropriate context, became Obrębski's PhD thesis, "Family Organisation Among Slavs as Reflected in the Custom of Couvade." Although he later worked on preparing it for publication—it was supposed to be published, as were books by other students of Malinowski, with his mentor's foreword—he did not manage to bring this project to its end.[16] The two-hundred-page typescript of the "Couvade" remains at the archive of the London School of Economics.

Obrębski's materials and writings from Macedonia are currently in the archive of the University of Massachusetts–Amherst, which received the scholar's legacy after his death in New York in 1967.[17] The collection consists of about fifteen hundred pages of manuscripts and typescripts in Polish, Macedonian (written in Serbian Cyrillic or transcribed into the Roman alphabet), and English, as well as photographs. Out of this abundant collection, only two articles were published during Obrębski's lifetime, both before the Second World War in a Polish popular science journal. These were "Black Magic in Macedonia" (1934) and "The Religious System of Macedonian Folk" (1936). Soon after the scholar's death, his text "Social Structure and Ritual in a Macedonian Village," first delivered as a lecture at the annual meeting of American Anthropological Association in Philadelphia in 1961, was edited and published in subsequent editions (Obrębski 2006 [1969]).

GENDER RELATIONS IN PORECHE AS
A "STRUCTURAL BISECTION"

Studying family and social organization and the system of kinship in their dynamic synthesis with the system of beliefs and rituals, including those that were asocial and carried out secretly, furnished Obrębski with a deep understanding of the local sociocultural system and many insightful interpretations. First of all, he delivered a consistent interpretation of the social reality of Poreche in categories that today would be associated with gender theories. Obrębski talked of a "structural bisection," characteristic of the social structure in Poreche—that is, "a division of the village society into groups of men and women, having different rights and being of different social standing. This differentiation results not only from biological speculation," he wrote, "[but] it is overflowing with significant social matter, it permeates all spheres of life: social organization, economy, law, moral customs, religion and art.... This division determines the [different] life aims and the [different] life careers ... of a man and a woman" (Obrębski 2022a, 242).

What is more, he pointed to the social inequality of the two sexes, governed by the rules of the patriarchy:

> Men are the privileged class, ruling over land and animals, having wealth at their disposal, deciding the matters of the village, household, family, and of the women, who are their subordinates. Women are subjugated by them, and the inferiority of their social standing is visible at every turn: in the limits of their right to own property, in their exclusion from family and village councils, in burdening them with work, in the restrictions imposed by etiquette and custom, and finally, in the peculiar gynophobia of the Macedonian, who attributes to the female nature malice, wickedness and deceptiveness. (Obrębski 2022a, 340)

At the same time, Obrębski steered far away from essentialism, revealing the sociocultural "nature of these factors which create and maintain the social differences between men and women in Eastern European society" (Obrębski 1933, 53). It did not end here; by no means did he narrow this division to male domination and female subordination, which he analyzed in socioeconomical as well as symbolic context, deconstructing "the ideology of man's superiority over women" (99). He warned "against applying any absolute criteria in summing up the women's position—or, to put it more clearly, against speaking of their 'inferiority' or 'superiority'—when various aspects of social life . . . give different answers to the problem" (22). He showed how flexible and inconsistent the dynamics of male-female inequality could be, depending on the circumstances. He meticulously unearthed incoherencies, contradictions, and paradoxes, pointing to those aspects of the relation between the sexes in which they were either equal in standing and privileges (as is the case for the oldest generation in a family group, with mother as mistress of the house and father as master of the house) or women had the dominating role. He allotted considerable space to analyzing the latter case. He focused on matrilocal marriage, in which the wife as master of the house played the social role of the man, and the husband-*domazet* (son-in-law living in the house of his in-laws) played that of the subjugated woman. He described in detail the role of superiority and agency that women played in magico-religious rituals.

Analyzing the particular position in this gender bisection of antisocial witchcraft, practiced by women, who occupied the inferior social position, Obrębski demonstrated that the dominating role of women in the ritual life of the society was a fundamental trait of the culture under scrutiny—a trait without which the entire sociocultural system would lose its balance. To quote the conclusions of his article "Social Structure and Ritual in a Macedonian Village":

> The responsibilities, privileges and rights granted to women in ritual activities compensate for their deprivation of status which is their share in secular life. . . . On the secular plane, there is a system of superordination and subordination, a system of solidarity circles, placing men above women and women below men. On the ritual level, the system gives way to a different type of social relations: those based on personal and family loyalties, sentimental attachments and cooperation. By the working of patriliny the secular community consists basically of men and their appendages. It divides its members into natives and strangers, men and women. It elevates men and their descendants and subordinates women to men, sisters to brothers and even mothers to sons. The religious community restores the balance. It embraces all: natives

and strangers, men and women, children and adults, the rich and the poor, the living and the dead. The secular community is founded on the unilateral patrilineal basis. The religious community is at least bilateral if not omnilateral; it is egalitarian and all-inclusive. (OC: "Social Structure and Ritual")

Obrębski's constructivist approach shows gender relations (in his terminology: "the social division into women and men") as immersed in social mechanisms, which imbue them with various functions and meanings. His "structural bisection," which cannot be reduced to either sexuality or ensuring the succession of generations, is dynamically, depending on the context, shaped by historical, economical, cultural, and symbolic factors, which themselves are subject to the rules of patriarchy. It is a flexible mechanism, the foundation and the primary constructional axis of the entire social and cultural system. And at the same time, it is a mechanism that warrants the system's completeness, coherence, dynamics, and continuation.

EMPIRICISM AND ANTI-ESSENTIALISM OF THE MACEDONIAN MONOGRAPHS

Obrębski, following Malinowski, remained at odds with "old-fashioned ethnology" (Obrębski 2022b, 47). He deconstructed the evolutionistic and diffusionistic myths and essentialisms entrenched in anthropology, including the romantic myth of the countryside as a thesaurus of archaisms amounting to the core of national culture, a myth that constituted European, including Polish, ethnography/ethnology. His critique was founded as much on theory (and his inspirations went beyond Malinowski's functionalism) as on empirical evidence—on his rich personal ethnographic experiences, including those before the fieldwork in Macedonia.[18]

I believe it is mainly because he knew the Eastern and Southern European villages inside out that he felt at home and competent among their inhabitants, he easily functioned in the field, and he could perceive the researched reality without ideology or prejudice, but far more realistically and critically. Although he was interested in (re)constructing that which was systemic in the culture, he saw and analyzed "what has so often been neglected and omitted from description of village life: class structure and class inequalities, individualism of families, the existence of conflicts and tensions stemming from contradictory interests, and the egoism of individual families—in a word, all the things that question the myth of social uniformity of the village, the myth of its collectivism and solidarity without exceptions" (Obrębski 2020, 68). In his descriptions and interpretations, he constantly accounted for the perceived facts, striving to understand "the reality and dynamics of village life" (67).[19] At the center of his interests remained the present, particular human being (not a "type"), with the individual's life experience, needs, emotions, agency, system of values, and beliefs. Obrębski was a humanist and at the same time a thinker with leftist sensitivity. This is why perceiving the studied reality "from the perspective of the local" was for him an injunction beyond discussion.

In his Macedonian works, which were addressed to readers from Western Europe, Obrębski built his ethnographic authority through the image of a researcher in close relationship with the locals, or even of a researcher that was as one among them—a Slav among Slavs. He highlighted his knowledge of Eastern and Southern European peasants gained from firsthand experience and wrote of his intimate friendships with them.[20] And even though there were, in fact, many things differentiating him from the Macedonian highlanders—most of all, his social status, with all the attributes of class difference (for the people of Poreche, he was an urbanite, he could read and write, and he had financial resources at his disposal)— the results of his fieldwork show that his statement "I simply ceased to be a foreigner. I became one of their own" (Obrębski 2020, 140) was not ungrounded in reality. This positive alliance between the anthropologist and the society he was studying was confirmed by the fact that his wife, Tamara Obrębska, visited Volche twice (in 1969 and 1971) after Obrębski's death where she was welcomed as "Yosifica" ("Yosif's wife" in Macedonian). Today it is confirmed by the, albeit mythologized, memory of Yosif (as his name is pronounced in Macedonian), still present in the conversations of the people of Poreche; a memoir about him published by one of the inhabitants of Volche (Veselinovski 2002); the name of the main street in Samokov, the biggest town in Upper Poreche, ulica Yosif Obrembski; and a marble statue of Obrębski in the central square of this town, seemingly the only statue of an anthropologist in the world—after all, even Malinowski does not have one.[21]

Obrębski's writings show open opposition to ethnocentrism. With at times malicious irony, he pointed out the way in which the West has frequently belittled the Eastern peasants through orientalization:

These European patriarchal people . . . are industrious agriculturalists and skilled stock-breeders, and even if they do perform various ceremonies incompatible either with Anglican Church services or with the proceedings of the Salvation Army, in their daily life they are perhaps not more superstitious than, let us say, Western European politicians or aircraft officers. . . . [A]lthough they do not belong to the leading nations of Western European civilization, it would be unwarranted . . . to charge them with mental indolence and unreasonable attachment to traditions—an opinion that as a matter of fact would be somewhat refuted by the event of the Bolshevik Revolution. (Obrębski 1933, 4)

Obrębski was a researcher of the contemporary world. The interpretations of his research were influenced by the global perspective and the sociocultural context—that is, the processes of modernization. He wrote:

The arena of world events is beginning to be frequented by people hitherto neglected—the Eastern European peasant and his brothers from the Ganges, the Yellow River, the Nile. Modern societies coming into being . . . based on the newly forming and quickly solidifying social layer of peasants . . . are one of the most momentous phenomena and processes of modern history. . . . By acquainting oneself with any of the spheres of life of the small, archaic farmer society of Europe, Asia, Africa, or America, we touch the foundation of the civilization of the future that is now being shaped. (Obrębski 2022a, 50)

UNFINISHED PROJECTS

The question remains why Józef Obrębski's Macedonian works and knowledge about them are virtually nonexistent in anthropological discourse.[22] Had he published at least the "Couvade" and "Witchcraft" with Malinowski's forewords in the 1930s, according to his plans, to say nothing of the monograph on Macedonian magico-religious system lost during the war, the information in those books would no doubt have influenced the subsequent development of anthropology. The beginning of anthropology of peasant societies would have dated to the 1930s instead of the 1950s.[23] Obrębski would have been seen, next to Malinowski and Mead, as an insightful forerunner of gender theory. Finally, not only would we have had a different image of the influence of functionalism on anthropological research in Europe, but this research would probably have been different as well, having taken into account Obrębski's achievements.

After Obrębski's return from Macedonia, Malinowski wrote of him to the Rockefeller Foundation:

> Obrebski, as you put it, is "rather vague." There is no doubt at all that he is one of the most capable young men in ethnology. He is a good worker, original, clear-minded, and efficient. He certainly has also a spark of genius. With all this it will be touch and go whether he will really come to the fore. To my knowledge, he has in his dossier at least two MSS practically ready for publication which I am afraid will never see the light. Most perfectionism, since I suffer myself from that Slav disease (and many others). I wish you to be very charitable towards Obrebski. I still hope he will come to the fore. (LSE: Malinowski to Kittredge, October 22, 1933)

Had Obrębski stayed in London in 1934 and continued to cooperate with Malinowski—that is, had he accepted the offer that he received from his mentor then—perhaps his perfectionism would have been better controlled and the "Couvade," as well as later monographs, would have seen the light.[24] He declined this offer, however, and instead returned to Poland, where no academic career, in the typical sense of being employed at a state university, awaited him, despite his having the highest degree of competence—competence, one might add, far outranking that of his Polish ethnologist colleagues from the same generation.

After returning to his home country, for two and a half years Obrębski had no permanent job, and his professional and financial circumstances were unstable. He joined an expert think tank researching the issue of national minorities in Poland and carried out a research project ordered by a government agency (see Engelking 2019b, 2022a). This project consisted of fieldwork in the Polesie region, focused on the processes of modernization, including national identity creation, of the Eastern European village.[25] It was not until 1936 that he was able to settle down, when he took the post of vice chancellor at the State Institute of Village Culture, a newly created sociological research institution.[26] It is not difficult to imagine that in a life filled with monthslong expeditions into the field, intellectual and institutional tasks at the institute, and smaller jobs such as delivering lectures at various institutions, translating, and editing, there was little time left to work on his Macedonian monographs. He wrote and published many things during this period of his life, but "Witchcraft" and other books remained on the back burner.

In 1939 the war broke out, bringing about a change of the political system in Poland and, as one of the consequences of this change, a deep reconfiguration of the institutional and intellectual field of science. Obrębski left the country. In the United States, where he lived starting in 1948, he did not achieve the same status in academic circles that he had when he left Poland.[27] In subsequent years, until his premature death at age sixty-two, he took up work anew on his Macedonian materials a couple of times. He had brought all his fieldwork materials to New York from Warsaw and began work on a monograph in English titled "The Giaours of Macedonia." He intended to finish it after he retired. Unfortunately, that did not happen.

Since the early 2000s there has been an undertaking to bring Obrębski's works postmortem into the anthropological discourse. First, his selected works and materials translated from Polish and English into Macedonian were published by a Macedonian folklorist, Tanas Vražinovski (Obrębski 2001a, 2001b, 2002). Then in 2005, "Scandal in the Village" and some fragments of the monograph on witchcraft were published in a modest selection of his works that I edited (Obrębski 2005a).[28] Finally, selected writings were published in English translation in 2020 (Obrębski 2020), followed by the full edition of Obrębski's Macedonian writings and fieldnotes in 2022 (Obrębski 2022a, 2022b).

With the gradual editing and publication of Józef Obrębski's works that had not been published during his lifetime, one hopes that he will finally come to the fore of European and world anthropologists—not only as a figure of great importance to the history of our discipline but also as a living figure, somebody who remains a source of inspiration and continues to stir anthropological undertakings and contemplations.

1. Obrębski was born in 1905 and died in 1967. For more information, see the Józef Obrębski website, https://jozef-obrebski.ispan.edu.pl/en/, and Engelking (2022b). At that time, Vardar Macedonia, also known as Southern Serbia, was part of the Kingdom of Yugoslavia.

2. Obrębski drew inspiration from all of Malinowski's works. The material from his fieldwork in Macedonia and his later elaboration on it show that he thoroughly studied such works as *Magic, Science and Religion* (1925), *Crime and Custom in Savage Society* (1926), *Myth in Primitive Psychology* (1926), *Sex and Repression in Savage Society* (1927), *Culture* (1931), and *Law and Custom* (1934). Malinowski's books on law, custom, and crime were translated by Obrębski into Polish in the late 1930s.

3. In the author's preface to his book *Coral Gardens*, Malinowski wrote, "In the working out of my material I received considerable help from research assistants provided by the Rockefeller Foundation; notably Dr J. Obrebski and Miss Agnes Drew, who assisted me in eliciting the material from my field notes. . . . Also the manuscript in its semi-final form was read at one of my seminars, a chapter by each member, criticized and discussed, and from this I, and I hope the book too, have derived considerable profit" (1966, xxii). Malinowski was spending his sabbatical in Oberbozen in Tyrol from July to September 1931 and in Tamaris on the Riviera from October 1931 to April 1932.

4. His companions at the seminar were, among others, Edward E. Evans-Pritchard, Raymond Firth, Meyer Fortes, Felix M. Keesing, Lucy Mair, Siegfried Nadel, and Audrey Richards.

5. Obrębski and Malinowski met in person in July 1930, during Malinowski's visit in Kraków. Malinowski wrote to Van Sickle, "During my stay in Cracow in July last, I tested Obrebski for his knowledge of English. . . . He understood me quite well, especially when I spoke about scientific matters, and I am certain he could follow my lectures from the very first moment. . . . Taking his scientific qualifications, his specialization in Slavonic kinship and family and his linguistic capacity, I should like to throw in all my weight in support of his application" (LSE, October 2, 1930).

6. For more information on the relationship between Obrębski and Malinowski, the Rockefeller Foundation, and Obrębski's involvement in propagating functionalism in Poland, see Engelking (2004, 2024).

7. Obrębski's master's thesis, "Folk Husbandry of the Eastern Part of the Balkan Peninsula," consisted of a series of four articles in the journal *Slavic Folk* in 1929–31.

8. I have written more broadly on the relationship between Obrębski and Moszyński in Engelking (2012).

9. He was viewed in a similar fashion by his peers, as is evident in mentions of him in his friends' memoirs: "Obrębski was thought to be the star of Polish ethnology. He was exceptionally intelligent. He had also an exceptional charm" (Weintraub 1994, 15–16). "He had a great disposition, unparalleled by anyone from his generation. He was being awarded scholarships. It was the common notion that he would go on to make a career. He was thought to be very talented" (Feliks Gross, pers. comm., 1996).

10. Obrębski wrote, "The author of these words has often functioned in the Poreche region as such a guest-friend of various Poreche families" (Obrębski 2022b, 52).

11. "In particular active participation in the life of the village which was the main area of my work, allowed me to discover the entire local system of witchcraft and penetrate it deeper not only theoretically, but even through participation in a couple of magic undertakings," he wrote in "Witchcraft of Macedonian Poreche" (Obrębski 2020, 70).

12. Obrębski wrote to Moszyński about the book:

> It was without a doubt the most difficult subject, due to its inaccessibility in Macedonia. *Nota bene* it seems to me that there is, up till now, no description of the system of medicine and magic of Southern Slavs. The work, undertaken initially because of anger at the secrecy and distrust of old Macedonian women, has developed in quite an interesting direction. The result of this will be a book about Macedonian witch doctors, which—if circumstances allow—I plan to prepare in English. . . . It will constitute a quite important contribution to the knowledge of the socio-cultural structure of patriarchal society. It has a rather ample collection of photographs, (IEiAKUJ: Obrębski to Moszyński, April 4, 1933)

> Substantial fragments of this book were published in English translation (Obrębski 2020), and the full edition was published in Polish (Obrębski 2022b). Among Obrębski's works in the archives, there are no texts written in English about magic in Poreche; there are only modest conspectus notes. The studies in English that we have concern the questions of family, marriage, and deconstruction of myths.

13. Obrębski was referring to his field expedition in Polesie (the Belarusian-Ukrainian region, then located near the eastern border of Poland), carried out by him in 1934–36 (see Obrębski 2007; Engelking 2022a).

14. *Sorcerers of Dobu*, published in 1932, is a monograph by Reo Fortune, a student of Malinowski, with a foreword by the latter. It describes witchcraft in New Guinea in the context of social structure.

15. This monograph was published in English translation in Obrębski (2020, 125–40), and in the Polish original in Obrębski (2022b, 135–64).

16. He wrote of his plan to publish this work:

> Some time ago you expressed the wish to write a foreword to the "Couvade". I greatly regret that hitherto I was not able to make avail of this proposal, as well as the support you have offered me in the prospective publishing of this work. After receiving, over a year ago, your letter on this issue, for a long time I labored under the illusion that I would be able to order my business in such a way as to be able to finally finish the "Couvade" and send it. However, I was able to work on it only v. sporadically and v. irregularly, so that only the first few chapters are more or less ready. All in all, it was v. discouraging. Even more so because I saw that this work requires a v. fundamental overdo.... Besides, the "Couvade" needs also for the bibliography and references to be completed, something I cannot do here. Therefore I have been constantly planning to go to London for at least a couple of weeks in order to finish this work; it became apparent, however, that I was too optimistic in assessing my possibilities. Perhaps I will be able to carry out this plan in the not too distant future. It is all the more desirable for me because I feel a strong need to breath in the atmosphere of your seminar and am afraid that without this journey to the ethnological Mecca my work and my intellectual development will be constantly suffering losses. (LSE: Obrębski to Malinowski, January 24, 1935)

17. This legacy has been compiled as the Obrebski Collection, http://scua .library.umass.edu/umarmot/obrebski-jozef.

18. Obrębski had been gaining fieldwork experience since the beginning of his ethnographical studies; he conducted fieldwork in many places in Poland. In 1927 and 1928 he worked for five months in the areas of Bessarabia, Dobruja, Bulgaria, European Turkey, Eastern Macedonia, Kosovo, Serbia, and Croatia.

19. On ethnological romanticization and mythologization of village reality, he wrote:

The falseness of this vision stems not so much from blindly following theoretical doctrine, but rather from insufficient empirical observation and from not drawing conclusions from that observation, which is thought to be of little importance and value. A typical ethnologist of the older school, going into the field with a previously prepared questionnaire, not interested in the reality and dynamics of village life, approaches the object of his studies with a particular attitude. The villagers who are to become the objects of his study are for him not members of a local society, members of institutions and groups which make up this society, not living people, whom one has to get to know and observe, but informants—good or bad informants.... He divides the researched society into those categories and sets for him the task to construct a certain pattern of customs—from information obtained through questioning—which he treats as typical or characteristic with little regard for whether, and to what extent, it is really observed, and if so, by whom. (Obrębski 2020, 67)

20. As he wrote in the foreword to the "Couvade":

I am, after all, a Slav myself, born and brought up in the most archaic and primitive parts of Eastern Europe. I have thus an inborn knowledge of my native land. I have, moreover, personal experience of my peasant countrymen—an experience which I have gained not only by anthropological fieldwork in Poland, White Russia, Ukraine, and Balkan States, but above all by intimate bonds of friendship with many natives of those countries.... If the reader will trust those experiences of mine and submit himself for the time being to my guidance, it will help us to approach the problem of the couvade in general unhampered by the inherent belief of the Western European in the superiority of his rational outlook and civilised habits over the incomprehensible ideas and strange customs of savagery. (Obrębski 1933, 5)

21. For more on the memory of Obrębski in Poreche, see Bielenin and Engelking (2015).

22. Until recently, anthropologists and folklorists interested in Macedonia, in addition to Obrębski's articles published in Polish and English, could only read his selected works and materials translated into Macedonian (Obrębski 2001a, 2001b, 2002). From this intellectual environment came both articles about Obrębski and his research (e.g., Bielenin-Lenczowska and Engelking 2015; Georgievski 2014; Risteski 2011) and, more important, works inspired by his achievements (e.g., Lubaś 2011; Rękas 2018;

Rękas and Lučeska 2015). Collective works stemming from undertakings devoted to Obrębski have also been published (Vražinovski 2002; Vražinovski et al. 2003; Vražinovski et al. 2006; Lucheska and Dimoski 2013; Bielenin-Lenczowska 2015).

23. "Although peasants up till quite recently were the most important part of the world's population, it was only in the 1950s when they became a separate object of anthropological studies, and in the 1960s and 70s when researchers were most interested in them" (Spencer 2008, 155).

24. I was told of this proposal by Józef's sister, Professor Antonina Obrębska-Jabłońska (pers. comm., 1994). I was later able to confirm it after finding the following passage in one of the letters Obrębski received from his mother when he was living in New York: "I will not forget this letter from Malinowski, in which Prof. Malinowski wrote to me, as your mother, if I could agree to your cooperating with him for some time. When I wrote to you about Malinowski's letter to me, you wrote back that one can study abroad, but one must work in Poland and only for the good of Poland" (OC: Maria Obrębska to Obrębski, April 27, 1957).

25. This research resulted in four articles published by Obrębski in 1936, in which he introduced an innovative, anti-essentialistic theory of ethnic groups and boundaries. 30 years before Fredrik Barth and Benedict Anderson, he conceptualized these phenomena as "imagined formations" and described the configuration of ethnic groups as a system of opposition between the perceptions of "other" and "ours" (see Obrębski 2005b [1936]).

26. I have written in greater detail about Obrębski's professional life and environment in 1934–36 in Engelking (2006).

27. He left as a habilitated doctor of ethnology, the chair of ethnology at the Sociological Institute, University of Lodz.

28. I am the scientific editor of Józef Obrębski's collected works. The first volume, comprising his works on Polesie, was published in 2007 (Obrębski 2007). The second volume contains his works on Macedonia (Obrębski 2022a, 2022b). Two more volumes are planned.

REFERENCES

Manuscripts and Archives

IEiAKUJ. Institute of Ethnology and Cultural Anthropology of Jagiellonian University in Kraków. Legacy of Kazimierz Moszyński.

LSE. London School of Economics and Political Science Archives. Correspondence of Bronisław Malinowski.

OC. Obrebski Collection, University of Massachusetts, Amherst. Legacy of Józef Obrębski, including these unpublished works: "Black Magic in Macedonia," "The Witchcraft of Macedonian Poreche," "The Giaours of Macedonia: An Account of the Magic and Religion of Shepherds in Poreche Against the Background of the Collective Life of Their Village," "Scandal in the Village," "Social Structure and Ritual in a Macedonian Village."

Published Works

Bielenin-Lenczowska, Karolina, ed. 2015. *Anthropology of Continuity and Change: Macedonian Poreče 80 Years After Józef Obrębski's Work*. Warszawa: Instytut Slawistyki PAN.

Bielenin-Lenczowska, Karolina, and Anna Engelking. 2015. "Józef Obrębski's Poreče: An Ethnographic Revisit." In *Anthropology of Continuity and Change: Macedonian Poreče 80 Years After Jozef Obrebski's Work*, edited by Karolina Bielenin-Lenczowska, 9–29. Warszawa: Instytut Slawistyki PAN.

Engelking, Anna. 2004. "Obrębski o Malinowskim. Z dziejów recepcji funkcjonalizmu w Polsce." *Studia Socjologiczne* 173 (2): 17–34.

———. 2006. "Józef Obrębski—etnolog i socjolog warszawski." *Sprawy Narodowościowe* 29:91–106.

———. 2012. "Kazimierz Moszyński i Józef Obrębski: nauczyciel i uczeń." *Lud* 96:139–56.

———. 2019a. "Krakowski projekt słowianoznawstwa zintegrowanego. Wizja, realizacje, kontynuacje." In *Niekonwencjonalne historie instytucji slawistycznych*, edited by Ewelina Drzewiecka and Ewa Wróblewska-Trochimiuk, 193–209. Warszawa: Instytut Slawistyki PAN.

———. 2019b. "Nauka na usługach polityki? Przypadek Józefa Obrębskiego." *Sprawy Narodowościowe* 51:1–24.

———. 2022a. "Anthropology in a Nationalizing State: Three Case Studies from Interwar Poland." *Nationalities Papers: The Journal of Nationalism and Ethnicity* 52 (1): 146–166.

———. 2022b. "From Archaic to Colonial Peasantries: An Intellectual Biography of Józef Obrębski, the (Forgotten) Polish Disciple of Malinowski." In BEROSE *International Encyclopaedia of the Histories of Anthropology*, article 2599. Paris: URL BEROSE.

———. 2024. "Under the Wing of the Rockefeller Foundation: On the Cooperation Between Bronisław Malinowski and His Polish Student Józef Obrębski." In *Bronisław Malinowski and His Legacy in Contemporary Social Sciences and Humanities: On the Centenary of Argonauts of the Western Pacific*, edited by Grażyna Kubica-Heller and Dariusz Brzeziński, 140–58. London: Routledge.

Flis, Mariola, and Andrzej Paluch, eds. 1985. *Antropologia społeczna Bronisława Malinowskiego*. Warszawa: PWN.

Georgievski, Petre T. 2014. "Karakteristike etnografskog istraživanja sela u Poreču tridesetih godina od polskog sociologa J. Obrembskog." In *Biti sociolog sela. Spomenica ħure Stefanovića*, edited by D. Ђorđević, 97–118. Nowi Sad: Prometej.

Kuper, Adam. 1987. *Między charyzmą i rutyną. Antropologia brytyjska 1922–1982* (przeł. K. Kaniowska). Łódź: Wydawnictwo Łódzkie.

Lubaś, Marcin. 2011. *Różnowiercy. Współistnienie międzyreligijne w zachodniomacedońskiej wsi. Studium z zakresu antropologii społeczno-kulturowej*. Kraków: Nomos.

Lucheska, Eli, and Zvonko Dimoski, eds. 2013. 105 godini od ragianieto na Jozef Obrembski. 105 years from the birth of Józef Obrębski, Prilep–Poznań: Institut za Staroslovenska Kultura, Instytut Filologii Słowiańskiej UAM.

Malinowski, Bronislaw. 1966. *Coral Gardens and Their Magic: A Study of the Methods of Tilling the Soil and of Agricultural Rites in the Trobriand Islands*. London: Allen and Unwin.

Obrębski, Józef. 1933. "Family Organisation Among Slavs as Reflected in the Custom of Couvade." Typescript. London: London School of Economics Archives.

———. 1934. "Czarna Magja w Macedonii." *Kuryer Literacko-Naukowy. Dodatek do Ilustrowanego Kuryera Codziennego* 111:6–8.

———. 1936. "System religijny ludu macedońskiego." *Kuryer Literacko-Naukowy. Dodatek do Ilustrowanego Kuryera Codziennego* 24:13–14, 26:11–12, 28:11–13, 29:11–12, 30:13.

———. 1969. *Ritual and Social Structure in a Macedonian Village*. Edited by B. Halpern. Northeast Meeting, American Association for the Advancement of Slavic Studies, Boston University.

———. 2001a. *Folklorni i etnografski materijali od Poreče*, vol. 1. Edited by Tanas Vražinovski. Skopje-Prilep: Institut za Staroslovenska Kultura, Matica Makedonska.

———. 2001b. *Makedonski etnosociološki studii*, vol. 2. Edited by Tanas Vražinovski. Skopje-Prilep: Institut za Staroslovenska Kultura, Matica Makedonska.

———. 2002. *Makedonski etnosociološki studii*, vol. 3. Edited by Tanas Vražinovski. Skopje-Prilep: Institut za Staroslovenska Kultura, Matica Makedonska.

———. 2005a [1936]. *Dzisiejsi ludzie Polesia i inne eseje*. Edited by Anna Engelking. Warszawa: IFiS PAN.

———. 2005b [1936]. "Problem grup i zróżnicowań etnicznych w etnologii i jego socjologiczne ujęcie." In *Dzisiejsi ludzie Polesia i inne eseje,* edited by Anna Engelking, 153–72. Warszawa: IFiS PAN.

———. 2005c. "Skandal we wsi." In *Dzisiejsi ludzie Polesia i inne eseje,* edited by Anna Engelking, 53–70. Warszawa: IFiS PAN.

———. 2006 [1969]. "Social Structure and Ritual in a Macedonian Village," edited by Joel M. Halpern. *Sprawy Narodowościowe* 29:286–95.

———. 2007. *Polesie. Studia etnosocjologiczne,* vol. 1. Edited by Anna Engelking. Warszawa: Oficyna Naukowa.

———. 2020. *The Giaours of Macedonia: Selected Writings.* Edited by Anna Engelking. Translated by Helena Teleżyńska. Warszawa: Oficyna Naukowa. https://jozef-obrebski.ispan.edu.pl/wp-content/uploads/macedonia-en .pdf.

———. 2022a. *Macedonia 1. Giaurowie Macedonii. Opis magii i religii pasterzy z Porecza na tle zbiorowego życia ich wsi.* Edited by Anna Engelking, Joanna Rękas, and Ilija Upalevski. Warszawa: Oficyna Naukowa. https://jozef -obrebski.ispan.edu.pl/wp-content/uploads/macedonia-1.pdf.

———. 2022b. *Macedonia 2. Czarownictwo Porecza Macedońskiego. Mit i rzeczywistość u Słowian Południowych. [Rozproszone teksty epickie i liryczne. Zapisy terenowe]. Struktura społeczna i rytuał we wsi macedońskiej.* Edited by Anna Engelking, Joanna Rękas, and Ilija Upalevski. Warszawa: Oficyna Naukowa. https://jozef-obrebski.ispan.edu.pl/wp-content/uploads /macedonia-2.pdf.

Rękas, Joanna. 2018. *Między słowami. Projektowanie folklorystyki konwersacyjnej na materiale celebracji Wodzic w Macedonii.* Poznań: Wydawnictwo Naukowe UAM.

Rękas, Joanna, and Eli Lučeska. 2015. "Wodzicka narracja Józefa Obrębskiego i zarys projektu jej współczesnej aktualizacji." In *Bałkański folklor jako kod interkulturowy,* edited by Vesna Petreska and Joanna Rękas, 25–41. Skopje–Poznań: Instytut Folkloru im. Marka Cepenkova, Instytut Filologii Słowiańskiej UAM.

Risteski, Ljupczo S. 2011. "Josef Obrebski's Anthropological Research on Macedonia." *Etnoantropoloszki problemi* 6 (4): 837–58.

Spencer, Jonathan. 2008. "Chłopi." In *Encyklopedia antropologii społeczno-kulturowej,* edited by Alan Barnard and Jonathan Spencer, 155–57. Warszawa: Oficyna Wydawnicza Volumen.

Veselinovski, Ariton. 2002. "Moite seḱavanja na J. Obrembski i negovata sopruga Tamara." In *70 godini od istražuvanjata na Jozef Obrembski vo Make-*

donija. Medžunaroden naučen sobir, Samokov, 14–16 septemvri 2001, edited by Tanas Vražinovski, 227–31. Prilep: Institut za Staroslovenska Kultura.

Vražinovski, Tanas, ed. 2002. *70 godini od istražuvanjata na Jozef Obrembski vo Makedonija. Medžunaroden naučen sobir, Samokov, 14–16 septemvri 2001.* Prilep: Institut za Staroslovenska Kultura.

Vražinovski, Tanas, Anna Engelking, and Joel M. Halpern, eds. 2003. *Jozef Obrembski, Poreče 1932–1933. Jozef Obrebski, Macedonian Porech 1932–1933.* Prilep-Skopje: Institut za Staroslovenska Kultura, Matica Makedonska.

Vražinovski, Tanas, Vladimir Karadžoski, and Sonia Jovanovska-Rizoska, eds. 2006. *Jozef Obrembski–značaen istražuvač na narodnata kultura na Makedoncite.* Skopje: Matica Makedonska.

Weintraub, Wiktor. 1994. *O współczesnych i o sobie. Wspomnienia, sylwetki, szkice literackie.* Kraków: Znak.

Internet Source

Józef Obrębski website, https://jozef-obrebski.ispan.edu.pl/en/.

3

"This Incredibly Fast Upswing of the American Negroes"

Felix von Luschan's "Die Neger in den Vereinigten Staaten" (1915)

JOHN DAVID SMITH AND SYLVIA ANGELICA SMITH

In July 1914 Dr. Felix von Luschan, a professor and anthropologist at Berlin's Friedrich-Wilhelms-Universität and former head of the Africa and Oceania Department of the city's Königliches Museum für Völkerkunde, ventured to Australia for research. Luschan (1854–1924), an Austrian by birth, emerged as imperial Germany's leading physical anthropologist after Rudolf Virchow's death in 1902. Luschan and Virchow ranked as the leading "liberal" German-speaking ethnologists before World War I. They shared "an approach to science and humanity that drew on liberal concepts," framing "their study of human groups around a firm conviction in the basic similarity of humankind" (Evans 2010, 64).

For his part, Luschan was one of the world's foremost scientists at the fin de siècle—a scholar of uncommon breadth, whose contributions spanned medicine, archaeology, anthropometrics, ethnography, linguistics, physical anthropology, and eugenics. He earned four doctorates: MD, LittD, and DSc from the Universität Wien (Vienna) and DPhil from the Ludwig-Maximilians-Universität (Munich). In 1911 the Austrian savant received the coveted Huxley Medal from the Royal Anthropological Institute of Great Britain and Ireland, which published his Huxley lecture, "The Early Inhabitants of Western Asia." Eight years later Luschan published the definitive, three-volume *Die Altertümer von Benin* (The Antiquities of Benin), based on his research in the Kingdom of Benin (part of present-day Nigeria). In it Luschan extolled the spectacular works of Benin sculptors as being on par with the art of famed Florentine Renaissance sculptor Benvenuto Cellini. According to H. Glenn Penny, "Luschan's analysis of the Benin Bronzes undercut racialized arguments about differences between Africans and Europeans ... and undermined colonial ideologies based on notions of biological racism" (Penny 2021, 91).[1]

Luschan's wife, Emma von Hochstetter, a prominent photographer who assisted her husband with his investigations, joined him on his trip to Oceania. Like other pioneer ethnologists, the Luschans employed cameras "to record racial types," and "the presumed objectivity of the photograph seemed to legitimize anthropological practice as a true science" (Kerr 2020, 68).[2] The couple sought to gather data on the theory of monogenism, to observe the Talgai skull (a human fossil found on the Talgai Station in Queensland, Australia), and to collect comparative anthropometric data on Australia's Indigenous populations. Luschan's field research during this period matters to scientists because it led to his metamorphosis from espousing first craniological, then cultural and behavioral explanations for racial differences, to adopting theories of Darwinian biological evolution. His empirical work underscored his intellectual development from biological determinism and a commitment to a racialist vision of the human species to the belief that the essential unity of humankind eliminated race as a meaningful factor in social relations.[3]

This chapter focuses on the Luschans' research project on Black Americans and race conducted in 1914–15.[4] It draws on an obscure primary source heretofore ignored by German and American scholars, "Die Neger in den Vereinigten Staaten" (The Negroes in the United States), published in Berlin in 1915.[5]

TRAVEL TO OCEANIA AND THE UNITED STATES

In the summer of 1914 the Luschans traveled from Germany to the Pacific, planning fieldwork not only in Australia but also in New Zealand (where Emma's father, Ferdinand von Hochstetter, had been a pioneer explorer), New Guinea, India, Indonesia, and Southern Babylonia. In Australia, Luschan presented a lecture on eugenics, "Culture and Degeneration," at a meeting of the British Association for the Advancement of Science in Sydney and received an honorary doctor of science from the University of Adelaide.[6] Despite the fortuitous start to their travels, on August 4 Great Britain declared war on Germany, and the Luschans suddenly became alien enemies. Fearing internment by the British, in early September the couple sailed to Hawaii, then an American territory, hopeful of returning to Germany via the United States, at the time a neutral power in the world war.[7]

The Luschans' one month in Honolulu proved productive. They organized the anthropological collection at the Bernice P. Bishop Museum of Ethnology, classifying and quantifying human remains and funerary objects of Lanai's first inhabitants, and measured contemporary adult males for anthropometric data.[8] By mid-October 1914 the Luschans had arrived in San Francisco. They spent the next several months conducting research at American museums, measuring human specimens largely in the American South. Felix presented lectures at several universities, including those of California, Chicago, Illinois, and Wisconsin, as well as at Cornell and Johns Hopkins.[9] While in the United States, he also addressed the American Anthropological Association in Philadelphia on "Convergency," arguing that physical and cultural characteristics were interrelated, not independent variables (Lowie 1915, 221).

Luschan considered his stay in North America a laboratory for the study of race, especially racial mixing, and what Progressive Era theorists considered the "Negro problem." In his U.S. lectures, he presented a preliminary analysis of what his contemporaries termed "miscegenation." "If two different races, a native one and strange invaders intermarry," Luschan explained, "the final result never corresponds to the arithmetical means, as has been so often said and believed. Above all we should be aware, that somatic type and language—the two principal features of the human races . . . are not influenced equally by such an intermarriage." Luschan recognized that only a handful of writers worldwide defined "race" as a social question, what he termed the "social meaning of pigmentation," and noted the "impossibility of giving a scientific definition of the white race."[10] Most European and American scientists held only a rudimentary understanding of racial mixing and Black culture, including whether Africans had brought their languages and cultural forms with them to America (Irek 1994, 54–55). "I am very unknowledgeable on these topics," Luschan confessed to the Austrian linguist Hugo Schuchardt.[11]

During his stay in the United States, Luschan took advantage of opportunities to study "race." He and his wife conducted fieldwork among living subjects, collecting quantitative data on Black Americans. "I would like to study some Problems of Heredity," he wrote to Booker T. Washington in December 1914. "I would like to study the exact pedigree of some hundred coloured families for 3 or if possible 4 generations and to note some anthropometric and other data on bodily and mental qualities of every single available member of these families." Luschan explained to eugenicist Charles B. Davenport, "I think this might give quite good results for some Heredity Questions and might perhaps be useful also for some questions connected with the great Negro-Problem" (Harlan 1984, 202–3).[12]

Washington recommended that the Luschans conduct their longitudinal research in several cities, including Boston, New York, Washington DC, Baltimore, Charleston, Savannah, Mobile, and New Orleans. He invited them to his training school for Black people, Tuskegee Institute in Alabama, where he served as principal, and recommended that they also travel to his alma mater, Hampton Institute in Virginia.[13] In late January 1915 Luschan reported to German readers that at these sites, he and his wife would "study several hundred Black families, record their family trees, and examine them all from an anthropological standpoint." He continued:

> We thereby hope to gather rich material for the study of heredity questions, as well as to contribute to the elucidation of the great mulatto problem. I consider this the most important social problem facing the United States today, yet one on which most people in the United States are not completely clear. Official statistics leave much to be desired; no great distinction is made between the very dark Africans and the much lighter-skinned mulattoes; usually they are all labeled "colored." Naturally, it is impossible to determine what the future of these over ten million coloreds is going to be, at least not before knowing how much white blood is mixed in with theirs, and whether or not the number of light-skinned mulattoes is increasing or decreasing within the total number of colored peoples. (1915b, n.p.)

Five months later Felix and Emma were in New York City, ensconced in an apartment at Columbia University. Felix informed W. E. B. Du Bois, who considered Luschan "one of the greatest of modern anthropologists," that the couple sought "perhaps 100 coloured families" to measure and describe "every single available member of such families." Aside from the "scientific interest" such research would provide, he was confident that it would unveil much "practical social value." Would Du Bois assist them in identifying such "coloured and halfcaste" families? Luschan also asked Du Bois if he was familiar with "*real Zulu's* [*sic*]" from South Africa who had allegedly been transported to North America and then presumably became enslaved. "I am sure," Luschan wrote, "that there is no man in the world, that is more competent on such a question as yourself and I would be very much obliged for your opinion on this matter. I know that some ships, with coloured people came from the Sansibar [*sic*] Coast, but never before had I heard of real Zulus brought to America" (Du Bois 1914).[14]

Before their return to Germany in March 1915, the Luschans measured Black people in all the cities Washington had recommended, plus St. Louis, Memphis, and Greenville, Mississippi. The couple worked eight-hour days, measuring on average three to five subjects per hour, including 814 African American schoolchildren. In terms of method, the Luschans recorded finger length and the size and form of nostrils. They coded skin colors, presumably employing the von Luschan skin color scale (*Hautfarbetafel*), which Felix had first developed in the 1880s, and analyzed photographs taken by Emma of Black children and adults.[15] Luschan informed Franz Boas of Columbia University, his former Berlin colleague and friend, that they had compiled valuable data while working in the South.[16] He wrote to Davenport, "We did very good work and brought back the pedigrees of about 100 families and the exact measurements etc. of about 350 persons. We saw also a good many Indians and Persons with mixed Indian and Negro blood."[17] Luschan told Edward S. Morse, director of the Peabody Museum of Salem, Massachusetts, that this data would enable him "to find some laws in heredity." He explained, "Principally we want to learn, how many single traits are transmitted by heredity independently from one another."[18]

RETURN TO GERMANY AND "DIE NEGER IN DEN VEREINIGTEN STAATEN"

Upon arriving in Germany, Luschan immersed himself zealously in war work for his adopted country, conducting "racial studies" of prisoners of war taken by German and Austrian troops (Evans 2002, 166–69, 2010, 2, 135, 138, 148). To prove his loyalty to German critics who charged that he had spent too much time in the United States and not in the *Vaterland*,

Luschan asserted disingenuously that the Americans had forced him to stay in the country against his will (1921, 571). Meanwhile, he quickly published a thirty-six-page summary analysis of his U.S. research, highlighting his coding, measurements, and observations of American Blacks during late 1914 and early 1915.

In "Die Neger in den Vereinigten Staaten," published in 1915 in the monthly popular magazine *Koloniale Rundschau* (Colonial Overview), Luschan explained that his empirical work in the United States focused on, among other things, collecting statistics on the physical characteristics of Black people and their mixed-race offspring, the demographic and social implications of racial mixing, alleged Black criminality, lynching, and solutions to the "Negro problem" generally. *Koloniale Rundschau*, according to a reviewer in London's *Journal of the Royal African Society*, offered "all-round discussion of colonial questions, taking into consideration the interest of the natives as well as that of the colonists." Intended for general readers interested in anthropological, colonial, ethnographic, and geographic questions, the publication looked beyond Germany's protectorates and sought "to draw the common life of primitive peoples into the circle of our consideration . . . and to examine it in relation to European culture" (Anonymous 1909).[19]

In his article, Luschan argued that despite white Americans' dire and hopeful predictions of Black retrogression, the population of African Americans (including mixed-race people broadly defined) had not decreased following emancipation; in fact, their gross population increased consistently. He enthusiastically praised the "admirable energy" that American Black people exhibited in terms of their social and moral development since 1863 (1915a, 508). Like Du Bois in his little-known biometric and auxological studies of one thousand Black students, Luschan repudiated the "retrogression hypothesis" of the degeneration of Black Southerners since emancipation (Farland 2006, 1017, 1021–23, 1034). He based this argument on data supplied by Tuskegee Institute statistician Monroe N. Work (see McMurry 1985). "This incredibly fast upswing of the American Negroes," Luschan averred, was "partially the result of the excellent schools which are equally typical for the entire Union, but the upswing is essentially also caused by the good natural gifts of the colored people and their strong desire to get an education" (1915a, 510).

Black people, whom Luschan referred to as "coloreds" (*die Farbigen*), mattered as workers on both sides of the Mason–Dixon line. "Negroes are cheap labor, in the South they are indispensable for plantation operations," Luschan wrote, "also in the North they would hardly be dispensable as servants, guards, waiters, chauffeurs and in dozens of other positions." He considered the leading source of racial hatred toward the formerly enslaved and their descendants to be the "growing literature, in which the Negro is being described in the most 'black' color (bad light) and is being described as a society different from the whites, monkey-like including cannibalism and other animalistic features" (507).

To punctuate his point, Luschan paid special attention to President Theodore Roosevelt's famous invitation to Booker T. Washington for dinner at the White House on October 16, 1901 (see Davis 2013). Referring to Washington as "one of the spiritual leaders of the colored Americans," Luschan charged that American journalists "reacted with outrage as if now the end of the Union were close." He considered the hyperbolic public response to Roosevelt's invitation in line with "the majority of the other popular literature on the Negro question" in the United States. On one hand, Luschan reported, "I know almost one hundred medicinal-statistical studies on the frequency of syphilis, tuberculosis and other diseases of the colored people; almost all of them are serious and instructive papers that are useful to those who are seriously interested in the social conditions of the Negroes." "On the other hand," he said, "the general literature on the colored people of the Union is all the more scarce" (507–8).

When assessing the extant literature on the "Negro problem," Luschan extolled the Mississippi cotton planter and self-proclaimed "sociologist" Alfred Holt Stone's *Studies in the American Race Problem* (1908) but excoriated William Benjamin Smith's *The Color Line: A Brief in Behalf of the Unborn* (1905) and Robert W. Shufeldt's *America's Greatest Problem: The Negro* (1915). Luschan befriended Stone, welcomed his economic analyses of post–Civil War race relations, and toured his Dunleith Plantation, near Greenville, Mississippi. Stone provided the Luschans with Black subjects to examine as well as contacts in the Mississippi Delta and in Memphis who identified additional Black people for them to measure (see Smith 2005; Hollandsworth 2008).

Luschan, however, tore into Shufeldt's proposals to deport American Blacks as counterproductive and intemperate, saying his book contained "uncontrolled insults and . . . false and stupid statements" (1915a, 508). Shufeldt denigrated two African Americans whom Luschan knew personally and held in the highest esteem—Washington and Du Bois. Exhibiting his own racial condescension, Luschan praised Du Bois, then editor of *The Crisis*, the monthly publication of the National Association for the Advancement of Colored People, as being "so light[-skinned] that in Southern Europe [he] would hardly strike any one as colored and he has an unusually beautiful head with an imposing 'thinker's brow'" (513). Luschan, when describing one of North America's foremost Black intellectuals, could not free himself of his long-outmoded deterministic anthropometric centrism.

Luschan came away from reading "race problem" texts published in the United States with an admiration for the freedpeople who, over five decades, had exhibited energy and commitment to advance their race in overcoming enslavement. He sympathized with the former bondspeople, not those who had been their enslavers. "Centuries of slavery did not only result in a sad lack of intellectual leaders and energetic initiative, but also necessarily and logically led to poverty, ignorance (lack of knowledge) and carelessness (thoughtlessness). Equally bad was the low esteem for physical labor which was intricately tied to remembering the old slavery" (511).

Anticipating by two decades the thrust of Du Bois's monumental *Black Reconstruction in America: An Essay Toward a History of the Part Which Black Folk Played in the Attempt to Reconstruct Democracy in America, 1860–1880* (1935), Luschan proclaimed that "the real liberation of the slaves in the Union took place when the southern troops capitulated in April of 1865, yet their emancipation had already been declared solemnly in January of 1863. From this day on one usually considers the beginning of the American Negroes upswing. In fact during these years a strong movement that is almost without parallel in human history, and which, apparently still lasting, promises a great future for the colored people of America" (508–9). He praised the military, industrial, and vocational training that faculty at Hampton and Tuskegee Institutes afforded upwardly mobile Black youth. Luschan described Booker T. Washington, with deep ties to both schools, as "the most popular colored man in the United States, a man of totally unusual and highly versatile talent and above all, an organizational genius of the first order, in any event also one of his countrymen's greatest benefactors" (512).

Luschan praised the moral standards exhibited by the students at Hampton and Tuskegee. Whereas white critics frequently complained about the high rate of premarital sexual relations between male and female students at schools that educated Black people, Luschan offered a dramatically different perspective. Based on his experiences as a professor at Berlin's Friedrich-Wilhelms-Universität, he declared, "It would be hard for me to measure these more than cloisterly customs with European standards. I am afraid similar institutes [in Germany] would deliver a much worse statistic." Luschan added, "Also in other respects I have the impression that the moral[s] of the colored people in the Union [are] not significantly different from that of the whites and as if the social class is much more important than the color, Hampton and Tuskegee are, without a doubt, exemplary upper-class-like institutions" (513).

Luschan also defended Black Americans from charges of an inherited propensity for criminality. During the Progressive Era, all manner of white supremacists besmirched Black people as uniformly inclined to commit illegal or immoral acts. "Where," the Austrian-German anthropologist explained, criminality "is greater for the colored people than for the whites, usually the social conditions are responsible, not race or color" (513–14). Luschan included damning quotations from Smith, Shufeldt (whom, exhibiting a rare sense of humor, he referred to as Smith's "soul mate" [527]), and John Temple Graves, a race-baiting Georgia journalist and defender of lynch law. The three men opposed racial mixing, which was then called "Negroization" of the country, and advocated not just rigid racial segregation but the forced repatriation of African Americans. Anything less would ruin the country, they said. Luschan quoted Graves, who in 1903 branded Black people the "pathological, undesirable, helpless and never assimilated element in our civilization." According to Luschan, such blatantly racist ideas stemmed from neither science nor sociology, but rather from simple "blind hatred" (514).[20] For his part, Luschan opposed the deportation of Black people to Africa or elsewhere (513). Responding to Graves's assertion that white European immigrants should replace American Black workers, Luschan quipped, "Indeed one only needs to imagine a Belgian factory worker with his high demands of wages, food, and lodging as a cotton picker in the Southern states in order to understand the sum total of folly and blindness lying in the sheer discussion of such a possibility" (516).

Luschan turned the tables on white Southerners, arguing that in fact whites, not Blacks, were responsible for the alleged "Negro problem." He admonished whites, especially white Southerners, to admit the fact that sexual liaisons between the races had existed for generations. The number of mixed-race people was on the rise, and in New Orleans, a place that Luschan considered "the capital of the South," cross-generational racial mixing was an open secret. During their stay in that city, the Luschans had read "scandalous stories" of respected white families discovering, to their shame, that their lineage included a "drop of colored blood." Political and social rivals employed such disclosures, even when they proved untrue, to discredit their enemies and ruin their social reputation. Such was the power of racial identification, the product of what Luschan termed "pure malice and meanness" in Jim Crow America (518). Such dog-eared "tragic mulatto" stories, he added, seemed "rather amusing to non-prejudiced Europeans." But to North Americans, such "social declassification" was not just apparent but real (519).

Deterministic racial classifications seemed alien to Luschan, who had spent decades conducting comparative ethnological measurements in southern Anatolia and the Kingdom of Commagene (modern-day Turkey), the Greek island of Rhodes, South Africa, and other sites. His years of field research suggested that racial classifications were more fluid than fixed. He marveled at "the lack of unity in the 49 American states with often quite different orders, regulations and laws, [suggesting] that the Union does not know a unified definition of the terms 'Negro' or 'colored' person." After delineating the various statewide definitions of "colored," based on a range of degrees of "Negro blood," Luschan found North Americans' preoccupation with their ancestors' racial genealogies hard to believe. "Considering how little even [those] in our middle-European order and culture . . . know . . . about their grandparents of their great-grandparents, it is easy to understand how such proof can really never be delivered" (520–21).

Nonetheless, the Luschans used the increasingly obsolete anthropometric research tools they had employed in Asia Minor to measure African American schoolchildren in Memphis, New Orleans, Greenville, and elsewhere. They coded skin color as measures of biological inheritance. "Usually we were able to execute our studies at the end of the class or at the beginning of the breakfast break where on certain days we had hundreds of school children individually march by us." He admitted, "I certainly know very well that such a 'moment's' mass recording contains lots of potential for errors, but on the other hand, it is still a whole lot better than everything that I know in this area in America." Luschan promised to publish his full findings at a later date, but for the time being, he presented his preliminary findings in *Koloniale Rundschau* (521–22).

Although he had failed to document the total number of Black students that he and his wife examined, Luschan presented the following approximate totals in his article:

3–5% purely white looking children,
18% purely African looking children,
39% about look like half-breeds,
18–20% apparently have very little and
20% apparently have very much colored blood. (522)

Luschan explained that he had also sent questionnaires to teachers with Black students, and he recognized that they presented methodological challenges. "Nobody needs to tell me that such material is much less reliable than mass recordings by an anthropological expert; in fact about 3% of the questionnaires returned to me I had to eliminate as completely misunderstood [by the teachers] but the total result of all the others apart from small fractions of percentages agree with my own recordings" (522).

Based on this limited sampling, Luschan determined that the largest number of African American students he examined were neither white nor Black, but rather of mixed racial heritage. In his opinion, "the penetration of white blood into the colored population" had increased in recent years, "an assumption corresponding with the general impression of many knowledgeable experts of the South." In the end, Luschan concluded that "one cannot ignore the fact of a steadily increasing racial mixing. Whether this happens primarily within matrimony or outside of marriage, is less important for the final result of the process." Based on his questionnaires, physical inspections of light-skinned people, and anecdotal information from white and Black sources, Luschan declared without evidence, "Hundreds of thousands of white men in the South have colored girl friends despite the social gap separating the two population classes and despite the resounding phrases that again and again are disseminated against such relationships" (523).

Luschan in fact drew an even broader conclusion from his research: that the "general morals" of all Americans—whites, Blacks, and "mixed race" people—left much to be desired. While in the United States, he had read newspaper accounts of "interstate commercialized vice," involving the disappearance of as many as fifty thousand girls, presumably in prostitution rings. He also commented on interracial marriages—a taboo among white people in Jim Crow America. Cognizant that "real marriages between whites and coloreds" were far less frequent than "loose relationships" between the races, he nevertheless emphasized that they existed. "From the beginning," Luschan noted, "I would have expected white men would marry colored girls . . . but three very experienced American physicians who[m] I asked about this, independently and assuredly asserted that far more white women marry Black men than the other way around. In both cases almost without exception it is the white partner not the colored one who initiated the marriage." Based on such random and anecdotal sources, Luschan remarked that this was "the case of the famous or rather infamous Black award-winning boxer [Jack] Johnson who for a while held the world record in boxing" (524).[21]

Luschan found the various state laws on marriages and punishments for interracial marriages fascinating and peculiarly American. Drawing on Davenport's research, he assessed the draconian penalties that thirty of the forty-nine states had imposed on interracial marriages. In Luschan's opinion, "The restrictions on marriages and the punishments for mixed marriages or other race mixing vary even more than the definitions for 'Negro' and 'colored' in the individual states of the Union" (524). That said, he underscored the point that every state, except Montana, provided the loophole that mixed couples wishing to avoid prosecution for miscegenation could marry in states where such marriages were not illegal and then return to their state of residence (526). Luschan considered this "part and parcel of the American freedom that in such questions a little more or less color does not matter . . . everyone can do what they please, if not in one state then in another. The more gaps are contained in the various laws, the more there are channels through which mixed marriages can be performed. The only problem is the social disregard for the offspring" (527).[22]

"Absolute unrestrainedness in sexual intercourse," Luschan declared, signified the most deleterious stereotype leveled against people of color by early twentieth-century white supremacists (527). To a certain extent, this trope was unsurprising, he said, given that the average American Black person was only five or six generations removed from "the African jungle and the large steppe of his old home country." Luschan supported this racist generalization by repeating the old proslavery argument that African slave traders sold socially inferior people (*Minusvarianten*), not the best people (*Plusvarianten*) in tribes, to European enslavers. To exacerbate the situation, "In America this quite mixed society happened to end up in the worst possible environment; all family ties were destroyed in the most gruesome ways by the new masters and the good old, often really patriarchal order and at least in many cases exemplary, strict and goodwill[ed] tribal organization was replaced by the most brutal arbitrariness" of chattel slavery. For many bondspeople, emancipation thus proved to be a bittersweet advantage: "A large part of [the] former slaves remained afterwards in often nearly unchanged situations with their old masters . . . [while] too many . . . found themselves thrown into the streets, helpless, without possessions, home, knowledge and abilities, without money and often without sufficient clothes" (528).

Luschan found it unsurprising that their environmental, historical, and sociological genealogies made it challenging for the freedpeople to live upright and wholesome lives. But, he argued, criticisms of Black people as genetically, morally, socially, and spiritually depraved were grossly inaccurate. Invoking the World War I context, Luschan averred, "In America this is part of the typical exaggerations and distortions—just as today, in July 1915, over there, there are 'educated' people who believe that German soldiers cut off the hands of Belgian children or that Berlin was destroyed by the Russians and leveled to the ground, one believes everything bad about Negroes. One can read in more than one book that in their home country the Negroes use their own children as lures for their wild animal traps and other similar silly stories." Luschan strongly disputed exaggerated assertions by Davenport, Graves, Shufeldt, William Benjamin Smith, and others that Black people uniformly suffered from "moral putridity," a phrase that William Hannibal Thomas, an African American author, coined in 1901 in his Negrophobic text *The American Negro: What He Was, What He Is, and What He May Become*, to describe alleged widespread bestiality, incest, rape, and all-encompassing retrogression by African American males (529).[23] "In fact," Luschan elucidated, "we can see from a careful [analysis of] crime statistics on which the census of 1890 is based, that in the Union a higher percentage of whites than coloreds have been punished because of incest and every anthropologist should have expected this who knows with what superstitious apprehension particularly African tribes avoid everything in conjunction with incest" (530).

As for the proverbial "Southern [white] rape complex," he contended, "Certainly, there are deplorable excesses, just as there are other sad accidents, but the idea that a white woman when her husband is gone always has to be ready to kill a colored attacker is as grotesque as if one advises us to sit on an isolating chair during a thunderstorm or, because we might encounter a rabies-infected dog to always hold a loaded gun in our hands.... Rapes by colored people are even rarer than injuries due to lightning or bites by rabies-infected dogs" (530). Luschan went on to say that based on his undocumented 1904 comparative research, "it is very clear that in the states of the Union not more coloreds participated in the crime of rape than French and Russians and only two fifth times as much as the Italians" (531).

Whereas Luschan defended Black men from allegations that they were degenerate rapists, he proved to be more ambiguous about the moral and legal meanings of their lynchings. Since 1895, he noted, around four thousand Black people had been lynched, both for alleged assaults on white females and for what he termed "totally unimportant crimes." In his opinion, "Cases of the latter kind certainly are most deplorable—even though if one is not willing to agree with the general condemnation of lynching." Rather than sympathizing with those who had been murdered in acts of extreme racial violence, Luschan blamed the judicial systems in the United States and Europe for being "too soft and slow" to adjudicate perpetrators of serious crimes. "My personal impression is indeed that there are crimes in which our law, European just like American, is much too mild and works much too slowly. I see not much reason why even an ordinary court of justice should not be able to bring to atone for an aggravated crime—rape, even attempted rape ... within 24 hours." Luschan remarked that he often explained to his applied anthropology students in Berlin how modern criminal law repeatedly worked "to protect the criminal rather than society." Without directly justifying lynching, Luschan still affirmed that unless American lawmakers reformed their judicial systems, "one can understand if people's offended sense of justice in extreme cases proceeds to help itself [by resorting to vigilante justice]. In this sense I have no doubt that—as brutal and reprehensible [as] lynching per se might be—it will not disappear from America as long as official administration of justice continues to ignore the teachings of eugenics and social anthropology" (531).[24]

Luschan concluded his impression of World War I–era African Americans by underscoring his belief that racial mixing in the United States was unstoppable: "No laws, regulations, even the best education and certainly not pathetic lamentations such as those by W. Benjamin Smith, Shufeldt and others help against human drives." Having said this, he asserted that the negative "consequences of such interbreeding are not in the least as strong [as] the majority of the Southern authors want us to believe." Luschan's anthropometric research among other ethnic groups, including Italians, Greeks, and "our Jewish friends," showed that they carried "Negro blood in their genes without seriously damaging their moral, intelligence and social value" (532). While fully convinced of the power of heredity in passing traits from parents to their offspring, Luschan argued passionately that the majority of mixed-race people were not inferior in any measurable way, including morals, health, and intellect. Undeniably, though, bad genes (*schlechtes Erbgut*) and social circumstances (*sozialen Verhältnisse*) contributed greatly to a person's development and behavior (533).

Luschan emphasized the significance of the physical environment, especially "sanitary conditions," more so than "race" or physiology, in influencing moral and intellectual characteristics. He charged that American authors had virtually ignored such variables when assessing human health and behavior. "The allegation that physiologically caused infant mortality is particularly widespread among mixed breeds [*Mischlinge*] is totally untrue, as is the theory of their low resistance against tuberculosis and syphilis. To be sure, the percentages for consumption and syphilis for Negroes and mixed breeds in many areas of the Union are higher than for most groups of the white population, but again, the causes are not physiological, but rather social." His pioneering excavations and research with Kurdish tribes in the 1880s in Sendschirli, a village in northwestern Syria, had taught Luschan the degree to which shifts in lifestyle, the mere "changing the habits of the people," could make the difference between life and death. "The situation of bad health of many Negro mixed breeds [*Negermischlinge*], especially in the Northern states of the Union is similar," he said. "Unfavorable and dangerous environment[s]," not genetics, contributed to countless deaths among African Americans. During his American visit, Luschan observed "many non-hygienical places which had been rented to poor coloreds by white usurers" (533–34).[25]

Like many American racial reformers during the Progressive Era, Luschan considered the repatriation of the nation's Black population to Africa a "utopian" pipe dream, as was the prospect of lessening or removing America's anti-miscegenation laws. "The threatening danger the coloreds pose for the Whites can be truly lessened only by way of a determined far-reaching elevation of the colored themselves. The true danger is not a matter of the African race's color, it is not a matter of race at all, but of the undesirable qualities of certain individuals, and thus it is not race but single inferior individuals against whom must be fought, fought with all means, tender and mild ones as long as possible, hard and cruel ones where necessary." Examined analytically and critically, the "American Negro problem" was not peculiar to the United States, Luschan said. It was "a merely social problem," much as in Germany, where governments had the eugenic responsibility to decrease "the number of morally, intellectually and hygienically inferior individuals," by imprisonment or in some way rendering them harmless, "and above all, exclude them from procreation" (1915a, 534–35).

Luschan, however, warned that proponents of "race hygiene" (*Rassenhygiene*) too often emphasized "race" and underemphasized "hygiene." "Mental, physical and moral health are everything," he charged, and "skull form and color almost nothing," seemingly rejecting his own anthropometric method (535). Again, Luschan implored governments in both countries to reform their criminal laws, de-emphasizing "healing"—no matter the gender, race, or social class of the offender—and isolating habitual offenders, alcoholics, and transmitters of sexual diseases and tuberculosis. Luschan supposed that the current number of American Blacks with such characteristics exceeded the number of whites and that they should "be caught and if need be, isolated for life." But he insisted that whites had the moral, "healthwise" [*gesundheitlich*], and intellectual responsibility "to elevate this race, oppressed for such a long time and kept away from the blessings of modern culture, morally, physically, and intellectually by all possible means. Only then will the coloreds cease to be a danger to the whites." Additionally, it was imperative for white people to confer true citizenship and equality—"which in the Union they now only have on paper," but not in reality—on the remaining Black people (536).

Luschan stressed that there were no facile solutions to the U.S. "Negro problem." Scientists, legislators, and jurists could not even agree how to define the term *colored*. Germans experienced the same difficulty in establishing and identifying racial categories in its vast overseas colonies (*Schutzgebieten*) (537). Racial mixing between African and Native Americans who married Caucasian Americans complicated the problem in the United States, he explained. So too did the dearth of reliable statistics to document assertions and different demographics in the North and South. "For the time being," then, "even a very careful observer can only report about opinions and impressions [*Meinungen und Eindrucke*]" (538).

Luschan was certain about one thing, however: The number of "mixed breeds" continued to rise, and white men were responsible 99 percent of the time. The same process had occurred between Jews and Gentiles over five or six generations in large Western European cities. He suspected that Southern Blacks might slowly migrate northward because of "the social discrimination . . . in the Southern states with their cruel and to us Europeans seemingly idiotic excesses" (538–39).

AFTERMATH

A year after the Armistice of November 11, 1918, Luschan expressed his disappointment that few people had paid attention to his North American research on African Americans. Perhaps, he said, his observations had offended white racists in Germany and the United States, who judged him to be too "Negro friendly" (*negerfreundlich*).[26] In *Völker, Rassen, Sprachen* (Peoples, Races, Languages), Luschan summarized his conclusions for a broad audience of German readers: "All of mankind consists of only one species: *Homo sapiens*. There are no 'savage' people, there are only people with a different culture than our own. The separating characteristics of the so-called 'races' have basically developed due to climatic, social, and other factors of the environment. There are no inferior races per se" ([1922] 1927, 374).[27]

In his book, Luschan praised American Black people for making across-the-board improvements in education, literacy, morals, and public health and dismissed the writings of their racist critics as unscientific. He blamed white slumlords for the poor living conditions many Blacks experienced, argued that Blacks were no more licentious than whites, and underscored the widespread racism of white people obsessed by the specter of racial mixing. Luschan, unlike white Southerners, accepted the reality of the practice of racial mixing, but like them, he refused to endorse it.

As in 1915 Luschan implored Americans to implement laws that isolated and thus controlled what he considered morally inferior citizens—criminals, drug addicts, epileptics, gamblers, impostors, the perverse, thieves, and unemployable vagabonds. But Luschan complained that in the United States, Jim Crow laws and de facto segregation unfairly hovered over responsible Southern Black people like a miasma. He doubted the success of the controversial plans of "Black Moses," Marcus Garvey, who in the 1920s promoted the repatriation of African Americans to Africa. That said, Luschan predicted that because of tense race relations in the United States, eventually a section of the American South might become an exclusively Negro state. In his opinion, the vexing "Negro problem" constituted "among the most interesting and hardest questions of social anthropology, that ever a Statesman or learned person studied" ([1922] 1927, 55, 59–61, 63–64).

One scholar, eminent American anthropologist Melville J. Herskovits, took the Luschans' field research seriously.[28] After Felix Luschan's death in February 1924, Emma had sold her late husband's papers and skeleton collection to the American Museum of Natural History in New York. In 1930 she urged Herskovits to examine their 1915 measurements of Black Americans. He did so, summarizing two of the Luschans' datasets from their work in St. Louis, Memphis, Greenville, New Orleans, Tuskegee, and Hampton. One included measurements of all 349 people that the Luschans had recorded during their American stopover. The other consisted of measurements of 155 people —52 men and 103 women—between the ages of twenty and seventy. Herskovits published his findings in *Zeitschrift für Ethnologie* (1930), then Germany's leading physical and cultural anthropology journal.

In terms of method, not surprisingly, the Luschans had measured characteristics (*die Merkmale*) of the African Americans as essential data in reaching scientific observations. These included head length, head width, length-width index, nose height, nose width, upper facial height, whole facial height, ear height, ear width, thickness of the lip, zygomatic arch width, and body size.

Herskovits drew three conclusions from this preliminary field data. First, men possessed a larger mean value for each characteristic than women, the one exception being lips. Second, the Luschans' limited sample identified "few pure Negroes." The majority of people they measured were descended from mixed racial stock—white and Black, Native American and Black, or an intermixture of white, Native American, and Black. Third, Herskovits argued, "because Luschan gathered his data from several locations and then combined the statistics, the variations from the average tended to be larger than they would have been had he sorted his data by individual location" (Smith 2011, 156). One wonders how Luschan would have judged such simplistic conclusions from a respected anthropologist like Herskovits.

In 1930 Herskovits might have paid more attention to Luschan's "Die Neger in den Vereinigten Staaten" than to the raw anthropometric statistics that originated from an already outmoded scientific method. Had he done so, Herskovits would perhaps have noted Luschan's intellectual and methodological maturation, from examining skulls and skeletons, to measuring bodies, to studying inheritance and heredity, to recognizing the influence of biological evolution and natural selection, and finally, to identifying cultural and environmental explanations for so-called racial differences. By the time he returned to Germany in 1915, then, Luschan had come to grasp the fluidity of human species types over time, the racial mixing that white supremacists in the United States so feared.

To be sure, Luschan, trained in medicine, science, literature, and philosophy, subscribed to *Rassenhygiene* to prevent disease, increase the number of "competent" people in Germany, and as he explained in 1921, "restrict the fecundity of the incompetent" (Zängl-Kumpf 1997, 1:623). But based on his field research in the United States and elsewhere, he increasingly merged hereditarianism and environmentalism to explain human differences (see Smith 2002, 36–38). As Penny explains, Luschan had defended German imperialism, believing that "if Germans and other Europeans involved in colonial enterprises learned to respect other people as humans, equal to themselves, then colonial regimes could do more good than harm" (2021, 105).

Markus Dressler writes that "von Luschan was a *racialist*, but *not a racist*" (2013, 54n33; italics added). Much like Du Bois, Luschan identified subtle and unsubtle characteristics that "have divided human beings into races, which, while they perhaps transcend scientific definition, nevertheless, are clearly defined to the eye of the Historian and the Sociologist" (Du Bois 1897, 7). One interpreter of Du Bois's racial ideology explains that he, too, "believed that races are real entities, that racial identities are real and valuable properties of human individuals, and that racial solidarity can help realize such human goods as equality and self-actualization" (Taylor 2000, 103). Luschan also employed "race" as a means of classifying and describing people, but he rejected the concept of "superior" and "inferior" races that lay at the heart of white racism in North America.

Unlike white supremacists in the United States, Luschan praised the progress of African Americans, their "upswing" since emancipation, and sympathized with their plight during the age of Jim Crow. He never accepted his friend Alfred Holt Stone's argument that Black people were retrogressing, "steadily losing ground to their white competitors in the labor market, not because of race prejudice, but because blacks in general were lazy, shiftless, improvident, and unreliable" (Oliver 2014, 61). Most African Americans could be educated and would become useful citizens, Luschan wrote, and they deserved equality with white people. Luschan considered Hampton and Tuskegee Institutes to be on par with contemporary German technical schools. At these institutes, Blacks learned vocational skills and morality.[29]

Du Bois, addressing a German audience in 1906, proclaimed that "the day of the colored race is dawning. It is madness to stop the development, it is wisdom to promote what it promises us in terms of light for the hope for the future" (79).[30] A week after the outbreak of World War I, he quoted Luschan (1911c): "So the question of the number of human races has quite lost its *raison d'être*, and has become a subject rather of philosophical speculation than of scientific research" (Du Bois 1914, 16).

While Luschan and Du Bois disagreed on many points, especially on the social and cultural meanings of "race" and, most notably, on eugenics, both were antiracists and concurred on the upward trajectory of African American people (see Smith 2002, 23–25, 37). In "Die Neger in den Vereinigten Staaten," Luschan, like Du Bois before him, praised "the admirable energy [with which] the colored people" since emancipation had improved "their social and moral development" (1915a, 508). "Today and in the next centuries I can see in the colored people of the Union only a very valuable and almost indispensable element of the population, whose loss would necessarily have to lead to an immense financial catastrophe and to a disturbance of public life that is hardly imaginable" (539).

NOTES

1. For an incisive account of the looting of the Benin treasures, see Hicks (2020). Also see Völger (2007); Grey (2020).

2. For an insightful and thorough study of how the Luschans employed photographs as ethnological sources, see Morris-Reich (2016).

3. On the nineteenth-century distinction between "racialism" and "racism," see Appiah (1992, 13–16). On Luschan's theoretical evolution and his contradictions on science and "race," see Smith (2002); Penny (2021, 92, 94–95, 107).

4. Portions of this chapter appeared in expanded form in Smith (2009, 2011). The publishers have graciously granted permission to reuse this material in this essay.

5. Sylvia Angelica Smith herein provides the first English language translations of this text.

6. Luschan (1911b, 600); Luschan's Estate: Charles R. Hodge to Felix von Luschan, July 29, 1914, and Luschan, "Culture and Degeneration" typed speech, August 1914; Königliches Museum für Völkerkunde: Luschan (1915b).

7. Morse Collection: Felix von Luschan to Edward S. Morse, September 9, 1914.

8. Morse Collection: Felix von Luschan to Edward S. Morse, October 15, 1914.

9. Kroeber Papers: Felix von Luschan to Alfred L. Kroeber, October 26, 1914.

10. Luschan's Estate: Miscellaneous lecture notes, n.d.; Luschan, "Unity of Mankind"; Luschan, draft book review of W. B. Smith, *Color Line*; Luschan, "Sociology," January 6, 1915, 5.

11. Luschan's Estate: Felix von Luschan to Hugo Schuchardt, January 16, 1914, Hugo Schuchardt Papers.

12. Davenport Papers: Felix von Luschan to Booker T. Washington, December 23, 1914; Felix von Luschan to Charles B. Davenport, December 21, 1914.

13. Luschan's Estate: Booker T. Washington to Felix von Luschan, January 2, 12, 1915.

14. Du Bois Papers: Felix von Luschan to W. E. B. Du Bois, July 1, 1915. Luschan and Du Bois may have met in Berlin in the early 1890s, when Du Bois studied there. Both men attended the 1911 Universal Races Congress in London.

15. James Papers: Felix von Luschan to Edmund J. James, February 28, 1915; Luschan's Estate: Felix von Luschan to Alfred Holt Stone, February 11, 1915. For decades anthropologists relied on Luschan's well-known scale to assess skin pigmentation; see Swiatoniowski et al. (2013).

16. Boas Papers: Luschan to Boas, March 5, 1915.

17. Davenport Papers: Luschan to Davenport, April 5, 1915.

18. Morse Collection: Luschan to Morse, April 5, 1915.

19. Following Versailles, contributors to *Koloniale Rundschau* vigorously promoted "pro-colonial interests," although Germany no longer held colonies. See Van Hoesen (2014, 306).

20. Summaries of Graves's arguments appear in Graves (1903a, 3; 1903b, 9).

21. On the global dimensions of Johnson's life, especially within the context of whiteness, racism, and social Darwinism, see Runstedtler (2012).

22. See Davenport (1913).

23. On William Hannibal Thomas and his notorious book, see Smith ([2000] 2019).

24. On lynching in the German context, with beatings as a form of communal justice against rapists and perpetrators of armed assault, see Berg and Wendt (2011, 2–3).

25. See Luschan and Orient-komitee (1911). For a contemporary account in English of Luschan's work in Sendschirli, see Müller (1894).

26. Boas Papers: Felix von Luschan to Franz Boas, November 22, 1919.

27. "Die gesamte Menschheit besteht nur aus einer einzigen Spezies: Homo sapiens. Es gibt keine 'wilden' Völker, es gibt nur Völker mit einer anderen Kultur als die unsere. Die trennenden Eigenschaften der sogenannten 'Rassen' sind im wesentlichen durch klimatische, soziale und andere

Faktoren der Umwelt entstanden. Es gibt keine an sich minderwertigen Rassen."

28. On Herskovits, see Gershenhorn (2004).

29. Luschan's Estate: Notes on Hampton Institute, n.d.

30. "Und vor allem bedenk Eins: der Tag der farbigen Rasse dämmert. Es ist Wahnsinn, diese Entwicklung aufzuhalten, es ist Weisheit das, was sie uns an Licht und Zukunftshoffnung verheißt, zu fördern." Du Bois contributed this article, in imperfect German, to Max Weber's journal.

REFERENCES

Manuscripts and Archives

"Acta betreffend Verschiedene Angelegenheiten der ethnologischen Abteilung." Vol. 21. Königliches Museum für Völkerkunde. Berlin.

Boas, Franz. Papers. MSS.B.B61. American Philosophical Society Library, Philadelphia.

Davenport, Charles B. Papers. American Philosophical Society Library, Philadelphia.

Du Bois, W. E. B. Papers. University of Massachusetts–Amherst.

James, Edmund J. Papers. University Archives, University of Illinois–Urbana.

Kroeber, Alfred L. Papers. Bancroft Library, University of California–Berkeley.

Luschan, Felix von. Luschan's Estate. Department of Manuscripts, State Library, Berlin.

Morse, E. S. Collection. Phillips Library, Peabody Essex Museum, Salem MA.

Schuchardt, Hugo. Papers. Karl-Franzens-Universität, Graz, Austria.

Published Works

Anonymous. 1909. Unsigned review of "*Koloniale Rundschau*. Monatsschrift für die Interessen unserer Schutzgebiete und ihrer Bewohner. Nos. 1 and 2. January, February 1909." *Journal of the Royal African Society* 8 (31): 328–29.

Appiah, Kwame. 1992. *In My Father's House: Africa in the Philosophy of Culture.* New York: Oxford University Press.

Berg, Manfred, and Simon Wendt. 2011. "Introduction: Lynching from an International Perspective," In *Globalizing Lynching History: Vigilantism and Extralegal Punishment from an International Perspective*, edited by Manfred Berg and Simon Wendt, 1–18. New York: Palgrave Macmillan.

Davenport, Charles B. 1913. "State Laws Limiting Marriage Selection Examined in Light of Eugenics." *Eugenics Record Office Bulletin* 9:37–40.

Davis, Deborah. 2013. *Guest of Honor: Booker T. Washington, Theodore Roosevelt, and the White House Dinner That Shocked a Nation*. New York: Simon and Schuster.

Dressler, Markus. 2013. *Writing Religion: The Making of Turkish Alevi Islam*. New York: Oxford University Press.

Du Bois, W. E. B. 1897. *The Conservation of Races*. American Negro Academy Occasional Papers 2. Washington DC: American Negro Academy.

———. 1906. "Die Negerfrage in den Vereinigten Staaten" [The Negro question in the United States]. *Archiv für Sozialwissenschaft und Sozialpolitik* 22 (January): 31–79.

———. 1914. "Does Race Antipathy Serve Any Good Purpose?" *Boston Sunday Globe*, July 19.

———. 1935. *Black Reconstruction in America: An Essay Toward a History of the Part Which Black Folk Played in the Attempt to Reconstruct Democracy in America, 1860–1880*. New York: Harcourt, Brace.

Evans, Andrew David. 2002. *Anthropology at War: World War I and the Science of Race in Germany*. PhD diss., Indiana University.

———. 2010. *Anthropology at War: World War I and the Science of Race in Germany*. Chicago: University of Chicago Press.

Farland, Maria. 2006. "W. E. B. Du Bois, Anthropometric Science, and the Limits of Racial Uplift." *American Quarterly* 58 (4): 1017–45.

Gershenhorn, Jerry. 2004. *Melville J. Herskovits and the Racial Politics of Knowledge*. Lincoln: University of Nebraska Press.

Graves, John Temple. 1903a. "For a Negro Republic." *New York Times*, September 4.

———. 1903b. "He Defends Lynch Law." *New York Times*, August 12.

Grey, Tobias. 2020. "A Virtual Homecoming for Lost Treasures." *Wall Street Journal*, May 16–17.

Harlan, Louis R., ed. 1984. *The Booker T. Washington Papers*. Vol. 13. Urbana: University of Illinois Press.

Herskovits, Melville J. 1930. "Felix von Luschans Messungen Amerikaischer Neger." *Zeitschrift für Ethnologie* 61:337–63.

Hicks, Dan. 2020. *The Brutish Museums: The Benin Bronzes, Colonial Violence and Cultural Restitution*. London: Pluto.

Hollandsworth, James, Jr. 2008. *Portrait of a Scientific Racist: Alfred Holt Stone of Mississippi*. Baton Rouge: Louisiana State University Press.

Irek, Malgorzata. 1994. *The European Roots of the Harlem Renaissance*. Berliner Beiträge zur Amerikanistik, vol. 1. Berlin: John F. Kennedy Institute for North American Studies.

Johler, Reinhard, Christian Marchetti, and Monique Scheer, eds. 2010. *Doing Anthropology in Wartime and War Zones*. Bielefeld, Germany: Transcript Verlag.

Kerr, Ashley. 2020. *Sex, Skulls, and Citizens: Gender and Racial Science in Argentina (1860–1910)*. Nashville: Vanderbilt University Press.

Lowie, Robert H. 1915. "The Philadelphia Meeting of the American Anthropological Association," *Science* 41 (1049): 221–22.

Luschan, Felix von. 1911a. "Anthropological View of Race," In *Papers on Inter-Racial Problems, Communicated to the First Universal Races Congress, Held at the University of London, July 26–29, 1911*, edited by Gustav Spiller, 13–24. London: P. S. King & Son.

———. 1911b. "Der Rassen-Kongreß in London." *Koloniale Rundschau* 3:600.

———. 1911c. "The Early Inhabitants of Western Asia." *Journal of the Royal Anthropological Institute of Great Britain and Ireland* 41 (July–December): 221–44.

———. 1915a. "Die Neger in den Vereinigten Staaten." *Koloniale Rundschau* 7:504–40.

———. 1915b. "In Australien und Amerika." *Berlin Vossische Zeitung*, January 31.

———. 1919. *Die Altertümer von Benin*. Berlin: Vereinigung Wissenschaftlicher Verleger.

———. 1921. "Franz Boas über Kultur und Rasse." *Deutsche Literaturzeitung: Kritische Wochenschau über die wichtigsten Neuerscheinungen in den gesamten Wissenschaften* 42 (43/44): 570–75.

———. (1922) 1927. *Völker, Rassen, Sprachen: Anthropologische Betrachtungen*. Edited by E. von Luschan. Berlin: Deutsche Buch-Gemeinschaft G.m.b.H.

Luschan, Felix von, and Berlin Orient-komitee. 1911. *Ausgrabungen In Sendschirli*. Berlin: Druck und Verlag von Georg Reimer.

McMurry, Linda O. 1985. *Recorder of the Black Experience: A Biography of Monroe Nathan Work*. Baton Rouge: Louisiana State University Press.

Morris-Reich, Amos. 2016. *Race and Photography: Racial Photography as Scientific Evidence, 1876–1980*. Chicago: University of Chicago Press.

Müller, David Henry. 1894. "The Excavations at Sendschirli." *Contemporary Review* 65 (April): 563–75.

Oliver, Lawrence J. 2014. "W. E. B. Du Bois and the Dismal Science: Economic Theory and Social Justice." *American Studies* 53 (2): 49–70.

Penny, H. Glenn. 2021. *In Humboldt's Shadow: A Tragic History of German Ethnology*. Princeton NJ: Princeton University Press.

Runstedtler, Theresa. 2012. *Jack Johnson, Rebel Sojourner: Boxing in the Shadow of the Global Color Line*. Berkeley: University of California Press.

Shufeldt, Robert. 1915. *America's Greatest Problem: The Negro*. Philadelphia: F. A. Davis.

Smith, John David. (2000) 2019. *Black Judas: William Hannibal Thomas and The American Negro*. Athens: University of Georgia Press.

―――. 2002. "W. E. B. Du Bois, Felix von Luschan, and Racial Reform at the Fin de Siècle." *Amerikastudien/American Studies: A Quarterly* 47 (1): 23–38.

―――. 2005. "Alfred Holt Stone and Conservative Racial Thought in the New South." In *The Human Tradition in the New South*, edited by James C. Klotter, 47–65. Lanham MD: Rowman and Littlefield.

―――. 2009. "'I Would Like to Study Some Problems of Heredity': Felix von Luschan's Trip to America, 1914–1915." In *Felix von Luschan (1854–1924): Leben und Wirken eines Universalgelehrten*, edited by Peter Ruggendorfer and Hubert D. Szemethy, 141–63. Wien: Böhlau Verlag Wien.

―――. 2011. "Transatlantic Anthropological Dialogue and 'the Other': Felix von Luschan's Research in America, 1914–15." In *Racism in the Modern World: Historical Perspectives on Cultural Transfer and Adaptation*, edited by Manfred Berg and Simon Wendt, 140–62. New York: Berghahn Books.

Smith, William Benjamin. 1905. *The Color Line: A Brief in Behalf of the Unborn*. New York: McClure, Phillips.

Stone, Alfred Holt. 1908. *Studies in the American Race Problem*. New York: Doubleday, Page.

Swiatoniowski, Anna K., Ellen E. Quillen, Mark D. Shriver, and Nina G. Jablonski. 2013. "Technical Note: Comparing von Luschan Skin Color Tiles and Modern Spectrophotometry for Measuring Human Skin Pigmentation." *American Journal of Physical Anthropology* 151 (2): 325–30.

Taylor, Paul C. 2000. "Appiah's Uncompleted Argument: W. E. B. Du Bois and the Reality of Race." *Social Theory and Practice* 26 (1): 103–28.

Van Hoesen, Brett. 2014. "The Rhineland Controversy and Weimar Postcolonialism." In *German Colonialism in a Global Age*, edited by Bradley Naranch and Geoff Eley, 302–29. Durham NC: Duke University Press.

Völger, Gisela. 2007. "Curator, Trader, Benin Scholar: Felix von Luschan—An Austrian in Royal-Prussian Museum Service." In *Benin Kings and Rituals: Court Arts from Nigeria*, edited by Barbara Plankensteiner, 213–25. Ghent: Snoeck.

Zängl-Kumpf, Ursula. 1997. "Luschan, Felix (Ritter Edler) von (1854–1924)." In *History of Physical Anthropology*, edited by Frank Spencer, 1:622–23. New York: Garland.

4

The Institutionalization of Anthropology in Portugal

Contributions from the University of Coimbra

PATRÍCIA FERRAZ DE MATOS

This chapter deals with the context of the institutionalization of anthropology in Portugal since the late nineteenth century, mainly in the realm of the University of Coimbra.[1] This context—in which several studies have been carried out, as well as the collection of objects, bones, and other specimens, in Portuguese territory and the former colonies—was valuable in terms of the creation of museums, scientific societies, and publications. Side by side with the Coimbra School of Anthropology's activities, other initiatives were developed in this city that have had effects at the local, national, and international levels. The path undertaken by anthropology in Coimbra illustrates the multiple facets this discipline has adopted in other places, which still elicit our thoughts and reflections.

Generally speaking, it could be said that the "modern world" was born between the Napoleonic Wars (1792–1815) and the First World War (1914–18). This period broadly coincides with the Industrial Revolution era. The various technological changes brought about and the increased ability for everyone to travel led to a greater dissemination of goods, information, and knowledge. At the same time, many power relations that had existed until that time were criticized and abolished or replaced by others. All these changes contributed to the emergence of anthropology as a science, which evolved under the influence of various thinkers' ideas following the transformations that Europe had undergone over several years, from the formation of capitalism to nationalism to a secularized science. According to Bruno Latour, the concept of an autonomous individual was a precondition for the concept of society ([1991] 1993). The free individual would be the measure of all things, and society could become the subject of a systematic reflection.

Both modern philosophy and scientific and technological advances in the eighteenth century were important for the collection of knowledge for anthropology, although it was not elevated to the status of an academic discipline until the nineteenth century. A change in perspective in the twentieth century, when the human being was no longer considered a subject and became an object, was described by Michel Foucault, who wrote that human sciences are a "body of knowledge" or a "body of discourse that takes as its object man as an empirical entity" ([1966] 1968, 447). However, as suggested by João de Pina-Cabral (1991), better than trying to define anthropology is to identify the contexts in which it is positioned. Thus I next present the context (historical and sociological) in which anthropology emerged and the way its objects were chosen.

The word *anthropology* often defines a science positioned between biology and culture. However, straddling the gap between biological and sociocultural factors frequently leads to more problems than solutions. Some modern authors have worked on this subject, such as Marshall Sahlins (2008), taking a rather interpretative perspective, or Tim Ingold (1988, 1990), seeking to establish a bridge between the biological and social aspects. The terminology employed can also be useful for the analysis of the distinction between the study of natural and social factors. The term *anthropology* arose in the late eighteenth century, and in 1855 it came to name a discipline at a French university; meanwhile, the term *ethnography* was not used until in the nineteenth century.

Over time, several approaches emerged, evolutionism being one of the most relevant and influential. Two books by Charles Darwin ([1859] 1968, 1871) helped systematize this idea, which later played a significant role in the current field designated as evolutionary anthropology. According to this approach, certain cultures were still in a relatively backward stage concerning civilization compared with Western societies. These cultures were allegedly like living fossils that exemplified how Western societies may have looked in the past.

Most of the time, the elements (objects or cultural practices) were collected not by the individuals who gathered and analyzed the data (desk scientists), but rather by travelers, missionaries, traders, or local employees. The evolutionary method used data confrontation, through which societies were compared with each other and recorded in a linear diachronic sequence, organized hierarchically from the one considered the least developed to the one allegedly most developed or evolved. Western society was seen as the standard based on which all others were differentiated, classified, and hierarchized. The main topics of evolutionism were religious, family, and legal institutions, as well as aspects related to material culture. The aim of this approach was to prove how culture was influenced by a unilineal universal evolution (Eriksen and Nielsen 2007).

One of the main criticisms of evolutionists was that so few of them performed fieldwork. For that reason, and because of their broad scope, including the study of culture but also the origins of human beings and their evolution, sciences such as prehistoric archaeology and human paleontology were filling the void. The resulting increase in activities related to these approaches led to important discoveries, such as Cro-Magnon and Pithecanthropus human fossils. Among the works produced at the Coimbra School of Anthropology (as well as the Porto School of Anthropology; see Matos 2023), several studies were inspired by the scientific method of evolutionism, which contributed to the development of these disciplines and to their autonomy. All in all, evolutionism did allow for better knowledge of the past of humanity and contributed to making the study of humans less compromised by religious dogmas.

It was Franz Boas (1858–1942), a dominant figure in American anthropology from the 1890s to the 1920s, who first emphatically opposed the procedures used by evolutionary anthropologists (Boas 1896) and introduced methods that were more suitable to the study of sociocultural factors. Boas opposed Victorian anthropology's dominant evolutionary paradigm and insisted that positioning individual cultures on a scale based on savagery-barbarism-civilization not only prevented us from seeing their singularity and integrity but also made it difficult to recompose the nonwritten stories of the individual cultures under study. The idea of each culture's singularity, with each having an individual story the knowledge of which called for fieldwork, was developed by Boas's school (Stocking 1974, 1996). Based on this, the concept of cultural relativism was developed, and it was also argued that evolution could occur from a more "complex" state to a "simpler" one.

THE PORTUGUESE CASE

The period of institutionalization of anthropology in Portugal, when these paradigms were still in force, included the last decades of the monarchy, which ended in 1910; the troubled First Republic (1911–26); and the years of consolidation of the dictatorship (1926–50). In the late nineteenth and early twentieth centuries, under the overall designation of anthropology, two approaches were practiced in the entire country: anthropology, which was more connected to physical anthropology and the interest for natural science, and ethnology, which was connected to the study of traditional literature and popular traditions, dating back to the Romantic period.

Anthropologist João Leal, whose research considers mainly the ethnological aspect, writes that the 1870s and 1880s "witnessed the emergence of Portuguese anthropology as an autonomous discipline." He highlights figures in this discipline such as Adolfo Coelho (1847–1919) and Teófilo Braga (1843–1924), as well as the works by Consiglieri Pedroso (1851–1910) and José Leite de Vasconcelos (1858–1941). These authors developed their works in an intellectual context that was influenced by the 1871 Casino Conferences (in which Coelho and Braga took part), which marked a "turning point in Portuguese culture and science" (Leal 2000, 29). Ethnologist Ernesto Veiga de Oliveira (1972, 5) names the founders of the "Portuguese ethnology school" as Coelho, Leite de Vasconcelos, and António Augusto da Rocha Peixoto (1866–1909). The prevailing issue in Coelho's work is that of knowing "who we are," notes Veiga de Oliveira, and this is what, according to geographer Orlando Ribeiro, underlies all the writings of Leite de Vasconcelos.

Between 1878 and 1885 historian Oliveira Martins (1845–94) organized the Social Sciences Library (Biblioteca de Ciências Sociais), an undertaking in cultural diffusion that "comprised the evolution of institutions and societies, from its primitive forms to the modern State" (Saraiva and Lopes 1996, 842). In this context, he wrote *Elementos de Antropologia: História Natural do Homem* (Elements of anthropology: Natural history of man, 1880); *As Raças Humanas e a Civilização Primitiva* (The human races and primitive civilization, 1881); *Sistema dos Mitos Religiosos* (System of religious myths, 1882); *Quadro das Instituições Primitivas* (Table of primitive institutions, 1883); *Tábuas de Cronologia* (Chronology tables 1884); *História da República Romana* (History of the Roman Republic, 1885); *História da Civilização Ibérica* (History of Iberian civilization, 1879); and *O Brasil e as Colónias Portuguesas* (Brazil and the Portuguese colonies, 1881). In *História de Portugal* (History of Portugal, 1879), a work that found continuity in *Portugal Contemporâneo* (Contemporary Portugal, 1881), he contended that the country owed "its existence, not to geographic, ethnic or economic conditions, but to a collective will" (Saraiva and Lopes 1996, 848). The works of the following were also precursors of ethnological studies: Joaquim Mendes dos Remédios (1867–1932), Antero de Quental (1842–91), Manuel Joaquim Pinheiro Chagas (1842–95), Joaquim de Vasconcelos (1849–1936), Alberto Sampaio (1841–1908), and Francisco Morais Sarmento (1833–99).

Leite de Vasconcelos was, in fact, a key figure. He founded the journals *Revista Lusitana* (Lusitana journal) in 1889 and *O Arqueólogo Português* (The Portuguese archaeologist) in 1895. He also directed the Portuguese Ethnographic Museum. He wrote *Religiões da Lusitânia* (Lusitanian religions) in three volumes and *Etnografia Portuguesa* (Portuguese ethnography) in eleven volumes, and his disciples, Orlando Ribeiro and Manuel Viegas Guerreiro, continued publishing the materials he had collected. He also had a strong influence on the works on archaeology, ethnography, and art by Father Francisco Manuel Alves, known as the Abbot of Baçal.

The year 1857 saw the creation in Lisbon of the Kingdom's Committee for Geological Works (successor of the Geological Committee, created in 1848), headed by geologist Carlos Ribeiro and to which geologists António Pereira da Costa and Nery Delgado also belonged. Pereira da Costa published on prehistoric anthropology; "anthropology was referred to" in Nery Delgado's work on the Caves of Cesareda; and Carlos Ribeiro's efforts allowed the organization in 1880 of the Congress for Prehistoric Anthropology and Archaeology, which encouraged anthropological studies (Leite de Vasconcelos 1928, 6). The Portuguese Ethnographic Museum (Portuguese Ethnological Museum from 1897) was created in 1893, following a proposal by Bernardino Machado (figures 1 and 2), then minister of public works, and by João Franco, who managed the kingdom's portfolio. Its structure was in a way an extension of the Museum of Anthropol-

Fig. 1. Bernardino Machado, 1903. Municipal Archive of Porto / Arquivo Municipal do Porto.

ogy, accommodated at the Geological Services Committee, and it had an archaeological section (up to the eighteenth century) and a modern section. The current Museum of Archaeology at the Jerónimos Monastery in Lisbon is a result of this late nineteenth-century creation.

According to Leite de Vasconcelos, the "first researchers of a properly Portuguese anthropology" were an initiative of Francisco Ferraz de Macedo (1845–1907), both a doctor (trained in Rio de Janeiro) and an anthropologist (trained at the Paris School of Anthropology), who in 1882 asked the Lisbon city hall if he could measure the skulls belonging to Lisbon's eastern and western cemeteries (1928, 7). Ferraz de Macedo devoted his efforts to "criminal anthropology" and published *Crime et criminel* (Crime and

Fig. 2. Bernardino Machado from the side, 1903. Municipal Archive of Porto / Arquivo Municipal do Porto.

criminal, 1892), *Bosquejos de Antropologia Criminal* (Summary of crimi-
nal anthropology, 1900), and *Os criminosos "evadidos do Limoeiro em 1847"*
(The criminals "evaded from Limoeiro in 1847," 1901). He also published
Lusitanos e romanos em Vila Franca de Xira (Lusitanians and Romans in
Vila Franca de Xira, 1893), although Leite de Vasconcelos expresses some
reservations as to the Lusitanians (Matos 2017).

Ferraz de Macedo's "observations" were probably what inspired António
Aurélio da Costa Ferreira (1879–1922) and Álvaro da Silva Basto (1873–
1924) when writing their works on the cephalic index and the cranial
capacity of the Portuguese, respectively. Although Costa Ferreira lived in
Lisbon in 1907, it was with Machado, in Coimbra, that he had taken his
first steps in anthropology in 1898. (He subsequently studied at the Faculties of Philosophy in 1899 and Medicine in 1905.) He wrote, among others, the following works: *Négroïdes préhistoriques en Portugal* (Prehistoric
Negroids in Portugal, 1907); *Sur quelques crânes de l'Alentejo et de l'Algarve*
(On some Alentejo and Algarve skulls, 1909); *Mésaticéphales du Sud de
Portugal* (Mesaticephales of southern Portugal, 1910); *La capacité du crâne
et la composition ethnique probable du peuple portugais* (The capacity of
the skull and the probable ethnic composition of the Portuguese people,
1903); and *La capacité crânienne chez les criminels portugais* (Cranial capacity among Portuguese criminals, 1905).

The separation between the study of natural and social factors can also
be illustrated by the creation of different institutions or the organization of
events that carried out several scientific studies. The names of some institutions are evidence of the position reached by anthropology in the context of
zoology or natural history. This is the case of the Bocage Museum (National
Museum of Natural History), which combines zoology and anthropology,
and of the Zoology Department of the Faculty of Sciences of the University
of Porto and the Museum of Anthropology of the University of Coimbra,
both connected to the Museum of Natural History (Matos 2013).

Some scientific societies allowed the study of interests and paradigms
that later enabled the formation of anthropology schools and vice versa.
Several of those scientific societies were centers for debate and information sharing, organization of scientific meetings, fundraising, publication
of works, and knowledge dissemination (Matos 2016; Ranzmaier 2011).

In addition, the study of the relationships between some of these institutions and societies allows us to analyze how scientific knowledge was produced and spread through a process of inclusion and exclusion of different scientists, schools, or countries (Matos 2018b).

ANTHROPOLOGY AT THE UNIVERSITY OF COIMBRA

The official study of anthropology in Portugal began with the creation of the discipline of anthropology, human paleontology, and prehistoric archaeology as a replacement for the subject of agriculture, zootechnics, and rural economy at the Faculty of Philosophy of the University of Coimbra (*Cem Anos de Antropologia em Coimbra* 1985, 14) by the legal charter dated July 2, 1885, written by Bernardino Machado (1851–1944) and Corrêa Barata (1847–1900) and published in *Diário do Governo* (no. 149, July 9, 1885). Barata wrote, among other works, *As raças históricas da Península Ibérica* (The historical races of the Iberian Peninsula, 1872) and *Origens Antropológicas da Europa* (Anthropological origins of Europe, 1873), both published by the University of Coimbra Press. In the academic year 1885–86 this discipline was coordinated by Henrique Teixeira Bastos, a replacement professor. He was followed by head professor Bernardino Machado, trained in physics and mathematics, who was mainly inspired by the works of Francisco Ferraz de Macedo. Besides anthropology, Machado also taught agriculture, physics, and geology at the university.

In 1898 Machado founded the Society of Anthropology, the first anthropological scientific society in Portugal, planned in 1896–97. It had three types of members: full, correspondent, and honorary. To be a full member, one had to "have special works in anthropology," "be proposed by two members," "obtain an absolute majority of the votes in the general assembly," and "reside in Coimbra" (*Estatutos da Sociedade* 1899). Except for the residency requirement, the same conditions were imposed on correspondent members. In comparison, the statutes of the Portuguese Society of Anthropology and Ethnology (SPAE, Sociedade Portuguesa de Antropologia e Etnologia), which followed in 1918, were longer and more detailed; in addition, full members did not necessarily have to live in Porto (Matos 2016, 56). The activity of Coimbra's society was short-lived, since Machado, its first and only president, became more involved with politics and the Republican Party, which he officially joined in 1903 and chose to focus on in 1907. He eventually left the university for political reasons and was twice elected president of Portugal.

The figure of Bernardino Machado was dealt with in several works (Lima 2007; Marques and da Costa 1978; Samara 2012) that describe his scientific and political path. When he left the university, Eusébio Tamagnini (1880–1972) contributed toward the consolidation and affirmation of the Coimbra School of Anthropology (Duro dos Santos 2005).

In 1911 Coimbra's museum and laboratory were considered a scientific research institution, which did not happen with its Porto counterparts until 1923. Coimbra's school can be compared, in some respects, to naturalist anthropologic traditions such as the Paris School of Anthropology (Duro dos Santos 2012). In the initial years, the research subjects chosen belonged mainly to the realm of physical anthropology. Under Machado's guidance, students performed osteometric works between 1884–85 and 1904, which were published under the title *Aula de Antropologia da Universidade de Coimbra—trabalhos dos alumnos* (Anthropology class at the University of Coimbra—student work 1904). For the academic year 1887–88, the recommended textbooks and readings were as follows: Paul Topinard, *Manuel d'anthropologie* (Anthropology manual, 188?); Paul Broca, *Instructions cranéologiques et cranéométriques, de la Société d'Anthropologie de Paris* (Craneological and craneometric instructions, from the Société d'Anthropologie de Paris, 1875); and Gabriel Mortillet, "Le Préhistorique, antiquité de l'homme" (The prehistoric, antiquity of man, in *Anuário da Universidade de Coimbra*, 1887–88, 173). The dissertations for the discipline of anthropology were focused on the domains of osteology, ethnography, sociology, anthropometry, and human ecology. The anthropological studies at the University of Coimbra, in a similar way to the Paul Broca school, were developed mainly as anthropometric practices that sought significant elements to establish human group classifications. The subject's bibliography shows not only the weight of physical anthropology at the time but also the influence of the French school in Coimbra (Matos 2023; Duro dos Santos 2012).

Between 1907 and 1950, following Machado's resignation, Tamagnini took the post of main professor of the discipline of anthropology and accepted the job of director of the Anthropology and Prehistoric Archaeology section of the Museum of Natural History. The subject was then divided into two distinct aspects: zoological anthropology, a designation created by Tamagnini, intended to be a general introduction to primatology, and ethnological anthropology, studying the characterization of "human races" (Rodrigues de Areia and Rocha 1985, 17–18).

Changes also occurred in other universities following the government's new university reorganization in 1911. On May 12 of that year, the government published a decree organizing the faculties of science in Lisbon and Porto, where it included the subject of anthropology, already existing at University of Coimbra. That same decree established the subject of ethnology at the faculties of arts and humanities of the three universities (Leite de Vasconcelos 1928, 12). In Lisbon's case, the anthropology subject was first coordinated by zoology professor Baltasar Osório (1855–1926), with Júlio Bettencourt Ferreira (1866–1948) as assistant and, later, Artur Ricardo Jorge (1886–1974).

From 1912 onward the university's Anatomy Institute of the Faculty of Medicine published the periodical *Arquivo de Anatomia e Antropologia* (Anatomy and anthropology archive), coordinated by Henrique de Vilhena, in which anthropology articles were published by its director and by Costa Ferreira, António Augusto Mendes Correia (1888–1960), and Joaquim Fontes (1892–1960), among others. In 1914, following the publication of *Aula de Antropologia* (students' works), the university's Anthropology Institute began publishing the journal *Contribuições para o Estudo da Antropologia Portuguesa* (Contributions to the study of Portuguese anthropology).

Concerning studies in the colonial field, in December 1901 the University of Coimbra proposed the creation of a colonial course at the Faculty of Law, which was coordinated by Rui Ulrich and Marnoco e Sousa between 1905 and 1910. The university also created the course of colonial ethnography, the curriculum of which, written by João Gualberto de Barros e Cunha (1865–1950) in the academic year 1912–13, advocated the importance for the colonizing peoples to know the ethnography of the Indigenous peoples of their colonies. Almost all matters were concerned with Africa and its peoples, their social organization, or the objects they produced, but those of India, Macao, and Timor were considered as well. There was also a different component concerning the course of criminal anthropology, authorized in the academic year 1908–9 and designated as the course of anthropometry.

The domain of ethnological anthropology did not witness a major development, despite the numerous collections gathered within the scope of the material culture. Nevertheless, the subject of ethnological anthropology, whose curriculum stated it was a "general introduction to the study of races," was in place for students of the Faculty of Arts and Humanities of the University of Coimbra. In 1929–30 the curriculum included, among others, the following courses: Ethnology and Ethnography, General Considerations; Notions on Species and Races; Distinctive Characters of Races; Skin Color, Melanines, etc.; The Various Anthropometric Indexes; and Classification of Human Races. In parallel with these subjects, Tamagnini and his disciples produced works in the areas of somatometry and osteometry, physiology, and biodemography. Coimbra was therefore developing a perspective that was similar to that of German anthropology in the sense of a *rassenkunde* (Proctor 1988). In the academic year 1939–40 the discipline of anthropology in the university's Faculty of Science still included classes such as Morphology Compared to Current Hominids, Anthropometry, Craniometry, and Notions of Species and Race in Light of the Principles of Genetics (Rodrigues de Areia and Rocha 1985, 21, 52).

One might suppose that there was academic sharing between the Coimbra and Porto schools, as well as political and ideological sharing, because of the positions held by some of the figures associated with these schools during the New State (1933–74) and possible personal proximity between their main representatives, Tamagnini and Correia. This was not the case, however, and there was great rivalry between Coimbra and Porto. When Tamagnini retired in 1948, his work in the discipline of anthropology was continued at Coimbra by José Antunes Serra (1914–90) and Alberto Xavier da Cunha (1908–?).

DEVELOPMENTS IN PARALLEL TO THE SCHOOL

Besides the activities organized by the Coimbra School of Anthropology, several initiatives were developed at the local, national, and international levels. As agreed among the Portuguese anthropologists, the headquarters of the Portuguese section of the International Institute for Anthropology was in Coimbra beginning in 1921. (The institute was founded in Paris and had a delegation in India, represented by researchers of the Goa Medical-Surgical School.)

In 1933 in Coimbra Eusébio Tamagnini presented the proposal for the creation of the Portuguese Society of Eugenic Studies, the statutes of which were approved in 1934. It was eventually founded on December 9, 1937, by Tamagnini; jurist, professor, and politician José Alberto dos Reis (1875–1955); and the professors of the university's Faculty of Medicine, Álvaro de Almeida Matos (1880–1954), Alberto Moreira da Rocha Brito (1885–1955), and Alberto Cupertino Pessoa (1883–1942). This foundation also counted on doctor and professor Henrique Jardim de Vilhena (1879–1958) from Lisbon and anthropologist and archaeologist Mendes Correia from Porto. The society was inaugurated during the university's centenary celebrations, with the presence of representatives from several countries (*Diário de Coimbra*, December 10, 1937), including Eugen Fischer (1874–1967), director of the Kaiser Wilhelm Institute of Anthropology, Human Heredity, and Eugenics in Berlin. It operated until 1974. Some of its counterparts were the German Society for Racial Hygiene (Deutsche Gesellschaft für Rassenhygiene, 1905), Eugenics Education Society in England (1907), Société Française d'Eugénique (1912), and American Eugenics Society (1921).

Despite having several advocates in Portugal, eugenics was considered mainly within the scope of hygiene—that is, researchers highlighted the influence of the environment and external factors. The hygienist way (supported by discoveries in the domains of chemistry, medicine, and pharmaceutics) eventually prevailed over the eugenic way, although both may have coexisted (Matos 2010). The measures of positive eugenics included a reinforcement of social assistance and mother-child protection, evidenced by, for example, the child-support homes created by doctors Fernando Bissaya-Barreto (1886–1974) and Elísio de Moura (1877–1977) in Coimbra. Another interesting aspect is the fact that the debate around eugenics began to add sociological, psychological, and even legal elements to the biological arguments regarding the regulation of marriages and divorces proposed by some doctors and the subsequent need to update the Portuguese Civil Code (Cleminson 2014). As to sterilization, it was the object of consensual disapproval. Only António Egas Moniz (1874–1955), who was a winner of the Nobel Prize in Medicine or Physiology in 1949, proposed sterilization to eradicate morbid heredity, a measure that was, however, restricted to special clinical cases (Pereira 1999, 588). Among the greatest advocates of eugenics were several psychiatrists connected to government institutions, such as Miguel Bombarda (1851–1910), Júlio de Matos (1856–1922), José Sobral Cid (1877–1941), and Henrique Barahona Fernandes (1907–92).

Between 1914 and 1982 the university's Anthropology Institute published eleven volumes of the journal *Contribuições para o Estudo da Antropologia Portuguesa*, each with a different number of installments. Although this publication received grants from the National Education Committee (Junta de Educação Nacional) and the institute, a lack of financing led to some installments being published as offprints of the journals *Revista da Universidade de Coimbra* (Journal of the University of Coimbra) and *Revista da Faculdade de Ciências da Universidade de Coimbra* (Journal of the faculty of sciences of the University of Coimbra). The last time this occurred was with the eighth installment of the sixth volume (1959).

In 1981 the journal printed a volume of all the indexes published in volumes 1–10 of this periodical (Figueiras 1981). The eighty-seven articles listed are divided into three topics: physical anthropology (seventy-nine), cultural anthropology (seven), and archaeology (one). This shows that the journal mainly published articles on physical anthropology (91 percent), with far fewer on cultural anthropology (8 percent) and archaeology (1 percent), unlike what could be found in SPAE's publications (Matos 2016, 75). What stands out in examining these indexes is not only the smaller number of articles within the scope of ethnology and ethnography compared with physical anthropology, but also the fact that none of the articles in either ethnology or ethnography analyzed the Portuguese population. Rather, they analyzed the populations of what were then colonies, mainly Angola, including the single article on the topic of archaeology (Martins 1976). Most of the articles on Angola were published in the 1970s by Manuel Laranjeira Rodrigues de Areia, a retired full professor in anthropology at the University of Coimbra (Matos 2023). In 1983 the journal *Antropologia Portuguesa* (Portuguese anthropology) was created as a continuation of the journal *Contribuições* and represented a new phase of anthropology at the university. The current journal still maintains an exchange with 181 journals and is referenced in several international databases (Research Centre for Anthropology and Health 2016).

The Museum of Anthropology's initiatives related to activities developed by the Educational Service and exhibitions directed at the general public were, and still are, a means of revealing the important heritage of this museum's collections, of which many are from Africa. These initiatives are an example of how the Museum of Anthropology in Coimbra was already beginning to develop an interest in African studies at a time when these were still incipient in Portugal.

Some of its exhibitions, such as the one titled *Africa: Musical Instruments* (figure 3), presented in 1984 and included in the Third African Culture Week, have considered the concerns of the "new museology" (*África* 1984). An international movement for a new museology was initiated in Portugal in 1985 as a group that reflected on the processes and practices of a museology that engaged with the communities and territories and was further developed in subsequent years. This movement was connected to the idea of social museology, largely inherited from the social movements that led to the revolution on April 25, 1974, and the end of the dictatorship in Portugal. The new museology, instead of focusing only on objects, considered the relationships that objects allow to be established among individuals. This concept was, however, marked by a tension between the safeguarding and diffusion of heritage. This notion would be developed in the subsequent years, but we should highlight the fact that the 1984 catalog draws attention to this aspect and states that contacts were being established with museums such as the Museum of Natural History in Maputo, the National Museum of Anthropology in Angola, and the National Museum and the Edison Carneiro Museum, both in Rio de Janeiro. Materials were actually received from some of these other museums.

FROM INSTITUTIONALIZATION TO TODAY

In Portugal, the institutionalization of anthropology, understood in its biological and sociocultural dimensions, is connected to the process of development of scientific organizations and of disciplines that arose, or expanded, in the nineteenth century. This process was intertwined with political and ideological factors. Among these were the desire for knowledge of the origins, ethnical identity, and cultural practices of the

ÁFRICA
instrumentos musicais

museu e laboratório antropológico
coimbra   maio 84

Fig. 3. Catalog for *África: Instrumentos Musicais*, 1984. Museu e Laboratório Antropológico da Universidade de Coimbra.

Portuguese people and concerns regarding the creation and consolidation of the colonial empire. The first initiatives to develop a discipline of anthropology were undertaken in Coimbra by Bernardino Machado. SPAE was created in Porto and was later the basis of the Porto School of Anthropology. In both cases, the study of social and cultural factors was present from the beginning but was often integrated into the study of natural factors.

Although more systematic research in colonial territory was carried out by anthropological missions in the 1930s (Matos 2018a), it was in the late nineteenth century and during the First Republic in 1911–26 that a colonial conscience was elaborated and defined, and with it arose the need to perform research on the colonies. Nevertheless, as highlighted by Gonçalo

Duro dos Santos, the fragilities of the Portuguese colonial project, its long duration in time, and the political context (dictatorship) "would not allow a colonial anthropology to grow as in other European nations" (2005, 18).[2] In the Portuguese case, anthropology, mainly as a result of its physical and racialist studies, eventually came to support some of the colonial domination processes (Asad 1973; Gallo 1988), such as when analyses were based on assumptions of the colonial projects' civilizational and racial superiority (Matos 2019; Roque 2010). When these assumptions were no longer shared, anthropology led the way in criticizing colonialism. Anthropology was not always conducted in the same manner, nor have anthropologists always shared the same opinions, even when contemporary.

The first university degree in anthropology was created in the 1960s at the Instituto Superior de Ciências Sociais e Política Ultramarina (Higher Institute of Social Sciences and Overseas Politics, ISCSPU) in Lisbon. In the years following the 1974 revolution, the ISCSP (its former designation, without the word *Ultramarina*) witnessed a struggle between young students associated with the left-wing political sphere and the conservative wing of the colonial ideologists, led by the former minister of overseas Adriano Moreira, who replaced Mendes Correia as head of this school.

In the late 1970s and early 1980s new departments were created, and others were replaced. Some anthropologists who had received their degrees were integrated into new schools. From a theoretical point of view, during the first phase of the 1980s, "the former concern with national identity gave way to a search for difference" (Pina-Cabral 1991, 37). Following the Department of Anthropology of ISCSP, another was created at Universidade Nova de Lisboa and what is today Instituto Universitário de Lisboa (ISCTE), both also in Lisbon.

In 1989 João Pereira Neto, a professor at ISCSP and then the director of Antropos-Sociedade de Estudos de Antropologia e Sociologia (Antropos-Society for the Study of Anthropology and Sociology), wrote an expert opinion on the creation of a degree in anthropology at the University of Coimbra (Neto 1988). This happened in 1992 at the university's Faculty of Science and Technology (FCT). About two years later, the university's former Anthropology Institute was given the status of a department. The implementation of the degree, the curriculum of which includes training in biological as well as social and cultural anthropology, both mandatory, was mainly due to the efforts of Manuel Laranjeira Rodrigues de Areia. Today this degree is part of the FCT's Department of Life Sciences, alongside degrees in biology and biochemistry. In the 1990s a degree in anthropology, in the form of applied anthropology (Pereiro 2014), also existed at the Fernando Pessoa University in Porto and the University of Trás-os-Montes and Alto Douro in Vila Real, but it was suspended during the next decade at both universities.

As to the anthropology carried out today, I ask the following: To guarantee a useful and creative scientific dialogue, is it necessary to have a common theoretical base or a common history or to identify with a set of antecedents? João de Pina-Cabral raises an issue that is at the same time synchronic and diachronic: "How [can one] describe a group of scientists that, despite being placed under the same discipline category, maintain incompatible theoretical and methodological positions and that, despite affirming a common past in the discipline, do not find there the inspiration for their work?" (1991, 13). According to Pina-Cabral (1989), it is a historicist sense, and not a theoretical and methodological one, that allows us to say that "there are anthropologists in Portugal, even if there is not just one anthropology." We will then be able to bring together the "diversity within this discipline's domain" by speaking less of disciplines and instead of discipline traditions (31).

Since the late 1970s, and especially more recently, the anthropology developed in Portugal and elsewhere has been turning to new fields or to fields that were not considered previously, which illustrates a new trend in the discipline toward learning to see the differences between closely related fields (de Lima and Sarró 2006). This is also connected to the theoretical evolution of the scientific area itself. What is understood by anthropology has come from a group of people, anthropologists, who may have had very different concerns, advocated diverging theories, and employed different methods and approaches. Moreover, not all anthropologists follow the same precursors in this domain, nor the specific work they developed. The analysis of the path of anthropology at the University of Coimbra throughout time is therefore a fine example of the various aspects of this discipline that compel us to reflect.

ACKNOWLEDGMENTS

This work was supported by the Portuguese Foundation of Science and Technology (FCT), under the project: https://doi.org/10.54499/dl57 /2016/cp1441/ct0001. The translation of this text was financed by national funds through the FCT, IP, within project UIDP/50013/2020.

NOTES

1. A more extensive analysis of this subject was published in Matos (2023).
2. What Duro dos Santos seems to be arguing is that the country did not have the economic or scientific conditions to make a more robust investment in the colonies, as happened in other European countries such as England or France.

REFERENCES

África: Instrumentos musicais. 1984. Coimbra: Museu e Laboratório Antropológico da Universidade de Coimbra.

Anuário da Universidade de Coimbra. 1887–88. Coimbra: Universidade de Coimbra.

Asad, Talal, ed. 1973. Anthropology and the Colonial Encounter. London: Ithaca.

Boas, Franz. 1896. "The Limitations of the Comparative Method of Anthropology." Science 4, no. 103 (December 18): 901–8.

Cem anos de antropologia em Coimbra, 1885–1985. 1985. Coimbra: Museu e Laboratório Antropológico da Universidade de Coimbra.

Cleminson, Richard. 2014. Catholicism, Race and Empire: Eugenics in Portugal, 1900–1950. Budapest: Central European University Press.

Darwin, Charles. (1859) 1968. A Origem das Espécies [On the origin of species]. Sao Paulo: Hemus.

———. 1871. The Descent of Man, and Selection in Relation to Sex. London: John Murray.

de Lima, Antónia Pedroso, and Ramon Sarró. 2006. Terrenos Metropolitanos: Ensaios sobre produção etnográfica. Lisbon: Imprensa de Ciências Sociais.

Duro dos Santos, Gonçalo. 2005. A Escola de Antropologia de Coimbra, 1885–1950: O que significa seguir uma regra científica? Lisbon: Imprensa de Ciências Sociais.

———. 2012. "The Birth of Physical Anthropology in Late Imperial Portugal." Current Anthropology 53 (5): 33–45.

Eriksen, Thomas H., and Finn S. Nielsen. 2007. História da Antropologia. Petrópolis: Editora Vozes.

Estatutos da Sociedade de Antropologia de Coimbra. 1899. Coimbra: Imprensa da Universidade.

Figueiras, Isabel. 1981. "Índices, vols. 1–10, 1914–1981." *Contribuições para o Estudo da Antropologia Portuguesa*. Coimbra: Instituto de Antropologia da Universidade de Coimbra.

Foucault, Michel. (1966) 1968. *As Palavras e as Coisas: Uma arqueologia das ciências humanas*. Lisbon: Portugália Editora.

Gallo, Donato. 1988. *O Saber Português: Antropologia e Colonialismo*. Lisbon: Heptágono.

Ingold, Tim, ed. 1988. *What Is an Animal?* London: Unwin Hyman.

———. 1990. "An Anthropologist Looks at Biology." *Man* 25 (2): 208–29.

Latour, Bruno. (1991) 1993. *We Have Never Been Modern*. New York: Harvester Wheatsheaf.

Leal, João. 2000. *Etnografias Portuguesas (1870–1970): Cultura Popular e Identidade Nacional*. Lisbon: Publicações Dom Quixote.

Leite de Vasconcelos, José. 1928. "A Antropologia portuguesa como fonte de investigação etnográfica." *Boletim de Etnografia* 4:1–19.

Lima, Joaquim. 2007. *Princípios de Antropologia em Bernardino Machado*. Porto: Campo das Letras.

Marques, António H. de Oliveira, and Fernando M. da Costa. 1978. *Bernardino Machado*. Lisbon: Montanha.

Martins, Rui de S. 1976. "A estação arqueológica da antiga Banza Quibaxe: Dembos—Angola." *Contribuições para o Estudo da Antropologia Portuguesa* 9 (4): 243–306.

Matos, Patrícia Ferraz de. 2010. "Aperfeiçoar a "raça", salvar a nação: Eugenia, teorias nacionalistas e situação colonial em Portugal." *Trabalhos de Antropologia e Etnologia* 50:89–111.

———. 2013. *The Colours of the Empire: Racialized Representations During Portuguese Colonialism*. Oxford: Berghahn.

———. 2016. "Anthropology in Portugal: The Case of the Portuguese Society of Anthropology and Ethnology (SPAE), 1918." In *Local Knowledge: Global Stage*, edited by Regna Darnell and Frederic W. Gleach, 53–97. Lincoln: University of Nebraska Press.

———. 2017. "Who Were the Ancestors of the Portuguese? Portuguese Debate on Their National Origins." *Portuguese Studies Review* 25 (2): 127–53.

———. 2018a. "Conhecimento científico como promotor de potência colonial: O caso das missões científicas de foro antropológico." In *Repensar el colonialismo: Iberia, de colonia a potencia colonial*, edited by B. Marín-Aguilera, 371–400. Madrid: JAS Arqueología.

————. 2018b. "Inclusions and Exclusions in the Production and Circulation of Scientific Knowledge: The Case of the Royal Anthropological Institute (RAI) and the Portuguese Society of Anthropology and Ethnology (SPAE)." In *Changing Societies: Legacies and Challenges*, vol. 1, *Ambiguous Inclusions: Inside Out, Outside In*, edited by Paulo Granjo, Sofia Aboim, and Alice Ramos, 407–29. Lisbon: Imprensa de Ciências Sociais.

————. 2019. "Racial and Social Prejudice in the Colonial Empire: Issues Raised by Miscegenation in Portugal (Late Nineteenth to Mid-Twentieth Centuries)." *Anthropological Journal of European Cultures* 28 (2): 23–44.

————. 2023. *Anthropology, Nationalism and Colonialism: Mendes Correia and the Porto School of Anthropology*. Oxford: Berghahn.

Neto, João P. 1988. "Parecer sobre a eventual criação da licenciatura em Antropologia na Universidade de Coimbra." *Estudos Políticos e Sociais* 26 (1–2): 130–31.

Pereira, Ana Leonor. 1999. "Eugenia em Portugal?" *Revista de História das Ideias* 20:531–600.

Pereiro, Xerardo. 2014. "Da antropologia à antropologia aplicada ou a afirmação da disciplina no Norte de Portugal." *Etnográfica* 18 (2): 425–40.

Pina-Cabral, João de. 1989. "Breves Considerações Sobre o Estado da Antropologia em Portugal." *Antropologia Portuguesa* 7:29–36.

————. 1991. *Os contextos da antropologia*. Lisbon: Difel.

Proctor, Robert. 1988. "From Anthropologie to Rassenkunde in the German Anthropological Tradition." In *Bones, Bodies, Behaviour*, edited by G. W. Stocking, 138–79. Madison: University of Wisconsin Press.

Ranzmaier, Irene. 2011. "The Anthropology Society in Vienna and the Academic Establishment of Anthropology in Austria, 1870–1930." In *Histories of Anthropology Annual*, vol. 7, edited by Regna Darnell and Frederic W. Gleach, 1–22. Lincoln: University of Nebraska Press.

Research Centre for Anthropology and Health. 2016. *Antropologia Portuguesa*, accessed November 12, 2019, http://cias.uc.pt/antropologia-portuguesa/.

Rodrigues de Areia, Manuel, and Maria Augusta Rocha. 1985. *O Ensino da antropologia em Coimbra*. In *Cem anos de antropologia em Coimbra, 1885–1985*, 13–60. Coimbra: Museu e Laboratório Antropológico da Universidade de Coimbra.

Roque, Ricardo. 2010. *Headhunting and Colonialism: Anthropology and the Circulation of Human Skulls in the Portuguese Empire, 1870–1930*. Hampshire, UK: Palgrave Macmillan.

Sahlins, Marshall. 2008. *The Western Illusion of Human Nature*. Chicago: Prickly Paradigm.

Samara, Maria A. 2012. *Bernardino Machado: Uma vida de luta.* Lisbon: Assembleia da República.

Saraiva, António J., and Óscar Lopes. 1996. *História da Literatura Portuguesa.* 17th ed. Porto: Porto Editora.

Stocking, George W., ed. 1974. *The Shaping of American Anthropology, 1883–1911: A Franz Boas Reader.* New York: Basic.

———, ed. 1996. *Volksgeist as Method and Ethic: Essays on Boasian Ethnography and the German Anthropological Tradition.* Vol. 8. Madison: University of Wisconsin Press.

Veiga de Oliveira, Ernesto. 1972. "Introdução." In *Museu de Etnologia do Ultramar: Povos e Culturas,* 1–16. Lisbon: Junta de Investigações do Ultramar.

5

Between Science and Ideology

An Intellectual Biography of António
Mendes Correia (1888–1960)

PATRÍCIA FERRAZ DE MATOS

Texts mentioning António Mendes Correia (figure 4) usually link his name to certain labels, but these often reveal scant knowledge of his life and work.[1] His life was filled with diverse activities, and thus it is difficult to categorize Mendes Correia in just one or two words. He was the figure who contributed most during the early years of the Portuguese Society of Anthropology and Ethnology (SPAE, Sociedade Portuguesa de Antropologia e Etnologia), a scientific society that was created in 1918 and still exists today. He sparked debate around subjects that were then considered of importance for anthropological science, and he encouraged studies in the field of ethnology, archaeology, and anthropology. SPAE contributed to what later became the Porto School of Anthropology, although the school was independent from the society. Mendes Correia was the most important person in this school and in anthropology in Portugal during the first half of the twentieth century.

His name is frequently mentioned, although his work is little known and is not always correctly quoted.[2] In other words, references are made to Mendes Correia based on those labels, but some of them show a lack of knowledge of his whole path, the diversity of his intellectual interests, the evolution of his theoretical formulations, and his contributions to the science produced in Portugal, which focused on not only the national but also the colonial context.

Examples of the varied perspectives on Mendes Correia can be found in tributes to him on three distinct occasions around the time of the fiftieth anniversary of his death. The first, at which I was present (Matos 2011),

Fig. 4. António Mendes Correia, 193? On the back of the photo is written "Foto Alvão, 5th September 193." Private collection.

was the *Primeiro Seminário de História do Património e da Ciência—A. A. E. Mendes Corrêa (1888–1960) entre a ciência, a docência e a política* (First Seminar on Heritage and Science History—A. A. E. Mendes Corrêa (1888–1960) Between Science, Teaching and Politics), organized by the Universidade Lusófona in Lisbon on December 9, 2010, following which a book was published (Martins 2011a). On this occasion, the participants associated Mendes Correia with several areas.

I associated him mainly with the history of the institutionalization of anthropology in Portugal. Within this history, Catarina Casanova (2011), a primatologist and professor at the Higher Institute for Social Sciences and Politics (ISCSP, Instituto Superior de Ciências Sociais e Políticas) of the University of Lisbon, considered him a "reference in biological anthropology in Portugal" and the father of primatology in the country. In fact, as with anthropologist Louis Leakey (1903–72), Mendes Correia encouraged some disciples to study nonhuman primates. The book *Gorilas do Maiombe Português* (Ferreira et al. 1945), for which Mendes Correia wrote the preface, is an example of his influence and illustrates that he was in the vanguard in relation to primatology in Portugal in the 1940s. At the same seminar, Teresa Salomé Mota (2011), a researcher in the field of geology, referred to him as a "front-line advocate of geology in Portugal," considering his efforts to institutionalize this discipline and legitimize the work performed by geologists. João Pereira Neto (2011), emeritus full professor at ISCSP-UL and a member of the Board of the Geographic Society of Lisbon (SGL, Sociedade de Geografia de Lisboa), an institution created in 1875, stressed the role played by Mendes Correia as a director (1946–58) and professor (1949–58) at the Higher Colonial College (ESC, Escola Superior Colonial), which was created in 1906 under the designation Colonial School and renamed in 1927. Finally, archaeologists Ana Cristina Martins (2011a, 2011b), who was then a researcher at Universidade Lusófona and played an important role in organizing the event, and João Luís Cardoso (2011), a professor at Universidade Aberta, highlighted Mendes Correia's role in the field of archaeology.

The second occasion, in which I also took part, was the transdisciplinary conference A Universidade e a Ciência, a Cidade e a Nação (University and science, the city and the nation) on January 6, 2011, organized by the Department of Science and Heritage Techniques of the Faculty of Humanities of the University of Porto (FLUP, Faculdade de Letras da Universidade do Porto), with the cooperation of the Faculty of Sciences (FCUP, Faculdade de Ciências da Universidade do Porto) and the support of the Porto Municipality (Câmara Municipal do Porto). This session, which took place at the Palácio dos Condes de Balsemão in Porto, illustrated the diversity of Mendes Correia's scientific activities in both the Faculties of Humanities and Sciences, as well as his involvement in politics, since he had been the mayor of Porto, among other positions.

On this occasion, several participants talked about his connection to FCUP: António Huet Bacelar, a retired advanced technician at the Museum of Anthropology of the University of Porto and a member of SPAE, focused not only on Mendes Correia's connection to archaeology but also on the impetus he gave to ethnology and folklore studies; Maria José Cunha, the coordinator of FCUP's Museum of Anthropology, highlighted some of the collections in this museum created by Mendes Correia; and Fernando Noronha, a professor at FCUP, analyzed the evolution of Mendes Correia's scientific career there. Others—Armando Coelho, an archaeologist and full professor at FLUP, and Sérgio Gomes, an archaeologist and member of SPAE—noted Mendes Correia's connection with FLUP and archaeology. Finally, Fernando Sousa, a full professor at FLUP and historian at the Center for the Study of Population, Economy and Society, associated Mendes Correia with the Porto Municipality and emphasized his work as its mayor from 1936 to 1942 (Sousa et al. 2009).

The third occasion was a tribute session dedicated to Mendes Correia, António de Almeida, and his daughter Maria Emília de Castro e Almeida, which took place on October 15, 2011, at the SGL. António de Almeida held a degree in medicine and was a professor at the Higher Institute for Overseas Social Sciences and Politics (ISCSPU, Instituto Superior de Ciências Sociais e Política Ultramarina), as the institution that preceded the current ISCSP was called (included in the University of Lisbon since 2012), where he taught Portuguese overseas ethnology and was responsible for the complementary course on anthropological and ethnological sciences. Maria Emília de Castro e Almeida was president and a member of the anthropology and ethnography sections of the SGL. Father and daughter performed joint studies on the Khoisan (which they referred to as Bushmen) in Angola. Several of Mendes Correia's activities were evoked in this tribute, mainly those in the scientific domain, such as his role as president of the SGL.

In addition, Mendes Correia was connected to several areas of political action. Besides being the mayor of Porto, he was also a member of the Corporative Chamber and deputy to the National Assembly, and he is sometimes considered an uncritical advocate of New State (Estado Novo) policies. This perspective, at least concerning Mendes Correia, is in my opinion reductionist and incomplete, particularly when there is a lack of knowledge of his true points of view and when his political actions and positions have not been duly studied, as I did elsewhere (Matos 2023). In other words, the fact of serving in public positions during the New State does not necessarily mean total alignment with the regime, but rather that politics can be used to defend various interests.

With this text, I intend to contribute to a better knowledge of a figure in the history of Portuguese anthropology who has long remained forgotten, or even excluded, to use the terminology of Richard Handler (2000), especially in the realm of anthropology, although his contributions in the fields of archaeology and geology are commonly known. Today the history of anthropology is recognized as a subdisciplinary field of anthropology. One example of this is the book series History of Anthropology, of which George Stocking was the editor in chief for many years. With a degree in history from the University of Pennsylvania, Stocking was inspired by the notion (in line with Franz Boas) of American anthropologist Alfred Irving Hallowell (1892–1974), who in 1965 considered the history of anthropology as an anthropological project. According to Hallowell ([1965] 1976), the history of anthropology should direct its attention toward the context and circumstances in which issues arose, which are the essence of anthropology today.

In Portugal, the institutionalization of anthropology occurred around the late nineteenth and early twentieth centuries. The historical, political, national, and colonial context in which this happened, as well as the issues considered pertinent for anthropology at the time, are worthy of in-depth analysis. Within this context, mainly regarding the first half of the twentieth century, the study of Mendes Correia's activities in several scientific areas (those with connections to anthropology or that could influence production in this disciplinary field) and in different instances of power (scientific and academic, but also political) can contribute to better knowledge of the history of anthropology in Portugal, from its institutionalization as a university discipline through paradigm shifts over time. Therefore, this text takes the form of an intellectual biography aimed at contributing to a history that has not yet been analyzed in depth.

Anthropology has a long tradition of life stories, and several biographies of past anthropologists have been published in the twenty-first century (Pina-Cabral 2008, 26). In his introduction to the special issue of *Reviews in Anthropology* titled "Biographies of Anthropologists," Roger Ivar Lohmann is emphatic that anthropologists' biographies are largely recognized as useful for the history of science and, specifically, for the history of anthropology (2008, 89). According to Lohmann, biographies of anthropologists do not merely describe people who dedicate their lives to anthropology; the study of their lives is anthropology (98). Therefore, by studying an individual with a central role, such as Mendes Correia, it is possible to learn about the wider cultural dynamics that allow us to better understand the history of anthropology in Portugal.

BIOGRAPHICAL ASPECTS

António Augusto Esteves Mendes Correia was born on April 4, 1888, into a privileged family in Porto, which provided him the foundation on which to build his future path. Son of a doctor, he was the eldest of four siblings and the only one who studied medicine. His family's life was fundamentally connected to the city of Porto, and although he had no children of his own, he had a close relationship with his nephews.

In his studies, he focused on medicine, science, and humanities. He became interested in both science and history while attending the Liceu Central do Porto, where he was a pupil of historian and art critic Joaquim de Vasconcelos (1849–1936). In 1911 he completed his degree in medicine at Porto's Medical and Surgical School, but he decided to pursue other areas as well. The Republican reform was implemented that same year, converting the Polytechnic School into the University of Porto.

Mendes Correia started his teaching career as a sub-assistant professor at FCUP, where he taught anthropology, geology, physical geography, physics of the earth, and paleontology. Two years later he also took on the role of assistant judge and doctor at the Central Youth Detention Center

(Tutoria Central da Infância) in Porto. In 1919 he became a member of the School Council at FLUP, where he taught the following subjects until 1928: Portuguese geography, Portuguese colonial geography, political and economic geography, general geography, ethnology, archaeology, ethnography, and general anthropogeography. He was among the founders of the International Institute of Anthropology in Paris in 1920, taking on the role of secretary of its Portuguese section. He finished his doctorate in natural history sciences at FCUP in 1921, and from 1923 he was director of the Anthropology Institute of the University of Porto (IAUP, Instituto de Antropologia da Universidade do Porto). FLUP's School Council awarded him the degree of doctor of letters in geographical sciences in 1925. (FLUP closed in 1928 and did not reopen until 1961.) In 1926 he became a full professor in the mineralogy and geology group at FCUP (despite being a permanent professor in anthropology), and he directed this faculty from 1929 to 1935. Also at Universidade do Porto, he was a member of the board and then president of the Peninsular Ethnology Studies Center (CEEP, Centro de Estudos de Etnologia Peninsular) from 1945 to 1956.

On the national level, Mendes Correia was a member of the Junta de Educação Nacional (in the archaeology subsection) from 1929 to 1936, and he belonged to committees in charge of studying the reform of university education. In 1936 the Junta de Educação Nacional was incorporated into the Junta Nacional de Educação (both of which translate as National Education Committee) and converted into the Institute of High Culture (Instituto para a Alta Cultura). That same year Mendes Correia cofounded the Portuguese Academy of History. In 1946 he became president of the Committee for Geographical Missions and Colonial Research (JMGIC, Junta das Missões Geográficas e de Investigações Coloniais) and directed the anthropological section. He maintained this position until 1959, although in 1955 JMGIC changed its name to Committee for Geographical Missions and Overseas Research (JMGIU, Junta das Missões Geográficas e de Investigações do Ultramar), following the constitutional revision of the Portuguese Republic of 1951, which replaced the terms *empire* and *colonies* with *overseas* and *overseas provinces*. During this period he also served as both the director (1946–58) and a professor (1949–58) at ESC; president of the SGL in 1951–60; and president of the National Committee for Demographic and Health Statistics (Comissão Nacional de Estatística

Demográfica-Sanitária) in 1955. He retired from teaching at ESC in 1958, and the following year he became president of his science section at the Lisbon Academy of Science. He died in Lisbon on January 7, 1960.

Mendes Correia's biography is also marked by activities in the domains of cultural diffusion and politics. He played an important role in participating in and organizing events and exhibitions. He was a co-organizer of the Fifteenth International Congress of Anthropology and Prehistoric Archaeology and the Fourth International Session of Anthropology, in Porto (1930); organizer of the Portuguese section of the Paris Colonial Exhibition (1931); co-organizer of the First National Congress on Colonial Anthropology, in Porto, an initiative by SPAE (1934); co-organizer of the Centennial Commemorations and the Congresses of the Portuguese World and president of the National Congress of Population Sciences, which was one of those congresses (1940); and co-organizer of the Second International Conference of the Western Africanists, in Bissau (1947). At the local level, he was the mayor of Porto (1936–42), and at the national level, he was a deputy to the National Assembly (1945–57) during the fourth, fifth, and sixth legislative periods of the New State (1933–74), a regime that in its early years was contemporaneous with other dictatorships, such as those in Italy (Mussolini, 1922–45), Germany (Third Reich, 1933–45), and France (Vichy, 1940–44).

In his roles as founder of IAUP and mentor of the Porto School of Anthropology (figure 5), he promoted the institutionalization and development of anthropology in Portugal. Because of his scientific activity, he was awarded with the title of doctor honoris causa by the Universities of Lyon (1931), Montpellier (1941), and Witwatersrand in Johannesburg (1949), as well as the title of excellency by the Pontifical Academy of Sciences in Rome (1940). He was also honored in two volumes of SPAE's journal, *Trabalhos de Antropologia e Etnologia*, in 1959 and 1969 (figures 6 and 7).

Today Mendes Correia is remembered only on rare occasions, such as the tributes on the fiftieth anniversary of his death. He is mainly associated with the institutionalization of anthropology in Portugal, as he played a fundamental role in the creation of SPAE, a scientific society in Portugal that encouraged the development of anthropological studies (Matos 2016, 2018). SPAE was connected to the Porto School of Anthropology and maintained decades-long relationships with national and foreign scientists. It

Fig. 5. Classroom of the IAUP. Natural History Museum, University of Porto / Museu de História Natural, Universidade do Porto.

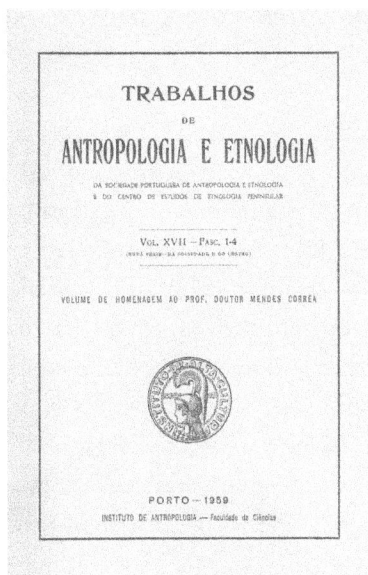

Fig. 6. LEFT: Volume de Homenagem ao [Volume of Tribute to] Prof. Doutor Mendes Corrêa. *Trabalhos de Antropologia e Etnologia* 17 (1–4).

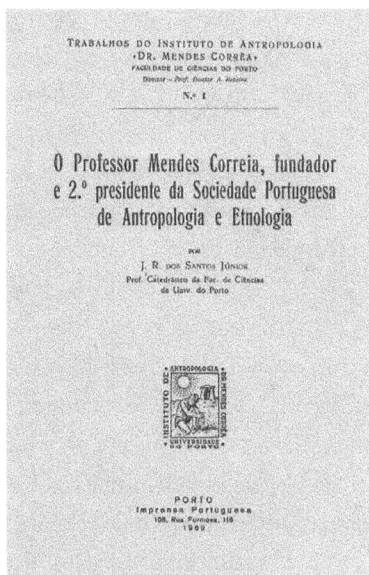

Fig. 7. RIGHT: J. R. dos Santos Júnior. 1969. *O Professor Mendes Correia, fundador e 2.º presidente da Sociedade Portuguesa de Antropologia e Etnologia. Trabalhos do Instituto de Antropologia Dr. Mendes Correia* no. 1.

was unique despite sharing similarities with other scientific societies that already existed abroad. From its inception, SPAE admitted women, one of whom later stood out—Leopoldina Ferreira Paulo (1908–96), Mendes Correia's assistant in anthropology at FCUP and the first woman to obtain a doctorate at the University of Porto. SPAE also amassed a considerable collection of books and journals from several countries, especially those in Europe and North, Central, and South America, as well as Russia. To some extent the Porto School of Anthropology was born out of the work of SPAE and the continued tradition at the core of the Carlos Ribeiro Society (1888–98) and its journal *Revista de Ciências Naturais e Sociais* (1889–98), succeeded by the journal *Portugália* (1899–1908), both of which published works on physical anthropology, ethnography, and prehistory.

SCIENTIFIC AND INTELLECTUAL ACTIVITIES AND IDEAS

Mendes Correia developed an interest in psychiatry and the study of human behavior during his studies of medicine. After completing his degree, he wrote *O génio e o talento na patologia* (Genius and talent in pathology) (Mendes Correia 1911). In 1913 he became a permanent assistant professor at FCUP and passed his public exams with the dissertation "Os Criminosos Portugueses" (Portuguese criminals) (Mendes Correia 1913). His early studies on human behavior, specifically on deviant behavior, presumably awakened his interest in anthropology. However, his scientific work eventually encompassed a wide variety of subjects that he associated with the study of the human being. Mendes Correia published 387 works (Santos Júnior 1969, 42), including several books, and he supervised numerous studies. His work reveals a broad and inclusive vision of anthropology; his topics were diverse, but on the whole, he felt they contributed to a better understanding of humanity. He treated biological, social, and cultural aspects with the same level of importance; however, the first was often presented as an explanation for the other two.

From 1913 onward he advocated the notion of a nonreligious but altruistic morality, deriving part of his inspiration from the work of Friedrich Nietzsche (1844–1900); this morality, however, did not renounce the benefits of individualism (Mendes Correia 1913, 1914, 1925a, 1931, 1946). In his curriculum for the discipline of anthropology in 1915 (Mendes Correia

1915), he used physical characteristics as his preferred method of differentiating human groups because he considered them the most "permanent" and easily observable, allowing for a more objective and precise analysis. During that same period, he criticized the authors who considered only somatic factors, such as monogenist Armand de Quatrefages (1810–92), Paul Broca (1824–80), and Paul Topinard (1830–1911). Mendes Correia argued that psychological and sociological data should not be excluded from the study of the human being. He was a monogenist, transformist, and Lamarckian evolutionist; according to him, natural selection could be explained by the neo-Lamarckian theory (Mendes Correia 1915). The topics he presented in his anthropology classes later formed the basis for the works he published over a period of about fifty years.

Mendes Correia is also known in archaeology for defending the hypothesis that Antarctica may have been a bridge that allowed human settlement in South America, enabling people to come from Australia and the Malay Archipelago (1925b). He proposed a scientific mission to Australia on the occasion of the International Geophysical Year (1957–58), with the aim of collecting elements that might point to the existence of that passage (Mendes Correia 1958). He believed that those people might have traveled in rafts or small boats, passing by the Auckland Islands and Tasmania, until they reached Antarctica (at a time when its climate was not as harsh as today) and then continued toward South America. This theory was suggested by his finding of several similarities between the peoples of Argentina (in Patagonia and Tierra del Fuego) and Aboriginal peoples of Australia. For Mendes Correia, these similarities were not strictly biological, such as blood group or cranial structure, but also ethnographic—for example, similarities existed in their languages and material culture, such as building structures and the use of the boomerang (Mendes Correia 1958). He also promoted several excavations through the CEEP in the Muge councils (*concheiros*) in Moita do Sebastião, Cabeço de Amoreira, and Cabeço da Arruda, such as those carried out by Jean Roche (1913–2008) and Octávio da Veiga Ferreira (1917–97), and he published on this subject (Mendes Correia 1940c, [1954] 1956).

From the 1930s onward his anthropological program was mainly connected to the Portuguese colonial project and the positions he later held in the CEEP, JMGIC, ESC, and SGL. This program had a clear nationalist inspiration, a sentiment that was dominant in his period—in regimes such as the First Republic (1911–26) and the New State (1933–74)—and he proposed to contribute to Portugal's reputation in a context of increasing international competition that was visible mainly in the conflicts surrounding the imperialist division of African territories. His solicitude for the nation and its empire and his belief in the importance of the study of the Portuguese population guided his intellectual life. By attending to the "vitality, health and robustness" of the Portuguese people, anthropology was destined, he wrote, to perform a "patriotic" task by contributing to the "improvement of the Portuguese with body and soul" (1933, 42). His concern with the health of the population, from hygiene to nutrition, was revealed in several of his writings (Mendes Correia 1951a). He intended to record the nation in a long-term history and advocated a relative homogeneity of the Portuguese population throughout time, insisting that the Lusitanians were the ancestors of the Portuguese (Mendes Correia 1918, 1919a, 1919b, 1924, 1928, [1938] 1944), an argument that was, however, based on a set of myths (Matos 2017).

According to Mendes Correia (1915), anthropology has "useful" or practical applications. In that sense, anthropological data, mainly psychological and ethnic data, could "guide political, religious, economic, trade or industrial action in many human agglomerations." Anthropology could be useful in the study of children in schools (pedagogical anthropology); in the study of delinquents and of the "pathologically abnormal" (criminal anthropology); in colonial administration and in the study of "indigenous populations" (colonial anthropology); and in art, philosophy, and history, among other areas (15). He added that doctors in schools and industrial facilities, as well as military doctors, should consider this discipline (28). This might have been why SPAE proposed that the country's medical schools should include anthropology in their subject matter (Matos 2016).

The studies most connected to criminal anthropology or to the politics of populations, considering social conditions, nutrition, and health, were focused mainly on the population of the metropolis, while the anthropobiological studies—those more dedicated to anthropometric practices and the analysis of what he considered a risk represented by racial mixings, sometimes including some ethnographic contextualization—were performed mainly in the colonial context. Subjects like miscegenation were approached differently: In the metropolis, although the existence of miscegenation was recognized, it was not seen as a problem, whereas in the overseas territories, miscegenation was seen as a potential threat that should be allowed only within certain limits (Mendes Correia 1934a, 1934b, 1934c, 1940a, 1940b, 1940d). In Mendes Correia's opinion, the Portuguese were different in this respect from other colonizing peoples (mainly meaning those from Northern Europe); however, the New State's political orientation did not promote miscegenation in the tropics, and he rejected the practice on several occasions, mainly in the 1930s and the first half of the 1940s (Matos 2019).

To Mendes Correia, the study of colonized populations from a physical perspective, as well as that of "primitive" cultures, was fundamental for future generations to know about examples of an almost extinct humanity. In that sense, he was one of the main promoters of research on the populations under colonial administration. Nevertheless, his studies on African and Asian social and cultural reality were sometimes used solely as a context for research in the scope of physical anthropology (Mendes Correia 1943). However, the works produced were related to the character of Portuguese colonialism and its policies, mainly during the New State. In the 1940s the subject of "race" was still a trend, miscegenation was being debated in Brazil, and Nazism was at its height. After World War II, Mendes Correia's formulations gradually began to change; the cultural approach slowly took the lead, and studies in the physical domain took on a new form (Matos 2013a).

Along his path, a number of his travels stand out, and those experiences contributed to his articles and books. One example is his efforts to increase intellectual relationships between Portugal and Brazil (Matos 2013b). Mendes Correia traveled to Brazil in 1934 and 1937 and published his impressions on the country and its population (*A Cultura Portuguesa no Brasil* 1935; Mendes Correia 1935a, 1935b). He met some Brazilian intellectuals, such as Gilberto Freyre (1900–1987); Renato Ferraz Kehl (1889–1974), president of the Brazilian League for Mental Hygiene, who had come to Portugal on his invitation in 1932; and Francisco José de Oliveira Vianna (1883–1951), with whom he had already established a relationship through correspondence and exchanging publications. Also in 1937 he took part in the centennial commemoration of the Royal Portuguese Cabinet of Reading (Real Gabinete Português de Leitura) in Rio de Janeiro, which houses the largest and most diverse library of Portuguese works outside Portugal.

From December 1945 to January 1946 Mendes Correia traveled to Guinea with Amílcar de Magalhães Mateus, who had a degree in biological science from FCUP, with the aim of preparing an anthropological mission (Matos 2020). Within the scope of that journey, he produced a field diary ("Diário"), an official report sent to the JMGIC ("Processo n.º 306"), and a book (1947). Before arriving in Guinea, they stopped in Casablanca, Morocco, where Mendes Correia met two of his former FLUP students, the Portuguese consul in Rabat and his wife. They then went to Dakar, Senegal, where they visited the Institut français de l'Afrique noire (IFAN, French Institute of Black Africa). On their way to and from Guinea, the two men spent part of their time at IFAN, which was described as "splendid facilities for scientific research" ("Diário") and was coordinated by Théodore Monod (1902–2000) of the Paris Natural History Museum. With Monod and Léon Pales (1905–88), a disciple of Paul Rivet (1876–1958) who had authored a volume on paleontology and led a scientific mission related to IFAN and the colonial health services, they visited the ethnology, botany, zoology, anthropology, and prehistory sections, as well as the library. They also met Georges Duchemin, head of the ethnology section; linguist Aimé Darot, who showed them graphics from phonetics equipment he had invented and proposed to travel to Guinea with Magalhães Mateus (this idea was approved by Mendes Correia, and in turn, a Portuguese representative would come to IFAN, a suggestion accepted by Monod); and J. Joire, a prehistorian and delegate of IFAN in Conakry, French Guinea. Mendes Correia took the opportunity to compare the work developed in Portugal and France.

In Senegal they also visited the Indigenous Medical School and the Anatomy Institute, where Mendes Correia reported that many "black students" were "dissecting dead black people" ("Diário"). He agreed to initiate closer collaboration and an exchange of publications with Monod. Júlio Martinez de Santa-Olalla, an archaeologist from Madrid, suggested to Monod that Portugal take part in the International Conference of Western Africanists, which the institute promoted in Dakar in January 1945—the first of a series that would take place in several colonies in the region of

Western Africa, north of Congo and south of Mauritania (Mendes Correia 1947, 32). Portugal did not take part then, but Mendes Correia sent a communication on the anthropological studies performed on the islands of Cape Verde and Guinea, and Judite dos Santos Pereira, an assistant professor at FCUP, sent a study on the geology of Guinea. The scientists also exchanged impressions on the centennial anniversary of the "discovery" of Guinea, which would take place in 1946, and discussed the possibility of cooperation between IAUP and the International Conference of Western Africanists in that event.

On this trip to Guinea, Mendes Correia revealed his interest in learning about other anthropological contexts and different individuals. He even stated that in the case of Guinea, considering the miscegenation among distinct groups and the migrations in the territory, the word *race* used to designate each ethnic group should be banned, since these groups were not distinct "races," but rather "cultural, linguistic, social, political or religious groupings, with no defined somatic individuality" (1947, 136). This explanation should, however, be understood in the context in which it was formulated—that is, during the post–World War II period, in which the idea of "race" started to be criticized and was being scientifically discredited (Matos 2013a).

In 1950 Mendes Correia traveled to the United States to attend the First International Colloquium on Luso-Brazilian Studies, which took place at the National Library in Washington DC. He gave a presentation titled "A cultura portuguesa na África e no Oriente" (Portuguese culture in Africa and the Orient) in the cultural anthropology section (1951b). Jorge Dias (1907–73), then an anthropologist at the CEEP of the University of Porto, also presented a lecture on the features of Portuguese culture. In Mendes Correia's presentation, he designated Portuguese culture as a "Luso-Christian culture" and stressed that, in agreement with Dias, one of the features that most strongly defined it was its psychological nature: affectivity (1951b).

He highlighted the fact that the colloquium was taking place in one of the most distinguished cultural facilities in the United States, the National Library; that it had gathered researchers from several countries dealing with the problems of the Luso-Brazilian culture; and that almost everyone there spoke Portuguese. To Mendes Correia, this showed the worldwide projection of the Portuguese language, culture, and history. Although he did not agree with all the solutions provided for the social problems in the U.S., Mendes Correia spoke positively of the "adopted salary system, the absence of classes on trains and the lack of concern for certain unnecessary and anachronic norms and hierarchies" (1951c, 11). While there, he also met Pedro Calmon (1902–85), the then Brazilian minister of education and health (1950–51) and head of the Brazilian delegation to the colloquium; Francis Millet Rogers (1914–89), a professor at Harvard University and president of the colloquium; and Bennett Harvie Branscomb (1894–1998), the chancellor of Vanderbilt University.

In the context of this journey, Mendes Correia recognized the rich development of cultural anthropology in the North American university centers. He believed that it would be important in the study of native populations in the Portuguese overseas territories and that the guidelines "as to their educational, political and legal system" should be adopted (1951c, 7). He visited the National Museum of the Smithsonian Institution and its natural history, ethnology, and archaeology collections. He met Thomas Dale Stewart (1901–97), one of the founders of modern forensic anthropology, who contributed to the areas of biology of the human skeleton, paleontology, and other domains of physical anthropology. Stewart was the successor of Aleš Hrdlička (1869–1943), a Czech physical anthropologist with whom Mendes Correia maintained an exchange for several years as the director of the Physical Anthropology Department of that institute. He also met Herbert William Krieger (1889–1970), head of the Division of Ethnology of the Department of Anthropology, and expressed his interest in the African documentation, which included various materials from Angola and Mozambique.

He visited the American Museum of Natural History in New York with António José de Liz Ferreira (1905–?), a disciple of Mendes Correia from Portugal who was completing his doctorate in anthropology at Columbia University. At the Department of Anthropology of Columbia University, he visited Margaret Mead (1901–78), whom he considered one of the greatest names in American cultural anthropology. In this department, he also met professors and anthropologists Julian Haynes Steward (1902–72), who developed a theory on cultural evolution, and William Duncan Strong (1899–1962), who was influenced by Alfred Louis Kroeber, Franz Boas's student. Additionally, Mendes Correia presented a lecture in Brooklyn, "Portugal: A terra e a gente" (Portugal: The land and its people), and another in New Bedford, Massachusetts, "Angola e Moçambique no Portugal de hoje" (Angola and Mozambique in today's Portugal).

That same year, he traveled to Kenya to attend the inaugural meeting of the Scientific Council for Africa South of the Sahara, accompanied by another Portuguese delegate, Professor Francisco Cambournac (1903–94), a malariologist and epidemiologist from the Institute of Hygiene and Tropical Medicine and the World Health Organization. In Nairobi, he reported that the Indians had "housings as luxurious and rich" as the Europeans but that there was great segregation between the two communities and also with regard to Black Africans. He stated that in British East Africa, although communism was not mentioned, there was a "commotion around national or racial prides" (Mendes Correia 1951c, 13). When he traveled to Guinea in 1945–46, he had mentioned the strikes by some Africans in Dakar (e.g., those who worked at hotels and restaurants). This social turbulence, which he witnessed in person, may have alerted him to the need for change in the Portuguese overseas territories as well. Language was yet another issue. The Bantu natives from the Quicuia and other "tribes" did not speak English, which was an additional "isolation factor" that the British did not seek to avoid (1951c, 13). At the hotel where he stayed, the Black servants did not understand the English language spoken by the guests and answered "Yes, sir" to everything. Nonetheless, he praised a series of endeavors that honored Britain and its administration. He considered that some initiatives in British East Africa and other African countries could serve as an example for the territories under Portuguese administration in that continent. At the Coryndon Museum, he took his time observing several prehistoric elements. He visited the Great Rift Valley with José Neiva and Professor Francisco Cambournac.

During that year, Mendes Correia also spent time in Cairo, Egypt, which had three universities, and went to the Egyptian Museum. At the new Fouad I Desert Institute, which contained sections on archaeology, zoology, botany, geophysics, mineralogy, and ethnography, he was received by its director, Naguib Paska Salem, and by the secretary, Mohammed Mitwalli, a physical geography professor. He was also received by director M. A. Sharkanry at the university's Institute of Geography. He toured the excavations at the predynastic stations of Heliopolis and Maadi, coordinated by professors Moustafa Amer, the rector of Faruq University; Sami Gabra, an Egyptologist who had been to Portugal for the International Congress of Anthropology of Coimbra and Porto in 1931; and Ibrahim Ahmed Rizkana, from the geography section. He lamented the fact that Portugal did not have a tradition in Arabic studies despite the Muslim occupation of its territory, the Arab princedoms in the Algarve, and the presence of Arabs and Muslims in the overseas territories (Mendes Correia 1951c).

In August and September 1953 Mendes Correia traveled to Timor as part of an anthropological mission promoted by JMGIU, where he established contact with the territory's population. Then seen as a small, remote country, Timor had suffered from Japanese occupation during World War II, which had killed several thousand Timorese. Despite Portugal's neutrality, many civilians in East Timor and several Portuguese settlers had fought for the Allies. During this journey, Mendes Correia visited the widow of the Timorese chief Aleixo Corte-Real, who was shot by the Japanese in 1943. He also paid several visits to António de Almeida, a doctor, anthropologist, and head of the anthropological mission in Timor, and Ruy Cinatti, an agronomy engineer and researcher at JMGIU who had worked in Timor for several years as head of the Agriculture Services. During this time, he wrote field notes, which he divided into anthropological, linguistic, and prehistoric sections.

In the book he published after this trip, he discussed its geographic aspects (e.g., soil, volcanoes, and climate); highlighted its care, education, and promotion works; and described the population. According to Mendes Correia, Timor had a long-standing autochthonous population, as evidenced by prehistoric traces, and was more a center or an area of racial, anthropogenic differentiation than a Babel where several human strains converged. He highlighted the absence of racial discrimination by the Portuguese, which he felt should have created good relationships with Timorese natives, and stated that in former Dutch (Indonesian) Timor, the natives were much less friendly to the Portuguese passing by than in Portuguese Timor. As to the cultural practices, he mentioned that the war tradition of beheading the vanquished seemed to be disappearing. However, he considered that there was no great difference between this practice and the barbaric cock fights, bullfights, or pigeon shooting that were then popular practices in Portugal. He concluded that the population's psychology and behavior revealed a progress that, in his opinion, was mainly due to the civilizing action of the Portuguese, the authorities' repression of the "barbaric" customs, and the work undertaken by missionaries (Mendes Correia 1955).

In 1957 at JMGIU, the Mission for the Study of Ethnic Minorities in the Portuguese Overseas (Missão de Estudos das Minorias Étnicas do Ultramar Português) was created. Jorge Dias was the head, and Margot Dias (1908–2001) and Manuel Viegas Guerreiro (1912–97) served as assistants. During the 1957 and 1958 Africa campaigns, in addition to the research work, about three hundred ethnographic objects of the Makonde of Mozambique were collected, which allowed the organization of the exhibition *Vida e Arte do Povo Maconde* (Life and Art of the Makonde People) in February 1959 (a year before Mendes Correia's death) at the National Secretariat for Information, Popular Culture and Tourism (Secretariado Nacional de Informação, Cultura Popular e Turismo). This collection formed the initial core of a museum, inaugurated in 1961, that mainly assumed a pedagogical character and was in the basement of the Higher Institute of Overseas Studies (ISEU, Instituto Superior de Estudos Ultramarinos) in Palacete Anjos in Praça Príncipe Real, Lisbon. The museum included the original collection and several acquisitions from study missions to the overseas territories and bought from collectors. Designated the Museum of Overseas Ethnology, it gave rise to the Center for Cultural Anthropology Studies at JMGIU. In 1962 the facilities of the museum were inaugurated at ISCSPU, and later it was transferred to the Palácio Burnay at Junqueira, where ISCSP maintained its activities until 2002. The current National Museum of Ethnology, founded in 1965, corresponds to the extension of the small museum initially operating at the ISEU.

POLITICAL ACTIVITY

In addition to his activities in connection with the university, education, and research, Mendes Correia also promoted initiatives connected to culture, the diffusion of knowledge, and the arts, both in Porto and at the national level. He was first involved in Republican projects, including the creation of the University of Porto in 1911. In regard to his career in politics and administration, he served as the mayor of Porto from 1936 to 1942 and was a member of the Corporative Chamber from 1935 to 1938 and from 1938 to 1942. At the parliamentary level, he was a deputy to the National Assembly from 1945 to 1957. But more than merely being a politician, Mendes Correia eventually became involved in certain issues and defended causes that were dear to him (Matos 2023).

His actions should be understood as those of a man whose life was guided by nationalism, which in turn was served by science, in a positivist sense as previously considered by doctors such as Júlio de Matos (1856–1922), Miguel Bombarda (1851–1910), and António Egas Moniz (1874–1955), also involved in politics—all Republican and the last an opponent of the New State. To Mendes Correia, science should be at the forefront in the efforts to guarantee the regeneration and the greatness of the motherland, both in the metropolis and in the colonies. In this context, he was eventually involved in the movement Renascença Portuguesa (Portuguese renaissance), which began in 1912 and gathered individuals from several strains of thought who shared a common nationalist ideal. This setting explains his interest in Portuguese archaeology and its historical heritage, ethnography, art, and music, as well as instruction and education. After analyzing his political interventions, I have concluded that they reflect his most frequent concerns: the origin and antiquity of sites; national memory and heritage; and specific social groups, such as children, so-called criminals, and individuals belonging to underprivileged social classes. Mendes Correia also spoke of the need to preserve and spread the Portuguese language and knowledge of its national heritage, including architectural monuments and ethnographic expressions, such as Portuguese folk traditions (Matos 2023).

With the intent of promoting good relationships with places outside of Portugal, Mendes Correia encouraged Luso-Brazilian connections at several levels. Other aspects that he believed might bring benefits to the nation were granting women the right to vote (an idea he proposed in 1945) and supporting artistic domains such as the fine arts, cinema, and music. The Portuguese people's living conditions and diet, as well as issues related to demography and emigration, were also part of his reflections (Matos 2023).

His vision of Portugal included the empire. Some of his proposals were therefore related to the need to improve the overseas populations' sanitary and health conditions, promote education in the colonies, and increase knowledge about these territories, thus developing a crucial role for the ESC and the JMGIC. In 1951 he proposed the elimination of the "indigenous status," which limited access to citizenship for the majority of the Native population in the Portuguese colonies, from the constitution; it was his belief that the populations included in this status should not be seen merely from a political and economic point of view and that the possibility of obtaining citizenship should be within their reach, if they desired and were able to do so. However, this status was maintained until 1961, after his death. Nationalist ideas, which involved the acceptance of the colonial-subordinate relationship, then considered as natural, were present in all his actions. Mendes Correia never questioned the legitimacy of colonial rule, assuming the superiority of the colonizer over the colonized (Matos 2023).

SUMMARY OF MENDES CORREIA'S ACHIEVEMENTS

Mendes Correia stood out for having created not only SPAE and the Porto School of Anthropology but also a network of collaborators and individuals with whom he corresponded about scientific matters. He created a museum and a laboratory, both of which were converted into IAUP in 1923. Both within the scope of the discipline of anthropology, which he taught, and in the context of his research, he encouraged his students to research new topics, stressed the importance of practical works in and outside of the lab, sought to obtain the necessary means for their execution, and kept track of those works. He also advocated the need to travel to the sites of the topics to be researched.

Those who, like Mendes Correia, had a medical education and were used to observing human bodies were particularly qualified to perform anthropometric studies. These early endeavors gave birth to an approach to anthropological knowledge, even if in a more bio-anthropological than sociocultural domain. British social anthropology and North American cultural anthropology probably did not have any influence on the Porto School of Anthropology, where the study of the somatic features of peoples was overemphasized and anthropology was set within the field of anthropobiology. Moreover, at the end of World War I, Mendes Correia expressed the same regard for anthroposociology, a pseudoscience that attempted to explain social facts based on "race" (Mendes Correia 1919b).

The physical anthropology that he developed did not distance him from his interests in prehistory, medicine, natural science, history, and ethnology. However, in some of his research, ethnographic elements appeared solely as a complement to the anthropobiological data he described and systematized. His beliefs on certain subjects, such as the origin of human beings, "race," and the Natives of the colonies, changed over the years. This can be seen as a necessary adjustment to the times, mainly in the post–World War II period, when there were important changes in perspectives.

Mendes Correia's main contribution to anthropology was to create conditions that allowed others to develop their future investigations in Portugal or the former colonies. Some of his ideas that most distinguished him were regarding African influence on the genetic heritage of the Portuguese (1917); Lusitanians as the main ancestors of the Portuguese (1919a); and the need for knowledge about the colonies and their inhabitants (1930s). As the mayor of Porto, he defended and implemented the construction of decent housing for the underprivileged, the common citizen's access to cultural and scientific life, and the appreciation of the country's heritage (1936). Later, as a deputy to the National Assembly, he supported the universal vote for women (1945); teaching careers in higher education (1945, 1946); the career of geologists (1952); the hiring of national artists (1946, 1947, 1949); the creation of a colonial university (1948); the appreciation of overseas heritage (1949); and the abolishment of the "indigenous status" (1951) (Matos 2023).

In addition to his most prominent proposals, one of his greatest legacies is the structures that were implemented and allowed research to be carried out. What also stands out is the fact that he gathered around him a diverse set of collaborators and disciples. When he traded Porto for Lisbon, where he took on other positions, Mendes Correia continued to follow the path of the school of anthropology he had created, mainly via the correspondence he kept up with Joaquim Rodrigues dos Santos Júnior (1901–90), graduate in historical-natural sciences (1923) and medicine (1932) and holder of a doctorate in historical-natural sciences (1944), who was his main collaborator and successor in Porto (at FCUP and SPAE). Mendes Correia presented topics to be debated at JMGIC and the National Assembly at Santos Júnior's request, leveraging the positions he held to intercede for the approval or financing of certain projects. On some of these occasions, he quoted the arguments of foreign experts to reinforce his reasoning.

In the eyes of his peers in Lisbon, he was still a man of the north, as he was from Porto and a full professor at FCUP. However, he left his mark in other places, such as at ESC, ISCSPU, JMGIC, and SGL. At ESC, he taught geography, was director of the school, and supervised final dissertations in advanced overseas studies. While he was president of the SGL, director of ESC, and deputy to the National Assembly, he invited young lawyer Adriano Moreira (1922–2022) by telegram to teach law at the ESC; Moreira eventually became the director of this school and minister for the overseas in 1961. Therefore, the reform in the country's overseas policies was also due to Mendes Correia. According to Rui Ennes Ulrich (1883–1966), who had a doctorate in law, his endeavors and enthusiasm led to the creation of the Research Institutes in Luanda (Angola) and Lourenço Marques (today Maputo, Mozambique) and the prestige of the ISEU ("Professor Mendes Correia" 1957, 128).

Mendes Correia was a university teacher, but he also held political positions. Because of his status in the area of science and the fact that he held positions that were decisive in the assessment of individuals' physical and mental health, he basically held a privileged position of power. He revealed what was almost an obsession for the study of the causes of disease, crime, the origins of human beings, and the Portuguese, as well as cities, languages, alphabets, and human migrations. His nationalism, compatible with various political regimes, was present in all his research, whether studying the origins of Portugal and the Portuguese, the country's position in the colonial system, the improvement of genetic heritage (eugenics), or the attempt to eliminate behaviors considered deviant. Although some of these concerns were common to successive governments, one cannot say that he reacted to them unthinkingly, that his works were at the service of political strategies, or that other scientists and politicians pursued the same agendas, the same sensitivity to resolving matters, or even the same principles and values. One must draw a line of distinction.

Even within the so-called single party, the National Union (União Nacional), in the New State, members held different mindsets, and the proposals presented for the resolution of the same problem could be very different, as could be seen in some of the debates in the National Assembly. In those circumstances, Mendes Correia used politics as a means to defend national interests—connected to obtaining better conditions for science and investigation, the diffusion of the Portuguese language, the conservation of heritage, and the protection of the arts—and to present his ideas on the overseas territories. He did not pursue a political career as such, although his actions were influenced by the specific restrictions of his context—a dictatorship. The relationships between the scientific and political milieus were not always peaceful, and his projects were not always supported and were sometimes directed toward other purposes.

In the scope of the history of anthropology in Portugal, and regardless of his research options, considering the object and the method, one can conclude that Mendes Correia was a driver of ideas, an entrepreneur, and a manager of people. The future of individuals such as Santos Júnior, Jorge Dias and his team, and Adriano Moreira resulted from an initial invitation by Mendes Correia to perform specific functions. I heard living first-person testimonies, not only from figures like Benjamim Enes Pereira (1928–2020), a member of Jorge Dias's team with whom I spoke, but also from other personalities connected to the ESC, such as Adriano Moreira and João Pereira Neto (1935–2023), both interviewed by me (Matos 2023).

Mendes Correia always wanted to promote a general study divided into several specific fields, which would contribute to a wide-ranging knowledge of the human being. Anthropology was, however, at the center of his interests, and other sciences like archaeology, geology, prehistory, and ethnology assumed a secondary role. To Mendes Correia, the specificity of the human being might have resided in his or her unspecific character; for studying them, it is not enough to simply consider some parts of history, of knowledge, of the physical body, and of the social and behavioral body. Precisely this specificity of the human being of not being specific—of not being easily identified or categorized—is also the challenge faced by anyone who seeks to study the diversity of the work produced by Mendes Correia. In any case, he was a dominant figure of anthropology in Portugal, rivaled only by José Leite de Vasconcelos (1858–1941), an ethnologist with a medical education who did not devote himself to physical anthropology, and it was not until the 1950s that he lost his significance to Jorge Dias.

One of the probable main factors that led to the end of the Porto School of Anthropology was Mendes Correia's death in 1960. His collaborators and disciples continued to produce some studies, but not for much longer. They grew apart as a result of both divergent scientific interests and personal incompatibilities. As a consequence of the division that followed, mainly caused by innovations from Jorge Dias and his team, anthropology started to favor the study of social and cultural factors to the detriment of the study of natural factors. That is, both the biological component (research in paleontology, genetics, and primatology, for example) and the social and cultural anthropology component took new paths, diversified their interests, and ventured into using new methods.

That Mendes Correia is a rather forgotten figure today is due to his being associated with the New State and its nationalist and colonial project, with which he identified, and to a form of anthropology that was marked by the importance given to "race" (and was often racist). This element was already being criticized in social and cultural anthropology in predominant centers, such as Great Britain and the United States, and also by prominent figures, and it was discredited in the post–World War II period. In other words, a change was necessary to allow the current form of anthropology to emerge. Both the French-German (ethnography) and the British-American centers abandoned the field of study of "race." Therefore, maybe social anthropology did not develop in Portugal during the period of Mendes Correia because the other areas of anthropology were still highly committed to the Portuguese national and colonial project. I will analyze this hypothesis in future works.

ACKNOWLEDGMENTS

This work was supported by the Portuguese Foundation of Science and Technology (FCT), under the project: https://doi.org/10.54499/dl57/2016/cp1441/ct0001.

ABBREVIATIONS
CEEP Centro de Estudos de Etnologia Peninsular (Peninsular Ethnology Studies Center)
ESC Escola Superior Colonial (Higher Colonial College)
FCUP Faculdade de Ciências da Universidade do Porto (Faculty of Sciences of the University of Porto)
FLUP Faculdade de Letras da Universidade do Porto (Faculty of Humanities of the University of Porto)

IAUP Instituto de Antropologia da Universidade do Porto (Anthropology Institute of the University of Porto)

IFAN Institut français de l'Afrique noire (French Institute of Black Africa)

ISCSP Instituto Superior de Ciências Sociais e Políticas (Higher Institute for Social Sciences and Politics)

ISCSPU Instituto Superior de Ciências Sociais e Política Ultramarina (Higher Institute for Overseas Social Sciences and Politics)

ISEU Instituto Superior de Estudos Ultramarinos (Higher Institute of Overseas Studies)

JMGIC Junta das Missões Geográficas e de Investigações Coloniais (Committee for Geographical Missions and Colonial Research)

JMGIU Junta das Missões Geográficas e de Investigações do Ultramar (Committee for Geographical Missions and Overseas Research)

SGL Sociedade de Geografia de Lisboa (Geographic Society of Lisbon)

SPAE Sociedade Portuguesa de Antropologia e Etnologia (Portuguese Society of Anthropology and Ethnology)

NOTES

1. For a detailed analysis of the life and work of Mendes Correia, see Matos (2023).
2. There is a lack of agreement on how to spell his name, as it is sometimes written as Correia, the name on his birth certificate, and other times Corrêa, a spelling he adopted later. In my works, because I had to apply a norm, I chose to use the former.

REFERENCES

Manuscripts and Archives

Mendes Correia, A. A. E. "Diário de campo de Mendes Correia sobre a viagem à Guiné," 1945–46. Private collection.

———. "Processo n.º 306 de António Augusto Esteves Mendes Correia." Vol. 1., doc. no. 1. Instituto de Investigação Científica e Tropical, Lisbon.

Published Works

A Cultura Portuguesa no Brasil: Missão do Professor Mendes Corrêa. 1935. Porto: Imprensa Portuguesa.

Cardoso, João Luís. 2011. "O Professor Mendes Corrêa (1888–1960) e a arqueologia portuguesa: breve síntese." In Martins, *Mendes Correia*, 75–84.

Casanova, Catarina. 2011. "O papel de Mendes Corrêa enquanto referência na Antropologia Biológica em Portugal: caminhos e percursos da Primatologia." In Martins, *Mendes Correia*, 85–127.

Ferreira, António José de Liz, Alfredo Athayde, and Hugo de Magalhães. 1945. *Gorilas do Maiombe Português*. Memórias. Série Zoológica 1. Lisbon: JMGIC.

Hallowell, Alfred Irving. (1965) 1976. "The History of Anthropology as an Anthropological Problem." In *Contributions to Anthropology: Selected Papers of A. Irving Hallowell*, edited by Raymond D. Fogelson, 21–35. Chicago: University of Chicago Press.

Handler, Richard, ed. 2000. *Excluded Ancestors, Inventible Traditions: Essays Toward a More Inclusive History of Anthropology*. History of Anthropology 9. Madison: University of Wisconsin Press.

Lohmann, Roger Ivar. 2008. "Introduction: Biographies of Anthropologists as Anthropological Data." *Reviews in Anthropology* 37:89–101.

Martins, Ana Cristina, ed. 2011a. *Mendes Correia (1888–1960): Entre a ciência, a docência e a política*. Lisbon: ACD Editores.

———. 2011b. "Mendes Corrêa (1888–1960) e a arqueologia coeva: (En) trechos." In Martins, *Mendes Correia*, 37–73.

Matos, Patrícia Ferraz de. 2011. "A vida e a obra do Professor Mendes Correia: Articulações entre antropologia, nacionalismo e colonialismo em Portugal." In Martins, *Mendes Correia*, 9–35.

———. 2013a. *The Colours of the Empire: Racialized Representations During Portuguese Colonialism*. Oxford: Berghahn.

———. 2013b. "Um olhar sobre as relações entre Portugal e o Brasil a partir da obra de Mendes Correia: desafios, pontes e interacções." *População e Sociedade* 21:53–69.

———. 2016. "Anthropology in Portugal: The Case of the Portuguese Society of Anthropology and Ethnology (SPAE), 1918." In *Local Knowledge: Global Stage*, Histories of Anthropology Annual 10, edited by Regna Darnell and Frederic W. Gleach, 53–97. Lincoln: University of Nebraska Press.

———. 2017. "Who Were the Ancestors of the Portuguese? Portuguese Debate on Their National Origins." *Portuguese Studies Review* 25 (2): 127–53.

———. 2018. "Inclusions and Exclusions in the Production and Circulation of Scientific Knowledge: The Case of the Royal Anthropological Institute (RAI) and the Portuguese Society of Anthropology and Ethnology (SPAE)." In *Changing Societies: Legacies and challenges*, vol. 1, *Ambiguous Inclusions: Inside Out, Outside In*, edited by Paulo Granjo, Sofia Aboim and Alice Ramos, 407–42. Lisbon: Imprensa de Ciências Sociais.

———. 2019. "Racial and Social Prejudice in the Colonial Empire: Issues Raised by Miscegenation in Portugal (Late Nineteenth to Mid-Twentieth Centuries)." *Anthropological Journal of European Cultures* 28 (2): 23–44.

———. 2020. "Modos de fazer da antropologia colonial: A missão científica de Mendes Correia à Guiné Portuguesa (1945–1946)." In *Modos de Fazer/ Ways of Making*, edited by Vítor Oliveira Jorge, 167–180. Porto: CITCEM (FLUP) and SPAE.

———. 2023. *Anthropology, Nationalism and Colonialism: Mendes Correia and the Porto School of Anthropology*. Oxford: Berghahn.

Mendes Correia, A. A. E. 1911. *O Génio e o Talento na Patologia*. Porto: Imprensa Portuguesa.

———. 1913. *Os Criminosos Portugueses: Estudos de Antropologia Criminal*. Porto: Imprensa Portuguesa.

———. 1914. *Os Criminosos Portugueses: Estudos de Antropologia Criminal*. 2nd ed. Coimbra: F. França Amado.

———. 1915. *Antropologia: Resumo das lições feitas pelo Assistente, servindo de Professor da Cadeira*. Porto: Imprensa Portuguesa.

———. 1917. "À propos des caractères inférieurs de quelques crânes préhistoriques du Portugal." Offprint of *Archivo de Anatomia e Anthropologia* 3 (3): 221–37.

———. 1918. "Estudos da etnogenia portuguesa: os habitantes primitivos do território." *Terra Portuguesa* 4:1–7.

———. 1919a. "Origins of the Portuguese." *American Journal of Physical Anthropology* 2 (2): 117–45.

———. 1919b. *Raça e nacionalidade*. Porto: Renascença Portuguesa.

———. 1924. *Os povos primitivos da Lusitânia*. Porto: A. Figueirinhas.

———. 1925a. "Antropologia criminal integral: O normal delinquente e a crise moral." Offprint of *Boletim do Instituto de Criminologia* 5:1–25.

———. 1925b. "O significado genealógico do "Australopithecus" e do crânio de Tabgha e o arco antropofilético Índico." *Trabalhos de Antropologia e Etnologia* 2 (3): 249–86.

———. 1928. "A Lusitânia pré-romana." In *História de Portugal*, vol. 1, edited by Damião Peres and Eleutério Cerdeira, 77–214. Barcelos: Portucalense.

———. 1931. *A Nova Antropologia Criminal*. Porto: Imprensa Portuguesa.

———. 1933. *Introdução à Antropobiologia*. Coimbra: Imprensa da Universidade.

———. 1934a. *Da Biologia à História*. Porto: Imprensa Portuguesa.

———. 1934b. "Os mestiços nas colónias portuguesas." In *Trabalhos do I Congresso Nacional de Antropologia Colonial*, vol. 1, 331–49. Porto: Edições da I Exposição Colonial Portuguesa.

———. 1934c. "Valor psicossocial comparado das raças coloniais." In *Trabalhos do I Congresso Nacional de Antropologia Colonial,* vol. 2, 385–93. Porto: Edições da I Exposição Colonial Portuguesa.

———. 1935a. "A etnogenia brasílica." Offprint of *Anais da Faculdade de Ciências do Porto* 19:1–22.

———. 1935b. *Cariocas e Paulistas.* Porto: Fernando Machado.

———. (1938) 1944. *Raízes de Portugal. Portugal "ex-nihilo"! ... Terra e independência. A raça.* Lisbon: Ocidente.

———. 1940a. "Discurso na Sessão Inaugural do Congresso Nacional de Ciências da População." Offprint of *Congressos do Mundo Português, Congresso Nacional de Ciências da População,* 1–20. Porto: Imprensa Portuguesa.

———. 1940b. "Factores degenerativos na população portuguesa e seu combate." In *Congressos do Mundo Português, Congresso Nacional de Ciências da População,* vol. 17, sec. 2, 577–89. Lisbon: Comissão Executiva dos Centenários.

———. 1940c. "Novas estações líticas em Muge." Offprint of *Congressos do Mundo Português, Congresso da Pré e Proto-História de Portugal,* 1–17. Lisbon.

———. 1940d. "O mestiçamento nas colónias portuguesas." In *Congressos do Mundo Português, Congresso Colonial,* vol. 14, sec. 1, 113–33. Lisbon: Comissão Executiva dos Centenários.

———. 1943. *Raças do Império.* Porto: Portucalense Editora.

———. 1946. *Em face de Deus: Memórias e Confissões.* Porto: Fernando Machado.

———. 1947. *Uma jornada científica na Guiné Portuguesa.* Lisbon: Agência Geral das Colónias.

———. 1951a. *A alimentação do povo português: Bibliografia prefaciada e coordenada pelo Prof. Doutor António Augusto Mendes Correia.* Lisbon: Centro de Estudos Demográficos.

———. 1951b. "A cultura portuguesa na África e no Oriente." *Estudos Coloniais. Revista da Escola Superior Colonial* 2 (1): 19–51.

———. 1951c. "Impressões de duas viagens." Offprint of *Boletim da Sociedade de Geografia de Lisboa* 69 (3–4): 1–23.

———. (1954) 1956. "Notice préliminaire sur les squelettes préhistoriques de Moita de Sebastião (Muge)." Offprint of *Crónica del IV Congreso Internacional de Ciencias Prehistóricas y Protohistóricas,* 133–39. Lisbon: Casa Portuguesa.

———. 1955. "Um Mês em Timor." Palestras na Emissora Nacional, na Série *A Ciência ao Serviço da Humanidade,* 1–24. Lisbon: Sociedade de Geografia de Lisboa.

———. 1958. "Sobre o Ano Geofísico Internacional." Offprint of *Boletim da Sociedade de Geografia de Lisboa* 76 (1–3): 3–20.

Mota, Teresa Salomé. 2011. "Mendes Correia, um 'posto avançado' na defesa da Geologia em Portugal." In Martins, *Mendes Correia*, 129–43.

Neto, João Pereira. 2011. "Preâmbulo." In Martins, *Mendes Correia*, 7–8.

Pina-Cabral, João de. 2008. "History of Anthropology and Personal Biography." *Anthropology Today* 24 (6): 26–27.

"Professor Mendes Correia. Homenagem dos seus amigos e admiradores." 1957. Offprint of *Boletim da Sociedade de Geografia de Lisboa* 4–6:119–52.

Santos Júnior, Joaquim Rodrigues dos. 1969. "O Professor Mendes Correia, fundador e 2.º presidente da Sociedade Portuguesa de Antropologia e Etnologia." Offprint of *Trabalhos do Instituto de Antropologia Dr. Mendes Correia* 21:37–45.

Sousa, Fernando de, Manuel Pires Ribeiro, and Ricardo Rocha. 2009. "António Augusto Esteves Mendes Correia." In *Os Presidentes da Câmara Municipal do Porto (1822–2009)*, vol. 2, edited by Fernando de Sousa, 479–85. Porto: CEPESE.

6

John Wesley Powell, John DeWitt Clinton Atkins, and the Battle over American Indian Languages

LEILA MONAGHAN

INTRODUCTION TO THE STUDY OF INDIAN LANGUAGES
AND HANDBOOK OF AMERICAN INDIAN LANGUAGES

In 1877 John Wesley Powell (1834–1902) published the *Introduction to the Study of Indian Languages with Words Phrases and Sentences to Be Collected* as part of his work for the Smithsonian.[1] This 104-page book was a field guide for researchers consisting mainly of tables with the first column listing English terms, phrases, and sentences, such as persons (e.g., "Man," "Woman," "Boy," and "Girl") (8); parts of the body (e.g., "Head," "Face," "Eye," "Left elbow") (9–12); relationships (e.g., "Husband's elder sister's husband, said by wife") (13–24); and general phrases and sentences (e.g., "John struck James") (86–103), along with blank columns in which to write the Native American language equivalents and make notes. The book begins with a systematic introduction to a phonetic alphabet for writing American Indian languages and then has a brief explanatory section with the cautionary note: "Care should be taken to collect words from the Indians themselves. Indians speaking English can be found in almost every tribe within the United States. Words cannot be accurately obtained from white men who are supposed to speak the Indian tongue, unless such persons have been long with the Indians and are intelligent and scholarly, and have some reasons for studying Indian languages on account of their being missionaries, teachers, or linguists" (7).

Powell became head of the Bureau of Ethnology in 1879, when it was officially established by Congress, but as Henrika Kuklick notes, "Congress's expectations were often at odds with Powell's" (2009, 39). His academic work respected American Indian languages, and his stance was quite different from that of other branches of the U.S. government, which were distinctly hostile. In 1885, 1886, and 1887, the commissioner of Indian affairs, John DeWitt Clinton Atkins (1825–1908), in his *Annual Reports of the Commissioner of Indian Affairs to the Secretary of the Interior*, tried to ban all languages but English in any school for Indian students. All three of his reports acted as, to use terminology from J. L. Austin (1962), "performatives," language that is an action; however, the increasing fervor of the reports serves as evidence of the imperfect nature of these performatives. This was true particularly in connection with the continuing use of the Dakota language (now known as Lakota). In his 1887 report, he felt the need to lay out the exact texts of orders sent, explaining, "I have given the text of these orders in detail because various misrepresentations and complaints in regard to them have been made, and various misunderstandings seem to have arisen" (Commissioner of Indian Affairs 1887, xxiii). He also provided extended arguments about citizenship and uplift from barbarism to support his edicts.

First Powell and then, a generation later, Franz Boas (1858–1942) worked to document and justify the importance of American Indian languages despite the commissioner of Indian affairs' ban on these languages in schools. Boas published part 1 of the *Handbook of American Indian Languages* in 1911. In the preface, he described the work as "an attempt to prepare a revised edition of 'The Introduction to the Study of Indian Languages,' by Major J. W. Powell." He argued that while "much linguistic material had been accumulated by filling in" the tables in that book, "the essential features of the morphology of American languages remained unknown" (1911, v). Boas's *Handbook* provided an "analytical study of grammar" (v) as well as an eighty-four-page introduction that included his famous distinctions between race, language, and culture. The fact that Atkins's reports confounded these issues to justify the repression of Native languages makes the importance of these distinctions all the clearer.

The difference between Powell and Boas reflected not only the growth and increasing complexity of the academic field of the study of American Indian languages but also momentous American political events, the international rise of nationalism, and changing constructions of the role of history in understanding events. While much of the general territory of this article has been covered by scholars such as Regna Darnell (1969, 2001), George Stocking (1992), Lee Baker (1998), and Henrika Kuklick (2009), these works have not looked at the connections and contrasts between Powell and the important documents in the *Report of the Commissioner of Indian Affairs*, more commonly read by historians. My argument here is that the distinctions between Powell and the views of language critics such as Atkins set the stage for Boas's work dismantling the connections between race, culture, and language.

THE POLITICAL DISCOURSES OF THE *REPORTS* OF THE *COMMISSIONER OF INDIAN AFFAIRS*

The election of 1876 featured a trove of coded telegrams; voter suppression and fraud in Louisiana, Florida, and South Carolina; economic crisis; and the election of Rutherford Hayes (1822–93), a Republican who won less of the popular vote than his Democratic opponent, Samuel Tilden (1814–86). The concessions made by Hayes to Southern politicians to ensure his election included the end of Reconstruction, which had provided a shield for the rights of African Americans in the South (Vazzano 2006). The election ushered in decades of closely contested elections and the widespread erosion of the rights of non-white inhabitants of the United States at the federal and local levels, including Jim Crow legislation and *Plessy v. Ferguson*, Chinese exclusion bills, Native American confinement to reservations, and the passage of the Dawes Act, which allowed the sale of parts of these Indian lands to white settlers (Clayton 2004; Vazzano 2006; Merjian 2010).

Language, both the way it was used as a tool within political discourses and ideologies about it nature, played an essential part in the creation and contestation of these inequalities. Within political discourses, overtly similar language can take on quite different meanings. As Matthew Levinger (2000) found in his study of nineteenth-century Prussian political discourse, some elements of the Prussian term *nation* were "strongly contested," while other features were ambiguous or largely agreed on. Benedict Anderson, looking at nationalist movements such as those in Prussia around this time period, pointed to how "'national print-languages' were of central ideological and political importance," in contrast to views of English in the American Revolution (2006, 69). This emphasis on "national print-languages" and their connection to citizenship is clearly found across a wide spectrum of U.S. and international writings by the 1880s. Oralist educators of deaf children in the 1890s, for example, connected "intelligently [exercising] the rights of citizenship" with English being "made the vernacular of the deaf if they are not to become a class unto themselves— foreigners among their own countrymen" (Baynton 1996, 27).

For the purposes of this chapter, the *Reports of the Commissioner of Indian Affairs*, including those by John DeWitt Clinton Atkins from 1885 to 1887, serve as an official example of such emphases on the connection between citizenship and language. Atkins was a Southerner and a professional politician: a lieutenant colonel in the Confederate army, a Democratic congressman from Tennessee, chairman of the Committee of Appropriations, and the commissioner of Indian affairs, appointed by Democratic president Grover Cleveland in March 1885 (U.S. House of Representatives, n.d.) and serving until June 1888. He wrote about language in all three of his reports, and all acted as performative decrees banning the use of Native languages in schools.

LANGUAGE IN THE REPORTS

One of Atkins's major arguments for the use of English in schools was its necessity as part of achieving and successfully practicing citizenship. This theme is apparent in his first report:

> When the farm and the school have become familiar institutions among the Indians, and reasonable time has intervened for the transition from barbarism or a semi-civilized state to one of civilization, then will the Indian be prepared to take upon himself the higher and more responsible duties and privileges which appertain in American citizenship. A wider and better knowledge of the English language among them is essential to their comprehension of the duties and obligations of citizenship. At this time but few of the adult population can speak a word of English, but with the efforts now being made by the Government and by religious and philanthropic associations and individuals . . . it is to be hoped, and it is confidently believed, that among the next generation of Indians the English language will be sufficiently spoken and used to enable them to become acquainted with the laws, customs, and

institutions of our country, and to regulate their conduct in obedience to its authority.

When this point in their upward progress has been attained they will be a part and parcel of the great brotherhood of American citizens, and the last chapter in the solution to the Indian problem will be written. After that we shall hear no more of the Indian as a separate and distinct race; we shall hear no more of him as a "ward of the nation" but like the alien and the negro, who by our laws are admitted to the great family of American citizens, each individual must stand upon his own bottom, enjoying equal rights and bearing equal responsibilities. (Commissioner of Indian Affairs 1885, vi–vii)

A letter included in the report from an anonymous student at the Carlisle Training School makes clear the pressures on Native Americans at this time. Explaining why he wanted to obtain U.S. citizenship rather than maintain his Native status, the student wrote, "Lose my rights as an Indian! What are the rights that an Indian has? Is it the drawing of rations and beef every week? No, the Indians have no rights. . . . The negroes became citizens while they were just as ignorant as can be, even now. Why cannot the Indians be allowed citizenship?" (Commissioner of Indian Affairs 1885, vii).

While Atkins argued for citizenship, he was clearly in favor of a restricted form. In response to a bill introduced by Senator Henry Dawes (presumably a precursor to the Dawes Act), he called for a gradual form of citizenship for "Indians who . . . are sufficiently prudent and intelligent to manage their own affairs" (1885, viii).

The following year Atkins reiterated his English-only stance:

In the extract from my first report . . . I expressed very decidedly the idea that Indians should be taught in the English language only. From that position I believe, so far as I am advised, there is no dissent either among the law-makers or the executive agents who are selected under law to do the work. There is not an Indian pupil whose tuition and maintenance is paid for by the United States Government who is permitted to study any other language than our own vernacular—the language of the greatest, most powerful, and enterprising nationalities beneath the sun. The English language as taught in America is good enough for all her people of all races. (Commissioner of Indian Affairs 1886, xxiii)

He also argued for 160 acres for any "Indian youth who shall graduate from school and marry an Indian maiden who has also graduated," saying, "If the homestead is not on an Indian reservation the man should also have the privilege of citizenship, including the right of suffrage. Such a law would greatly encourage Indian youths and maidens in their resistance to the evil and savage influences of their untutored friends, and would do much to keep them from a return to savage life" (Commissioner of Indian Affairs 1886, xxv).

In the opening lines of his 1887 report, Atkins maintained that it "gives substantial evidence of continued progress on the part of Indians toward civilization. This is gratifying to every American patriot and humanitarian of any clime or country" (Commissioner of Indian Affairs 1887, iii). A six-page section titled "The English Language in Indian Schools," however, reflects that the implementation of English-only policies as part of this "continued progress" was not absolute. In this section, Atkins cited a portion of the 1885 report and then quoted a document from an 1868 "Peace Commission" that included "Generals Sherman, Harney, Sanborn, and Terry," which contended, "Through sameness of language is produced sameness of sentiment, and thought; customs and habits are moulded and assimilated in the same way, and thus in process of time the differences producing trouble would have been gradually obliterated. By civilizing one tribe others would have followed. Indians of different tribes associate with each other on terms of equality; they have not the Bible, but their religion, which we call superstition, teaches that the Great Spirit made us all. In the difference of language to-day lies two-thirds of our trouble" (Commissioner of Indian Affairs 1887, xx).

This passage seems particularly odd both in its inception and its inclusion in Atkins's arguments. The Peace Commission was made up of generals who had just fought and won the long and bloody Civil War, a war that had little to do with language differences and much to do with notions of property and authority. The presence of the passage in the report is made all the odder by the fact that Atkins had fought on the side of the Confederacy. His use of the passage seems to emphasize that the unifying force between the North and the South after the war was their common reassertion of the power of the white male elite.

The last two-thirds of the "The English Language in Indian Schools" section of the 1887 report seems to be railing against the teaching of Dakota. Atkins cited previous regulations issued in 1880 and 1884, as well as his 1886 report banning English in schools. The 1884 regulations declared, "If Dakota or any other language is taught such children, they will be taken away and their support by the Government will be withdrawn from the school" (Commissioner of Indian Affairs 1887, xxi). This was perhaps a reference to the work of Jesuits such Father Francis Craft, a missionary to the Lakota at Standing Rock who was injured at Wounded Knee, a man familiar enough with their language to include it in his journals (Foley 2002).

One of the points of contestation seems to have been over preaching in local languages. According to Atkins, his orders did not "touch the question of the preaching of the Gospel in the churches nor in any wise hamper or hinder the efforts of missionaries to bring the various tribes to a knowledge of the Christian religion. Preaching of the Gospel to Indians in the vernacular is, of course, not prohibited" (Commissioner of Indian Affairs 1887, xxiii). In a prior passage Atkins had doubled down on arguments about citizenship:

> Only through the medium of the English tongue can they acquire a knowledge of the Constitution of the country and their rights and duties thereunder. Every nation is jealous of its own language, and no nation ought to be more so than ours, which approaches nearer than any other nationality to the perfect protection of its people. True Americans all feel that the Constitution, laws, and institutions of the United States, in their adaptation to the wants and requirements of man, are superior to those of any other country; and they should understand that by the spread of the English language will these laws and institutions be more firmly established and widely disseminated. Nothing so surely and perfectly stamps upon an individual a national characteristic as language. So manifest and important is this that nations the world over, in both ancient and modern times, have ever imposed the strictest requirements upon their public schools as to the teaching of the national tongue. (Commissioner of Indian Affairs 1887, xxi)

Here, he added an evolutionary argument: "The first step to be taken toward civilization, toward teaching the Indians the mischief and folly of continuing in their barbarous practices, is to teach them the English language. . . . Bands of the same tribes inhabiting different localities . . . sometimes can not communicate with each other except by the sign language" (xxiii).

Finally, he included three attachments to the section. One was from a "former missionary among the Sioux," who wrote approvingly of Atkins's English-only policy: "Before you came to administer the affairs of the country the Republicans thought well to undertake similar work in the work in the Government schools, but lacked the courage to touch the work of the missionary schools where it was needed" (xxiv). The second was from an Indian agent: "Nothing can be gained by teaching Indians to read and write in the vernacular, as their literature is limited and much valuable time would be lost in attempting it. Furthermore I have found the vernacular of the Sioux very misleading, while a full knowledge of the English enables the Indians to transact business as individuals and to think and act for themselves independently of each other" (xxiv). The third attachment was from "one of the leading religious weeklies," which argued that "there are two hundred thousand Indians old enough to talk who use a hundred dialects, many of which are as unintelligible to those speaking the other dialects as Sanscrit is to the average New England schoolboy" (xxiv-xxv). It would be useful to have the original sources of these documents, as major differences between religious communities, including Catholic and Protestant missionary activities, are being papered over here. A search for the original text from the religious weekly, however, has not revealed anything.

In Atkins's three reports, a number of distinct ideologies, including language ideologies, emerge. These include the following:

1. Citizenship
    a. The importance of citizenship but also the need to limit it to those with "comprehension of the duties and obligations of citizenship."
    b. English as an essential part of this "comprehension of duties."
    c. The equating of Native Americans with other second-class citizens, "the alien and the negro."

2. Individualism
   a. An emphasis on individual homestead farming, which comes through a little in this discussion of Atkins's views on language and clearly in other parts of the reports.
   b. A focus on how "each individual must stand upon his own bottom."
3. Secular nationalism
   a. The Constitution as the touchstone document. While references to God would not have been uncommon during this period, the only mention of religion is to separate government functions from religious ones.
   b. The clear connection between nationalism, English, and importance of the Constitution, creating a situation that neared the "perfect protection of its people." Given the brutal Great Plains Wars, the rise of Jim Crow laws, and few rights for women, "people" here can be read at best as meaning white men. This nationalistic emphasis on English does, however, echo Anderson's imagined monolingual communities.
4. Economic ideologies
   a. The connection between the proscribed English curriculum and governmental monetary support.
   b. The connection between English, individualism, and the status of independent economic actor. In this there is an echo of fear of the collective action possible when Natives worked as a group.
5. Evolutionary models
   a. An assumption of monolineal evolution from barbarism to civilization.
   b. The equating of English with civilized culture as opposed to the barbarous practices and languages of Natives, including "the sign language." This dismissal of sign language was happening at the same time that sign language teaching was being banned from schools in the United States and internationally.
6. Linguistic ideologies
   a. The use of the term "vernacular" to refer to both English and Native American languages, a circumlocution that allowed Atkins not to use terms such as "the Dakota language," thus diminishing the nature of Native languages.

b. A belief that "through the sameness of language is produced sameness of sentiment and thought," despite clear evidence to the contrary in the use of English by both sides in the Civil War.
c. A lack of connection with academic models of language. The Indian agent quoted "found the vernacular of the Sioux very misleading," while the religious weekly quote refers to the uselessness of "Sanscrit"—a brief but dismissive reference to contemporary philological studies including the connections between English and the larger Indo-European language family.

Other commissioners had different takes on language. Ohioan John H. Oberly (1837–99) was appointed commissioner after Atkins in 1888 ("John H. Oberly Dies" 1899; BIA 2008). In his report that year, Oberly restated the "orders forbidding the teaching of the vernacular in Indian schools" laid out by Atkins but also mentioned letters by religious organizations about "reading the Bible in the vernacular." In response, Oberly noted, "It is not intention of the Indian Bureau to prohibit the reading of the Bible by any Indian in any language," walking back at least some of Atkins's rhetoric (Commissioner of Indian Affairs 1888, xvii). The commissioner in Boas's time, 1910–11, was Robert G. Valentine, a Republican and later Progressive New Englander appointed by William Taft (Valentine Papers 1805–?). His reports do repeat concerns about farming and "the assimilation of the Indians into American life" but do not mention using English for this purpose (Commissioner of Indian Affairs 1910, 15).

CONNECTING POLITICAL AND ANTHROPOLOGICAL DISCOURSES

Powell's 1877 and 1880 versions of the *Introduction to the Study of Indian Languages* were both designed as notebooks for collecting data, something clearly reflected on a table early in the book asking for information on the tribe and collector (1880, iii–iv):

(DO NOT FAIL TO FILL THIS BLANK.)
Tribe, _____
Locality, _____
Recorded by _____
Date of Record, _____

Even Powell's brief cautionary note in the earlier edition about how linguistic forms should be collected differed radically from Atkins's take on language: "Care should be taken to collect words from the Indians themselves" (Powell 1877, 7). Adult Indians were seen as experts, not as failed citizens or unwanted wards of the state. The missionaries and teachers who had learned the languages were seen as other sources of valuable information, not people to be railed at in repeated reports and orders.

There was a marked change in environment between 1877, a year after Little Bighorn and a period when Native people in the West and Southwest still had some independence, and 1880, when most had been forced onto reservations. While the 1880 edition was still a collection notebook, it was a greatly expanded version of the 1877 text. The first edition was 104 pages long, with a 4-page introduction on how to write American Indian languages; half a page of "Explanatory Remarks," including the admonition to gather information from "the Indians themselves" or at least persons who "are intelligent and scholarly"; 95 pages of schedules to be filled in with linguistic examples, each section accompanied by further introductory remarks; and finally, half a page of "Remarks," including brief discussions of how to learn an Indian language and very basic grammar. The book's introduction also lays out its formative influences: a 51-page pamphlet by George Gibbs (1815–73), published by the Smithsonian in 1861, that was a general guide to ethnographic collecting and included a list of 211 terms to translate; a reference to a work on mythology by Lewis H. Morgan (1818–81); and an acknowledgment of the philological work of Professor W. D. Whitney, who wrote the section on "The Alphabet," describing how to write previously unwritten languages.

In comparison to Atkins's reports, even the brief material presented in the 1877 edition reflected a radically different approach. Two examples from "Explanatory Remarks" and the final "Remarks" illustrate this:

To collect words from an Indian requires great patience, as it is difficult to hold his attention for any great length of time. . . . Sometimes an Indian will deceive by giving foolish or vulgar words, considering it a good jest; for this and other reasons, everything collected should be carefully verified. (7)

In obtaining the phrases and sentences above, the student will be initiated into the best method of mastering and Indian tongue. The attempt to learn Indian words and then to construct sentences from them will only result in failure. The student has also learned that the Indian tongue contains very few synonyms of English words, which is also true to an important extent in the more cultivated languages of the Indo-European stock; but the statement has a much wider application when we speak of Indian languages. (104)

The 1880 edition is a longer and more polished work. It starts with a March 1880 introduction from Powell in which he mentioned his "exploration of the Colorado River of the West"—that is, the Grand Canyon—and briefly reviewed the development of the Bureau of Ethnology, again acknowledged the influences of Whitney and Morgan, and then introduced the work of J. Hammond Trumbull, which he included for "a more advanced stage of linguistic study" (v–vii). He ended the book's introduction with a description of the state of American Indian languages and a plea for help: "Hundreds of languages are to be studied; hundreds of governments exist, the characteristics of which are to be investigated and recorded. All these peoples have, to a great extent, diverse arts, diverse mythologies, as well as diverse languages and governments; and while the people are not becoming extinct but absorbed, languages are changing, governments are being overthrown, institutions are replaced, and arts are becoming obsolete. The time for pursuing these investigations will soon end. *The assistance of American scholars is most earnestly invoked*" (viii).

The rest of the book is more than double the size of the 1877 edition, at 228 pages long, and includes both more background material and more schedules for collection. The most interesting new section in light of Atkins's divisions between barbarous Indian languages and civilized English is Powell's discussion of the standing of Native languages:

§32.—THE RANK OF INDIAN LANGUAGES.

Students of Indian languages have sometimes fallen into error about their rank or value as instruments for the expression of thought, as shown in many of the dissertations on Indian languages found in the literature of the subject.

The assumed superiority of the Greek and Latin languages to the English and other modern civilized tongues, has in part been the cause of the many erroneous conceptions of the rank of Indian tongues. . . . The many curious linguistic devices by which great specification of expression is attained has led some scholars into undue admiration, as they have failed to appreciate the loss in the economy and power which these peculiar methods entail. (70)

There seem to be two endings to this discussion about rank. The first one is at the bottom of page 74:

In all these particulars it is seen that the Indian tongues belong to a very low type of organization. Various scholars have called attention to this feature by describing Indian languages as being holophrastic, polysynthetic, or synthetic. The term synthetic is perhaps the best, and may be used as synonymous with undifferentiated.

Indian tongues, therefore, may be said to be highly synthetic in that their parts of speech are imperfectly differentiated.

In these same particulars the English language is highly organized, as the part of speech are highly differentiated. Yet the difference is one of degree, not of kind. (74)

A short paragraph on inflection follows this discussion. My argument that the above was the original ending or portion thereof is in part based on the pagination. While the rest of the book has the pages numbered sequentially (. . . 72, 73, 74), the numbering after page 74 continues with 74a, 74b, and 74c, and then a blank page before the next section, "Chapter III—Schedules," begins on page 75. As the linotype machine was not invented until 1886, major revisions at a late stage of proofs would have required the arduous task of resetting of handset type (Hendel 2011).

The other evidence for a new ending having been added is that the next three new pages doubled down on an evolutionary argument:

Economy in speech is the force by which its development has been accomplished, and it divides itself properly into economy of utterance and economy of thought. Economy of utterance has had to do with the phonic constitution of words; economy of thought has developed the sentence. (74b)

A Ponca Indian, in saying that a man killed a rabbit, would have to say the man, he, one, animate, standing, in the nominative case, purposely killed, by shooting an arrow, the rabbit, he, the one, animate, sitting, in the objective case; and the form of the verb would in like manner have to express [many particulars] . . . . Perhaps one time in a million it would be the purpose to express all of these particulars, and in that case the Indian would have the whole expression in one compact word, but in the nine hundred and ninety-nine thousand nine hundred and ninety-nine cases all of these particulars would have to be thought of in the selection of the form of the verb, when no valuable purpose would be accomplished thereby.

In the development of the English, as well as the French and German, linguistic evolution has not been in vain.

Judged by these criteria, the English stands alone in the highest rank; but as a written language, in the way in which its alphabet is used, the English has but emerged from a barbaric condition. (74c)

Unlike Atkins, Powell did not use "barbaric" to describe Indian languages here. While he did imply that they were of low rank, he reserved "barbaric" for English spelling conventions.

Powell's 1891 classificatory work "Indian Linguistic Families of America, North of Mexico," also presents a modified version of evolutionary history. While the introductory overview of the text includes a discussion of the savagery of Indian philosophy, the article itself is mainly a historical summary of linguistic classifications found in others' work. For example, the introductory overview to the volume argues, "In savagery the observed facts of the universe, relating alike to physical nature and to the humanities, are explained mythologically, and these mythic conceptions give rise to a great variety of practices" (Powell 1891a: xxxvi). The discussion of savagery within the article is more related to the tendency of others to classify Native groups:

When brought into close contact with the Indian, and into intimate acquaintance with his language, customs, and religious ideas, there is a curious tendency observable in students to overlook aboriginal vices and exaggerate aboriginal virtues. It seems to be forgotten that after all the Indian is a savage, with the characteristics of a savage, and he is exalted even above the civilized man. The tendency is exactly the reverse of what it is in the case of those who view the Indian at a distance and with no precise knowledge of any of his characteristics. In the estimation of such persons the Indian's vices greatly outweigh his virtues; his language is a gibberish, his methods of war cowardly, his idea of religion utterly puerile. . . .

[The student of language] is led to overlook the great truth that the mind of man is everywhere practically the same, and that the innumerable differences of its products are indices merely of different stages of growth or are the results of different conditions of environment. In its development the human mind is limited by no boundaries of tribe or race. (1891b: 35–36)

Powell started with the understanding that "attempts at a classification of these languages and a corresponding classification of races have led to the development of a complex, mixed, and inconsistent synonymy." However, he also argued that "while the analogies between linguistic and biotic classification are quite limited . . . still in some particulars the requirements of all scientific classifications are alike" (8).

At an 1882 memorial service for Charles Darwin (1809–82) held by the Biological Society of Washington in conjunction with the Philosophical and Anthropological Societies of Washington, Powell laid out his definition of scientific classification, saying, "The revelation of science is this: Every generation in life is a step in progress to a higher, fuller life; science has discovered *hope*" (1882, 66). His idea of "no boundaries of tribe or race" reflected this hope.

Powell's method for analyzing language families, instead of internal philological characteristics of languages, relied on historical names of communities and the work of previous scholars who did use linguistic data to connect particular groups. Although he did not present specific information from languages, he did make judgments about the nature of languages that accorded more with the view of a student than someone who observed from a distance. He wrote, "The author has everywhere been impressed with the fact that savage tongues are singularly persistent, and that a language which is dependent for its existence upon oral tradition is not easily modified" (1891, 141).

A number of implicit and explicit comparisons can be made from these passages within some of the ideological categories developed in analyzing Atkins:

1. Citizenship
    a. While Powell did not mention notions of citizenship in the 1877 edition of *Introduction,* his appeal to *"American scholars"* and discussions of governments in his 1880 preface offer a strong counterdiscourse to politicians like Atkins who would deny Indians citizenship.
2. Individualism
    a. If Atkins saw individualism as an ideal, it was one that could be achieved only by removing Natives from their communal environment. Powell's language here is patronizing but clearly recognizes the issues of individual (presumably white male) researchers with individual Indian informants.
    b. Powell's recognition of the biased views of outside observers in his 1891 "Indian Linguistic Families" reinforces the idea of his recognition of individual variation.
3. Evolutionary models
    a. Powell's ideas of evolution reflected his knowledge and specific misreading of Darwin's ideas as a philosophy of hope.
    b. The 1877 edition of his *Introduction* presents differences between Indian languages and "the more cultivated languages of the Indo-European stock," a milder form of the differences between barbarism and civilization assumed by Atkins. The terms are further tempered by connecting features of these two groups of languages.
    c. The 1880 edition includes a discussion of the rank of languages. Specific arguments about evolution, however, including invoking that term and discussing a "force" in the development of language, are tacked on to an original argument in additional pages numbered as 74a–74c.

d. In both his 1880 *Introduction* and 1891 "Indian Linguistic Families," Powell threaded a careful path between criticizing "students" who exalt Indian languages and outsiders who label them "gibberish." If, as Atkins stated, he had congressional and community support for banning the teaching of Native languages in schools, Powell's argument that English was linguistically evolved would have found support from both the public and his government funding agencies.

4. Linguistic ideologies

   a. Unlike Atkins, Powell was closely connected to the academic study of ethnology and philology. His referencing of Morgan and inclusion of Whitney's writings on "The Alphabet" in the 1877 *Introduction* reflected his specific scholarly traditions. In particular, the use of Whitney's work and reference to "Indo-European stock" situate the work within the German philological tradition (Whitney possessed a rare, for the time, German PhD) and tie it to the American Philological Association, founded in 1869.

   b. While he distanced himself from Whitney in the 1880 *Introduction* (vi), he used the work of Whitney's colleague from the American Philological Association, Trumbull. This is made more marked by the fact that at the time, the association was moving away from the study of Indian languages under the influence of Southern apologist and classicist Basil Gildersleeve, founder and editor of the first formal journal of the association.

POWELL AND BOAS IN PERSPECTIVE

As Regna Darnell has noted about Powell's main power base, "The autonomy of the Bureau [of Ethnology], particularly its immunity from political changes, could not . . . be taken for granted" (1969, 32). Looking at Powell's work in light of the writings of the highly political Atkins shows the larger political discourse he was operating within. While Powell followed the evolutionary schema of the time, it was a "weak version" of the ideology as opposed to the "strong version" of Atkins.

It was left to Boas to emphasize actual linguistic data and to break away from the evolutionary perspective altogether. He was able to do this because he was not a direct employee of the government. Boas had a secure position at Columbia University, possessed the technical skills to present actual examples of American Indian languages, and had remarkable control over the content of the 1911 *Handbook of American Indian Languages*. As Carl Voegelin has pointed out, Boas could have been regarded "as the author of nine out of the ten sketches" (Stocking 1992, 63). While Powell did not have Boas's independence or long commitment to civil rights, he did provide a space for the serious intellectual study of Native American languages.

NOTE

1. Professor Monaghan passed away in 2022 as this volume was in preparation. We thank her husband, Robert McGovern, for his approval and help in keeping this chapter in the volume.

REFERENCES

Manuscripts and Archives

Valentine, Robert G., Family. Papers. 1805–1996. Massachusetts Historical Society, Boston. http://www.masshist.org/collection-guides/view/fa0383.

Published Works

Anderson, Benedict. 2006. *Imagined Communities: Reflections on the Origin and Spread of Nationalism*. London: Verso.

Austin, J. L. 1962. *How to Do Things with Words*. Cambridge MA: Harvard University Press.

Baker, Lee D. 1998. *From Savage to Negro: Anthropology and the Construction of Race, 1896–1954*. Berkeley: University of California Press.

Baynton, Douglas. 1996. *Forbidden Signs: American Culture and the Campaign Against Sign Language*. Chicago: University of Chicago Press.

BIA (Bureau of Indian Affairs). 2008. *The Commissioners of Indian Affairs, 1824–1981*. U.S. Department of the Interior. January 5. https://www.bia.gov/sites/bia.gov/files/assets/public/pdf/idc-001881.pdf.

Boas, Franz. 1911. *Handbook of American Indian Languages*. Bureau of American Ethnology Bulletin 40, pt. 1. Washington DC: Government Printing Office.

Clayton, Dewey M. 2004. "A Funny Thing Happened on the Way to the Voting Precinct: A Brief History of Disenfranchisement in America." *Black Scholar* 34 (3): 42–52.

Commissioner of Indian Affairs. 1885. *Annual Report of the Commissioner of Indian Affairs to the Secretary of the Interior, for the Year 1885.* Washington DC: Government Printing Office.

———. 1886. *Annual Report of the Commissioner of Indian Affairs to the Secretary of the Interior, for the Year 1886.* Washington DC: Government Printing Office.

———. 1887. *Annual Report of the Commissioner of Indian Affairs to the Secretary of the Interior, for the Year 1887.* Washington DC: Government Printing Office.

———. 1888. *Annual Report of the Commissioner of Indian Affairs to the Secretary of the Interior, for the Year 1888.* Washington DC: Government Printing Office.

———. 1910. *Annual Report of the Commissioner of Indian Affairs to the Secretary of the Interior, for the Year 1910.* Washington DC: Government Printing Office.

———. 1911. *Annual Report of the Commissioner of Indian Affairs to the Secretary of the Interior, for the Year 1911.* Washington DC: Government Printing Office.

Darnell, Regna. 1969. "The Development of American Anthropology, 1879–1920: From the Bureau of American Ethnology to Franz Boas." PhD diss., University of Pennsylvania.

———. 2001. *Invisible Genealogies: A History of Americanist Anthropology.* Lincoln: University of Nebraska Press.

Foley, Thomas. 2002. *Father Francis M. Craft, Missionary to the Sioux.* Lincoln: University of Nebraska Press.

Hendel, John. 2011. "Celebrating Linotype, 125 Years Since Its Debut." *Atlantic,* May 20.

"John H. Oberly Dies in New Hampshire." 1899. *Washington Times,* April 16.

Kuklick, Henrika. 2009. *New History of Anthropology.* Malden MA: John Wiley and Sons.

Levinger, Matthew. 2000. *Enlightened Nationalism: The Transformation of Prussian Political Culture, 1806–1848.* Oxford: Oxford University Press.

Merjian, Armen H. 2010. "An Unbroken Chain of Injustice: The Dawes Act, Native American Trusts, and Cobell v. Salazar." *Gonzaga Law Review* 46:609.

Powell, John W. 1877. *Introduction to the Study of Indian Languages with Words Phrases and Sentences to Be Collected.* Washington DC: Government Printing Office.

———. 1880. *Introduction to the Study of Indian Languages with Words Phrases and Sentences to Be Collected.* 2nd ed. Washington DC: Government Printing Office.

———. 1882. "Darwin's Contributions to Philosophy." *Proceedings of the Biological Society of Washington* 1:60–70.

———. 1891a. "Introduction." *Seventh Annual Report of the Bureau of Ethnology to the Secretary of the Smithsonian, 1885–86,* xv–xli. Washington DC.

———. 1891b. "Indian Linguistic Families of America, North of Mexico." *Seventh Annual Report of the Bureau of Ethnology to the Secretary of the Smithsonian, 1885–86*, 7–148. Washington DC.

Stocking, George W. 1992. *The Ethnographer's Magic and Other Essays in the History of Anthropology.* Madison: University of Wisconsin Press.

U.S. House of Representatives. n.d. "Atkins, John DeWitt Clinton, 1825–1908." Accessed June 27, 2020. https://history.house.gov/People/Listing/A /atkins,-John-DeWitt-Clinton-(a000327).

Vazzano, Frank P. 2006. "Rutherford B. Hayes and the Politics of Discord." *Historian* 68 (3): 519–50.

7

The Relationship between Literature and Ethnography

The Example of Edward Sapir, 1917–22

JAMES M. NYCE

To date little attention has been paid to the three prose pieces and a poem that anthropologist and linguist Edward Sapir wrote on Tom, his Nootka informant: "Tom" (1918), "The Blind, Old Indian Tells His Names" (1921a), "The Life of a Nootka Indian" (1921b), and "Sayach'apis, a Nootka Trader" ([1922a] 1967).[1] To be more precise, what is difficult to find is any discussion of these four pieces as a group.

They do, however, represent a whole, because one central figure, Tom, unites them, as well as does the refraction of Tom's life history and experience through various literary conventions and genres. Not until Richard Handler's 1984 article do we find a discussion of them as corpus (although Handler tends to treat them as all variations of a single theme). In short, like Richard Preston (1966), Handler tends to see these four as simply individual experiments in Sapir's psychiatric science. When Regna Darnell turns to the 1922 piece, she does recognize that this was not, for Sapir, an isolated project (2001, 226) and that all four of the Tom pieces are related to each other. What ties them together for her is not Sapir's psychiatric science so much as that they represent expressions of Sapir's artistic interests at the time and that they attempt to move beyond (and critique) standard ethnographic form. Darnell returns to these themes in her biography of Sapir, without direct reference to Tom (1990), and (with Handler and Judith Irvine) in volumes 3 and 4 of *The Collected Works of Edward Sapir* (Darnell and Irvine 1994; Darnell et al. 1999). Philipp Schweighauser (2017), while citing Darnell and Handler, offers a different take on Sapir's

Tom. Mainly, he traces what he terms Sapir's poetic license and artistic or ethnographic bad faith, which he claims underlies (and connects) all of Sapir's portraits of Tom. Although he is not clear as to which sins Sapir is most guilty of, he singles out Sapir's 1921 poem as the most egregious for how it mishandles the Nootka naming conventions that inform Tom's life and biography. In his discussion of "The Blind, Old Indian Tells His Names," Schweighauser sums up his criticisms of Sapir:

> [He] plays fast and loose with an especially sensitive area of Nuu-chah-nulth culture: naming. Of course, his exertion of poetic license is perfectly in sync with a modern understanding of artistic autonomy, but it also betrays a carefree, perhaps careless use of ethnographic data that appropriates biographical and cultural knowledge gained during fieldwork in ways that are difficult to reconcile with and possibly offensive to members of the culture subjected to the anthropologist-poet's gaze. (Schweighauser 2017, 118)

Benedict noted that while Sapir's fieldwork among the Nootka "greatly influenced his own thinking in ethnology . . . he never prepared either the ethnology or the grammar for publication" (1939, 466). Sapir did, however, draw on the material he had collected. A sketch (1918), a poem (1921a), and a life history (1921b, 1922a) in which Tom, his primary Nootka informant, is the central figure were published. These pieces are of interest in themselves, but even more importantly, when they are correlated with a paper of Sapir's on literary technique (1917) and his correspondence with anthropologist Robert Lowie, it is possible to arrive at some understanding of what Sapir wanted ethnography to become. Although his design for ethnography and for a science of man are deeply related (and this so far has received little attention), this essay attempts to address the issue.

In July 1918 Sapir wrote to Lowie, "Your plans for the indefatigable continuance of ethnological research impress me very much . . . (*it's high time I bestirred myself and began to shell out a little on the Nootka stuff!*)" (Lowie 1965, 27–28). However, during the next four years he published little of the material. What Sapir did publish for the most part was neither ethnographic descriptions nor writing related to traditional ethnological concerns.

A reason for this can be found in his correspondence with Lowie. After comparing E. A. Robinson's poetry to that of Edgar Lee Masters, Robert

Frost, and Amy Lowell, Sapir concluded, "But probably you don't care much for these things. Everyone to his own taste. Problems interest me less and less; impressions and temperaments more and more" (Lowie 1965: 32). No doubt Sapir's experience with his own poetry, which he had just begun to publish (Newman 1951, 182), helped turned his attention in this direction.

This shift away from the kinds of issues that were preoccupying Lowie led Sapir to experiment with genres of writing that would support inquiry of this nature. Sapir had become concerned not with rhetoric or grammar but rather with how precisely states of mind can be articulated and which forms of expression could best represent them to others. Precision here is not meant in any quantifiable sense but rather is a concern with having personal interaction and response portrayed accurately—that is, to have the reader respond as the person originally in the situation did.

In a letter he wrote to Alfred Harcourt of Harcourt, Brace and Company on June 17, 1922, Sapir described a study of perhaps eighty thousand to eighty-five thousand words that he proposed to do: "This account of a Vancouver Island tribe would not take the form of a monograph but would rather present the results of the ethnographic work he did among these people in a form that would give the reader a real feeling for life in a community such as this."

Implicit in Sapir's proposal was the belief that he had at last found a medium capable of handling this problem. I argue that composing and working through the pieces already mentioned helped Sapir come to this decision. Others have noticed that problems of form and expression had begun to interest him: "His writing continued to be clear and ordered . . . but he emphasized more and more the control of evocative overtones in any topic he discussed . . . [and] instead of continuing to master the one style of conventional academic writing, he became adept at handling many styles" (Newman 1951, 182–83).

As his work on Tom is examined, this becomes clear. In December 1918 Sapir published his sketch of his Nootka informant. "Tom" begins with a description of the rainy season on the west coast of Vancouver Island: "Rain, rain, rain day after day—not your light frisking showers alternating with sunny cloud—patched sky, nor those whirling rackety down—pours, climaxes of cosmic dramas, but just good old honest Philistine rainfall, coming down with heavy respectability." Sapir then turned to Tom's village of Alberni, Tom's family, then to Tom himself: "Nothing more shabby than his clothing could well be imagined" (Sapir 1918, 7).

Sapir's interviews with him are described much the same way. The subject has been treated lightly. This is because the conventions that define our expectations about what we read (Frye 1963, 39, 44, 50–51) allow only a single point of view, the author's, to be presented. (These literary conventions, Frye argues, apply both to readers and authors.) The work in fact has the reader respond to Tom and his surroundings as the author must have, at least at first.

Another convention at work here is a concern with the picturesque. But when the circumstances of the old man are touched on, this relatively superficial interest that pervades the rest of the piece is put aside. "And yet there was nothing shamefaced or apologetic about his manner. His present abject poverty was not the reward of past shiftlessness. . . . He had had his days of prestige and now rested content in their memory" (Sapir 1918, 7). This highly visible evidence of poverty, squalor, and deterioration is not the only thing described here, and the focus is instead on the meaning poverty had for Tom.

This aspect of Nootka life continued to interest Sapir. The month "Tom" appeared, he sent Lowie notes on the concept of ownership among the Nootka. A month later Sapir, apparently in response to another letter of Lowie's, discussed the difficulty in characterizing different groups as individualistic or communistic and warned him that "such conceptualizing need have no great culture—historical value after all, as so much depends on just what the natives considered value and property" (Lowie 1965, 33). For Sapir, then, discussions of wealth and property must take into account how the people themselves viewed this dimension of their lives.

Evidently, how to proceed in this direction was becoming a matter of concern to him. In 1921 Sapir published another study of Tom—a poem, "The Blind, Old Indian Tells His Names," that describes how Tom himself perceived his poverty:

And 'Stand-up-high' became a name that day
And comes to me, for I am looking down
Though poor, with squandered wealth and rich renown.
My songs have rung in feasts, my wealth has thundered,

Tribes have feasted and the slaves have wondered.
His staff was beating to a feast song
And feeble, stumbling words now sang along:
My wealth is drumming in the air. (1921a, 38)

This passage and poem reflect his concern with portraying the meaning that the various elements of Native life had for those immersed them.

Sapir also dealt with this subject in "Tom" (1918). Even though style and interest on occasion overlap in the two works, their intentions (and the conventions that inform them) are quite different. The author's first impressions of Alberni inform the sketch. Tom is only one of the objects that evokes an aesthetic response. "The Blind, Old Indian Tells His Names" (1921a), however, is not concerned with the perceptions and feelings of the author. Tom is no longer an occasion around which a causerie, a literary piece, can be built, and unlike in "Tom," personal (and aesthetic) response does not entirely inform the work. Given Sapir's empathy and control of language, it is clear that the poem was a means through which his knowledge of the Nootka could be accurately presented and readily understood. Schweighauser (2017) disagrees. He argues that Sapir got his facts wrong in "Tom" and that this ethical lapse makes "Tom" the worst of a bad lot.

The same year, "The Life of a Nootka Indian" (1921b), Sapir's last study of Tom, also appeared. This subtly "insightful" life history (Preston 1980, 3) reflected Sapir's concern with representing experience as the person in the culture perceived it. To achieve this, "the conventional categories of ethnography" are represented, "as they have meaning, both conscious and unconscious, for the individual" (Preston 1966, 1112).

As insightful as it is, the life is not entirely convincing—something Sapir acknowledged himself (1922b). To understand why, an essay by Sapir on realism in literature needs to be considered. For a work to be found compelling, Sapir argued, the "reader has to be made to live through the experiences, thoughts, feelings of the characters." The difficulty is that "once we have identified ourselves with a definite personality, our imaginative pride demands, provided always the artist can hold our interest, that we watch the progress of events from our own point of vantage" (Sapir 1917, 503–4). This, of course, is what Sapir intended to have us do with the figure of Tom, but the work is flawed. The reason for this is not that he lacked the ability to capture the reader's attention, but that he did not keep the perspective under control.

An example from the life of Tom illustrates this. First, here is how the Nootka concept of esteem is handled: "Tom is now old and poverty-stricken, but the memory of his former wealth is with his people. The many feasts he has given and the many ceremonial dances and displays he has had performed have all had their desired effect—they have shed lustre on his sons and daughters and grandchildren, they have 'put his family high' . . . and they have even carried his name to other, distant Nootka tribes and to tribes on the east coast of the island that are of alien speech" (Sapir 1921b, 232).

Sapir's intention and artistry came together, and "elements of inner and outer life [were placed] in comprehensible, living relations" (Sapir 1917, 504). They are presented as Tom would have perceived them. But when Sapir described the manner in which a Nootka obtained respect, note the change in voice. Decidedly ethnological, it represents a dramatic shift of perspective to the impersonal and external:

> To earn the esteem of his fellow-tribesmen by a lavish display of wealth . . . He must from time to time invite other families of his tribe, and the neighbouring tribes, to public ceremonies known as "potlatches," in which one or more of the important privileges to which he is entitled are shown and glorified by the distribution of property to the guests . . . he must be careful to distribute at least as much property as has already been distributed in his family in connection with the public presentation of the privilege. If it is at all possible, he will try to exceed the record, so as to add to the public prestige not only of himself and his immediate family but of the privilege itself. (1921b, 356–57)

The presence of more than one point of view, and the alternation between them, is sufficient reason for the reader not to be able to identify with Tom. The objective nature of one of the perspectives further increases the distance between audience and character. For "even when we cordially like such [explicit] analysis, we cannot altogether ward off a sneaking irritation at the disturbing influence it exercises on the flow of narrative" (Sapir 1917, 506).

The partial failure of a life history has been accounted for thanks to Sapir's ability to delineate the literary techniques and conventions that characterize realism. The relationship between the conventions of literature and the structure of ethnographic writing needs to be better understood. Some of the reasons other forms of ethnography fail to be convincing will then become evident.

While the writing culture movement that started in the mid-1980s (Clifford 1983) returned to some of the issues Sapir raised a half century ago, the effect the movement had on writing in anthropology has not been long-lasting. It led to calls for innovation, introspection, and change but few actual changes in how the discipline writes. The writing culture movement certainly can be credited with helping blur the line between ethnography and memoir (what is acceptable to depict as fact and what is self-production) and inaugurate some new prizes for ethnography and poetry competition, but not much has changed in how anthropologists write. For the most part, we publish the same kind of articles and ethnography that Franz Boas and Ruth Landes did. Some of this is due to the dead hand of tradition—that is, academia's innate conservativism—but not all of it.

The writing culture movement tended to be preoccupied with issues of style and authorial intention, important in the literary criticism of any form. However, this focus has obscured some even more fundamental issues—ones Sapir started to address years ago in respect to ethnography. These, as Toms Kencis notes, have somehow "slipped under the radar of ideology claiming transparency of representation and immediacy of experience" (2012, 38). These are the primary issues that need to be addressed if we are to reinvent and critique writing in anthropology.

Before turning to the more fundamental issues, let us look at where the writing movement's focus on style and self emerged from. This focus almost directly reproduces the Romantic notion of the author as an autonomous self and agent struggling against tradition. All that has to change to bring about innovation is the author's intention. To believe that either the writer (or for that matter, the reader) can have such full control of their responses to the world and literature expresses something much like the intentional fallacy—a fallacy already widely discussed in literary criticism (Wimsatt and Beardsley 1954).

This is not to say that the writing movement has not paid attention to factors other than the self that influence the ethnographic form. In fact, Clifford gives an encyclopedic list of the factors that can influence ethnography as writing, and he also gives us some idea of their relative importance and origins: "(1) contextually (it draws from and creates meaningful social milieux); (2) rhetorically (it uses and is used by expressive conventions); (3) institutionally (one writes within, and against, specific traditions, disciplines, audiences); (4) generically (an ethnography is usually distinguishable from a novel or travel account); (5) politically (the authority to represent cultural realities is unequally shared and at times contested); (6) historically (all the above conventions and constraints are changing)" (1986, 6).

But note the last parenthesis. If we read it the way Clifford wants us to, this implies a radical nominalism when it comes to both written conventions and authorial constraints, as well as the role they play in ethnography. Their relative unimportance is underscored by Clifford mentioning them last, only within parentheses, and stressing their historical mutability.

So where does this leave us? If all the issues related to ethnography as writing have seemingly been subordinated to questions about the text and author, the only thing that remains is some commitment to the writing of the fact, no matter how much we might want to deny this. Ironically, the movement's strong ideological commitment to exploring the idea of representation simply reaffirms and strengthens this commitment. In other words, denying the influence of things like convention and genre is "completely overwhelmed by the writing of fact, as by the flattened form and static temporality [of] such writing" (Trumpener 1997, 106). This denial of any literary consanguinity also helps legitimize the idea that ethnography, whatever its problems, suffers from none of the defects of fiction. The result is that the writing movement has almost single-mindedly focused on the issues of authenticity, truthfulness, and believability, and further, it has tended to reduce them to psychologisms—things like character, intention, and motivation. For much the same reason, recent challenges to the movement have also been unable to handle the issues that radical alterity poses for ethnography and anthropology (Willerslev 2013, 42). "We are struggling here with a fundamental issue that still eludes us, and although few in anthropology would put it this way, it is the extent to which ethnography makes itself believable even today" (Clifford, 1986, 13). Despite the discipline's perennial anxieties about reflexivity, this issue still more or less is framed as one about the extent to which "This text has been dictated to you by Reality itself" (de Certeau 1984, 148). If this is not discomforting enough, consider what Roland Barthes asks us to believe: "Representation is defined directly by imitation [instead, and] even if one gets rid of notions of the 'real,' of the 'reasonable,' of the 'copy,' there will be still representation as long as a subject (author, reader, spectator or voyeur) casts his gaze towards a horizon" (1977, 69).

The question then is, if we accept Barthes's challenge, What in ethnography and anthropology are we representing and imitating? Gregory Bateson has given us perhaps the clearest answer to this question. The task of the ethnographer is "to present the whole of a culture, stressing every aspect exactly as it is stressed in the culture itself, [so that] no single detail would appear bizarre or strange or arbitrary to the reader, but rather the details would all appear natural and reasonable as they do to the natives who have lived all their lives within the culture" (1936, 1).

What makes Bateson's argument seem plausible is that it relies on a correspondence theory of truth and representation. While correspondence theory has often been refuted and is seemingly exhausted in anthropology, its persistence, despite the ascendancy of interpretivism in American anthropology, owes much to its Foucauldian effects.

To show that this argument is not (entirely) out of left field, let us look at Clifford Geertz's famous "Deep Play: Notes on the Balinese Cockfight." In it, he writes, "Finally, the Balinese peasants themselves are quite aware of all this [the rules that inform these cockfights] and can, at least to an ethnographer, do state most of it in approximately the same terms as I have" (1973, 440). Let us ignore for the moment Geertz's "approximately the same terms," for this may be nothing more than some topos of modesty—used preemptively to defuse any criticism of an author's work.

To go on, it is clear from the above that not even Geertz is immune to the seductions of correspondence theory. For Geertz the proof of an ethnographic argument still rests on the extent to which the argument, as Barthes put it above, can be portrayed directly through imitation and mimesis. In short, the validity of Geertz's argument in "Deep Play" rests on correspondence theory—that is, how closely his cockfight rules and those held by his informants mirror each other.

While correspondence theory has been successfully challenged in other disciplines since Bruno Latour and Steve Woolgar in *Laboratory Life: The Construction of Scientific Facts* (1979) began to unpack the role that simplification and context have in scientific work, it is an open question why the news has not really reached anthropology or had much impact on ethnography. Perhaps holding on to correspondence theory helps the discipline strengthen its legitimacy because, we, as a four-field discipline, (theoretically) can hold the mirror up not only to the social but to nature as well.

Whatever the reasons, the explorations anthropologists label under the "crisis in representation" have not yet gone far enough. We have not yet been able to challenge the discipline's deep commitment to a kind of primitive realism and empiricism. To put it another way, the discipline seems unable to acknowledge that it is more pictorial than photographic in its ethnographic representations. Further, the fact that ethnography might be pictorial at all challenges any number of central beliefs the discipline has about itself.

The struggle here is over whether we should continue to operate, knowingly or not, under the spell of correspondence theory or whether we will consider the challenge that the mimetic fallacy raises for anthropology and ethnography. This takes us back to Sapir. Through his various ethnographic experiments—that is, by working through his stories of Tom and Nootka life—he became aware of exactly how mannered not only ethnography but also literature itself is. Sapir, however, did not take the next step of considering what role mimesis plays in any of this, which is odd because of how often this issue appears in his linguistics.

Whether we borrow the term from Aristotle's *Poetics*, Samuel Coleridge's *Biographia Literaria*, or Michael Taussig (1993), the mimetic fallacy argues that it is impossible for any kind of representation, no matter how well drawn or argued, to portray things as they are in the world. Further, any attempt to circumnavigate mimesis will, if the representational project is sufficiently interrogated, ultimately confirm this. So Sapir left us in a kind of epistemological and ontological dilemma—one that even today has not received the kind of attention it deserves.

As long as this is the case, we will remain committed, despite much rhetoric to the contrary, to the discipline's present representational strategies. Therefore, it is difficult to foresee that any substantial change or innovation will occur in anthropology's written universe. This will leave us, unwittingly or not, no other choice but to try to make our stories seem "credible, logically motivated or morally [intelligible] lifelike in short" (Frye 1961, 603). However, there is a considerable divide that separates the lifelike from the real even if we anthropologists try to pretend that either it does not exist or it does not matter. As Northrop Frye has done, Katie Trumpener also reminds us that "all scholarly attempts to describe a culture . . . remain caught within text-based modes of knowledge, dependent on textual sources for their investigation and on textual forms for the transmission of their discoveries" (1997, 107).

In other words, we need to pay more attention to the similarities and differences and their origins between, say, an Azande poison oracle, E. E. Evans-Pritchard's recording of and writing about this, and how the anthropological reader responds to and is informed by it. Until we do, no higher-order understanding or criticism of ethnography will be possible.

NOTE

1. This chapter was first written as a paper for the 1977 Halifax Congress of the Canadian Ethnology Society, and revised twice before publication in this collection of essays.

REFERENCES

Manuscripts and Archives

Sapir to Harcourt, June 17, 1922. Correspondence files of Harcourt Brace Jovanovich, New York.

Published Works

Barthes, Roland. 1977. *Image-Music-Text*. New York: Hill and Wang.
Bateson, Gregory. 1936. *Naven*. Cambridge: Cambridge University Press.
Benedict, Ruth. 1939. "Edward Sapir." *American Anthropologist* 41:465–69.
Clifford, James. 1983. "On Ethnographic Authority," *Representations* 2:118–46.
———. 1986. "Introduction: Partial Truths." In *Writing Culture: The Poetics and Politics of Ethnography*, edited by James Clifford and George E. Marcus, 1–26. Berkeley: University of California Press

Darnell, Regna. 1990. *Edward Sapir: Linguist, Anthropologist, Humanist*. Berkeley: University of California Press

———. 2001. *Invisible Genealogies: A History of Americanist Anthropology*. Lincoln: University of Nebraska Press.

Darnell, Regna, and Judith T. Irvine, eds. 1994. *The Collected Works of Edward Sapir*. Vol. 4, *Ethnology*. Berlin: Mouton de Gruyter.

Darnell, Regna, Judith T. Irvine, and Richard Handler, eds. 1999. *The Collected Works of Edward Sapir*. Vol. 3, *Culture*. Berlin: Mouton de Gruyter.

de Certeau, Michael. 1984. *The Practice of Everyday Life*. Berkeley: University of California Press.

Frye, Northrop. 1961. "Myth, Fiction, and Displacement." *Daedalus* 90 (3): 587–605.

———. 1963. "Nature and Homer." In *Fables of Identity: Studies in Poetic Mythology*, 55–70. New York: Harcourt, Brace and World.

Geertz, Clifford. 1973. "Deep Play: Notes on the Balinese Cockfight." In *The Interpretation of Cultures*, 412-453. New York: Basic Books.

Handler, Richard. 1984. "Sapir's Poetic Experience." *American Anthropologist* 86:416–17.

Kencis, Toms. 2012. "A Disciplinary History of Latvian Mythology." PhD diss., University of Tartu.

Latour, Bruno, and Steve Woolgar. 1979. *Laboratory Life: The Construction of Scientific Facts*. Princeton NJ: Princeton University Press.

Lowie, Robert H. 1965. *Letters from Edward Sapir to Robert H. Lowie*. Berkeley CA: Luella Cole Lowie.

Newman, Stanley. 1951. "Review: Selected Writings of Edward Sapir in Language, Culture and Personality." Edited by David G. Mandelbaum. *International Journal of American Linguistics* 17:180–86.

Preston, Richard J. 1966. "Edward Sapir's Anthropology: Style, Structure and Method." *American Anthropologist* 68:1105–28.

———.1980. "Reflections on Sapir's Anthropology in Canada." Canadian Review of Sociology and Anthropology 17 (4): 367–75.

Sapir, Edward. 1917. "Realism in Prose Fiction." *Dial* 62:503–6.

———. 1918. "Tom." *Canadian Courier*, December 7, 7.

———. 1921a. "The Blind, Old Indian Tells His Names." *Canadian Bookman* 3 (2): 38–40.

———. 1921b. "The Life of a Nootka Indian." *Queen's Quarterly* 28:232–43, 351–67.

———. (1922a) 1967. "Savach'spis, a Nootka Trader." In *American Indian Life*, edited by Elsie C. Parsons, 298–323. Lincoln NE: Bison Books.

———. 1922b. "A Symposium of the Exotic." Review of E. C. Parsons, ed., *American Indian Life*. *Dial* 73:568–71.

Schweighauser, Philipp. 2017. "Playing Seriously with Genres: Sapir's 'Nootka' Texts and Mead's Balinese Anthropology." RANAM: *Recherches anglaises et nord-américaines* 50:107–21.

Taussig, Michael. 1993. *Mimesis and Alterity: A Particular History of the Senses*. London: Routledge.

Trumpener, Katie. 1997. *Bardic Nationalism: The Romantic Novel and the British Empire*. Princeton NJ: Princeton University Press.

Willerslev, Rane. 2013. "Taking Animism Seriously, but Perhaps Not Too Seriously?" *Religion and Society: Advances in Research* 4 (1): 41–45.

Wimsatt, W. K. Jr., and Monroe C. Beardsley. 1954. *Verbal Icon: Studies in the Meaning of Poetry*. Lexington: University of Kentucky Press.

8

Edward Sapir, Harry Stack Sullivan, and Harold Lasswell Collaborations

Real and Imagined

RICHARD J. PRESTON

Where was Edward Sapir headed in the late 1930s, during the last few years of his life? The indications are various; he has sometimes been represented as heading where scholars have retrospectively wished to see him follow their own specialties, perhaps thereby constituting his final vote of confidence for their own particular disciplinary goals. But this is projecting our wishes onto his intentions and special preferences; in fact, he maintained many major interests, continuing his work on Indo-European (Malkiel 1984) and American Indian (Golla 1984) languages and on the psychology of culture (Preston 1984) and other topics.

This essay affirms his overarching humanistic philosophy of the psychology of culture and focuses specifically on the intellectual context that was developed in his collegial exchange with two other major thinkers: psychiatrist Harry Stack Sullivan and political scientist Harold Lasswell. My thesis is that the three men were engaged in remarkably convergent paths in their individual intellectual careers, each reacting creatively to what he believed to be unsupportable and unscientific narrowness of inquiry in his respective profession. The 1920s and 1930s were formative years for major syntheses in psychiatric theory and practice and for policy formulation regarding mental health and psychopathology. Freud, his disciples, and his dissenting students were of great interest, not so much as a professional force (this was to come in the late 1930s with the exodus of psychoanalysts from Europe under Hitler's domination) as the asking of fundamental questions regarding human emotion and mentation. The answers to these questions had potential application to understanding the willingness of millions of Europeans to espouse militant fascism, thus enabling Hitler's rise to power. Today these answers may apply to understanding and ameliorating the rise of new militancies, including Islamist, Zionist, and Christian.

Sapir, Sullivan, and Lasswell were a part of a lively context of argumentation regarding future directions in theory, method, and applications of psychiatric and social scientific knowledge. They were not alone in this, although they were aware of the general attitude of skeptical distancing preferred by most of their colleagues. One like-minded colleague was sociologist W. I. Thomas, who convened a conference in 1927 on the theme of the form-giving or synthetic tendencies of the unconscious as a corrective to the Freudian emphasis on the disorganizing or dysfunctional attributes of the unconscious. Among the contributors were Sapir, gestalt psychologist Kurt Koffka, psychiatrist William Alanson White, and other major figures of this period (Dummer [1928] 1966). Other manuscripts that are of particular value in documenting the period are the transcripts of the Social Science Research Council Hanover Conferences and the National Research Council Committee on Personality and Culture. Sapir, Sullivan, and Lasswell participated in a number of these meetings.

For Sapir, the time and effort required to further most or even a few of his projects were diminished by illness several years before his death in 1939, but he continued to work and offer guidance for the work of others. His situation at Yale was a difficult mix of some admiring students and colleagues, coupled with negative pressures of both a professional and a personal nature. Given these pressures and his limited energy for teaching, it is not surprising that he considered resigning from Yale to support Sullivan's scheme to establish, under the auspices of the William Alanson White Psychiatric Foundation, a genuinely interdisciplinary research program (Perry 1982, 366–76). What was he willing to try to move into at this point in his life? Sullivan wrote the following:

> The Foundation proposes expressly to concentrate research on a small number of fundamentally important issues. Its initial research program comprises a group of interconnected investigations to supply relevant data for the checking of major hypotheses. A comparative study of personality will be undertaken, concentrating on individuals from 15

to 35 years of age, since their difficulties in adapting to the standards of their given cultures render them singularly accessible to investigation, and expose the stresses which are induced by contradictory tendencies within the culture.

These personality maladaptations are joined to "material" and "administrative" factors in determining the line of collective discontent which furnishes the immediate dynamic of political change. This emphasizes the necessity for a continuing survey of fluctuations of discontent throughout the world. . . . The cultural situations which are significant for the comparative analysis of personality and social unrest must be investigated in order to furnish the necessary backgrounds for the sound interpretation of specialized details. (1938, 135–36)

The instigator of this scheme was Sullivan, and our most complete record of the context of the scheme is in Helen Swick Perry's biography, *Psychiatrist of America: The Life of Harry Stack Sullivan* (1982). Perry's book is graceful, thorough, and clearly partisan. As a biography of the innovator of a theory of interpersonal psychiatry, it is also appropriately interpersonal, detailing the most significant relationships (including Sapir and Lasswell) in his career. For Lasswell, we have a substantial essay by Dwaine Marvick introducing his edition of Lasswell papers (1977), and some short items by others. For Sapir and Lasswell, though, we are faced with shorter, fragmented individualist portrayals with too much eclectic effect, and none of these contain more than a brief mention of their intellectual convergence. This makes the task of evaluating the three points of view on the interrelationship a matter of very unequal evidence. Perry spoke persuasively of Sullivan's views, but it is less clear how Lasswell and Sapir regarded the goals and means of the scheme, what they hoped to do in collaboration with Sullivan, and how they saw their continuing relationships.

We know that they had been intensely engaged as friends and colleagues since soon after Sapir's arrival at the University of Chicago and that they shared remarkably similar theoretical concerns and interests in sustained exchanges over a dozen years. Some appraisals of Lasswell's career come close to being a fair description of the intellectual style of all three of them:

The innovations and scope of his research, the fertility of mind and fluency of style, the freedom from pomposity and cant, the throw-away generosity with ideas and insights, make him unique among contemporary scholars. ("Review of *Politics*," 1970, 168)

Lasswell's deepest personal commitment was to the creation of a comprehensive theory for inquiry about the individual human being in social process. His goal was to develop a theory which could be made sufficiently precise to facilitate performance of all the different intellectual tasks necessary to the rational clarification and implementation of individual and community policy. (McDougal 1979, 676)

A more irreverent phrasing is given by Robert Redfield, writing to his wife while attending the 1930 Social Science Research Council Hanover Conference as a junior colleague:

The principal psychiatrist present is Harry Stack Sullivan, a droll person, and interesting. He is another one, like Sapir and Lasswell, with the gift of tongues. When the three of them get together the polysyllabic confluences are amazing. (1978, 12)

But even his humorous remarks are in a context of something closer to awe:

I feel very poorly equipped in this company. They are so wise in the ways of the academic world, and make so many brilliant suggestions. I don't even answer the questions adequately, for while I am considering the question, they answer it for me and go on to something else. I do not feel completely at ease in the company of such scintillating intellects. (11)

The interest in the interplay of culture, personality, society, and politics was a significant part of the intellectual milieu of the period between the two world wars, a powerful motive, for instance, in the development of the "Chicago school" with Charles E. Merriam, William I. Thomas, James Angell, Charles H. Cooley, William F. Ogburn, and others. Applied social science was a major part of the scene, motivated by an interest in the effective implementation of experimentally proven or systematically hypothesized ideas, as the best and ethically most sound route to the amelioration of social problems in Chicago and elsewhere. Of comparable relevance to then-current sociopolitical threats and a similar scope of inquiry was the development in Germany of gestalt psychology by Max Wertheimer,

Wolfgang Kohler, Kurt Koffka, and later Kurt Lewin. Sapir, Sullivan, and Lasswell were not alone in their more particular concern with the problem of personality pathology in social, cultural, and political contexts either. But if they had some good company, they also had opposition from the general tendency within social science toward more narrowly professional interests in the definition and maintenance of boundaries of careers and disciplines, away from the larger issues of *Personal Psychopathology* (Sullivan 1972), spurious cultures (Sapir 1949), and "The Garrison State" (Lasswell 1941).

Lasswell wrote more than thirty books and 250 articles, Sapir's *Collected Works* fills sixteen volumes, and Sullivan was also generous with words. Their gift of tongues creates a logistical problem to which I will respond here by examining only a small sample at an appropriate place and time: the first issue of Sullivan's journal *Psychiatry* (1938). Each of these men contributed an article, and Sullivan also provided a prospectus for their sustained collaboration as a research nucleus at the White Foundation.

Sapir's contribution, "Why Cultural Anthropology Needs the Psychiatrist," is best known for his explication of the statement "Two Crows denies this." The point was a criticism of the degree of impersonality in anthropology, a product of a more or less deliberate method of generalizing through the overoptimistic use of the technique of normative overinclusion. The fallacy of normative overinclusion arises out of the difficulty and necessity of generalizing about the phenomena of social life, against the backdrop of the intellectual drive for making elegant, powerful, and parsimonious statements to one's peers or, perhaps, even more powerful statements for the public media and policymakers. In Sapir's words, "The assumption was that in some way not in the least clearly defined as to observational method it was possible for the anthropologist to arrive at conclusive statements which would hold for a given society as such" (1949, 569). In his seminars, he specifically criticized both Ruth Benedict and Margaret Mead for the overgeneralized and implicitly homogeneous psychological characterizations that are made to stand as normative metaphors for Zuni or Samoan people. Because of its tendency toward oversimplification, the method is better suited to art than to science, and Sapir's example of Two Crows is intended to tell us why this is so.

At the level of method, "Two Crows denies this" is both a reproach and an opportunity. The reproach is to question the degree of consensus implied in our pattern statements, for culture is rarely so unanimously validated by its carriers. The opportunity is to define our method to account for variance and thereby to get to the psychology of cultural processes. It is not only bad science to fail to account for variation; in a few instances, what begins as individual variation takes hold on a large social scale. The process by which new patterns form, to augment or to displace existing patterns, is appropriate for study by intensive psychological inquiry.

What starts as a thoroughly irresponsible and perhaps psychotic aberration seems to have power, by some kind of "social infection," to lose its purely personal quality and take on something of that very impersonality of custom that, in the first instance, it seemed to contradict so flatly (Sapir 1949, 571).

A truly rigorous analysis of any arbitrarily selected phase of individualized "social behavior" or "culture" would show two things: First, no matter how flexible, how individually variable, it may in the first instance be thought to be, it is, as a matter of fact, the complex result of an incredibly elaborate cultural history, in which many diverse strands intercross at that point in place and time at which the individual judgment or preference is expressed (this terminology is *cultural*). Second, conversely, no matter how rigorously necessary in practice the analyzed pattern may seem to be, it is always possible in principle, if not in experiential fact, for the lone individual to effect a transformation of form or meaning that is capable of communication to other individuals (this terminology is *psychiatric* or *personalistic*). What this means is that problems of social science differ from problems of individual behavior in degree of specificity, not in kind (572–73).

Statements defining the "effective consistencies" (576) in the variations and uncertainties in human behavior are the psychiatric science's replacement for the impersonally defined "patterns." We risk missing the objective reality of culture unless we are able to go behind impersonal pattern statements to perceive people's actual interrelationships and discern their variations in relation to their central tendency. Through this close and psychiatric analysis, we are able to discover the meaning of norms as they really are, as effective consistencies in behavior. In Sapir's example, Two Crows disagrees with other Omaha people on the matter of whether there are eight clans in Omaha society. By inquiring, we may find that, for example, one clan is now extinct. Therefore, in a practical sense, represented by Two Crows' statement, there are only seven clans; in a theoretical sense, represented by the other Omaha informants, there are eight. But the variance may be psychologically more complex, and it may be that Two Crows, for instance, is not simply motivated to be practical rather than theoretical but also is motivated by some satisfaction at the demise of this particular clan for some remembered slight it had caused to his own clan. Now we can see both a practical and an emotional basis for denying the claims of the other informants. And through this and further inquiry into the psychological reality of the informants' statements, we will be able to discern more precisely the form and meanings of "effective consistencies" in statements and perceptions regarding Omaha clans. In this way we are able to clarify the actual processes involved, not only in informants' pragmatic use of language but also in the ways that perception and conception change through time in culture.

Sapir's example of Omaha clans is illustrative of the value of a psychiatric approach in a more deeply systematic sense than the discernment of effective consistencies, or patterns in behavior. The interpersonal context of inquiry allows for the determination of causality. Sapir was convinced that the search for causality in social phenomena was impossible so long as they were defined as if they were a separate order from actual behavioral phenomena.

An effective philosophy of causation in the realm of social phenomena does not seem possible if these phenomena are judged to have a valid existence and sequence in their own right. It is only when they are translated into the underlying facts of behavior from which they have never been divorced in reality that one can hope to advance an understanding of causes. The test can be made easily enough. We have no difficulty in understanding how a given human being's experiences tend to produce certain results in the further conduct of their life. Our knowledge is far too fragmentary to allow us to understand fully, but there is never a serious difficulty in principle in imputing to the stream of the person's experiences that causative quality we take for granted in the physical universe. To the extent that we can similarly speak of causative sequences in social phenomena, what we are really doing is to pyramid, as skillfully and as rapidly as possible, the sorts of cause-and-effect relations that we are familiar with in individual experience, imputing these to a social reality that has been constructed out of our need for a maximally economical expression of typically human events. It will be the future task of the psychiatrist to read cause and effect in human history (576).

Actual events, whether purely physical or dynamically psychological, are more amenable to causal analysis, while abstractions from events, particularly from those influenced by mentation, are more appropriately limited to functional analysis. Sapir was quick to add that psychiatry is far from being able to approach the goal he had set, but the path to the goal must be through a more precise understanding of human beings, their personalities, and interrelationships with other personalities.

Sapir, Lasswell, and Sullivan were conjointly developing similar ways to understand behavior. In "What Psychiatrists and Political Scientists Can Learn from Each Other," Lasswell addressed comparable issues within political science, with a similar strategy of exposition, contrasting the discipline's use of formal generalization with the immediate phenomena of events. The *phenomenon* of political behavior is the lively exchange between rules and persons:

> The "great game of politics" as we know it operates within the rich context of rules which are commonly held to be authoritatively binding. These rules may be stated in statutes passed by legislatures, ordinances made by executives, regulations laid down by administrators. Such authoritative words are generally presumed to guide the official in the exercise of his judgement. The working politician knows that the rules give different results in the hands of different men, and of the same men under different incentives: what, after all, he asks, is the constitution among friends? (1938, 33)

But the discipline of political science is not organized to reflect this, Lasswell told us. Instead, it focuses on the study of public law, political ethics, and especially political institutions. Much of what is done by its practitioners is the description of the structure and function of government, most commonly as follows:

Efforts are made to connect the agencies of public law with the context in which these agencies operate. This requires the collection of data about the relative rise and fall of agencies in relation to one another through selected periods of time. . . . If this change is once established, the path is clear to consider aspects of the context which can be said to cause the change. . . . This explicitly connects the authoritative rules with the context in which they are found, and furnishes a procedure for the statement of the conditions under which laws will "work", that is, when events will conform to the express requirements of the law. (35)

Both the terminology and the method of abstracted empiricism (taking normative statements *as if* they accurately represented experience) are similar to the cultural view that Sapir was criticizing and contrast with the complementary but underutilized psychiatric view that both men advocated. Lasswell went on to espouse this complementarity of what he termed "extensive" (Sapir's "cultural") and "intensive" (psychiatric) research. Like Sapir, Lasswell hoped to use psychiatric study to discern the actual processes of symbolic formulation and use and to find, through an analysis of variation, the reality of a norm. Speaking more of himself than his colleagues, Lasswell said:

In recent times there has been a rapidly increasing emphasis among political scientists upon the symbolic and personality aspects of the context in which rules operate. . . . The moment any serious attempt is made to understand the conditions which determine the successful manipulation of symbols, the aid of the psychiatrist is bound to be enlisted. . . . Qualified political scientists are well acquainted with the facts about the distribution of many symbols in definite historical situations, and they are accustomed to consider these symbols as aspects of the context in which they occur, and as interacting upon other aspects of this context. But, the political scientist has developed no strict procedure for the investigation of the finer texture of this context.

The contribution of the psychiatrist is chiefly his standpoint of observation: he focuses attention upon the individual career line for protracted periods of time, and he utilizes special ways of exposing the structure of personality. Hence he can examine in great detail the degree to which a given set of political symbols is integrated with the other features of the total personality. (35–36)

Lasswell made a similar case for the intensive study of particular leaders, the problems of recruitment of competent administrators, and the potential contributions of social psychiatry to the advisory staff of these persons, so that they would gain greater expertise for guiding the use of symbols in directed culture change.

Both Lasswell and Sapir directed us to the value of adding the study of "personal symbolisms in the use of cultural patterns" (Sapir 1949, 568) to more abstracted types of studies that are made in terms of the key social scientific "technical metaphors" for organized behavior (e.g., pattern, norm, rule, institution, process) per se. Sullivan came at the problem from the other extreme. The formulation of *The Interpersonal Theory of Psychiatry* (1953) and *The Fusion of Psychiatry and Social Science* (1964) arose in criticism of the individualist metaphor and its consequence—a narrow focus on subjective experience taken by most of his predecessors and contemporaries in psychiatry.

The dynamic psychiatry of the present is chiefly interested in bringing order into the subjective elaboration of experience, without much concern for implications as to the culture complex, accidents of acculturations, and implicit culture invention or disintegration. The next task of psychiatry is to seek out the actual processes that manifest in human differentiation and deviation. Its basic formulations must be derived from analyzing these processes of personality growth and function in terms of a temporal series of distributed interactions of a highly integrated organism with other people as cultural surrogates. It must view each person as an emergent configuration referable to the interplay of factors of native endowment, physicochemical and biological environments, and personal interaction. It should interpret the phenomena of interpersonal relations in terms of more or less extensive references to unrealized personal goals and find one of its most valuable tests in the prediction of future behavior. Unfortunately, the inhibitions and facilitations more or less universally effective in any elaborated culture complex tend to minimize the range of personal differentiation and stereotype both personal goals and performances for their achievement. The special need of psychiatry is the comparison of life courses that have been studied in this culture with intensive studies of personalities in culture areas widely divergent from ours. This type of investigation will show the limitations of many of our current formulations and point accurately to advantageous fields of investigation (Sullivan 1938, 136).

Clearly, the main point of convergence is between the social scientific overemphasis on extensive method for large-scale abstractions from the phenomena of human interactions, which both Sapir and Lasswell found methodologically and theoretically insufficient, and the psychiatric and psychoanalytic overemphasis on an intensive method for the understanding and amelioration of the subjective states of individuals, which Sullivan found methodologically and theoretically insufficient. Their convergence is toward the social psychiatry of cultures, drawing on the historical developments of the psychiatry of mental health as well as the psychiatry of mental illness. From this they hoped to develop a significantly more powerful and synthetic social science. And on the more applied, ameliorative side, they hoped to develop a social psychiatry of personal and patterned maladaptations, of which the rise of Hitlerian fascism was the most immediately pressing example. In a letter to anthropologist Alfred L. Kroeber dated August 25, 1938, Sapir put it bluntly:

Dear Alfred,

Of course I'm interested in cultural patterns, linguistic included. All I claim is that their consistencies and spatial and temporal persistences can be, and ultimately should be, explained in terms of humble psychological formulations, with particular emphasis on interpersonal relations. I have no consciousness whatever of being revolutionary or of losing an interest in what is generally phrased in an impersonal way. Quite the contrary. I feel rather like a physicist who believes the immensities of the atom are not unrelated to the immensities of interstellar space. In spite of all you say to the contrary, your philosophy is pervaded by fear of the individual and his reality. You find anchorage—as most people do, for that matter—in an imaginatively sundered system of cultural and social values in the face of which the individual has almost to apologize for presuming to exist at all. It seems to me that if people were less amenable to cultural and social mythology we'd have less Hitlerism in the world.

But my basic philosophy has little to do with my specific interests. I am as much as ever interested in large scale patterning, in such problems as reconstructing Athapaskan and placing Tokharian accurately in a genetic and historical sense (which last, incidentally, I think I shall be able to do if my allotted span is long enough)....

The rumor you picked up is hardly justified. There has been talk of my joining a unit at Washington but, as far as I can see now, I continue at Yale in 1938–39. Needless to say, I'm a bit fed up with teaching, for it takes a lot out of me and my health is probably going to be precarious for the balance of my life. And there are many points on this planet that are more attractive than New Haven.

Yours as ever,
[Edward]

Sapir immediately reiterated his central point. Yes, patterning is the prime interest of social science. But the shape of content in any pattern is a complex of effective consistencies with individual variations. That is to say, what humans think, feel, and do is guided by a historically based consensus, as each individual happens to embody that consensus. Two Crows is an example of the way that the consensus may look different from different individuals' points of view. So the task of a more scientific study of patterned behavior is to be able to more precisely and intensively define the range and dynamics of variation. This must be selective in its application, of course, for the task would otherwise be overwhelming. But a practical application of selective psychiatric inquiry is a recognition of the essential philosophical point that social scientists are addressing phenomena that are in reality the behavior of individuals, however these phenomena may be abstracted into folk or scientific categories. It is similarly a recognition that individual behavior is powerfully guided by consensus—by unconscious and conscious patterning—and that social science is therefore fundamentally a psychiatric science. Sapir's distress at the tendency of social scientists to regard their task as "sundered" (to use his term) from actual individuals was in considerable measure shared by Lasswell and some others of the period, while the reciprocal error, an overexclusive emphasis on specifics of individuality by psychiatrists and psychoanalysts, caused Sullivan comparable distress and was a motive for developing a more adequate psychiatric science.

The letter to Kroeber speaks, individual to individual, to his insistence on a superorganic, "sundered" from the intensive study of actual persons, and then speaks to the particular projects that Sapir was engaged in during the last year of his life. "But my basic philosophy has little to do with my specific interests" is a statement worth our reflection. He was at work, but not in a way that he felt was a satisfying expression of his fundamental values and goals. He is, in most of his writings and in the great bulk of data in his memory, a superb linguist. But his philosophy does not rest only within the discipline of linguistics. Rather, he was, as Kroeber argued in a retrospective assessment (1959), a humanist more than he was a linguist or an ethnologist. Perhaps his philosophy would have been partly expressed in a book on the psychology of language, and we have good indication that it was to be given substantial statement in his proposed book, "The Psychology of Culture." He had a genius for language, but for all his facility and the richness of his technical resources, he found in it the limited satisfactions that accrue to the contemplation of pure form, "the serenity of a self-contained system" and the relative ease of working within a domain of inquiry that offers well-defined technique and method. According to his wife, Jean Sapir, "His work on languages was such a pleasure to him that he was able to remain 'busy' in that manner, but he did deeply feel that he died without saying his full say" (Preston 1980, 374).

These statements by Sapir, Kroeber, and Jean Sapir should persuade us that no one discipline can fairly claim Sapir as essentially its own; he was indeed a humanist first, as well as an interdisciplinary pioneer. Linguistics was the field of his most perfect achievement; psychiatric anthropology was an emerging field that he provided with a schematic program. His work in the arts may be fruitfully researched for statements and aesthetic images that are complementary to, and in this way clarifications of, his other work. To evaluate the whole man as if he were best remembered as a linguist is to diminish him and to diminish the significance of the relationships between language, culture, psychiatry, criticism, and art.

We can only wonder at the effects on his morale and intellectual efforts of the personal disappointments at Yale, of his failing health, of the tendencies of intellectuals to prefer narrow goals, and of the depressing outlook for

Europe as war loomed ever larger. In this context, "Psychiatric and Cultural Pitfalls in the Business of Getting a Living" (1939) is all the more poignantly autobiographical in tone and in substance, probably written with a feeling of deep pessimism about his prospects and those of the world at large. The closing paragraph of the letter to Kroeber shows his sense of resignation toward a return to Yale for lack of a viable alternative in Washington DC.

Sullivan had tried and failed to find funding for their unit, including a salary for Sapir and support for his family upon the eventuality of his death. At Lasswell's urging, he hired a fundraiser Lasswell knew, but this also failed (Perry 1982, 366–71). Had funding been found by 1938, it is fair to suggest that a productive collaboration would have gotten underway. But reality was less kind. Lasswell resigned from Chicago in 1938, and the van moving his papers to New York crashed and burned. Sapir returned from his sabbatical in New York, where he had visits from Sullivan three or four afternoons a week, and died at Yale early in 1939. Sullivan then moved to Washington, and while both he and Lasswell were based there during the war years, they worked separately. The White Foundation furthered its work in the professional training of psychiatrists and publication of its avowedly interdisciplinary journal. Sullivan worked there and continued his work for government agencies. During a 1949 trip to Europe to a meeting of the founders of the World Federation for Mental Health, he made a side trip to speak with General Lucius Clay regarding East-West communications. Both events were discouraging to him, and he was found dead, perhaps a suicide, in a Paris hotel (Perry 1982, 414–24). Lasswell, much younger than the other two, took a position at the Yale Law School, where he felt that his influence might work better on future leaders during their professional training than would be likely in a department of political science. He died in 1978.

It is intriguing to imagine what might have been the outcome of their planned collaboration, but today this remains only imagination. It is worth noting here that one aspect was to be work by Stanley Newman on some of the psychiatric aspects of language use, perhaps along lines that he subsequently did on his own initiative. Newman and Sapir were looking to small examples to reveal the precise detail of actual psychological processes (Sapir 1927; Newman and Mather 1938; Newman 1939, 1941, 1944).

Another possibility is the furthering of what became known as paralanguage studies. As far as I know, the major study of personality that Sullivan referred to in the first issue of *Psychiatry* has not yet begun, although it would be of great interest to better understand the cross-cultural basis of political discontent in terms similar to those proposed. Perhaps the study of the dehumanizing effects of social and cultural mythologies that Sapir mentioned in the letter to Kroeber would have been another topic for their collaborative research. There are many fascinating possibilities.

Finally, I must mention the relation of all this to Sapir's unwritten book on the psychology of culture. He continued to teach his graduate seminar from the outline of the book up until his last sabbatical. And the concerns to redefine the study of culture toward a blend of cultural and psychiatric terminology were a large part of his outline. Further, his emphasis on dealing intensively and comparatively with the problem of individual adjustment in society, and ultimately to discern the processes of cultural decay and renaissance (Preston 1984), speaks directly to the goals of the planned collaboration. Put simply, "The Psychology of Culture" was very much a part of the planned collaboration; the convergence of interests of the three men was fundamental and extensive.

The fact that these goals exceeded the abilities of the psychiatric and social sciences (which is still the case) does not make the effort unworthy or impractical, to be buried away as opportunities never realized. It is still, today, a major direction for the furthering of these sciences. The appalling willingness of young adults to "escape from freedom" is still enabling militancy globally. Three brilliant men saw the challenge as both possible and necessary during the 1930s. The succeeding years have served to further emphasize both the challenge and the importance of these directions for research.

REFERENCES

Manuscripts and Archives

Kroeber, Alfred L. 1959. "A. L. Kroeber and Others Talk about Edward Sapir." Recorded by David M. Schneider at the University of California–Berkeley. Online Language Archive, University of Chicago. Audio.

Sapir, Edward. "The Psychology of Culture." Unpublished book outline proposed to Harcourt in 1928.

Sapir to Alfred L. Kroeber, August 25, 1938. Bancroft Library, University of California–Berkeley.

Published Works

Cowan, William, Michael K. Foster, and Konrad Koemer, eds. 1984. *New Perspectives on Edward Sapir in Language, Culture and Personality. Proceedings of the Edward Sapir Centenary Conference*. Philadelphia: John Benjamins.

Dummer, Ethel S., ed. (1928) 1966. *The Unconscious: A Symposium*. Freeport NY: Books for Librarians.

Golla, Victor. 1984. "Sapir, Kroeber, and North American Linguistic Classification." In Cowan, Foster, and Koemer, *New Perspectives on Edward Sapir*, 533–51.

Lasswell, Harold D. 1938. "What Psychiatrists and Political Scientists Can Learn from Each Other." *Psychiatry* 1:33–39.

———. 1941. "The Garrison State." *American Journal of Sociology* 46:455–68.

———. 1977. *Harold Lasswell on Political Sociology*. Edited by Dwaine Marvick. Chicago: University of Chicago Press.

Malkiel, Yakov. 1984. "Sapir as a Student of Linguistic Diachrony." In Cowan, Foster, and Koemer, *New Perspectives on Edward Sapir*, 533–51.

Marvick, Dwaine. 1977. "Introduction: Context, Problems and Methods." In *Harold Lasswell on Political Sociology*, 1–72. Chicago: University of Chicago Press.

McDougal, Myres S. 1979. "Harold Dwight Lasswell, 1902–1978." *Yale Law Journal* 88:675–80.

Newman, Stanley. 1939. "Personal Symbolism in Language Patterns." *Psychiatry* 2:177–82.

———. 1941. "Behavior Patterns in Linguistic Structure: A Case Study." In *Language, Culture and Personality: Essays in Honor of Edward Sapir*, edited by Leslie Spier, A. I. Hallowell, and S. S. Newman, 94–106. Menasha WI: Banta.

———. 1944. "Cultural and Psychological Features in English Intonation." *Transactions of the New York Academy of Sciences* 7:45–54.

Newman, Stanley, and Vera G. Mather. 1938. "Analysis of Spoken Language of Patients with Affective Disorders." *American Journal of Psychiatry* 94 (4): 913–42.

Perry, Helen Swick. 1982. *Psychiatrist of America: The Life of Harry Stack Sullivan*. Cambridge MA: Belknap Press of Harvard University Press.

Preston, Richard J. 1980. "Reflections on Sapir's Anthropology in Canada." *Canadian Review of Sociology and Anthropology* 17:367–75.

———. 1984. "Sapir's Psychology of Culture Prospectus." In Cowan, Foster, and Koemer, *New Perspectives on Edward Sapir*, 533–551.

Redfield, Robert. 1978. "Letters to Margaret Park Redfield, 1930." Excerpted in *History of Anthropology Newsletter* 5 (2): 11–12.

"Review of *Politics, Personality, and Social Science in the Twentieth Century*. Arnold A. Rogow, ed." 1970. *Psychiatric Quarterly* 44:167–69.

Sapir, Edward. 1927. "Speech as a Personality Trait." In *Selected Writings of Edward Sapir in Language, Culture and Personality*, edited by David G. Mandelbaum, 533–43. Berkeley: University of California Press.

———. 1938. "Why Cultural Anthropology Needs the Psychiatrist." *Psychiatry* 1:7–12.

———. 1939. "Psychiatric and Cultural Pitfalls in the Business of Getting a Living." *Mental Health* (9): 237–44.

———. 1949. *Selected Writings of Edward Sapir in Language, Culture and Personality*. Edited by David G. Mandelbaum. Berkeley: University of California Press.

Sullivan, Harry Stack. 1938. "Editorial Notes: The William Alanson White Psychiatric Foundation." *Psychiatry* 1:135–40.

———. 1953. *The Interpersonal Theory of Psychiatry*. Edited by Helen Perry and Mary Gawel. New York: W. W. Norton.

———. 1964. *The Fusion of Psychiatry and Social Science*. New York: W. W. Norton.

———. 1972. *Personal Psychopathology: Early Formulations*. New York: W. W. Norton.

Silenced Bodies

The Accession of Mortal Remains in the Museum of Ethnography,
1904–16, during the Argentinian Gran Chaco Military Campaigns

SANDRA TOLOSA AND LENA DÁVILA

> *Esa cabeza toba! Debéis verla.*
> *Si es la cabeza de un muerto, digo que hay en la muerte,*
> *como en la vida, algo que relampaguea.*
> *That Toba head! One must see it.*
> *If it is the head of a dead person, I say that there is in death,*
> *as in life, a sudden flash.*
> —Lucio V. Mansilla

The Museum of Ethnography, founded in 1904 as an academic institution affiliated with and financed by the College of Philosophy and Letters at the University of Buenos Aires, was intended to be a center for teaching and research to address the need for disciplinary professionalization, rather than just a space for exhibits (Arenas 1989; Perazzi 2005). This scientific objective underpinned its prestige, which was fostered through national and international networks that its director Juan Bautista Ambrosetti (1865–1917) developed at the institution, capitalizing on his position as a member of the period's elite social circles and drawing on his personal relations within and outside of the scientific milieus in the academy.

As had directors at other institutions, such as Francisco P. Moreno at the Museum of La Plata, Ambrosetti took on the task of building the museum's collections and holdings with the goal of using them for instruction, research, or exchange with other scientific programs.[1] However, in the La Plata model, the display of not just objects but also human remains was part of its objectives, whereas the Museum of Ethnography distinguished itself through the years by not displaying skulls and skeletons for public viewing in its exhibition cases.

Despite many other similarities with his scientific peers, Ambrosetti differed in his insistent claim to systematicity in his objectives. The relationship between the institution and its director was reflected in the historiography of Argentine anthropology, to some extent shielding this relationship from critical analyses in comparison with other contemporary scientists. Thus the more polemic and ambiguous aspects of this history have been perpetuated as simply the period's modus operandi and have not been more closely scrutinized.

Research on the Museum of Ethnography has been scant and relatively recent, focusing mainly on the history of its museology practices and to a lesser degree on particularly problematic aspects of specific collections (Pérez Gollán and Pegoraro 2004; Gustavsson 2008; Pegoraro and Elías 2010; Pegoraro and Spoliansky2013). Departing from these precedents, we address a specific issue in this essay: the acquisition during the museum's early years of sets of mortal remains belonging to Indigenous peoples of the period.[2] Gustavsson (2011) has already pointed out the ambiguity surrounding the classification of these bodies, shunted to the museum's Anthropology Section, which was largely made up of "archaeological" remains. We agree with her that this general classification contributed to erasing the differences among Indigenous remains from different time periods and that this is why the issue we are raising has received little attention.

To broach the issue, we focus on the human remains from the Chaco region that were accessioned in the museum in the early twentieth century as part of a series of projects and requests that Ambrosetti conveyed to residents—both permanent and transient—in different areas in the territory.[3] While the ways in which these requests were made involved a variety of individuals and institutions that fit his purpose, the Chaco case represents a particular conundrum as some of the submissions to the museum—which currently remain part of its collections—were obtained by members of the military who were engaged in territorial campaigns against local Indigenous peoples.[4] Drawing on existing archives, we examine how Ambrosetti managed to capitalize on the military advance on Gran Chaco, in the early twentieth century to expand the museum's ethnographic and anthropological holdings.[5]

One can also discern parallels between the transmittal of Indigenous objects, which Ambrosetti promptly camouflaged, and the dismantling of Indigenous resistance at the hands of the national military. While local cultures were being raided and destroyed, science cast itself in the role of protector, albeit merely for the purpose of conserving fragments, resignified in glass cases along with new interpretations for the edification and instruction of the urban middle and upper classes. But the most blatant expression of this paradox between destruction and preservation was the amassing of Indigenous skeletons and crania, along with objects from their material culture. Some of these were collected by officers of the same national army that brought to bay, exterminated, and conquered the Gran Chaco's original inhabitants. This situation begs for a deep inquiry into the collusive ties between science and war, much addressed in relation to the Museum of La Plata but less so regarding the Museum of Ethnography.

In what follows, we briefly establish the context of the strategies that Ambrosetti used to stock the Museum of Ethnography and, in particular, to create the Anthropology Section. Against this background, drawing on archival documents, we analyze several examples of requests for objects and bodies that were directed to territorial interlocutors. We then briefly contextualize the main military campaigns in the Chaco territory and the relations that developed between the college and the army. Finally, we touch on two cases we find in sources: Cacique Carayá's cranium and the skeletons of Cacique Illirí and his child, both added to the museum's collections in the 1910s. By drawing on data we have managed to cull, we attempt to recover aspects of Cacique Illirí's subjectivity that have been erased by his materialization as an "object" for anthropological inquiry. While taking the immediate historical context into account, we aspire to foster reflection on these past practices and their consequences, past and present, for Indigenous peoples, both directly and on sociocultural and academic imaginaries.

THE MUSEUM OF ETHNOGRAPHY AND ITS COLLECTING STRATEGIES

The Buenos Aires Museum of Ethnography was founded by the decree of Dr. Norberto Piñero, dean of the College of Philosophy and Letters, and on the strength of Juan B. Ambrosetti's "alma mater" advocacy.[6] He envisioned it as the first South American institution of its kind, in the context of the professionalization and institutionalization of archaeological, anthropological, and ethnographic instruction independently of the natural sciences of which it had been part (Pegoraro 2005; Perazzi 2011).

The museum was intended to document American humankind as well as the geography and cultures of all other continents. Three general sections— the Ethnography, Archaeology, and Anthropology Sections—were organized to fulfill this goal. The first would document cultural diversity, the second would reconstruct the past of American humankind, and the third would compare physical and "racial" characteristics among human groups (Pegoraro 2005). As the director, a position he held until his death in 1917, Ambrosetti launched the museum's collections, beginning with a bare minimum. He augmented the collections over the course of his stewardship to reach 19,543 pieces by 1916, according to his last *Memoria*, submitted just before his death. He aimed to amass materials specifically designated for research and study, although he largely employed the period's collectionist practices.

Diverse strategies were used to achieve this expansion. First, the College of Philosophy and Letters financed expeditions, most of them focused on Argentina's northwest territories, in accord with the director's preferred approach of "Calchaquí archaeology."[7] Second, Ambrosetti mobilized his personal networks, sustained by his position and his social and professional prestige, to encourage individual donations, engage in institutional exchanges of holdings, and contact antique dealers. Finally, he established special outposts and reporting agents in the Argentinian hinterland. This facilitated access to the territories, diminishing the need to organize and invest in expensive, labor-intensive expeditions, while capitalizing on local knowledge and relationships. Ambrosetti detailed the collections' consequent growth in the annual *Memorias* that he submitted to the dean of the college.

A sort of "collectionist fever," particularly between 1909 and 1916, is evidenced in the exponential increase of both activity and objects at the museum. The expansion of the ethnographic collections was a salient objective within this trend. Notably, by 1907, the Ethnography Section remained quite small: between donations and 16 objects that had been gathered in expeditions, it amounted to a total of 41 objects, compared with the Archaeology Section's 2,380 pieces, a difference that hampered the institution's aspirations (Pegoraro 2009, 55). In his pursuits, Ambrosetti's territorial imaginary expanded toward the spaces recently brought under national sovereignty through political and military encroachments: the national territories. These new regions were approached through the aforementioned collaboration channels and specific institutional relationships. As much was conveyed in that year's *Memoria* (1915), submitted to dean Rodolfo Rivarola: "Good material has also been received from different expeditions and missions, particularly as requested from a variety of the museum's friends and collaborators, among them, Mr. Eduardo A. Holmberg (Junior), Mr. Enrique Lynch Arribálzaga, Mr. Luis González Leiva, Francisco Cubas, and Eugenio J. Leroux, who have maintained their submissions from the National Territories of the Chaco, Formosa, Chubut, and Santa Cruz."[8]

To convey his intent across the contexts of dissimilar and remote "specialists," Ambrosetti generally provided "instructions" for the preservation and appropriate treatment of museum material during its collection, storage, and transportation. These became a basic tool so that the academics at the center could institute certain systematic guidelines even in the most remote branches of the territory, a matter of great concern for Ambrosetti, who stressed the importance of keeping precise records of the collected items to preserve their scientific value. He thus conveyed an expansive series of requests to a variety of individuals by means of ad hoc instructions detailing the objects in which the institution was interested. All the items were valued because they would be used either to expand the collections or to exchange with other institutions, as would be done, for example, with duplicates.[9]

A notable instance of this practice was the support Ambrosetti received from Isidoro Ruiz Moreno, who headed the National Territories Directorate, facilitating access to objects from the territories. In a July 22, 1915, letter, Ambrosetti acknowledged Ruiz Moreno's goodwill and attached "the lists and instructions for the submission of the objects we are missing to complete our ethnographic and archaeological collections from the National Territories."[10] The directorate circulated this material through an announcement to the territorial governments, which was conveyed from these to the departmental police commissars so that they could "search, among the residents in their jurisdiction, for objects that the Museum of Ethnography wishes to acquire, as these functionaries are in the best position to submit the most exact information of the knowledge and relationships among the inhabitants of their departments."[11] The surviving dossier shows that the announcement, with the attached list of objects, was sent to the governments of Misiones, Santa Cruz, and Chaco, although with disappointing outcomes, as reflected in multiple negative responses from Misiones and scant responses from the other two.[12]

Two issues should be noted: The first was that personal ties—here between Ambrosetti and Ruiz Moreno—were becoming increasingly relevant as vehicles for mobilizing requests from one state institution to another. This was a common modus operandi of the period, and institutional operations were often subservient to this sort of personal relationship between directors, who usually belonged to elite circles. Ruiz Moreno was quite cognizant of the Indigenous issues in the territories, thus being a most helpful mediator for the museum's objectives.

The second issue leads directly to our argument in this essay and is linked to the specificity of the "orders," particularly the inclusion of human remains. Although the files at the Museum of Ethnography do not include the listings of objects, the request for human bones is textually implied in some of the replies.[13] For example, the Apóstoles commissar explained, "I could not locate any of the listed objects, and the existence of indigenous skulls or skeletons is unknown in this department."[14] The Santa Ana commissar focused toward skeletons "of yore" and pointed out that "the ancient inhabitants of this department don't know where the Jesuits sited the cemetery."[15] We must underscore that the likelihood of not finding objects and bodies was being attributed to the absence of Indigenous peoples in missionized areas. "Although in past times, groups of three or four Cainguá Indians have been known to be in the area," wrote to the Corpus commissar, "nowadays, with the production stoppages, they have migrated toward the northern part of the territory, [and I] do not know where they might have buried any of their bodies nor of the existence of objects they might have used since, nowadays, they all have modern weapons and utensils. According to information gathered from some travelers, there are two colonies of Guayaná and Cainguá Indians close to the Paraguay border."[16]

In the response from a "specialist," Francisco Fouilliard, the items Ambrosetti requested were explicit, including weapons, agricultural implements, musical instruments, pottery, decorations, textiles, antique objects, urns, vases, pots, axes, stone tools, balls, fishhooks, lip plugs—and skulls and skeletons. Fouilliard expounded on the technicalities regarding the impossibility of finding appropriately preserved bodies:

Requests from the Museum of Ethnography: Skulls and skeletons.

Only purchasing some recently deceased Indians in Paraguay could skulls and skeletons be obtained, since the lack of sodium chloride in the Misiones soil precludes the preservation of interred bones except for a few short years and particularly because the Indians don't season their food with salt. Besides, there are no Indians in Misiones except for a small group of mestizos who call themselves Guayanás [and] who prowl around San Pedro, and whose cCacique, one Maidana, was a white guy born in Santo Tomé. Another inconsequential group prowls between Once Vueltas Creek and Campo Grande; perhaps in the Mbororé ruins, which have never been found.[17]

We are left with no choice *but to purchase some dead Guayaquí in the Paraguayan coastal area where those Indians are plentiful so as to send their bones to the museum.* The Guayaquí is the quintessentially primitive Guaraní, as he's stuck in the Stone Age, doesn't know art nor fire, nor the construction of houses (italics in original).[18]

This tellingly documents how the acquisition of crania and bones of the recently deceased seems not to have created an ethical dilemma. One needs then to consider whether the purchase of the newly dead by scientific institutions might have been a more common practice than is commonly assumed. Also to be considered is that these exchanges are part of official institutional records, which implies knowledge on the part of, involvement by, and support from the National Territories Directorate—in other words, they are evidence of the nation state's direct and explicit collaboration.

Other official correspondence documents that Ambrosetti circulated requests for items and human remains to all sorts of networks and contacts. On June 3, 1913, he wrote to Dr. Jorge Larrosa, who was on a trip to the country's south with his girlfriend, attaching a list of objects and specifying that anything Larrosa could obtain would be useful, including duplicates for exchange, explicitly adding, "If you can get us a cranium on your trip, it will be splendidly received."[19] On August 6, 1914, two months before his death, former president, Julio Argentino Roca (1880–86) wrote to Ambrosetti, "In response to your kind letter of the 29th, I am pleased to inform you that I have once again ordered that the indigenous objects and skeletons found in my properties be collected. I will gladly send any findings to the Museum of Ethnography, thus contributing to the project that you are carrying on with such intelligence and zeal."[20]

Going by these examples, it is important to note some initial points. Most of the scholarship addressing the problem of Indigenous human remains in museums and, consequently, the politics of restitution has generally dealt with the Museum of La Plata, where a substantial quantity of cases have been identified (e.g., Arenas and Pinedo 2005; Badenes 2006; Colectivo Guías 2008; Curtoni and Chaparro 2011; Tamagno 2009; Verdesio 2011). Our focus on the Museum of Ethnography to examine this issue allows us to compare and analyze, on a more extensive factual basis, whether these practices were the exception, and thus should be imputed to particular individuals, or were a routine institutional practice of the period, shared and commonplace—which nevertheless does not make them any less objectionable.

We must first consider differences in the development of the "subdisciplines" at each institution. While the Museum of La Plata's Anthropology Section was established earlier, its counterpart was not as important at the founding of the Museum of Ethnography, possibly an outcome of Ambrosetti's personal preferences toward cultural, archaeological, and folkloric practices. Thus the development of this section was relatively slower than the other sections.[21] Consequently, publishing on this subdiscipline practically nonexistent during this period.[22] Nevertheless, as a developing institutional space, anthropology needed be integrated, and its course offerings required the acquisition of osseous holdings, occasionally specifically purchased for such purposes.[23] This was documented in the request submitted to the dean to solicit from the Medical Sciences College the following material, described as "indispensable for anthropological comparative research":

A complete skeleton of a 25–30-year-old man
A complete skeleton of a 25–30-year-old woman
A cranium of a 7–8-year-old boy
A cranium of a 7–8-year-old girl
A cranium of an older, 65–75 years old man
A cranium of an older, 65–75 years old woman

Since in this museum there are no appropriate facilities nor staff, these should be clean and bleached for their usefulness. This material should be of pure White individuals, preferably Italians.[24]

As one can see here, the "exemplars" were used for the comparative study of racial anatomy. But one wonders in this case whether the bodies that the medical school could contribute were those of poor immigrants or other marginalized subjects, whose remains had been tagged as useful for scientific inquiry. We also consider it possible that the creation of the Anthropology Section precipitated the problem of overlap, confounding "archaeological" remains excavated from pre-Columbian interments with contemporary remains without a registry that documented origins with precision. Gustavsson (2008, 2011) has analyzed this problem of classification, which extended over time. One might wonder whether the search for skulls and skeletons in the national territories could have gained impetus from the need to shape the Anthropology Section, which stood unfinished before Ambrosetti's untimely death. And if so, one might consider how useful the military advance into the Gran Chaco was for this purpose, especially in view of the seldom challenged usual scientific practices wrought on Indigenous bodies, which would be ever less questioned in the context of territorial conquests. Adding to this was the scarcity of ethnographic material from that region in the museum's cases. The military campaigns were thus a valuable conduit for accessions that Ambrosetti could capitalize on.

MILITARY CAMPAIGNS AND THE EXPANSION OF THE ARGENTINIAN NATION STATE INTO THE GRAN CHACO

To understand how the "collecting" campaigns in the Gran Chaco could be undertaken, we must establish the context of the nation state's military advances in the territory in the late nineteenth and early twentieth centuries. In contrast to what transpired in other Argentinian regions, territorial control in this case was compounded by the need to discipline the Indigenous peoples in order to convert them into a labor force, due to the demands of different agroindustrial sectors.

The expansion into the Gran Chaco began in 1870 and lasted until the 1930s. It involved a direct and systematic encroachment into the territory by military forces that developed a variety of strategies to expand the nation state's sovereignty and subordinate its population. Most of the military expeditions carried out in the late 1800s relied on the collaboration of the scientific societies as well as the participation of geographers, naturalists, and botanists (Arenas 1989), among other professionals specializing in the study of the wealth and natural resources of the territories and their potential for exploitation. Thus did the political and military field and the scientific one mutually benefit from a long-lasting relationship.

We now briefly describe three of these military campaigns. The first, headed by General Benjamín Victorica in 1884, during Julio Argentino Roca's first presidency, is considered among the most important of the campaigns for its systematicity and violence, especially in comparison with those that preceded it. The show of armed forces included infantry, cavalry, and navy line regiments whose main objective was consolidating the territory's occupation and redrawing the sovereign nation state's borders, while subjugating the Indigenous populations of the Chaco.

Although construed as a successful campaign in official discourses proclaiming that it had effectively achieved absolute control over both the territory and its inhabitants, parts of the region remained beyond the nation state's grasp. The succeeding campaigns were directed toward consolidating supremacy and quashing Indigenous resistance. Those who survived these campaigns were stripped of their lands and barred from access to the forests and rivers that constituted their traditional means of subsistence. The lands conquered by the state were later redistributed, with the consequent emergence of substantial estates, largely for cattle raising and sugar production, as well as exploitative forestry (Iñigo Carrera 1984; Gordillo 1995; Trinchero 2000; Brunatti et al. 2002). The need for Indigenous peoples to seek new subsistence resources thus gradually emerged, which necessarily led them to sell their labor, mostly in manufacturing and sugar refining.

The second campaign, decreed by President Figueroa Alcorta in July 1907 and led by General Teófilo O'Donnell, continued the advance of the fortified line, aiming for total territorial occupation and the establishment of non-Indigenous settlement. Its objectives included the construction of roads to facilitate transportation, provisioning, and commerce, as well as laying telegraph lines for improved communication, particularly between the occupied areas and the new settlements that were emerging as the military campaigns advanced. The caciques who resisted and revolted were murdered or captured as prisoners of war until their ultimate fate was determined, which often meant being transferred to concentration camp–like spaces or forced to join the industrial labor force or the frontier troops.

The third was Colonel Enrique Rostagno's campaign, labeled the Chaco's Operational Forces, which immediately followed in 1911. This was considered the last great advance on the territory. It brought about the definitive incorporation of the central-west areas, now the provinces of Formosa and Chaco, into the territory and marked the "ultimate pacification" of the Indigenous peoples that had so far not been subjugated.

If the objectives designated in 1884 were deemed achieved with this campaign (Iñigo Carrera 1984), and the subjugation of the Indigenous peoples seemed a done deal, it was not considered sufficient. It was deemed crucial to discipline the Indigenous peoples and transform them into "productive labor." In this context, in a report submitted to Defense Minister Gregorio Vélez, Rostagno referenced the need to teach Indigenous people to cultivate the land and, to that end, establish a place where the "spontaneously" submissive "tribes" could be relocated (Rostagno [1911] 1969). Among his arguments, Rostagno alluded to the inhabitants' vulnerability, which allegedly gave caciques grounds for soliciting aid:

> In addition to the 1600 Indians under the Caciques Coyahiqui, Sobiacay, Solinkí, *Ilirí*, Santiaguito, and Natochí of the Caballero tribe who have agreed to learn farming; of the 1000 Mocovíes of Pedro José who are asking not just for land, but even schools, are the self-same Cacique Caballero and the Cacique Jara with 2000 of their members requesting the 9c [Ninth Cavalry] to let them work wherever it may be, with the only condition that the regiment manage their contracting, such is their concern that they might be robbed. I can add as well that more than 1500

Pilagaes [Pilagás] who follow Cacique Nella-Lagadik in the Killolkai lagoons (tiger's head) and Pedagananaes of Central Pilcomayo, who traverse much of the upper Pilcomayo [River], have expressed to me their desire for permanent work. (Rostagno [1911] 1969, 22; emphasis added)

Rostagno's request was heeded, and consequently, on October 27, 1911, the national government decreed the establishment of the Napalpí Indian reduction.[25] It was configured as the prototypical forestry and farming reduction that was expected to be adopted in the territory, and its first appointed director was renowned naturalist Enrique Lynch Arribálzaga.[26] In those regions where the Indigenous population had been vanquished, the national army opted for withdrawal; here the reductions would fulfill the "civilizing mission." In this way, physical subjugation was complemented by new forms of social control for the production of docile bodies (González Stephan 1999; Foucault 1975), now fostered by the state in lockstep with national market needs. This mode of subjection was concretized in the establishment of three Franciscan missions that preceded Napalpí—San Francisco de Laishí (1900), Nueva Pompeya (1900), and San Francisco Solano de Tacaaglé (1901)—and the foundation of three reductions that followed: Bartolomé de Las Casas (1914), Francisco Javier Muóiz (1935), and Florentino Ameghino (1935).[27] In less than forty years, a system of control over the Indigenous labor force was thus consolidated in the national territories of Chaco and Formosa. Insofar as anthropology was concerned, the missions, the reductions, and the sugar and manufacturing enterprises became desirable targets for those interested in studying the living, as well as for those who pursued expanding institutional collections through the acquisition of diverse goods and objects.[28]

THE MUSEUM OF ETHNOGRAPHY AND THE MILITARY CAMPAIGNS

Pegoraro (2005) points out that the Museum of Ethnography's first incursion to the Chaco region was the expedition to the Chaco and to Jujuy in 1909, headed by Salvador Debenedetti, who collected 348 ceremonial and household objects from the region's Indigenous groups. Previously, though, Ambrosetti had written to the college's dean, raising the need to approach the national army as it launched its regional campaign about collaborating with the museum. Ambrosetti was confident that O'Donnell was enlightened enough to grasp the initiative's import:

> At the very outset of the national troops' advance through the Chaco territory, I think it would be very opportune to ask the head of these forces, General Don Carlos O'Donnell, that he should command those in charge of the advance operations to collect and remand ethnographic objects to our college's museum. *The Chaco tribes tend to disperse further away or to disappear as they come in contact with the White man; and because of this, it is urgent to collect the largest amount of material as is possible,* with which one may be able to study their uses and customs and engage in their much-needed ethnographic comparison (emphasis added).[29]

From then on, the museum received multiple contributions from army officers. Salient among them are those of Major Pedro Cenóz of the Ninth Cavalry Troop and Lieutenant Colonel Francisco Magín Guerrero of the Seventh Regiment, who sent ethnographic and anthropological collections they had gathered from Chaco peoples.[30] Although the detailed list of requested objects in Ambrosetti's letter to the dean did not include human remains,[31] when Cenóz reported to the museum's director in an October 1909 letter that he had entrusted the dean with Indigenous objects, he clarified, "I am sorry to report that, *as far as your foremost request is concerned, which is for Indian skeletons,* I have been unable to obtain any even with all sorts of offers of compensation, since the very missionary fathers, who are in the better position for their time among the Indians, have been unable to show me where any burial ground might be" (emphasis added).[32]

In this sense, it is noteworthy that the request for skeletal remains does not appear in the listing attached to the letter to the dean. As the original has disappeared, we are unable to prove any hypothesis, since the request could have been included in a separate attachment or sent—for reasons we cannot yet establish—unofficially and on a personal basis. Ambrosetti was openly thankful for the more than twenty ethnographic objects Cenóz sent on that occasion, pointing out to the dean several days later: "Beyond the objects' value, this development is significant as a first step taken toward National Army officers contributing to this college's museum and this is why I am asking our dean to thank Mr. Major Cenóz for this shipment as he deserves it and so as to stimulate this collaboration that we so much need."[33]

Pegoraro notes, "The idea of mobilizing the army and the local [territorial] governments through institutional hierarchies became a way to facilitate the transmittal of instructions, given that they came from official circles and met the administrative requirements established by each government agency" (2009, 209). Certainly, Ambrosetti highly valued the "efficacious participation of members of our National Army," much as he expressed it in relation to Cenóz or when he received the first two donations from Guerrero: a cranium and a set of Toba arrows.[34] For their part, army officers were equally happy with the possibilities in cooperating in this kind of scientific mission and providing "good service to the country and to science," as Cenóz put it.[35]

Beyond the pragmatism inherent in the objective of developing collections, we are interested in bringing to light the implications of these connections, in that they set up a veritable alliance between the Museum of Ethnography, a scientific institution committed to the study of the Indigenous peoples, and repressive military forces that were tasked with their extermination or subjugation for exploitative purposes. In other words, the Indigenous "removal" and "disappearance" that Ambrosetti noted were part and parcel of the same military actions directed toward the "rescue" of Indigenous objects and, eventually, of their very bodies. It is from this standpoint that we analyze three specific applications in the collection practices of Chaco Indigenous objects and human remains for the Museum of Ethnography in violent contexts: prison, reductions and missions, and caciques killed in military encounters.

Prison

As we noted, the letter for O'Donnell that Ambrosetti submitted to the dean carried an encompassing and detailed listing of ethnographic objects to be sent to the museum. It also stated, "It does not matter if we get many duplicates as there may be many interesting differences among similar ethnographic objects. If at all possible, the objects should be sent with whatever Indian name they might have, *and this should be easy to elicit from the pris-*

oners [or] the domesticated Indians. It is essential that all objects come labeled with the name of the tribe or nation to which they belong" (emphasis added).[36]

This passage indicates how the Indians' carceral condition was perceived as a propitious circumstance for stockpiling objects of scientific interest and for eliciting useful data for precision in their cataloging. Even if it cannot be ascertained that these instructions were effectively acted on, the fact that they were stated gives credence to a total lack of empathy toward the subjects that Ambrosetti claimed to study, whose sole value seems to have been as producers of objects and facilitators of information. Science thus added its own brand of violence to the context of submission, depriving Indigenous peoples—whether "domesticated" or the imprisoned hostiles—of their valuables and their knowledge, thus coercing them into being museum "collaborators."

Reductions and Missions

As disciplinary spaces, the reductions and missions played a crucial role in pacifying the Indians and facilitating their transformation into seasonal workers. Both spaces are usually referred to as suppliers of cheap labor; less common is to consider their role as "centers" for data collection and scientific research. In this sense, continuing the trend to capitalize on the conditions of incarceration, the transfer of anthropologists to the sugar mills and reductions fostered their contact with the concentration of potential ethnographic subjects therein gathered, without exposing themselves to danger and suffering the vicissitudes of fieldwork. Such were the circumstances for Debenedetti's 1909 expedition, the only "ethnographic mission" the museum undertook under Ambrosetti's directorship (Pegoraro 2009, 22). These spaces were also considered privileged sources for the provision of objects for the collections.

Thus the directors of reductions and missions not only could facilitate access to the field but also were useful as "collectors." For this purpose, Ambrosetti capitalized on his personal relationship with Lynch Arribálzaga, then director of the Napalpí reduction, to whom he wrote a letter with a special request.[37] Ambrosetti's thoughtlessness toward incarcerated Indigenous people is dwarfed in comparison to the request he made to his friend for ethnographic objects and Indigenous skeletons. Lynch Arribálzaga, who usually collaborated with a variety of institutions, sending them natural specimens and ethnographic objects, replied:[38]

> I could not but laugh *at your avidity in asking me for my charges' crania and skeletons,* whose lives and welfare are precisely of my greatest concern. Besides, if I became involved in digging up Indians, don't you think my prestige among them would diminish?
>
> But calm down; there is something I can do for that great Museum of Ethnography that I so desire to know and to whose progress I would be very pleased to contribute. Indeed, there are several old Indian burial grounds in these environs that I could get some information about; some are Toba and other Vilelas. Having some funding and availing myself of some trustworthy people [to keep silent] my intervention in the matter, I could make them search to remove from them adult bodies and any other object buried with them.
>
> Additionally, in the Napalpí Reduction and other places where I work with the Indians, I will buy weapons, textiles, and utensils of their use on your account (emphasis added).[39]

Drawing ethical boundaries around his "charges," Lynch Arribálzaga would only accept the task of getting ethnographic objects, delegating the culling of bones to others. What he wrote in his letter seems to document that exhuming human remains and sending them to scientific institutions were problematic for those who headed institutions meant for the custody of Indigenous peoples. Nevertheless, Lynch Arribálzaga apparently did not think this action itself illegitimate but preferred that it be conducted outside the reduction under his aegis, as he proposed these alternatives: "According to the Reduction's administrator—great friend and knowledgeable about the Chaco Indians—*it is not hard to extract skeletal remains of unknown individuals such as those who are his enemies;* he has thus promised me that he will search for them and dig out all he can. Indeed, he points out that there was significant combat with the armies of the famous 'English Cacique'[40] and the Tobas, confirming that the name given to those parts means 'the dead,' in reference to the many resting there" (emphasis added).[41]

The reference to the "English Cacique" helps us place these war casualties in the period between the mid-1870s and 1884, when the cacique was murdered—that is, only twenty-eight years before this letter. Moreover, acting on Ambrosetti's request for mortal remains, Lynch Arribálzaga contacted González Leiva, a forest ranger for the region "that Eduardito heads," [Ambrosetti's brother-in-law and Eduardo Holmberg's son]. In a letter of May 7, 1913, Lynch Arribálzaga reported to Ambrosetti news from González Leiva: "[I]n the killing fields of the Seventh Cavalry on the other side of the Bermejo [River], Indian skeletons have been [found] as well as household utensils left behind. He told me, too, that if Eduardito orders him to travel to those places and he is given means of transportation, he will go and collect them for the museum. Take advantage ASAP, then, of this chance to get an abundance of all you are desiring."[42] On May 20 Eduardito himself wrote a warm letter to Ambrosetti reporting a donation by his wife, Libia de Holmberg, of a "cranium" of Rigoleto found in the interior of the Chaco.[43] Concerning González Leiva's proposal, Lynch Arribálzaga shared with Ambrosetti a year later what had happened:

[T]his past November, he [González Leiva] went in search of the skeletons on the Seventh Cavalry battlefield to discover *the beasts had destroyed them and they took some bones, which is worse, as they lacked skulls because the Indians used, according to him, to bury warriors who died in battle.* But he has recently learned where an Indian who died from a snake bite is buried and adds *that he knows as well where the renowned Cacique called Viejo or Ñato has been buried for the last seven years.* He is willing to search for these skeletons if we get permission from the area's military commander to disinter them and $150 for the costs of mobilization and transportation the excursion entails. "Once with a crew," Mr. González Leiva told me, "I will not return without two [skeletons] at the very least" (emphasis added).[44]

Although going only by the documents in the collections and the 1914–15 *Memoria*, we cannot be certain that this excursion was successful, we can assume that at least some of the human remains sent by González Leiva that were accessioned at the museum may be those referred to in this letter. Concerning Cacique Ñato, there is no entry recording his accession, at least not under that name. It is important to stress that the agents involved or authorized to appropriate the Indigenous mortal remains referred to in archival sources—forest rangers, caretaking staff, administrators, and military personnel—were public functionaries who were sheltered by the state in their operations, an indisputable and direct participant in such practices. Moreover, the references to battle casualties are strong evidence confirming that the search for Indigenous human remains transpired in the same spaces where they had been slaughtered by military forces, now with the explicit goal of sending them to the museum.

Trophy Caciques

What we have been describing brings to light how the collection of objects and human remains destined for the Museum of Ethnography took place. By cross-referencing different sources, we have created a table to recap the actual accession of human remains among the consignments from the Chaco during the period we are concerned with (see table 1), several of which were directly undertaken by military personnel.[45] Drawing on the scant information at hand, we can determine the accessioning of at least fifteen crania and sixteen full skeletons between 1904 and 1916. The lack of uniform classification schema and the multiple ways in which these accessions have been recorded make for informational disparities. Some remains are cataloged merely as "humans," although most are referred to as "Indians," and at times the Indigenous identity is given: Toba, Pilagá, Mocoví, or Chiriguano. Only twice are the remains gendered as female, and individual identity is noted only if it involves a cacique's remains: Cacique Carayá's skull and the skeletons of the Cacique Illirí and his son.[46]

While most of the bodies are anonymous and labeled merely with their data of origin and their donor, seller, or conveyor, the fact that the names of these caciques are included allows us to trace their personal histories. Nevertheless, given the scarcity of information we have found about them so far and the methodological difficulties of working with fragmented information, which calls for further research, we need to reiterate that this essay is but a first step in this journey. In this sense, we are committed to continue documenting the trajectories of the victims of these practices, identifying their nations of origin, and discovering their ties with living descendants for the purpose of recovering the subjectivity of those who have gone unidentified and were objectified in the context of scientific practices.

As concerns Cacique Carayá's skull, data on its accession at the Museum of Ethnography barely exist. It is briefly referred to in the printed 1904–

12 *Memoria* as a donation from the Museum of Beaux Arts, but it goes unmentioned in the related Collections files. Indeed, no human remains of any origin are noted on the list of donated objects. Minnitti Morgan refers to Carayá as a tongue-tied local guide and army collaborator who was taken to Buenos Aires in the 1880s along with Cacique Pichón, where the national government vested them with "a safe-conduct pass protecting them from interference from any Chaco authority" and "$100 in silver coins" (2011, 27). He seems to have returned north after visiting the capital city. There are references noting that he was involved in the ambush and murder of the prominent Cacique Cambá, who, according to a 1908 description by Colonel Ignacio Fotheringam, was "a huge Indian, very dark, of athletic build, and very highly regarded among the Tobas" (Ruiz Moreno 2012, n.p.). Cambá had challenged the troops, and his capture had been entrusted to Captain Rosendo Fraga, who relied on Cacique Carayá and six Indians as "auxiliary Indians." In early December 1884 Fraga, warned by Carayá that they were being observed, finally came upon Cambá and his two hundred Indians. A single shot took down Cacique Cambá, and then "Carayá identified his fallen enemy and before he could be rescued by his own men, a corporal by the name of Luna ran to him, stabbed him repeatedly, cut his head, and impaled it on [Cambá's] own spear" (Ruiz Moreno 2012, n.p.).

We have not managed to gather any more information on Carayá, nor on how his cranium ended up in the National Museum of Beaux Arts, from where it went to the Museum of Ethnography. We wonder, though, whether this consignment came from the military officers he collaborated with. It is possible, then, that the distinction between Indian "collaborator" and "enemy" became irrelevant when it came to submitting Indigenous remains to museums, all being considered chattel for the purpose of "scientific inquiry."

As to Cacique Illirí, we know that his full skeleton and that of his son were sent by Lieutenant Francisco M. Guerrero to be accessioned by the Museum of Ethnography. Correspondence between Guerrero and Ambrosetti, preserved in the Photography and Documentary Archive at the Juan B. Ambrosetti Museum of Ethnography (AFDME), demonstrates that the officer, who sent several Indigenous human remains from the Chaco region (see table 1), was more than willing to collaborate with the project of acquiring ethnographic objects, bones, and crania for the museum, as he expressed his "pride, as an Argentinian, for our ethnographic museum's expeditious prosperity." In reference to the consignment of Illirí's remains, in a letter of October 2, 1913, Guerrero shared with Ambrosetti: "Fulfilling the promise I made when there, I am sending the museum, through Mihanovich Transports, two boxes with the remains of Cacique Illirí and his son who were killed on November 4, 1912, in an ambush. This Cacique was the most renowned in the Collagá Tribe, which is on its way to extinction."[47]

Although information on Illirí's life and death is fragmentary and confusing, referring to "an ambush" leads us to infer that this might have been one that the army engineered. To flesh out these data, we have triangulated several sources, allowing us to recover portions of his biography even if some of its details may be contradictory. Beck (1994, 60) points out that O'Donnell himself convened with Caciques Illirí and Matolí in October 1907, while he was reconnoitering a three-hundred-league area in the Formosa and Chaco territory, and "he persuaded [them] to acquiesce to the colonization project." In 1909 Matolí headed an uprising, which led to a series of attacks on Forts Brown, Warnes, Urquiza, and Arenales (Beck 1994; Tamagno et al. 2015). Some of O'Donnell's meetings with Indigenous groups were captured in photographs taken by Major Pedro Cenóz (see figure 8).

Illirí's death is described in the memoir of Agustín Santiago, who had been a soldier in Formosa's Ninth Cavalry Regiment.[48] O'Donnell had founded this regiment, which was described as being "on the warpath, under severe disciplinary codes, interned in virgin jungles, where the savage Indian's hostile presence would be crushed by military forces for civilizing purposes." (De Marco 2003, 212). In a context of scarcity and multiple dangers, a basic training activity was "to pay attention and bolster [what one learned from] instructing officers about the aboriginal mind—rather known for his continual cowardice, malicious cunning, concealed in the jungle, besieging the missions that constantly circulated among the forts—than for his bravery. Different tribal races: Tobas, Pilagás, Guaraní, Lenguas, Chunupís, and others" (215).

Among other general accounts that the by-then-old Santiago memorialized, he chose to convey the following as a "memorable experience," titling it "The capture of a Cacique 'alive or dead'":

Fig. 8. Colonel Teófilo O'Donnell meeting with Toba caciques. Cenóz (1913, 129).

On orders from the War Ministry, we sought the Cacique known as
Illirí, of the Toba race, who, along with his numerous tribe, ambushed
and killed Captain Solari when he was crossing a mountain trail with
six soldiers. The trail is an opening that the soldiers, using machetes
and axes, hew among the trees for the circulation of mules transporting food and official service goods that [the mules] can only traverse
one after the other. For the Indians, it is of much use, as it allows them
to launch surprise attacks with arrows by concealing themselves in the
foliage and close to the trail.

The Second Squadron, in which I served, achieved the objective of
capturing him alive or dead when we were surrounded by a tribe after
three days on the trail. A skirmish ensuing—the Indians used arrows
as they had no firearms, which left them disadvantaged for action, however brief—the cacique, among others, was killed. *The most harrowing
part of it was transporting the body wrapped up in bags, on the back of a
mule, to Gran Guardia, which was the order. We arrived after two days
on the road, with the Indian's rotten body. He was immediately defleshed,
by boiling, scraping his flesh with a knife, until the bones, now clean, were*

immersed in containers filled with kerosene and lye, so as to send them to Buenos Aires. They might possibly be in some museum. In the vicinity of Santa Fe in the Chaco, there is a town named after Captain Solari. (De Marco 2003, 216–17; emphasis added)

This account coincides with and supplements others that foreground Captain Solari's heroic death in what is known as the Wetlands Surprise of June 1, 1912. These other sources refer to a generic "group of Indians" that allegedly ambushed and killed the captain. For example, López Piacentini (1979) reports that Solari would have arrived from Resistencia to Presidencia Roca in late 1911 as chief of the Seventh Cavalry Regiment's Second Squadron (five hundred strong) and received instruction there to proceed to the Ninth Regiment encampment, headquartered in Formosa, in compliance with Rostagno's order to secure the construction of the Embarcación-Formosa rail line and the February 8, 1912, presidential decree to "populate" the territory. This decree shows that the head of the Ninth Regiment was Colonel Francisco M. Guerrero, founder of the Comandante Fontana settlements and, according to the Museum of Ethnography archives, Illirí's skeleton's donor (see table 1). Solari was sent in late May 1912 to patrol the string of forts on the Bermejo River, setting out from Fort Lapachito in the Elisa Colony with Sergeant Domingo Arce and fifteen to twenty recently recruited men. The first account of what transpired, presented by López Piacentini, maintains that the encounter with the Indians ensued right at the beginning of their trek toward Formosa:

After a brief march . . . the soldiers of the Seventh's Third Squadron made out an Indian encampment between the slope and the marsh.

Captain Solari scanned the Indian encampment through his spyglass and comments that it was empty. However, a sergeant, Arce, warns that a surprise attack must be foreclosed, insisting that they draw their firearms.

When the column advanced toward the encampment, there came a dense firearm volley from a nearby slope, following a first shot from a rifle, which would definitely be the one that caused Captain Solari's death. Sergeant Arce, also wounded, nevertheless ran to his commanding officer's aid. Once dismounted, he shelters behind Solari's horse, which was also dead, and uses his commanding officer's pistol to resist the Indians. But Arce, wounded, can only retreat, but was unable to take his officer's body. (Cúndom 1962, quoted in López Piacentini 1979, 91–93)

According to the second version, once the attack ensued, since Arce was wounded and Solari dead, one of the soldiers took over the squadron and ordered its retreat, leaving behind its captain, whom the Indians allegedly were already undressing to take his clothes. By order of the regimental head, Colonel Mariano Aráoz de Lamadrid, a troop was organized and placed under Lieutenant José María Ruda's command to return for the captain's body along with a forty-man squad, in view of the situation's dangerousness as described in the previous account. Solari's body was found a day later, partially submerged in the marshland waters, naked and decomposed. It was transported to Presidencia Roca, where the captain was waked with an honor guard. His remains were later sent to Puerto Bermejo and shipped to Corrientes, where they remain to this day (López Piacentini 1979).

Six months later, in October 1912, a commission from the Seventh Regiment on its way to Formosa found an Indian wearing the captain's jacket. When Sergeant Félix Benítez questioned him on the garment's source, he was fatally felled by a bullet. A new squad, fifty men strong, was sent out of Presidencia Roca under Mayor Marcos Hermelo's charge to search for the Indians, of whom many were murdered and a number of others imprisoned. According to Cúndom, "The punishment inflicted on the Indians, Solari's presumptive assassins, can only be likened to a horrible massacre. Mayor Hermelo himself—in valiant battle—killed Cacique Coyaiquí with a single sword thrust to the heart and his soldiers split the barbarians' skulls like ripe squash, writing in the deep red of their own blood the last chapter of their everlasting misfortunes" (Cúndom 1962, quoted in López Piacentini 1979, 96).

The reference to Cacique Coyaiquí in this version raises a series of questions that compound the absence of proper names in the preceding narratives. Moreover, the date indicated in Santiago's memoir—which appears to be the most precise account of Illirí's murder vis-à-vis Solari's death and accords with the fate of his remains—does not match the date Guerrero gave for the cacique's death (1912), although the recruit, by his own report, joined the troops in early 1913. These contradictions compel us to point out that the information on the cacique and other Indigenous leaders in the region is scarce, incomplete, or unreliable, which creates methodological issues. Our inquiry therefore continues to strive to dispel the doubts thus raised.

One last document is crucial for our purposes: a photograph of Cacique Illirí (figure 9) printed in Pedro Cenóz's memoir, titled *The Gran Chaco*. Given the fragmentary nature of the archival data, this discovery represents a significant advance for our project of uncovering the cacique's persona, since he—as were others—was dehumanized when transformed into an object of anthropological inquiry. The photographic image facilitates a direct reencounter with the cacique, silenced first by firearms and then by science. His account acquires corporeality, his name gains a link to a concrete visual, and the person emerges. Illirí, whose remains, we believe, are still resting among the Museum of Ethnography holdings, reveals himself to us through his own facial features.

FINAL CONSIDERATIONS

We have examined how Ambrosetti's prominent role in the systematization, methodologizing, and professionalization of the discipline of anthropology in Argentina (Cáceres Freyre 1967) shielded him, at least partially, from critical challenges regarding his professional practice. In this sense, certain strategies for acquiring holdings to establish and expand the Museum of Ethnography's collections merit review and contextualization vis-à-vis similar ones applied by actors and institutions that have already been subjected to greater critique.

The sources we have drawn from confirm that under Ambrosetti's directorship, human remains of contemporary Indigenous inhabitants of territories that had recently been annexed into the nation through the use of military force were accessioned at the Museum of Ethnography. The connections the director forged with such institutions as the National Territories Directorate attest to the ways in which requests were facilitated and legitimated by state decree. But it is particularly the accession of human remains from the Gran Chaco at the exact moment when its Indigenous peoples were being decimated that raises issues about the relationship, fostered by Ambrosetti himself, between this academic museum and the national army. Meticulous archival work and the cross-referencing of

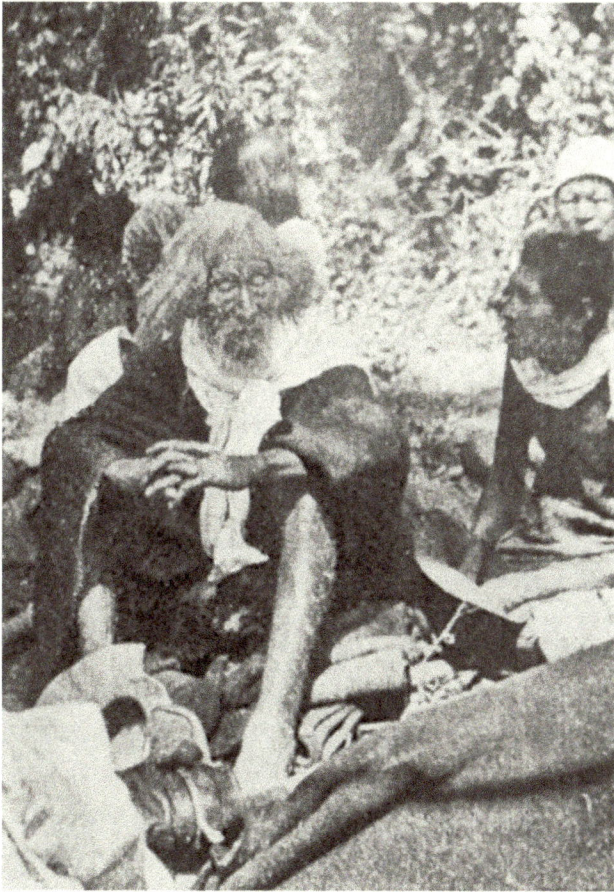

Fig. 9. Toba cacique Illirí. Cenóz (1913, 109).

archival documents of various origins allowed us to confirm the accession of at least fifteen skulls and sixteen full skeletons whose provenience lay in this region, not accounting for those that came from other regions, such as Patagonia.

The cases of Carayá and Illirí are evidence that some of the Chaco's Indigenous chiefs, slain during military campaigns, were incorporated into the Museum of Ethnography's collections, much as had been the case at the Museum of La Plata with the remains of caciques from Pampa and Patagonia, along with some of their kin. Examples from La Plata are Cacique Inacayal; his wife, Margarita Foyel (the daughter of Cacique Foyel); and Panguitruz Güor. Notably, at the Museum of Ethnography, human remains were kept from the public eye, unseen by anyone not engaged in research.

We do not think it mere happenstance that only the mortal remains of the two Chaco caciques were precisely identified on consignment by members of the army. It seems to have been a gesture expressing the triumph of "civilization over barbarism," a demonstration that those lands, formerly considered untamed, had finally been domesticated.

Moreover, on the basis of the cases we have addressed, we conclude that the acquisition practices of Indigenous remains—promoted by anthropology museums, deployed through institutional channels, and fulfilled through military interventions—were not exclusive to a particular museum or anthropological institution but common to all of them. These practices were not confined to the Museum of La Plata, whose cases have gained greater notoriety, particularly in recent years. We consider, then, that the examination of specific situations will contribute to a deeper and more thorough reading of anthropological practices, as well as of the complex relationship between science and the nation state's repressive apparatus at the beginning of the twentieth century in a context of extreme violence against Indigenous peoples. Finally, we hope that the factual documentation of specific and hitherto less-known cases will contribute to the continual progress in the recovery of the individual histories of those who lost their humanity when accessioned as objects of inquiry into anthropological museums and institutions. Ultimately, this will open up the possibility that those remains that are identified will be returned to their place of origin if their descendants determine they should be.

Table 1. Ethnographic objects and human remains from the Gran Chaco region accessioned at the Museum of Ethnography[49]

Year entered	Original cataloging	Origin	Description	Sender	Source
1906	314 to 319	Pilcomayo, Chaco	2 arrow sets 2 battle breastplates 2 plant fiber bags	Juan Manuel Ezcurra	AFDME: Memoria 1906–12; AHFFyL: b. B5–10, d. 9

1906	Unspecified	Chaco	1 Toba pottery jug collected from an abandoned Indian encampment	Guillermo Navarro	AHFFyL: b. B5–10, d. 13
1907	2447	Fort Tostado, Santa Fe Chaco	**1 Mocoví Indian skull** 2 ethnographic objects (lead-filled mate bowl and lead boleadora mold)	Dr. Teófilo Weschler	AFDME: *Memoria* 1906–12; AHFFyL: b. B5–10, d. 60
1909	6612 to 6615	Ledesma, Jujuy	**4 Chiriguan Indian skeletons from the Bolivian Chaco**	Dr. Juan Paglia	AFDME: Collections dossier #19 J; Paglia and *Memoria* 1906–12; AGFFyL: b. B5–10, d. 71
1909	6858 to 6885	Southern Chaco	2 wooden maces, 1 jug, 1 leather bag, 7 plant fiber cuffs 4 wool headbands, 1 ornament and 3 bead necklaces, 2 bows, 4 arrows and 1 to hunt birds	Mayor Pedro Cenóz	AFDME: *Memoria* 1906–12 and Collections documents 3; AGFFyL: b. B5–10, d. 72
1909	6919/6920	Resistencia, Chaco	**1 Toba skull** and a few arrows, and a Toba bow and arrows set	Tte. Colonel Francisco M. Guerrero	AFDME: Collections dossier #18 F, Guerrero; *Memoria* 1906–12 Collections documents 3; AGFFyL: b. B5–10, d. 77

Year entered	Original cataloging	Origin	Description	Sender	Source
1909	Unspecified	Juja Chaco, between San Pedro de Jujuy and Calilegua, Ledesma Sugar Mill	348 Chiriguan, Mataco, Chulupí, and Chorote Indian ethnographic objects, among them bows, arrows, farming tools, cuffs, pipes, battle whistles, and headbands	FFYL: Debenedetti Expedition	AGFFYL: b. B5–10, d. 64–65
1909	Unspecified	Bolivian Chaco and Bolivia	Over 230 archaeological and ethnographic objects	Purchased from Eduardo Holmberg [Jr.]	AFDME: Collections dossier 46, E. Holmberg [Jr.]
1911	8473	Paraguay Highland	1 Guato bow and 6 arrows	Juan Roth	AGFFYL: b. B5–10, d. 93
1911	8881	Chaco	**Toba skull (Cacique Carayá)***	National Museum of Beaux Arts, authorized by the Ministry of Education	AFDME: *Memoria* 1906–1912
1911	9597	Chaco	1 Mataco bow and set of 8 arrows	Engineer Livio Castilla	AFDME: *Memoria* 1906–12; AGFFYL: b. B5–10, d. 100
1911	10719 to 10721	Chaco	2 Toba wood maces, 1 farming tool, and 1 bow	Alberto Escalada	AFDME: *Memoria* 1906–12
1911	10643 to 10681	Paraguay	Ethnological collection of 38 Guayaquí and Kainguá items from Paraguay	Luis Patri	AGFFYL: b. B5–10, d. 105

1911	10805 to 10823	Upper Paraná	Collection of 19 Guayakí items	Berta Wernicke	AGFFyL: b. B5–10, d. 109
?	11258 to 11260	Chaco	1 Toba woven girdle and 2 Mataco items	Miss Victoria Aguirre	AFDME: *Memoria* 1906–12
1911	Unspecified	Upper Paraná Chaco Paraguayo	22 Guayaquí items, among them 1 stone axe with a wooden handle	Federico Mayntzhusen	AGFFyL: b. B5–10, d. 95
1911	Unspecified	Paraguay River	53 Chamacoco items	Alberto V. Fric	AGFFyL: b. B5–10, d. 94
1912?	12698	Formosa, item found on the Pilcomayo River right bank, in the area known as Puerto del Dorado, three leagues from Fort Yunká	1 stone axe	Tte. Colonel Francisco M. Guerrero	AFDME: Collections dossier 18, F. Guerrero, and Collections documents 3
1912	12700 to 12713	Chaco	14 Pilagá personal use items	Captain Alberto Benavídez	AGFFyL: b. B5–11, d. 4
1912?	12700/713	Chaco and Formosa	Bows and arrows	Lt. Colonel Francisco Guerrero	AFDME: Collections documents 3
1913	13.339 to 13.400	Chaco	1 Toba poncho, 1 small stone file, and 1 box of Indian objects per the attached list (not found in the dossier)	Enrique Lynch Arribálzaga Mission	AFDME: Collections dossier 60, Lynch Arribálzaga

Year entered	Original cataloging	Origin	Description	Sender	Source
1913	13.778 to 13.818	Chaco	**1 Toba female "tiny" skeleton and Pilagá items**	Lt. Colonel Francisco M. Guerrero	AFDME: Collections dossier 18, F. Guerrero, and Collections documents 3
1913	14.442	Chaco	**1 Indian skull**	Libia E. de Holmberg	AFDME: Collections dossier 52, Libia de Holmberg, and Collections documents 3
1913	15.421 to 15.475	Chaco	1 Toba shovel, bow and arrows	Enrique Lynch Arribálzaga Mission	AFDME: Collections dossier 60, L. Arribálzaga Mission
1913	15.482 to 15.483	Southern Chaco, "Langostal" area (sent along with another deposit from Chubut)	**1 human skull**	Prof. Juan A. Domínguez	AFDME: Collections dossier 3
1913	Unspecified	Chaco and Neuquén	17 unidentified items	Jorge González Larrosa	AFDME: *Memoria* 1913–14
1914	16136 to 16137	Formosa	**Cacique Illirí's skeleton and that of his son**	Lt. Colonel Francisco M. Guerrero	AFDME: Collections dossier, F. Guerrero; Collections documents 3, and *Memoria* 1913–14; AGFFYL: b. B5–11, d. 7

1914	16696/ 17016	Chaco	Toba ethnographic objects	Enrique Lynch Arribálzaga Mission	AFDME: Collections documents 3
1915	20744/45		2 Toba items		
1914	17.053	Chaco	**1 human skull**	Carlos Brackebusch	AFDME: Collections documents 3 and *Memoria* 1914–15
1914	17219	Napalpí, Chaco	**1 Toba human skull**	Hipólito Poyssegur	AFDME: *Memoria* 1914–15
1914	17718 to 17719	Formosa	**Toba human skeletons**	Luis González Leyva Mission	AFDME: Collections documents 3 and *Memoria* 1914–15
1914	19063 to 19069	Chaco Austral	Toba items and **Toba woman human skeleton**		
1915	19971	Rio de Oro, Chaco	**Toba human skeleton**		
1914	Unspecified	Chaco	Unidentified	Alberto Escalada	AFDME: *Memoria* 1914–15
—	Unspecified	Chaco, Jujuy, and Paraguay	Unidentified	Salvador Debenedetti	AFDME: *Memoria* 1916
1915	Unspecified	Resistencia	Toba shovel, bows and arrows crafted by a Toba elder	Lynch Arribálzaga Mission	AFDME: Collections dossier 60, L. Arribálzaga Mission
1915	Unspecified	Chaco	Unidentified	Alfonso Najera	AFDME: *Memoria* 1916
1915	Unspecified	Argentinian and Bolivian Chaco	Unidentified	Cristobal Hicken	AFDME: *Memoria* 1916

Year entered	Original cataloging	Origin	Description	Sender	Source
1915	Unspecified	Chaco	Unidentified	Isaac Fernández Blanco	AFDME: *Memoria* 1916
1915	Unspecified	Chaco	Unidentified	Sergei Geiman Mission	AFDME: *Memoria* 1916
1915	Unspecified	Salto Chaco	**1 Pilagá skeleton Esqueleto de indio** from those who practice the funerary rite of placing their dead on treetops **8 Mataco and Chiriguano crania**	Juan Ascher Mission	AFDME: *Memoria* 1916; AGFFYL: b. B5–11, d. 24
1916	Unspecified	Chaco	**3 Toba skeletons**	Ulpiano Cáceres	AFDME: *Memoria* 1916; AGFFYL: b. B5–11, d. 23

Note: Created by Sandra Tolosa and Lena Dávila.

*The institutional reference to Carayá's skull, dated April 15, 1911, is from the 1904–11 *Memoria*. The skull's accession is not noted in the 1911 report, although the donation's transmission document refers to Calchaquí items and about one hundred other unspecified objects as part of a lot received on April 21, 1911, from the Museum of Beaux Arts. However, the cataloging number notes 1911 as the accession year.

TRANSLATION BY
VILMA SANTIAGO-IRIZARRY

NOTES
Argentinian general, politician, and journalist Lucio Victorio Mansilla sent his musings over Jorge Luis Fontana's drawing of a Toba warrior to president Nicolás Avellaneda (1874–80):

> The attached drawing represents the head of a dead warrior of the Toba Nation, copied from nature, moments before it was hewn from the body that sustained it, while its flesh still throbbed and my ears rang with the brave

and resounding voice that prevailed over the roar of arms and the hot-bloodedness of battle, emboldening the Indians' spirit. I had forgotten to tell you that I defleshed this head, and the cranium was showcased at the most recent Scientific Society Exposition, and is today at my friend, Francisco de Paula Moreno's Museum of Anthropology. (Fontana to Mansilla Villa Occidental, September 30, 1878, in Mansilla 1995, 198)

1. On the founding of the Museum of La Plata, see Farro (2009); on the Museum of Ethnography, see Pegoraro (2009).

2. Throughout this chapter, we use the term "mortal remains" per Law 25517 (2001), enacted by Decree 1022 (2004). Article 1 of the law establishes that "the mortal remains of aboriginal persons, whatever their ethnicity, collected in museums and/or public or private collections will be made available to those indigenous nations and/or communities to which they belong [and] that are claiming them." We also use the variant "human remains." Honorable Congress of the Argentine Nation, "Indigenous Communities," December 20, 2001.

3. Ambrosetti made his first trip to the Chaco–Santa Fe region when he participated in a military expedition under A. Romero, captain of a marine infantry battalion. They assembled in natural historian and writer Eduardo L. Holmberg's home, where renowned contemporaries often met, among them naturalist Enrique Lynch Arribálzaga, whom we refer to later in this essay. Several years later, Ambrosetti made multiple visits to Misiones, by then with the goal of collecting information about these territories. His second trip was under the aegis of the Museum of La Plata's director, Francisco P. Moreno, as a naturalist affiliated with the Northeastern Scientific Expedition (Ambrosetti 2008; Chébez and Gasparri 2008; Arias and Dávila 2014).

4. Some of these submissions are part of the Toba Collection, subject of a joint cataloging project between museum adjuncts and a Qom community in Derqui, a province of Buenos Aires. The catalog was issued in a CD that was distributed among affiliated associations, organizations, and institutions (Pegoraro and Elías 2010).

5. The Gran Chaco encompasses the south-central region of Brazil, western Paraguay, western Bolivia, and Argentina's north-central region. We here focus on the Argentinian sector.

6. Translator's note: In its original sense of "nurturing mother."

7. Translator's note: *Argentine Archaeology: Bronze in the Calchaquí Region* (1904) was among Ambrosetti's most influential publications. The Cal-

chaquí, now extinct, were renowned for their resistance to European colonialism. This characterization is meant to convey a conservative approach to the project.

8. *Memoria* submitted by Ambrosetti to Rodolfo Rivarola, dean of the College of Philosophy and Letters, Buenos Aires, April 1, 1915, AFDME: Ambrosetti Files.

9. With the college's authorization, per a note submitted by Ambrosetti to José N. Matienzo, dean of the College of Philosophy and Letters, Buenos Aires, December 7, 1907, AGFFyL: b. B5–10, d. 35.

10. Letter from Ambrosetti to Isidoro Ruiz Moreno, Buenos Aires, July 22, 1915, AGN: Isidoro Ruiz Moreno Files, d. 5, f. 2.

11. Reply from the Misiones Governance, Misiones, September 28, 1915, AFDME: Ambrosetti Files, National Territories Dossier, f. 1, 401.

12. Most of the responses in the Museum of Ethnography archives are from the Misiones Territory, which Ambrosetti had visited even before he became the museum's director. For a more thorough examination of this matter, see Ambrosetti (2005, 2008).

13. The evident "irregularity" in a file from the National Territories Directorate being in Ambrosetti's private papers in the museum's archives demonstrates as well how personal links overrode orderly institutional practices.

14. Response from the Apóstoles commissar to the Misiones government in reference to Official Notice #555, August 30, 1915, AFDME: Ambrosetti Folder, file labeled "Initiatives in the National Territories for the Purpose of Augmenting the Collections," f. 9.

15. Response from the Santa Ana commissar to the Misiones government, in reference to Official Notice #555, Misiones, August 26, 1915, AFDME: file labeled "Initiatives in the National Territories for the Purpose of Augmenting the Collections," f. 7.

16. Response from the Corpus commissar to the Misiones government, in reference to Official Notice #555, Misiones, August 30, 1915, AFDME: Ambrosetti Folder, file labeled "Initiatives in the National Territories for the Purpose of Augmenting the Collections," f. 13.

17. As in the case of Corpus, as described by the commissar, happens with the previous quotation or in that of the Azara commissar, Clementino Esquivel Misiones was considered a territory without Indigenous peoples. This correlates with official discourses claiming that once national borders were redrawn after the War of the Triple Alliance, the Indigenous peoples in this territory ended up in Paraguay and thus were not included in Argentina's population counts (Segundo Censo de la República Argentina, 1895).

18. Engineer Francisco Fouilliard's reflections on how to find what the museum was requesting and where to find it, attached to the response of Soriano Romero to the National Territories Directorate regarding Official Notice #82, Posadas, August 10, 1915, AFDME: Ambrosetti Folder, file labeled "Initiatives in the National Territories for the Purpose of Augmenting the Collections," f. 2–3.

19. Letter from Ambrosetti to Jorge Larrosa, Buenos Aires, June 3, 1913, AFDME: Ambrosetti Folder.

20. Note from Julio A. Roca to Ambrosetti, August 6, 1914, AFDME: Ambrosetti Folder.

21. The 1908 *Memoria* documents that the collection of two hundred crania was being organized and allocated "to lay the foundation and install the Anthropology Section, which currently has adequate space with seven cabinets with glass cases and drawers, and two glass-topped tables." AGFFyL: Ambrosetti to José N. Matienzo, Buenos Aires, April 10, 1908, b.B5–10, d.41.

22. To this end, Ambrosetti sought permission from the dean to allow Dr. Robert Lehmann-Nitsche to study the "human skull fossil from Arrecifes, Buenos Aires Province," acquired by the college and cataloged as Number 1953. The analysis could be "published in the publication series in anthropology the college has already launched." AGFFyL: Ambrosetti to Jorge N. Matienzo, Buenos Aires, December 10, 1906, b.B5–10, d.37. The following year, the anthropological material had "expanded with the addition of eleven mounted human skeletons." Once more, their antiquity was not noted. AGFFyL: Ambrosetti to José N. Matienzo, Buenos Aires, April 14, 1909, b. B5–10, d. 48.

23. A year's acquisitions listing noted "a human adult skeleton and another of a seven-month-old fetus for the anthropology course." AGFFyL: Ambrosetti to José N. Matienzo, Buenos Aires, April 14, 1909, b. B5–10, d. 48. Another example was the donation of "a gorgeous cranium of a microcephalic female." AGFFyL: Dr. Alejandro Korn, b. B5–12, d. 68.

24. AGFFyL: Ambrosetti to the dean of the College of Philosophy and Letters, Buenos Aires, September 24, 1907, b. B5–10, d. 29.

25. Translator's note: In Spanish, a *reducción*, the term for Indian communities originally established by the church under Spanish colonialism to facilitate religious conversion and colonization. The reductions involved the relocation of Indigenous communities into highly regimented settlements where they were "taught" basic farming techniques, trained for menial labor, and expected to work in farming and industrial colonial enterprises.

Some of them were headed by local caciques. In Argentina, however, the reductions were established by the state and were thus civil institutions, distinct from the church's missions.

26. Enrique Lynch Arribálzaga was born on August 26, 1856, in Buenos Aires, Argentina, and died on June 28, 1935. Along with Eduardo L. Holmberg, he founded the journal *The Argentinian Naturalist* (1878), the first of its kind in the country. In 1881 he traveled for the first time to the national territories, in an expedition headed by Jorge Luis Fontana. He was appointed underminister for agriculture in 1887 and later became ministry delegate to the Indian reduction. Years later he settled permanently in the Chaco, and in 1911 he became Napalpí's director, a position he occupied until 1916 (Lynch Arribálzaga 1924; Viyerio 1999).

27. For an expanded account on the policies on Indian reductions in Argentina, see Musante (2013).

28. For anthropologists, the reductions, religious missions, and sugar mills represented the possibility to observe and study individuals from a variety of societies without having to travel from one place to another, given the large concentration of members from diverse Indigenous groups in a single space.

29. AGFFyL: Ambrosetti to José N. Matienzo, Aires, November 2, 1907, b. B5–10, d. 31.

30. Also mentioned is Captain Alberto Benavídez, who donated several objects, although we do not yet have enough information to detail how the link was established with him in particular.

31. It is very important to point out that the list attached to the note to the dean—and which was transcribed in Pegoraro, 2009—found in the AGF-FyL is not an original document, but a photocopy of a manuscript, which it is not possible to confirm if it was originally written by Ambrosetti, since it does not match the typed letter. On the other hand, the existence of an earlier correspondence (Letter from Pedro Cenóz to Ambrosetti, Formosa, June 27, 1909. AFDME, Fondo de gestión institucional académico-administrativa, Serie historia de las colecciones, Legajo de colecciones Nº 17, Cenóz.) allows inferring that, after the communication from the dean's office, Ambrosetti would have maintained a personal correspondence with Cenóz.

32. Pedro Cenóz to Ambrosetti, Formosa, October 29, 1909, AFDME: Academic-Administrative Collection, History of the Collections Series, f. 17, Cenóz.

33. AGFFyL: Ambrosetti to José N. Matienzo, Buenos Aires, November 6, 1909, b. B5–10, d. 72.

34. AGFFYL: Ambrosetti to José N. Matienzo, Buenos Aires, December 29, 1909, b. 5–10, d. 77.
35. Pedro Cenóz to Ambrosetti, Formosa, June 27, 1909, AFDME: Academic-Administrative Collection, History of the Collections Series, f. 17, Cenóz.
36. AGFFYL: Ambrosetti to José N. Matienzo, Buenos Aires, November 2, 1907, b. B5–10, d. 31.
37. According to Chébez and Gasparri (2008), when he was only 13 years old Ambrosetti was introduced to Enrique Lynch Arribálzaga, at Eduardo Holmberg's house. The fact that the personal bond between the two had existed for so many years, that this enabled a communication without too many objections, which could explain the "directness" of the request.
38. In 1908 Lynch sold to the National Museum of Buenos Aires a collection of 13 objects of the Toba Indians that were listed in the catalog with their indigenous name (Pegoraro 2008).
39. Lynch Arribálzaga to Ambrosetti, Resistencia, December 7, 1912, AFDME: Ambrosetti File.
40. The "English Cacique" refers to Cacique Salarnek-alou, Juan el Raí (phonetic rendition of Juan el rey), called "English" for his light complexion and physique. He was a great cacique who commanded a vast amount of resources, minor caciques, and warriors. His power was already being acknowledged by 1879 by Colonel Napoleón Uriburu. Along with Cacique Cambá, he laid siege to the city of Resistencia, whose attack was prevented by Colonel Manuel Obligado's withdrawal from the city in 1879. Around 1883 the Chaco governor, Francisco Bosch, initiated a new campaign against the Cacique, with high losses of Toba warriors in their encounter at Napalpí. In 1884 Minister General Benjamín Victorica mobilized three regiments of cavalry, two of infantry, and three warships in an attack that dispersed the main Indian forces, slaughtering major caciques and imprisoning warriors. Along with three of his sons, the cacique was killed in an encounter with the Twelfth Cavalry under Colonel Obligado on June 17, initiating a cycle known as "the end of the great Cacicazgos." The cacique had previously tried to lay down arms but was late:

> Three of the English Cacique's envoys emerged from the tents before said Cacique was attacked and he ordered them to submit to the government's orders and asked where he should convene with his people. I have explained to them what has happened, which was not what the government desired, and I will be sending them to bring that tribe to Resistencia. Through these self-same envoys, I know that José Petiso is

on the Campos del Cielo trails, to our extreme left, and they have vol-
unteered to go there to try to subdue him. I have also tasked them with
that and given them till next August for their surrender. Petiso's tribe
is the only remaining one among the Mocovíes that could threaten the
settlements and this is why I am so set on subduing it since the Tobas
have become so hostile that they are now on Bermejo's side. (Obligado
to army and navy minister, telegram, Reconquista, July 29, 1884, in Minnitti Morgan 2011, 42)

41. Lynch Arribálzaga to Ambrosetti, City, December 22, 1912, AFDME:
Academic-Administrative Collection, History of the Collections Series, f.
60, Lynch Arribálzaga Mission.

42. Lynch Arribálzaga to Ambrosetti, Resistencia, May 7, 1913, AFDME:
Academic-Administrative Collection, History of the Collections Series, f.
60, Lynch Arribálzaga Mission.

43. Eduardito Holmberg to Ambrosetti, City, May 20, 1913, AFDME:
Academic-Administrative Collection, History of the Collections Series, f.
52, Libia de Holmberg.

44. Lynch Arribálzaga to Ambrosetti, Resistencia, May 9, 1914, AFDME:
Academic-Administrative Collection, History of the Collections Series, f.
60, Lynch Arribálzaga Mission

45. In addition to the crania and bones from the Chaco territory that we
have described, the *Memorias* detail the accession of crania from a variety
of territorial regions (e.g., Buenos Aires, Chubut, Santa Fe, Rio Negro,
Tierra del Fuego) but without the data that would establish whether they
involved old or contemporary remains.

46. In references we have examined, one specifies a "daughter," while the rest
note a "son." It was likely just a slip, so we have chosen to correct it.

47. Francisco M. Guerrero to Ambrosetti, location unspecified, October 2,
1913, AFDME: Academic-Administrative Collection, History of the Collections Series, f. 18, Guerrero.

48. Agustín Santiago, born in Casilda in 1892, wrote one of the scarce firsthand accounts produced by a soldier who participated in the campaigns,
doing so at his grandson Marcelo's behest. He documented details on
the Gran Guardia recruitment and the organizing of Forts Yunká, Pilcomayo, Lagadik, Kilómetro 500, Las Lomitas, and Pozo del Tigre and the
outposts of Guaruruú, Las Saladas, Manzanitas, Palo Blanco, Paso de las
Tobas, and Fortune, where there were twenty or thirty armed recruits and

one mule per person. The soldiers would practice marksmanship and train their mules into docility (De Marco 2003).

49. We have compiled only what we have been able to cross-check with cited sources, which implies that there might be gaps in the data. With some donors or interlocutors referred to in the *Memorias* of 1914–16—such as Jorge González Larrosa, Alberto Escalada, Salvador Debenedetti, Alfonso Najera, Cristobal Hicken, Isaac Fernández Blanco, Mrs. E. M. de Saint-Germain, and the Dergei Geiman Mission—we have not been able to identify the specifics of the donation. Although this chapter focuses solely on the Argentinian Chaco, the table includes Gran Chaco donations from Paraguay and Bolivia. We have not included entries on human remains from other Argentinian regions or those whose origin we cannot establish. By thus clarifying the data, we can document that larger numbers of crania and skeletons were accessioned at the museum in the time period we analyze than is here noted.

REFERENCES

Manuscripts and Archives

AFDME: Archivo Fotográfico y Documental del Museo Etnográfico Juan B. Ambrosetti (Photography and Documentary Archive at the Juan B. Ambrosetti Museum of Ethnography)

AGFFyL: Archivo General de la Facultad de Filosofía y Letras (College of Philosophy and Letters Archive)

AGN: Archivo General de la Nación (National Archive)

Published Works

Ambrosetti, Juan Bautista. 2005. *Viaje de un maturrango y otros relatos folklóricos.* Buenos Aires: Taurus.

———. 2008. *Primer y segundo viaje a misiones.* Buenos Aires: Editorial Albatros.

Arenas, Patricia. 1989. "La antropología en la Argentina de fines del Siglo XIX y principios del XX." *Runa* 2:89–104.

Arenas, Patricia, and Jorge Pinedo. 2005. "Damiana vuelve a los suyos." *Página 12,* November 20.

Arias, Ana, and Lena Dávila da Rosa. 2014. "Prácticas de viaje y autoridad científica. Una comparación de experiencias de D'Orbigny, Ambrosetti y Lehmann-Nitsche." *Revista de Ciencias Sociales.* Bernal, Argentina: Universidad Nacional de Quilmes.

Badenes, Daniel. 2006. "Restos humanos en el Museo de Ciencias Naturales de La Plata. Trofeos de Guerra." *La Pulseada* 43 (September).

Beck, Henry. 1994. "Relaciones entre blancos e indios en los territorios nacionales de Chaco y Formosa. 1885–1950." *Cuadernos de Geohistoria Regional* 29:7–209.

Brunatti, Olga, Maria Colángelo, and Germán Soprano. 2002. "Observar para legislar." In *Historias y estilos de trabajo de campo en Argentina,* edited by Sergio Visacovsky and Rosana Guber, 79–123. Rosario, Argentina: Editorial Antropofagía.

Cáceres Freyre, Julián. 1967. *Juan Bautista Ambrosetti.* Buenos Aires: Ediciones Culturales Argentinas.

Cenóz, Pedro. 1913. *El Chaco Argentino.* Buenos Aires: Talleres de la Casa Jacobo Peuser.

Chébez, Juan Carlos, and Bárbara Gasparri. 2008. "Presentación de primer y segundo viaje a Misiones por Juan Bautista Ambrosetti." In *Primer y segundo Viaje a Misiones,* edited by Juan Ambrosetti, 12–14. Buenos Aires: Editorial Albatros.

Colectivo Guías. 2008. *Identificación y restitución: "Colecciones" de restos humanos en el Museo de La Plata.* La Plata, Argentina: Huellas.

Cúndom, F. P. 1962. "La tragedia del Capitán Solari. Una breve version." In *Historia de la Provincia del Chaco,* edited by C. P. López Piacentini, 94–97. Chaco, Argentina: Editorial Región.

Curtoni, Rafael, and Maria Chaparro. 2011. "Políticas de reparación: Reclamación y reentierro de restos indígenas. El caso de Gregorio Yancamil." *Corpus* 1 (1). https://doi.org/10.4000/corpusarchivos.931.

De Marco, Miguel. 2003. "Apuntes de un ex soldado conscripto durante la Campaóa del Chaco." *Temas de historia argentina y americana* 2:211–20.

Farro, Maximo. 2009. *La formación del Museo de La Plata. Coleccionistas, comerciantes, estudiosos y naturalistas viajeros a fines del Siglo XIX.* Rosario, Argentina: Prohistoria Ediciones.

Foucault, Michel. 1975. *Vigilar y castigar. El Nacimiento de La Prisión.* Translated by Aurelio Garzon del Camino. México: Siglo XXI editores.

González Stephan, Beatriz. 1999. "Cuerpos de La Nación: Cartografías Disciplinarias." *Anales* 2:71–106.

Gordillo, Gastón. 1995. "La subordinación y sus mediaciones: Dinámica cazadora-recolectora, relaciones de producción, capital comercial y estado entre los tobas del Oeste de Formosa." In *Producción doméstica y capital: Estudios desde la Antropología Económica,* edited by Héctor Trinchero, 105–38. Buenos Aires: Biblos.

Gustavsson, Anne. 2008. "Documentation, Research, Conservation, Restitution and Exhibition of Human Remains Collection at University Museums in Argentina. The Case of the Museo Etnográfico Juan B. Ambrosetti in Buenos Aires." Master's thesis, Gottenburg University.

———. 2011. "Estrategias del Museo Etnográfico J. B. Ambrosetti frente a la restitución de restos humanos." *Corpus* 1 (1). https://doi.org/10.4000 /corpusarchivos.950.

Iñigo Carreras, Nicolas. 1984. *Indígenas y fronteras. Campaóas militares y clase obrera. Chaco, 1870–1930.* Buenos Aires: Centro Editor de América Latina.

López Piacentini, Carlos Primo. 1979. "La Conquista del desierto verde." In *Historia de la Provincia del Chaco*, 1–142. Chaco, Argentina: Editorial Región.

Lynch Arribálzaga, Enrique. 1924. "Materiales para una bibliografía de Chaco y Formosa." Resistencia, Argentina: Establecimiento Tipográfico Juan Moro.

Mansilla, Lucio. 1995. *Esa cabeza toba. Horror al vacío y otras charlas.* Buenos Aires: Editorial Biblos.

Minnitti Morgan, Edgardo. 2011. *El cacique Inglés.* Córdoba, Argentina: Ediciones Eta Carinae.

Musante, Marcelo. 2013. "Las reducciones estatales indígenas. ¿Espacios concentracionarios o avance del proyecto civilizatorio?" *Jornadas Santiago Wallace de Investigación en Antropología Social.* Facultad de Filosofía y Letras, Universidad de Buenos Aires. https://www.aacademica.org/000-063/359.

Pegoraro, Andrea. 2005. "Instrucciones y colecciones en viaje. Redes de recolección entre el Museo Etnográfico y los Territorios Nacionales." *Anuario de Estudios en Antropología Social* 5:49–64.

———. 2009. "Las colecciones del Museo Etnográfico de la Universidad de Buenos Aires: un episodio de la historia del americanismo en la Argentina 1890–1927." PhD diss., Facultad de Filosofía y Letras, Universidad de Buenos Aires.

Pegoraro, Andrea, and Mariana Elías. 2010. "Documentación de colecciones etnográficas: Los desafíos de los tiempos actuales. El caso de las colecciones etnográficas del Museo Etnográfico Juan B. Ambrosetti de la Universidad de Buenos Aires." 1° Congreso Nacional de Museos Universitarios, Universidad de La Plata, Argentina, October 20–22. http://sedici.unlp .edu.ar/bitstream/handle/10915/41723/%20documento_completo.pdf ?sequence=1.

Pegoraro, Andrea, and Vivian Spoliansky. 2013. "El Archivo del Museo Etnográfico Juan B. Ambrosetti: Documentos para la historia institucional y disciplinar." *Revista Electrónica de Fuentes y Archivos* 4 (4): 180–89.

Perazzi, Pablo. 2005. "Los Institutos de Investigación de la Facultad de Filosofía y Letras de la Universidad de Buenos Aires: Una síntesis de sus acciones,

1896–1975." *Proyectos y actividades de los Institutos de Investigación de la Facultad de Filosofía y Letras*, 13–44. Buenos Aires: Universidad de Buenos Aires.

———. 2011. "La antropología en escena: Redes de influencia, sociabilidad y prestigio en los orígenes del Museo Etnográfico de la Universidad de Buenos Aires." *Anthropologica* 29 (29): 215–31.

Pérez Gollán, José Antonio, and Andrea Pegoraro. 2004. "La repatriación de un *Toi Moko*." *Relaciones de la Sociedad Argentina de Antropología* 29:331–38.

Rostagno, Enrique. (1911) 1969. *Informes fuerzas en operaciones en El Chaco 1911.* Buenos Aires: Biblioteca de actualización militar.

Ruiz Moreno, Isidoro. 2012. *Campaóas militares argentinas: Luchas contra indios y sediciosos (1878–1884).* Buenos Aires: Editorial Claridad.

Segundo Censo Nacional de la República Argentina. 1895. Buenos Aires: Taller Tipográfico de la Penintenciaría Nacional,

Tamagno, Liliana. 2009. "Saberes, ética y política. La restitución de restos humanos en el Museo de La Plata." In *Pueblos indígenas: Interculturalidad, colonialidad y política*, edited by Liliana Tamagno, 105–13. Buenos Aires: Biblos.

Tamagno, Liliana, Carolina Maidana, and Alejandro Martínez. 2015. "Rebeliones indígenas, movimientos socioreligiosos y procesos de territorialización. El Dios Luciano y la iglesia evangélica unida en Argentina." *Tabula Rasa* 22:147–66.

Trinchero, Héctor. 2000. *Los Dominios del demonio*. Buenos Aires: EUDEBA.

Verdesio, Gustavo. 2011. "Entre las visiones patrimonialistas y los derechos humanos: reflexiones sobre restitución y repatriación en Argentina y Uruguay." *Corpus* 1 (1): 1–6. https://doi.org/10.4000/corpusarchivos.989.

Viyerio, Julio César. 1999. "Vida, pensamiento y obra de Enrique Lynch Arribálzaga." *Nordeste*. Universidad Nacional del Nordeste. https://hum.unne.edu.ar/publicaciones/tesis/stesis1.htm.

A Special Style

Nancy Oestreich Lurie's Legacy of Engaged Anthropology

SPECIAL SECTION EDITED BY
GRANT ARNDT AND LARRY NESPER

10

Introduction to Nancy Lurie's Work

LARRY NESPER

Shortly after my arrival at the University of Wisconsin–Madison, where I took a position that was shared between the Department of Anthropology and the American Indian Studies Program, Ada Deer, the director of the latter and the person most responsible for my being hired, shared with me her desire to get the university to confer an honorary doctorate on her longtime friend and collaborator Nancy Oestreich Lurie. Lurie had been intimately involved with both the Menominee Tribe's restoration to federal recognition and the Ho-Chunk Tribe's reorganization, both watershed historic moments for both communities.

Deer knew Lurie for many decades and was most impressed with her generosity in availing her home as a meeting place for the Menominee members living in Milwaukee who needed a gathering place to organize for tribal restoration. Deer was also appreciative of Lurie's respect and admiration for Indian people and the differences between the tribal cultures of the state.

Ada Deer and I worked together on the project of getting UW-Madison to recognize Lurie's contributions to society and scholarship with an honorary doctorate. She used her remarkable network of relationships to secure letters of support from other professionals and tribal leaders. I assisted her by coordinating the effort and doing some of the writing that the application required. It was through this project that I came to know Lurie personally and her work more deeply.

Nancy Lurie was an alum of the university and had a career that engaged with the Native Nations of the state of Wisconsin in way that was exemplary of action anthropology. Her work is explored in detail in this collection by Judy Daubenmier, concentrating on the American Indian Chicago Conference of 1961 in chapter 11; by Grant Arndt, focusing on the Ho-Chunk tribal reorganization in chapter 12; by Patrick Jung's chapter on Nicolet and the Ho-Chunk; and by Alice B. Kehoe and Dawn Scher Thomae and Joshua Smith in chapters 14 and 15, based on their presentations at a 2017 memorial panel held at the annual meeting of the American Society for Ethnohistory. Lurie's work is also exemplary of the Wisconsin Idea, the commitment that education should influence people's lives beyond the boundaries of the classroom; alternatively, it is the commitment that the work of the university should extend to all the families in the state, and here we are particularly concerned with the tribal families.

An accomplished academic anthropologist, Lurie was inclined toward the subdiscipline of ethnohistory. This is evidenced in the detailed bibliography compiled by Patrick J. Jung in chapter 17, which supports the argument in Arndt's chapter as well as Kehoe and Thomae's review of her academic writing, but mostly in Jung's contribution on Lurie's ethnohistorical sophistication in chapter 13. Jung collaborated with Lurie on a mythbusting and iconoclastic book project on the early contact history of Wisconsin. Lurie was one of the founding ancestors of the American Society for Ethnohistory. She had an article in volume 2 of the society's journal titled "Problems, Opportunities, and Recommendations" (1955), which came out of a symposium, Anthropology and Indian Claims Litigation: Papers Presented at a Symposium Held at Detroit in December, 1954. Another of her articles, titled "Ethnohistory: An Ethnological Point of View," was published in volume 8 (1961a).

In their contribution to this collection, Kehoe and Thomae offer an overview and conclude with a review of the ways in which Lurie synthesized her interest in ethnography and commitments to social justice in her museum exhibits. Joshua Smith introduces a previously unpublished paper by Lurie, written in 1971 in the course of her work on the Menominee's legal case for restoration to federal recognition. The manuscript shows how her ongoing research interest in the history of anthropology (here the history of applied anthropology) contributed to the development of her more well-known account of Menominee termination as a colonial project (Lurie 1972).

This collection of essays about Nancy Lurie's life and work begins with the introduction to the dossier that was submitted in the application for an honorary degree, as it is built on appraisals of Lurie's career by her peers who supplied letters of support (University of Wisconsin–Madison archives, Honorary Degree Committee Records, 2002–13, n.p.).

NOMINATION OF PROFESSOR NANCY OESTREICH LURIE FOR AN HONORARY DEGREE OF DOCTOR OF HUMANE LETTERS

Nancy Oestreich Lurie is an accomplished scholar committed to the discipline of anthropology and dedicated to the well-being of the people who have been the subjects of her scholarship. She is an educator in the very best and widest sense of that term, as she has generously and imaginatively shared the knowledge that has emerged in her ethnographic work with the public. She has exemplified the Wisconsin Idea in a few different ways. Professor June Helm writes, "In meticulous ethnological and historical research . . . in educational accomplishment . . . in service to her discipline . . . and in enduring commitment to the hopes and aims of the first Americans, Nancy Oestreich Lurie has pursued a career of outstanding achievement and value." In Professor Raymond Fogelson's words, "Leadership in scholarship, education and public service is rarely so intimately embraced and so effectively integrated in the career of a single individual."

Clearly, Nancy Lurie has exemplified the Wisconsin Idea in many dimensions of her career. If you were to ask any anthropologist in the United States to name a colleague from the state of Wisconsin, Nancy Lurie's would be the first. President of the American Anthropological Association, the largest and most prestigious organization of anthropologists in the world, her academic, applied, and activist work is world-renowned.

Nancy Lurie took her BA from the University of Wisconsin–Madison, MA from the University of Chicago, and PhD from Northwestern University. She went on to a distinguished teaching career at the University of Michigan and the University of Wisconsin–Milwaukee; the latter awarded her an honorary doctorate of humanities in 1994. She was able to realize her vision of educating the wider public for twenty years as the Curator of Anthropology of the Milwaukee Public Museum. Her work as an expert witness with seven tribes for the Indian Claims Commission, her coordination of the American Indian Chicago Conference, and numerous action anthropology projects with the tribes of Wisconsin and the urban Indian people of Milwaukee over the length of her career are all evidence of the "sustained and characteristic . . . meritorious activity . . . that are esteemed by a great university," in the words of the Committee on Honorary Degrees.

As a scholar, Nancy Lurie has spent her professional life working among Native American people, chiefly in the state of Wisconsin but also among the Dogrib people of sub-Arctic Canada. She is the author of four books. The first, *Mountain Wolf Woman, Sister of Crashing Thunder: The Autobiography of a Winnebago Woman* (1961), is the first autobiography of an American Indian woman, and according to Professor Raymond Fogelson, "an insightful perspective on a Winnebago woman's life, an account that is clearly culturally contextualized and not rhetorically disembodied." Helen Tanner points out that this "illuminating volume is constantly used in a variety of college and university courses." Her book, *Wisconsin Indians* ([1969] 2002), is a much-needed, concise, yet accurate depiction of the political, historical and cultural elements of each tribe in the state. She has updated this book twice. Professor Paul Prucha characterized it as ". . . an unparalleled source of information on the Indians of Wisconsin." *Women and the Invention of American Anthropology* (1999), is ". . . a landmark in feminist scholarship within anthropology," according to Professor Alice Kehoe. Professor June Helm points out that *A Special Style: The Milwaukee Public Museum, 1882–1982* (1983), ". . . foster(s) appreciation of Wisconsin's heritage." She also notes that Nancy Lurie's ". . . writings, although directed to academic audiences, address themes in the history and cultures of American Indians that offer perspectives and challenges to all questing minds." Professor Lurie is also the author of two edited books and numerous scholarly articles, ". . . written without jargon, to reach and engage the broadest audiences," in Alice Kehoe's words echoing Helm.

Nancy Lurie was the Head Curator of the Milwaukee Public Museum from 1972 to 1992. Her contributions to that institution and through it to the city of Milwaukee and the state of Wisconsin are described in the accompanying letters of support. Helen Tanner indicates the breadth of that vision: ". . . she utilized her unique opportunities to carry out an expanding educational endeavor through the school programs at the Museum and innovative exhibits." She not only extended the resources of the museum to citizens of Wisconsin but also was also able to navigate the ethical and political complexities of both representation and repatriation working collaboratively with the Indian nations of the state.

Nancy Lurie came of age as a professional anthropologist when the policy of the federal government regarding Indian people was to terminate their special legal status that had been guaranteed by treaty in the nineteenth century, widely considered to be an ill-advised shift. The Indian Claims Commission was established in the post–World War II era as a means of settling outstanding issues with the tribes to achieve that end. As a measure of her "constant dedication to the welfare of Indian people," in Fogelson's words, and "support of struggles for justice" in Kehoe's, Nancy Lurie testified on behalf of seven different tribes in these hearings. Consistent with this commitment to the lives of the people she wrote about in her scholarly work, she co-coordinated the Chicago American Indian Conference with Sol Tax, professor of Anthropology at the University of Chicago. A week-long meeting of nearly 500 Indian people from 90 different tribes to discuss current problems in the troubled relationship between Indian people and the federal government, this conference in 1961 was one of the most consequential gatherings of Indian people in the 20th century as it articulated an agenda for action in the "Declaration of Indian Purpose" and gave birth to other Indian organizations. The conference set Nancy Lurie on a career of action anthropology, ". . . and brought Lurie to the forefront of that field" according to June Helm, wherein collaboration with Indian people in identifying problems and solutions becomes the starting point of scholarship. She would share her understanding of that event in an article in *Current Anthropology* (1961), which Paul Prucha appraises as ". . . the best report on the conference" that has been done. From her involvement in a ground-breaking conference, she would go on to work closely with the Menominees in their successful effort to restore their tribal status playing a valuable role in a historical reversal of federal policy. She went on to work with the Ho-Chunk, (formerly Winnebago) and with urban Indian people in Milwaukee in a series of projects.

Nancy Lurie is affectionately referred to as "Nancy-ga" by her Ho-Chunk friends and relatives, an indigenization of her name and a measure of endearment and respect. As Buck Martin points out in his letter, "She was embraced by the Indian community for her work and joined us at our PowWows, our birthdays and our funerals." It is clear from her record of generosity and hospitality, detailed in the accompanying letters, that she has taken on many of the values of native peoples. Nancy Lurie assisted the Ho-Chunk in writing their first grant at a time when the federal policy began to shift in the direction of self-determination. In Susette LaMere-Arentz's words, this was "the first 'big step' to improve educational opportunities for our children, create better housing opportunities for the people, and help get jobs for the men and women of working age." She also guided the development of a tribal archive. Her expert testimony on their behalf, her encouraging Indian people to continue their educations, and her ethnographic writings have been of immeasurable value to the Ho-Chunk people. The letters document the wide variety of contributions she has made; Pamela Winneshiek's noting, ". . . she has become an integral member of this community."

Truly a national treasure, Nancy Lurie is esteemed and admired by her academic colleagues, students and fellow citizens. She is loved and respected by Indian people across the nation for her abiding concern, commitment and involvement. To honor the depth and breadth of her humanity and a distinguished life in service of others, the Department of Anthropology and the American Indian Studies Program respectfully urge the Committee on Honorary Degrees to recommend the award of an honorary degree of doctor of humane letters to Nancy Oestreich Lurie.

REFERENCES

Lurie, Nancy Oestreich. 1955. "Problems, Opportunities, and Recommendations." *Ethnohistory* 2 (4): 357–75.

———. 1961a. "Ethnohistory: An Ethnological Point of View." *Ethnohistory* 8 (1): 78–92.

———. 1961b. *Mountain Wolf Woman, Sister of Crashing Thunder: The Autobiography of a Winnebago Woman*. Ann Arbor: University of Michigan Press.

———. 1961c. "The Voice of the American Indian: A Report on the American Indian Chicago Conference." *Current Anthropology* 2 (5): 478–500.

———. (1969) 2002. *Wisconsin Indians*. Madison: Wisconsin Historical Society Press.

———. 1972. "Menominee Termination: From Reservation to Colony." *Human Organization* 31 (3): 257–69.

———. 1983. *A Special Style: The Milwaukee Public Museum, 1882–1982*. Milwaukee: Milwaukee Public Museum.

———. 1999. *Women and the Invention of American Anthropology*. Long Grove IL: Waveland Press.

11

"Pow-Wow-How-Taxed-We-Are"

Nancy Lurie and Sol Tax

JUDY DAUBENMIER

In the history of action anthropology, the names Nancy Oestreich Lurie and Sol Tax are linked tightly. Can you think of the 1961 American Indian Chicago Conference without both of them coming to mind? Yet the relationship between the two nearly ended before it started. How that happened and how the relationship was rebuilt is the story of two people who set aside ego and hurt feelings in favor of the demands of a profession to which both were dedicated. This chapter looks at how Lurie and Tax managed to create a fruitful working relationship despite the rocky beginning. It discusses how two extremely talented individuals had the character to put aside personal matters of the past because of their mutual dedication to collaborating with American Indians at a time of great ferment in federal Indian policy and the stirrings of change within anthropology itself. Each of them had a talent for action anthropology. And each also had a talent for recognizing merit in the other's work, although it took a while for Tax to recognize Lurie's talent.

Sol Tax was a professor of anthropology at the University of Chicago when Nancy Lurie arrived in 1945 as a graduate student. In many ways, she was not the typical graduate student. For one thing, she was a woman dealing mostly with male faculty at a time when gender stereotypes were firmly held. She was also young, just twenty-one, but anthropology had already been her lifelong dream. In an interview with the author in April 2002, she reflected, "I knew from the time that I was six years old that I was going to be an anthropologist, and I knew from the time I was eight years old that someday I would be the head of anthropology at the Milwaukee Public Museum, and I was *dedicated*."[1] Lurie's path to a doctorate in anthropology was far from smooth, however. She had her heart set on attending the University of New Mexico. Her parents wanted their only child to stay close to home for her first couple of years and then transfer to New Mexico, so she enrolled at the University of Wisconsin–Madison. With the onset of World War II, which made long-distance travel difficult, Lurie was stuck at Madison, where she came under the influence of the brilliant but difficult J. Sydney Slotkin.

Slotkin was a short man who did not bear it well, in Lurie's view. He wore elevator shoes to make himself seem taller, for example, and disguised his insecurity about his height by adopting a superior attitude toward others. "He expected to be rejected," Lurie recalled. "He was arrogant or gave the appearance, and he turned people off, but if you stuck with him, which I did, he couldn't do enough for you." At their first meeting, Slotkin's sexism also was on full display, as he seemed unwilling to believe that a woman could be a serious scholar. "He said, 'You either plan to get married and have a family or your own family is wealthy enough to support you through your—' I think he used the word *dilettantism*. I was outraged, absolutely outraged." Encouraged by her family to "use some backbone," Lurie went back to Slotkin and argued with him. Yet when she turned in a paper that she was very proud of, he told her it was "pretty thin stew." Again she marched in to confront Slotkin. Because of the war, the students in the anthropology program had dwindled so much that she was the only one left. "And then he sat down with me and said, 'This is how you do research.' I had a tutor. He was wonderful."

Slotkin impressed on Lurie the importance of publication, encouraging her to do fieldwork with the Ho-Chunk between her junior and senior years. By age twenty she already was a published scholar, with her article "Cultural Change Among the Winnebago" appearing in *Wisconsin Archeologist* in 1944. Lurie went on to dedicate her 1961 book *Mountain Wolf Woman, Sister of Crashing Thunder: The Autobiography of a Winnebago Indian* to both her biological father and her intellectual father, Slotkin. And it was Slotkin who encouraged her to go to graduate school at the University of Chicago, which Lurie said was "absolutely the worst place for a person like me, because I'm not terribly competitive . . . and kind of naive."

When Lurie showed up at the University of Chicago in 1945, the war had just ended, and university enrollment was swelling with returning veterans. The department was in a state of flux and internally divided into factions, one made up of Robert Redfield, Sol Tax, and Fred Eggan and another headed by W. Lloyd Warner, author of the Yankee City series of socio-anthropological studies of life in a typical American community. "And I was too naive to really appreciate it, but talking to people there ... it appears that if you were W. Lloyd Warner's student, you wouldn't stand a prayer with Redfield, Tax, Eggan, and vice versa," she recalled. Despite the factional problems, Lurie said she "walked on air" during her first year of graduate school:

> It was heavenly. I hadn't been allowed to take any anthro at Madison until I was a sophomore because of prerequisites. I went up there, and [if] I'd gone to New Mexico, ... I could have taken anthro. So here [in Chicago] I could just take anthro. I didn't have to take anything else, and Sol and Fred had developed a wonderful syllabus, and they were trying it out on this class of '45 that came in. And it was nice, but by my second year, I became aware of the fact that you did not share your best ideas in seminar, because the other students would pirate them. And then I realized there are people here who are twenty-five and thirty who are still working on their master's degrees because they were terrified to take the qualifying exams. It was an awful place. It was really terrible.

Lurie got her master's in 1947 and took the PhD qualifying exams. The university required a grade of "high pass" in all four fields—cultural anthropology, physical anthropology, linguistics, and archaeology—to qualify for advancement, but she fell short of that threshold in two fields. With a job waiting for her back in Milwaukee at the University of Wisconsin extension division, Lurie decided to retake the exam later and to start teaching in the meantime. Despite a grueling work schedule of five three-hour classes, including ones at night and on weekends, Lurie retook the exam at the end of the first semester. She earned a high pass in one of the remaining two fields but fell short in her own field of cultural anthropology. Still teaching, she added a new course to her workload and then took the qualifying exam again in the spring, falling short once more. A fourth try yielded a pass, but not a high pass, leading Lurie to the revelation that she was subconsciously trying to put off getting her PhD for personal reasons. "And I got a letter from Sol and Eggan ... telling me that I should consider my master's degree terminal and that they did not really think I was PhD material. Well, needless to say," Lurie said.

Lurie considered her options. Being at a Chicago university was important because it allowed her to keep her job in Milwaukee. She was already a published scholar with an article in print based on the fieldwork she had done between her first and second years and could have argued that her fieldwork and publication demonstrated her qualifications. But, she said, "by this time I was sick and tired of Sol Tax." At meetings of the American Anthropological Association, Lurie had seen Melville Herskovits, the head of the Anthropology Department at Northwestern University, who had a lot of graduate students. Here the gender stereotyping she had initially confronted with Slotkin was less a factor. "And of course, he was a Boas product, and Boas had welcomed women into anthropology," she said. "And so there were women, and they would crowd around him like a flock of turkeys around a mother hen, and they called him Papa Herskovits." Lurie marched over to Northwestern, made an appointment with Herskovits, and told him she would like to transfer. When Herskovits asked why, she gave him Tax's letter and told him that Tax "doesn't think I'm PhD material and I think I am, and I think I could do well with a fresh start."

Herskovits told Lurie after receiving her letter, he had called Tax and could not understand what the problem was. "So he took the letter out of my hand, tore it up in little pieces, dropped it in the wastebasket, and said, 'That's over.' So I got my PhD at Northwestern. Many, many—most people think because of my later association with Sol that I got it at Chicago." So it was that Lurie left the University of Chicago just as Tax's Fox Project—the incubator for action anthropology—was about to get underway in 1948. (Tax had encouraged Lurie to do fieldwork for her master's with the Fox, or Meskwaki, Indians in Iowa, but she wanted to continue her association with the Ho-Chunk.) Lurie began crossing paths with Tax, however, as she attended conferences and gave papers. In the process, they discovered how similar their attitudes were toward fieldwork and relations with Native people. In lieu of paying informants, Lurie said, "you do it in-kind. Participant observation means helping to wash dishes and do a lot of other things."

Tax and Lurie also were on the same side when it came to opposing the federal government policies of the 1950s that were so devastating for

Native communities, including termination and relocation. "We just gravitated to each other," Lurie recalled. One factor may have been their shared Milwaukee roots. Lurie remembered one of Tax's daughters saying to her during a meeting at his home for the American Indian Chicago Conference, "'Oh, you come from Milwaukee, maybe that's why you get along so well with Daddy,' which sort of tells you something. But it's true [that] Milwaukee is kind of our distinctive [tie]."

By the late 1950s Nancy had married Edward Lurie, a historian, and moved to Ann Arbor, where her husband had a tenure-track position at the University of Michigan. Again her gender posed a hurdle to her advancement. Nepotism rules at the time barred spouses from holding positions in the same department, which tended to disadvantage women. She wound up officially in the public health school and later at Wayne State University. But she told Tax in a 1958 letter that she felt isolated in an academic environment that shunned cultural relativism and the works of scholars such as Ralph Linton and Edward Sapir. Her letter reveals how much she shared Tax's views that Native people were not going to disappear. She decried termination and relocation projects as isolating them in low-income areas of major cities and argued that Native people should keep their distinctiveness because it brought honor to them from the larger population. "Second, those Indian communities that are still going concerns, offer the pleasure and security of that which is familiar and to break them up and make them find new sources of security and pleasure is to waste a social resource that would be improved economically and need not be discarded utterly," she wrote, noting that was basically what Tax was saying.[2]

Exchanges like those were in the background when Tax began formulating the concept of the American Indian Chicago Conference as the Eisenhower administration ended and the nation prepared for a new president and, many hoped, a new federal Indian policy. In the fall of 1960 he approached the Emil Schwarzhaupt Foundation for a $10,000 grant to pay for a conference at the University of Chicago to write a report on the failures of past Indian policy and suggest a new path for federal policy. In November he met with the National Congress of American Indians (NCAI) in Denver and put forward ideas for the conference, securing the NCAI's backing.

Three weeks before he met with the NCAI, however, Tax approached Lurie to work on the conference. He laid out his idea in an October 24, 1960, letter, claiming that he was being pressured (he did not say by whom) to write an updated version of the 1928 report on economic, social, and educational conditions for Native peoples called the Meriam Report which had been commissioned by the Brookings Institution. "I cannot undertake to do this unless I get the good and willing help of somebody with skill and energy, like you, who also has more time than I have," he wrote. Having her do research and help "bat out a draft" of the report would be preferable to a committee of three or four anthropologists, Tax told her. He promised to try to get money for her expenses. And then he closed with a hard sell: "If you are not in a position to help, I would probably not undertake this at all, and unfortunately I have to decide within a week."[3] In other words, Tax was purporting to put the future of one of the most influential gatherings of Native people in the twentieth century into the hands of a scholar whom he had earlier said was not PhD material. That dismissive characterization of Lurie, however, was in the distant past. It may have been around this time—Lurie was not clear when—that she and Tax had a pivotal conversation. "And Sol looked straight at me and said, 'We have made some serious mistakes with regard to our graduate students.' Breach healed. And . . . he was big enough to say it," Lurie recalled.

Lurie accepted Tax's job offer. She became assistant coordinator for the American Indian Chicago Conference (AICC). More people joined later to fill various roles, but only Lurie's name was on the letterhead, right under Tax's. Working together brought them even closer, although Lurie remained in Ann Arbor most of the time. They were in constant communication by letter and phone, covering the most minute details of the conference. In one handwritten letter on hotel stationery, Tax explained exactly how he wanted a printed statement announcing the AICC to appear.[4]

Other letters covered the need to assemble a Steering Committee of Native people to plan the conference, the difficulties of putting together a mailing list to reach as many Native people as possible in an era before email, and how to combat rumors that the AICC was either "an Indian Bureau plot" or a new organization to compete with the NCAI. Lurie also handled sensitive issues such as how to navigate the racial politics of holding a meeting in the South, where some Native people were also of African

American ancestry. When the AICC Advisory Committee met in Chicago in February 1961, Lurie served as recorder for the meetings, taking notes and producing reports summarizing the proceedings. The task required delicacy, as Steering Committee members debated the name of the Chicago meeting, whether the Bureau of Indian Affairs would be offended by the gathering, whether people would vote as individuals or as tribes, and how to balance representation of reservation Indians, urban Indians, federally recognized tribes, and unrecognized tribes.[5]

Later, volunteers joined Lurie in working on the AICC, including Tax students Joan Ablon, Bob Thomas, and Albert Wahrhaftig. Although Lurie described Tax as a "terrible task master" who had high expectations for his associates, the team bore it all in good humor. They composed lyrics, sung to the tune of "Ta-Ra-Ra-Boom-De-Ay," complaining, "Pow-Wow-How-Taxed-We-Are, Pow-Wow-How-Taxed-We-Are," with the fifth and last verse ending, "We are Tax's faithful crew. / Indian Friends, what we've gone through / He would never ask of you. / But blithely says what we must do."[6] Stereotypes about gender roles may have again played a role. Lurie recalled that Tax struggled to understand why problems such as a sick child sometimes interfered with a team member's ability to do their job. His wife, Gertrude, handled the family's domestic affairs, relieving him of most of that burden, Lurie said.

Tax's high expectations extended to his colleagues too. Once during AICC preparations, Lurie had composed a letter of thanks to some people who had been helping out, but Tax dismissed it, saying, "What do we need that for? They should be happy to do it." Lurie found that Tax's lack of personal ego and his endearing Charlie Chaplin-esque appearance made it easier to put up with his demands. "He was lacking in compassion for people's personal needs. But he looked upon anthropology as a calling, not a profession. It was his religion, it was his philosophy, it was his life," Lurie said. It was also hers, and that was the crucial tie between them.

The AICC was pivotal for Lurie. Decades later she wrote a key article explaining its significance in reviving the concept of tribal sovereignty as a legal strategy for American Indian tribes, arguing that the conference helped "introduce 'tribal sovereignty' into the general Indian-English lexicon far beyond the little coterie that embraced it in 1961" (Lurie 1999). Within her own career, the AICC was crucial in her evolution into an avowed action anthropologist. The AICC spurred her involvement with the Ho-Chunk in helping them obtain federal recognition under the leadership of Helen Miner Miller and the Wisconsin Winnebago Business Committee. She wrote to Tax in October 1962 in regard to a grant she was seeking from the U.S. Department of Health, Education, and Welfare: "I keep saying I'm not a groupy person and big undertakings scare me and after AICC I'd never get involved personally in action anthropology as much as I approve of it in principle for those with the stamina and personality constellation for it—and here I am joyously wallowing in action anthropology. The thing is, of course, the Winnebago understand action anthropology! As I've said before, I'm their anthropologist, they are not my tribe, and I helped get the money, but it was their idea to get it and they are calling the shots." A few days later, Tax wrote that HEW asked him about the grant and "needless to say I said it was the most important thing in the world and that the Indians are too modest in their request and would need more money than they asked for," suggesting that was the reason the grant amount was increased to $7,300 from $6,500.[7]

Besides helping with that grant, Tax went on to write glowing recommendations for Lurie. When she sought a Fulbright-Hays grant to go to the University of Aarhus, Denmark, to lecture on action anthropology and American Indian ethnology and ethnohistory, Tax gave her the highest possible recommendation, pointing out he had known her for twenty years as a student and then a colleague. On the form, Tax checked "truly exceptional" in every box and told the grant reviewers he had never before marked anyone truly exceptional in all categories.

The two remained close and continued to correspond. Lurie kept Tax informed on her work to help the Ho-Chunk win federal recognition under the 1934 Indian Reorganization Act and to help the Menominee reverse their termination, for example. When a celebration was held for Tax at Panajachel, Guatemala, where Tax had done research for his 1953 book, *Penny Capitalism*, Lurie was invited along with many of his former students.

Lurie eventually achieved her dream of working for the Milwaukee Public Museum, serving as the curator of anthropology from 1972 until her retirement in 1992. It was a dream she held on to and achieved despite— and because of—Sol Tax.[8]

NOTES

1. Unless otherwise noted, all quotes and information are from Nancy Lurie, interview by the author, April 2002.
2. Lurie to Tax, June 10, 1958, STP, box 132, folder 1.
3. Tax to Lurie, October 24, 1960, AICC, box 8, folder Sol Tax-N.O.L.
4. Tax to Lurie, October 22, October 24, December 17, 1960, AICC, box 8, folder Sol Tax-N.O.L.
5. Lurie to Tax, January 28, 1961, AICC, box 8, folder Sol Tax-N.O.L; Notes on AICC Meeting of Indian Advisory Committee, February 10–14, 1961, AICC, box 2, folder Sol Tax Chicago Indian Advisors.
6. "Song for Singing by Bob, Al, Joan and Nancy—Dedicated to Sol Tax," June 1961, AICC, box 8, folder Sol Tax-N.O.L.
7. Lurie to Tax, October 18, 1962, STP, box 132, folder 1; Tax to Lurie, October 22, 1962, STP, box 132, folder 1.
8. Lurie to Tax, October 16, 1964, STP, box 132, folder 1.

REFERENCES

Manuscripts and Archives

AICC. Papers of the American Indian Chicago Conference. National Anthropological Archives, Federal Records Center, Suitland MD.
STP. Sol Tax Papers. Special Collections Research Center, Regenstein Library, University of Chicago.

Published Works

Lurie, Nancy Oestreich. 1944. "Cultural Change Among the Winnebago." *Wisconsin Archeologist* 25 (4): 119–25.
———. 1961. *Mountain Wolf Woman, Sister of Crashing Thunder: The Autobiography of Winnebago Indian.* Ann Arbor: University of Michigan Press.
———. 1999. "Sol Tax and Tribal Sovereignty." *Human Organization* 58 (1): 108–17.
Tax, Sol. 1953. *Penny Capitalism: A Guatemalan Indian Economy.* Washington DC: U.S. Government Printing Office.

12

Nancy Lurie and Ho-Chunk Reorganization

Action Anthropology, Indigenous Nation Rebuilding,
and the Struggle for Decolonization

GRANT ARNDT

Nancy Oestreich Lurie was a key figure in the development of a decolonial mode of anthropological practice years before decolonization became a concern for most American anthropologists (Dinwoodie 2023; Arndt 2019). She championed the critique of anthropology in Vine Deloria's *Custer Died for Your Sins* and exemplified the sort of responsive commitment to Indian concerns and issues that he called for from anthropologists (Deloria 1969, Lurie 1971b; Arndt 2023). Lurie understood her anthropological activism as part of a tradition of individual anthropologists seeking ways to support Indigenous peoples in their ongoing struggles for survival and self-determination, a tradition she saw as being theorized and championed most clearly in the work of her former professor Sol Tax and the "action anthropologists" who emerged from the University of Chicago in the late 1940s (Lurie 1999).

The action anthropology of Tax, Lurie, and others grew out of their engagement with American Indian communities that were facing a renewed assault on their self-determination and survival in the years following World War II. Participation in the social struggles of Native communities confronting new threats to their sovereignty, pursuing treaty claims, and responding to the challenges of urban relocation caused action anthropologists to rethink disciplinary assumptions about the inevitable disappearance of Indigenous cultures and communities. Doing so allowed them to recognize innovative political projects guided by long-standing but dynamic social, moral, and political values (Provinse and Useem 1954; Lesser 1961; Tax; Lurie 1961) and led them to seek ways to support the projects through which Indigenous people were asserting their right to choose their own futures (Tax [1958] 1975, 516).

This chapter presents an account of Nancy Oestreich Lurie's first independent project of action anthropology in the early 1960s, as she worked for the leadership of the Ho-Chunk Nation in Wisconsin in their effort to create a federally recognized tribal government. Through their creation of a new government, the Ho-Chunk Nation reestablished themselves as an economically and politically significant polity in their traditional homeland by the end of the twentieth century. Lurie's contribution to their work was part of an ongoing relationship with and commitment to Ho-Chunk people in Wisconsin that lasted for seven decades. Here I consider Lurie's published accounts (1973, 1989) along with archival documents to describe her contributions to the project, emphasize its importance to her efforts to develop a theory of Indigenous activism, and provide a more complex account of the engagement of American anthropologists with American Indian nation-rebuilding projects in the twentieth century.

FROM EXPERT WITNESS TO ACTION ANTHROPOLOGIST

Nancy Oestreich Lurie began her anthropological research as an undergraduate at the University of Wisconsin. She spent the summer of 1944 working with Ho-Chunk people in the cherry orchards of Door County, Wisconsin, where she met the tribe's elders and intellectuals, in particular John C. Decorah and Mitchell Red Cloud Sr., who mentored her in the belief that her work could later prove valuable to their people (Lurie 1972b). Her experiences led her to focus on Ho-Chunk culture and history for graduate work at the University of Chicago (MA 1947) and Northwestern University (PhD 1952).

After graduation, she became a researcher and expert witness for the Ho-Chunk claim against the United States before the Indian Claims Commission, testifying on their behalf for the first time in 1957 (Ganteaume 1989). It was one of a number of claims cases she worked on as an expert witness during the emergence of the discipline of ethnohistory (Harkin 2010). Lurie became a leading voice in the debate over the role of anthropologists as expert witnesses, writing a series of articles analyzing the complexities of anthropological work in a contentious legal setting (Lurie 1955, 1956, 1957). Her close work with communities during the claims process led Sol Tax, one of her former professors at the University of Chicago, to ask her to be his assistant coordinator for the American Indian Chicago Conference (AICC) in 1961, a weeklong set of meetings of representatives of American Indian communities from around the country with the goal of producing a statement outlining their vision of American Indian policy and the needs of Indian people (Lurie 1961, 1999). The AICC was Lurie's official introduction to action anthropology and remained a model of this approach throughout her career.

While Lurie was working with Tax to organize the AICC, Ho-Chunk people in Wisconsin held discussions about the problems of education, employment, housing, healthcare, and discrimination they faced in Wisconsin. By January 1961 the existing Wisconsin Winnebago Business Committee, a representative body that had been coordinating the tribal case before the Indian Claims Commission, had started to discuss the possibility of participating in the upcoming AICC. Committee member Robinson Johnson, a longtime Chicago resident, relayed information on the planned conference to Ho-Chunk tribal members at a meeting in February. A larger Ho-Chunk group began to organize around the idea of participating in the AICC to gain a hearing for the concerns of nonreservation Indians such as themselves.[1] During this period, another member of the committee, Rev. Mitchell White Rabbit of the Black River Falls Mission church, representing the Ho-Chunk group at a regional meeting of the federal government's Task Force on Indian Affairs, presented a statement on nonreservation concerns authored by committee member Helen Miner Miller:

> We Winnebago Indians of the state of Wisconsin are unique in that we live on non-reservation land or homestead land. The only help we receive is of an emergency nature and only when we are completely morally and physically broken down do we receive such help. We exist in the worst slum areas, we are the worst fed, the worst clad, and the worst housed group in Wisconsin. We are the recipients of the poorest education and medical services in the state. . . . We encounter historical and deep-rooted obstacles to the full development and employment of our abilities.[2]

The statement called for "the same care and understanding that is accorded other races in dire need" and outlined the community's immediate needs, including a food program, "opportunities for more extended education for young Indians," and "equal job opportunities and equal pay in the communities in which we reside." It also asked for "a health program to provide for our medical and dental needs . . . without begging for it when we are in need."[3]

In April Ho-Chunk and Lakota activist Benjamin Bearskin came from Chicago to a general tribal meeting in the Wisconsin Dells to explain the purpose and philosophy of the AICC. He read the text of a Sol Tax speech on action anthropology in which Tax stated that he believed the United States would never be able to help Indian people "adjust economically and socially to American life" until it recognized that "Indians have a right to make this adjustment as Indians" and should be "free to make their own choices."[4] At the end of the meeting, representatives of community and religious groups within the Ho-Chunk Nation expressed their support for participation in that summer's meeting. The group recommended that Helen Miner Miller become their representative at the upcoming regional planning meeting in Milwaukee. Miller was a college-educated, bilingual Ho-Chunk woman who lived with her non-Indian husband in the Chicago suburbs, where she taught high school (Lurie 1989). She subsequently joined the AICC's national planning board. Miller was also part of the thirty-three-member Ho-Chunk delegation from Wisconsin that took part in the conference meetings that June. This delegation was the largest to represent any single community, and its concerns about the issues facing nonreservation communities were included in the final AICC document, "The Voice of the American Indian" (Lurie 1961, 1989).

The experience of the AICC proved to be pivotal for Ho-Chunk organizational efforts. That fall a tribal meeting of Ho-Chunk people heard reports on the AICC and the idea emerging from it that they should create a federally recognized tribal government to organize and lobby on their behalf with local, state, and federal agencies. At that meeting, committee member Alberta Day introduced a proposal to enlarge the Business Committee to fifteen members so that it could take on an expanded mission, from its existing focus on pursuit of the tribal claim to acting as an "informal communicating body" for investigating of the possibili-

ties of reorganization. Participants also voted to have the Business Committee become a member of the National Congress of American Indians (NCAI) and designated Helen Miller as its official representative for
NCAI functions.[5]

The Business Committee arranged to have former NCAI director Helen
Peterson address a general tribal meeting that December. Peterson used
the occasion to explain the benefits of organizing at the federal level
under the Indian Reorganization Act as a way to reclaim the "threads
of sovereignty left to you as an Indian nation."[6] At a meeting later that
month, the Business Committee appointed Miller to head a subcommit-
tee tasked with writing a draft constitution and bylaws and to consult
with the Bureau of Indian Affairs (BIA) and others toward the goal of
federal reorganization.[7] Miller also began publishing a tribal newspaper
to make the Business Committee's nation-rebuilding effort visible to all
Ho-Chunk tribal members and to seek a tribal consensus for the committee's projects. The newspaper's first issue was dedicated almost entirely
to the text of Peterson's speech explaining the importance of reorganization (Peterson 1962).

Miller and the other members of the Business Committee spent 1962
developing a draft constitution. That project led them to enlist a number
of outside advisors, including the NCAI's Helen Peterson, scholar D'Arcy
McNickle, former commissioner of Indian Affairs William Zimmerman,
and Nancy Lurie, then an assistant professor at the School of Public Health
at the University of Michigan. At the time, Lurie was involved in ongoing
work on the Turtle Mountain Chippewa claim and also in field research
with June Helm with the Tlicho First Nation in Canada, but she consulted
with Miller as she worked on drafts of the constitution.

Lurie began to take on a more active role as advocate in the fall of 1962,
when, after months of negotiations, the BIA suddenly notified the Ho-
Chunk leadership that bureau lawyers had found the tribe ineligible for
reorganization (Lurie 1989, 18). Miller and the Business Committee ral-
lied Lurie and other outside supporters, especially Zimmerman, to lobby
Commissioner of Indian Affairs Philleo Nash to reconsider the decision.[8]
Lurie appealed to Nash in her role as "the anthropologist most closely
associated with the Wisconsin Winnebago over the last 18 years," providing him with "outside and academic substantiation" of the facts about Ho-

Chunk history and the context of the reorganization effort. She told him in particular about a series of remarkable leaders since the 1870s who had been "hampered" by a lack of money and also explained why Ho-Chunk people had originally decided to "table" the idea of reorganization in 1937. She warned Nash of the negative consequences that the failure of the reorganization effort would have on the Ho-Chunk community.[9]

The combination of the direct appeal of Helen Miller and the Business Committee, Lurie's letters, and in-person lobbying by Zimmerman persuaded Nash, an anthropologist by training (see Nash 1937; Landman and Halpern 1989, Lewis 2024), to intervene with the bureau's lawyers to request a review of the decision to reject the Ho-Chunk application (Lurie 1989). In early December he telephoned Miller to let her know that the legal obstacles to reorganization had been overcome and wrote to Lurie that "as of today, the train is again back on the track" (Lurie 1973, 1989). At a tribal referendum in January 1963, eligible Ho-Chunk tribal members voted for reorganization by a margin of 514 to 5. Lurie attributed the success of the vote to the Business Committee's communication efforts, including a series of regional meetings and a tribal newspaper created and published by Miller.[10] In June the Business Committee held the first general election for tribal office, and the Ho-Chunk electorate chose Miller to serve as the first tribal chair (WWBC 1963b).

In September 1963 the Business Committee held a general council and powwow to celebrate the reorganization effort. They welcomed William Zimmerman and Philleo Nash as special guests of honor and recognized Zimmerman's role in the reorganization effort by bestowing on him a ceremonial Ho-Chunk name. In archival accounts and correspondence, Lurie described the event as a catalyzing moment in the development of a new tribal structure. Planning for the general council and powwow led to a revival of the traditional functions of the bear and buffalo clans, with the bear clan members acting as police at the gathering and the buffalo clan members, traditionally the "town criers," fulfilling the duty of emceeing. The family of the traditional chief took charge of hosting and feeding the guests. All these traditional institutions were mobilized to complement the Business Committee, allowing it to take on projects of liaison and representation with the dominant society, which the older tribal structure had not provided for(Miller and Lurie 1963).

The vote to reorganize was only the first step toward Ho-Chunk self-governance and development. Lurie's supportive role in the reorganization effort was followed by her close collaboration with Helen Miner Miller on an innovative self-study undertaken by the Business Committee. Conceived early in 1962, even as the Business Committee was still developing drafts of the constitution and bylaws, the self-study was a response to the recognition that even if the Ho-Chunk effort to reorganize proved successful, the committee would be unable to carry out its mission unless it obtained external funding. Miller and Lurie investigated funding possibilities for a "community development study" to be carried out by Ho-Chunk people themselves, using questionnaires, interviews, home visits, and group discussions to collect data from Ho-Chunk people on issues of health, education, living conditions, as well as their "expressed needs and preferences in programs for economic improvement and community development." The project's findings would be used in planning organizational structures and projects for community development in line with Ho-Chunk values and goals. In a draft proposal for the project, Miller and Lurie emphasized that the members of the Business Committee were determined "to encourage those features of their native heritage which continue to have meaning and value in the modern world," creating a "formal organization for dealing with the larger world and to represent their interest" toward the "ultimate goal of a decent level of living as Winnebago Indian people." They also explained that Ho-Chunk people would insist on being the "decision-makers, drawing on expert advice as they see its need and pertinence but not simply [being] passive recipients of programs designed for their own good by outsiders."[11]

Miller and Lurie sent the proposal for the self-study project to over a dozen agencies. Although they received a number of supportive letters in response, only one, from the Department of Health, Education, and Welfare (HEW), included an offer of funding (Lurie 1965a, 1973). In correspondence with Sol Tax, Lurie reported that their proposal had succeeded in part because one of the reviewers for the grant was Leo Srole, who had worked with Ho-Chunk people in Wisconsin as a postgraduate student in anthropology at the University of Chicago in 1938–39. Srole, she noted, "had pushed our request" and "expressed an eagerness to help the effort in any way" he could.[12] He later visited Wisconsin to consult with the Business Committee and also donated his field notes to the committee as a resource for the creation of a roll of eligible tribal members. Based on feedback from the grant program's director, Ida Merriam, Miller and Lurie revised the proposal to better fit the parameters of the grant and resubmitted it that June. In early October they received word that the proposal had been accepted.[13]

Miller and Lurie began to organize the self-study just after the January 1963 tribal referendum vote. Miller wrote a survey questionnaire, while Lurie researched methodologies of tabulating the data. In late January Miller and Lurie held training sessions for the Ho-Chunk researchers in Chicago and Wisconsin.[14] At the same time, Miller used the tribal newspaper to encourage Ho-Chunk constituents to participate. She explained that the self-study was a means through which the Business Committee could "fulfill its recently expanded functions in serving the general welfare of the Wisconsin Winnebago Tribe." The Ho-Chunk people would "provide accurate and complete information about themselves that would be useful in making concrete recommendations for community betterment." She also noted that while the Ho-Chunk people obviously already knew the issues they faced and had good ideas about how to address them, their ability to gain the external support they needed to carry out their plans was dependent on having "all of this information brought together . . . and written out so that even white people can understand it" (wwbc 1963a).

With the hew funding in hand, field research for the self-study began in March 1963. By the time it was concluded in April, the research team had collected responses from 315 households (Miller and Lurie 1963). Most of the field researchers were also members of the Business Committee and, as Lurie later reported, combined their research with problem-solving activities in the field. They addressed complaints of local discrimination, provided help with bureaucratic paperwork, and intervened with local school boards on behalf of Ho-Chunk parents. In a later memo describing the lessons of the project, Lurie explained that Helen Miner Miller viewed it as a means of creating a sense of collaboration, vital to ensuring trust and cooperation between the Business Committee and local Ho-Chunk communities.[15]

Although Miller and the rest of the Business Committee valued the knowledge and collaboration the self-study entailed, they considered its primary value to be the external funding it provided for needed tribal projects and programs, so they developed a strategy to channel the HEW money into their tribal treasury. HEW had granted the Business Committee $7,400 on the understanding that the committee would provide an additional $2,479 in matching funds. The committee budgeted the funds it received from HEW to cover the salaries of Miller, as codirector, and part of the survey team and proposed to use its matching funds to pay the salaries of Lurie and the rest of the survey team. By prior agreement, all those who received salaries from the HEW portion of the funds signed the checks they received back to the Business Committee to be redistributed as needed for tribal projects. All payments to Lurie and others from the committee's portion of the budget were purely notional (Lurie 1989).

In a letter to Miller on June 14, 1962, Lurie wrote that she had mentioned receiving a salary for her work on the project in a letter to Merriam while indicating indirectly to Merriam that she was not really expecting to receive any money: "I figure to take my salary out in 'trade' that is, I'd like to get an article out of the work (though won't insist on it) and I figure that in opportunities to chat with Winnebago people more frequently with the project going I will be picking up all kinds of useful anthropological data on which no price can be put but which has personal and scholarly value for me." She added, "But please don't think I'm trying to twist anyone's arm for information they would be reluctant to give. . . . As I've said before, I owe a debt to the Winnebago but since HEW doesn't seem to like retroactive accounting, I couldn't say that in my letter to Miss Merriam."[16]

In the summer of 1962 Lurie moved from the University of Michigan to a new job as a tenured associate professor at the University of Wisconsin–Milwaukee. She explained in a letter to Helen Miller that she had accepted the new position over competing offers because it would allow her to be near the Wisconsin Winnebago and to "act in a bridging role between tribe and University."[17] Miller and Lurie worked to assemble the data produced by the survey that summer and then presented the first draft of the self-study to a general tribal council held in conjunction with the annual Labor Day powwow in September. They then spent the rest of the fall finalizing the report. It was published by the Business Committee in December (Miller and Lurie 1963).

In their introduction to the self-study, Miller and Lurie described their report as the product of a "unique situation wherein a tribe is collaborating in the writing of its own current ethnography." Their conclusion emphasized that although the conditions facing Ho-Chunk people seemed "bleak," even those suffering the most were participating in the project, contributing their leadership, insight, and energy alongside those who were better off. Emphasizing that the actions of the Business Committee were a total group effort by the Ho-Chunk people, Miller and Lurie explained that the committee built "on existing traditions" based on a principle of dualism within traditional Ho-Chunk political institutions that allowed for the creation of "new institutions" like the Business Committee, oriented to "new endeavors" while still "mutually supportive of existing institutions" (Miller and Lurie 1963, 53).

THEORIZING INDIGENOUS ACTIVISM

Throughout her work on the reorganization effort, Lurie produced scholarly accounts of the project as an example of a new mode of American Indian activism. Her first attempt came amid the push to organize the tribal referendum on reorganization in late 1962, in the form of a paper for an American Association for the Advancement of Science (AAAS) symposium on minority groups. Her paper suggested that the "momentous" actions of the Wisconsin Ho-Chunk provided a test of the assumptions about the inevitable disappearance of American Indian identities and communities shared by the general American population and many scholars. Lurie drew on her work with Miller to argue that the Ho-Chunk people had begun to develop an organizational structure based on Ho-Chunk values and aims—"syncretized with such [structures] of the dominant society that serve Winnebago purposes and command general respect"—to address "immediate and definable economic goals." She noted that military service in the First and Second World Wars had revived the Ho-Chunk warrior tradition, providing "a new sense of unity and satisfactory patterns for dealing with the dominant group," setting in motion the creation of the provisional Business Committee and reviving the powwow as a central community cultural institution. She concluded that the Ho-Chunk people were showing that "under fortuitous circumstances of open choice," Indian people could develop innovative forms of "tribalism" as a viable approach to contemporary life.[18]

Lurie mentioned in correspondence with Sol Tax and with Helen Miller that she had conceived the paper as addressing both Ho-Chunk and academic audiences. Miller had made Ho-Chunk archival files available to Lurie, stipulating that she "make [this] research available to the Winnebago and maybe publish the paper in their new news-sheet" to provide tribal members access to information about otherwise poorly documented periods in their history. Lurie used the material from these files in her advocacy with the BIA and in drafting her AAAS paper. She subsequently submitted the AAAS paper to the Business Committee for its approval and also for its internal use, and she continued adding updates about ongoing events. Lurie encouraged Miller to distribute the paper to regional meetings during the reorganization process "so that when people were discouraged by the difficulty of the struggle they could be reassured by all they had already accomplished."[19] Although the paper was never published, Miller later adapted it as a printed pamphlet to be distributed to Ho-Chunk students, and the Ho-Chunk government published a number of editions of the pamphlet throughout the 1960s (WWBC 1964).

In the summer of 1964 Lurie presented another academic paper on Ho-Chunk reorganization at the VIIth International Congress of Anthropological and Ethnological Sciences in Moscow. In it, Lurie argued that the Wisconsin Winnebago "constitute a particularly striking example of the determination to maintain tribal identity while improving their standards of living," through a "judicious utilization . . . of those facets of the larger socio-economic system which could serve their needs." She drew on the vision of the dual institutional structure in the self-study to explain how the Business Committee took on a liaison role "between the tribe and the larger society" in conjunction with "the revival of clans and other traditional institutions designed to maintain order and [lend] dignity to collective activities." The committee's goal was to raise the Ho-Chunk people's "material living standard" without abandoning "those viable and meaningful features of their tribal heritage which have always sustained them" (Lurie 1971a).

The Moscow presentation came during a time of transition for Lurie's action project. Just a few weeks before Lurie left for Moscow, Helen Miner

Miller had resigned from the Business Committee for health reasons. Lurie continued to consult with the committee throughout the fall of 1964 and spring of 1965 as it worked to identify new sources of funding for its housing and educational projects. But she also began to think about future research and applied for a Fulbright fellowship in Denmark, where she planned to teach at Aarhus University and explore the possibility of ethnographic research with Sami peoples.

Without other offers of funding, the Business Committee decided to pursue a second wave of funding for its HEW grant. The committee had been informed that the Ho-Chunk people's active explorations of resources and alternative ideas for self-help would count as appropriate "research." With Miller's departure, Lurie agreed to continue to work on the second phase of the project with the committee's approval, and Nadine Sieber took Miller's place as the project's codirector. Lorraine Swan Winneshiek, the wife of the traditional chief and one of Lurie's oldest Ho-Chunk friends, came on board to handle the finances as an extension of her duties as the committee's treasurer. Planning began in November, and in December the Business Committee officially voted to proceed with the project, with regional meetings and discussions held throughout the spring.[20]

In the midst of the new project, the Business Committee began to experience some unexpected challenges. Ho-Chunk people living near Black River Falls had requested funds from the BIA to rehabilitate the recently abandoned school building in their community. Instead, the BIA proceeded to rehabilitate the building itself without consulting the Business Committee. While a well-intentioned gesture, the new building soon became a source of strain on the committee because it had indoor plumbing, requiring the use of expensive oil heating during colder months to prevent the pipes from bursting. The BIA had assumed that the Business Committee would be able to cover such operational costs out of its own funds; however, given the minimal existing tribal treasury and lack of ongoing means of generating revenue, the expenses of maintaining the building rapidly began to drain the tribal treasury. This created tensions within the Ho-Chunk community, between Black River Falls and other community centers, since it drew on resources intended to be shared equally among Ho-Chunk people and undermined plans for local development and land acquisition projects in other settlements.

In correspondence with BIA officials, Lurie tried to explain the problems with the bureau's actions, focusing in particular on its failure to consult with the Business Committee: "Well-meant but precipitous action undertaken in the belief that it was the 'practical' and 'realistic' course has resulted in bankrupting the tribe and producing a building which is not even useful." As she wrote to Philleo Nash, it was an object lesson in one of the basic principles of action anthropology—that communities know themselves and their needs better than outsiders.[21] As a partial apology for the issues with the school building, Nash and the BIA offered the Business Committee a new housing project, with guaranteed funding from a bureau program meant to provide housing for those most in need.[22]

As she prepared to leave for her Fulbright fellowship, Lurie wrote a long memorandum thanking the Business Committee for the "vindication" of her "optimism and faith that people can help themselves and one another and will do so given any kind of proper opportunity." She then offered an anthropological analysis of the academics and professionals the committee would have to deal with as it moved forward with its projects, warning of the stereotypes and tactics it would face from the BIA and others who worked with Indians, whose expectations were likely to be a poor fit for Ho-Chunk people. "It is almost inevitable that unless you prove otherwise outsiders are going to generalize about you on the basis of [the] stereotype of 'Woodland Indians.' It will influence their policies and actions toward you—and with only the greatest good-will intended because they think they really 'understand' you."[23]

Lurie also drew on her observations from the past years to describe the tendencies she felt set Indigenous planning apart from the Euro-American ways exemplified by federal agencies and academic consultants. "Euro-Americans meet a new situation or problem by creating a structure to solve the problem and then perhaps adjusting the structure or trying new ones [while] Indian people let the structure for solving a problem grow out of the problem or situation itself." She noted that the Indigenous approach seemed to work better, and if they knew how to present their plans to outsiders, they would be able to get programs accomplished "without compromising [their] values and methods."[24]

The worries that motivated Lurie's advice about dealing with external agencies proved to be prophetic. Over the next year, desperate for money for tribal projects, the Business Committee turned to the new federal Office of Economic Opportunity for funding. The funds the committee received allowed it to make progress in land reacquisition and the development of education and vocational programs, but the money was administered in ways that undermined Ho-Chunk decision-making, leading to the sort of internal political struggles that the leaders had previously worked to avoid. When Lurie returned from Aarhus, she found "new houses on newly acquired land in tribal trust status, a community building at one settlement, [and] many new students in college and vocational programs," but she also discovered that the Business Committee had become "riven into warring camps" by disagreements caused by the external administration of the new funding (see Gudinas 1974, 173–88, for an account). With friends in both camps and a sense that any involvement by her would only exacerbate the conflict, she withdrew and turned her action efforts elsewhere.

RECOVERING THE LESSONS OF HO-CHUNK REORGANIZATION

Nancy Lurie's work on the Ho-Chunk effort to create a federally recognized tribal government was the first in a series of action projects that culminated in her participation with activists from the Menominee Nation in their ultimately successful bid for restoration to tribal status in 1973 (Peroff 1982; Shames 1973; Lurie 1972a; Arndt 2023). While engaged in these action projects, Lurie continually drew on her experiences with the Ho-Chunk project as a basis for an ongoing effort to develop a theory of contemporary Indian action (Lurie 1965, 1968, 1971; Arndt 2019). Yet in her writing, she rarely discussed her own work or the Ho-Chunk project. She reduced the argument of her 1962 AAAS paper to a footnote in the special issue of the *Midcontinental Journal of American Studies* on the "American Indian Today" that she coedited, focusing instead on insights from other scholars into the relevance of the concept of renaissance as a framework for understanding what was going on in Native communities (Lurie 1965, Levine and Lurie 1965). Her 1964 paper for the Moscow conference was published only years later by a Soviet publisher in the predominantly Russian language conference proceedings (Lurie 1971a). Long before it appeared, the international group of Americanists who had met at the Moscow conference began to plan a collaborative volume, initially conceived as a Soviet textbook giving evolutionary and historical perspectives on Native peoples, but eventually becoming *North American Indians in Historical Perspective*, which Lurie edited with Eleanor Leacock (Leacock and Lurie 1971; Arndt 2019). During the long gestation of that volume, Lurie developed a general theory of the "articulatory" movement emerging across Native North America, but her account included only oblique references to the Ho-Chunk project (1971c).

It was only in the 1970s that Lurie finally began to discuss the Ho-Chunk project, first in her subsequently misunderstood contribution to a symposium on Vine Deloria's *Custer Died for Your Sins*, in which she suggested that her work on Ho-Chunk reorganization provided one model of anthropological praxis addressed to contemporary Indigenous mobilizations and critiques (Lurie 1973, 4; Arndt 2023), and later as part of a tribute to the career of Philleo Nash (Lurie 1989). The latter account came as part of an emergent effort to explain the misunderstood legacies of action anthropology and commemorate the efforts of anthropologists including Sol Tax, D'Arcy McNickle, Philleo Nash, Alexander Lesser, Robert Rietz, and Robert Thomas, all of whom had practiced an engaged anthropology rooted in a commitment to Indigenous self-determination and well-being long before such engagement enjoyed mainstream acceptance in the discipline (Lurie 1998, 1999). In these contributions, Lurie wrote to address misrepresentations of action anthropology at a time when anthropologists around the world were once again confronting the challenges of Indigenous action and activism, but even those most actively engaged with Indigenous issues did not recognize that they were joining an ongoing, if often marginalized, tradition within the discipline (e.g., Stocking 2000, 255).

That ignorance has continued in the discipline's most recent engagement with the politics of decolonization, despite the ongoing efforts of a number of historians of action anthropology and Americanist anthropology more generally (e.g., Smith 2015, 2021; Cobb 2019; Dinwoodie 2023; Bashkow 2019, 2023; Barron 2023). In this context, I hope that this account of Nancy Lurie's work with Helen Miner Miller and other Ho-Chunk leaders in their project of nation rebuilding contributes to the project of developing a new, more complex understanding of the history of Americanist anthropology while also providing a model for contemporary anthropologists seeking to make their own contributions to Indigenous struggles.

ACKNOWLEDGMENTS

I would like to thank the participants in the memorial panel that Larry Nesper and I organized for the annual meeting of the American Ethnohistorical Society in 2017, especially the late Ada Deer, and the contributors of essays to this special section on Nancy Lurie, many of which are derived from that panel. I am also grateful to Regna Darnell for being in the audience for our panel and for supporting the subsequent development of the project. Thanks to Fred Gleach for all his editorial and organizational work on this volume. This chapter reflects my initial efforts to reconstruct Nancy Lurie's action anthropology projects and is therefore indebted to the work of prior scholars seeking to recover the legacies of action anthropology and its relationship to contemporary Indigenous activism, especially Joshua Smith, Daniel Cobb, and Judy Daubenmier. The project as a whole has also been enriched by those who have commented on my other publications on Nancy Lurie, including Nick Barron, Ira Bashkow, David Dinwoodie, April Eisman, Herbert Lewis, Alice Kehoe, and Max Viatori. I would like to acknowledge the archivists at the Newberry and Regenstein Libraries in Chicago, and especially Dawn Scher Thomae at the Milwaukee Public Museum, for facilitating my research. I am also grateful to Iowa State University for its support.

NOTES

1. HMMP: "Reports of Meetings Beginning Jan. 1, 1961, Wisconsin Dells, Wisconsin at NAC," box 1, folder 7.
2. HMMP: "Wisconsin Winnebago to Presidential Task Force on Indian Problems, Mar. 27, 1961," box 1, folder 4.
3. HMMP: "Wisconsin Winnebago to Presidential Task Force."
4. HMMP: "Reports of Meetings Beginning Jan. 1, 1961."
5. HMMP: General Wisconsin Winnebago Tribal Meeting, Wisconsin Dells WI, September 9, 1961, box 5, folder 52.
6. For the text of Peterson's speech, see Gudinas (1972, 103–4).
7. HMMP: Minutes, Wisconsin Winnebago Business Committee, Wisconsin Dells WI, December 9, 1961, box 5, folder 52.
8. STP: Nancy Lurie to Sol Tax, October 18, 1962, box 132, folder 1.
9. NOLP: Nancy Lurie to Philleo Nash, November 24, 1962, HCN Ho-Chunk Nation Chronological Files, 1961–83 (hereafter HCN).

10. NOLP: Nancy Oestreich Lurie, "The Wisconsin Winnebago: Tribe-Minority Group-Tribe," paper presented at the symposium Ethnic Minorities Around the World, American Society for Ethnohistory, Philadelphia, December 27, 1962, with cover sheet "To the Wisconsin Winnebago Tribe" and 1963 addendum, HCN.

11. NOLP: Helen Miner Miller and Nancy Oestreich Lurie, "Prospectus for Community Development Study of the Wisconsin Winnebago Indians," January 29, 1962, HCN.

12. STP: Nancy Lurie to Sol Tax, October 18, 1962.

13. STP: Lurie to Tax, October 18, 1962; Lurie 1973.

14. NOLP: Helen Miner Miller and Nancy Oestreich Lurie, "Franklin Park Seminar," January 23, 1963, HCN.

15. NOLP: Nancy Oestreich Lurie to Carl Olien and Robert Smith, "Regarding: Effective Working Relations Between the Wisconsin Winnebago People and the Office of Economic Opportunity as well as Other Agencies," March 27, 1967, HCN.

16. NOLP: Nancy Lurie to Helen Miner Miller, June 14, 1962, HCN.

17. NOLP: Nancy Lurie to Helen Miner Miller, March 11, 1963, HCN.

18. NOLP: Lurie, "Wisconsin Winnebago." Lurie's prescient observations about the revival of the warrior tradition and its impact on leadership roles remained unpublished until 1994, when she invoked them in an article for the Ho-Chunk Nation's newspaper in association with the thirtieth anniversary of reorganization (Lurie 1994).

19. NOLP: Lurie to Miller, March 11, 1963.

20. NOLP: Minutes on Nancy Oestreich Lurie and WWBC meeting with Matthew Pilcher (HEW) on continuation of funds for research, November 9, 1964, HCN.

21. NOLP: Nancy Oestreich Lurie to Philleo Nash, June 30, 1965, HCN.

22. NOLP: Nadine Sieber, Nancy Oestreich Lurie, and Wisconsin Winnebago Business Committee, "Preliminary Draft for HEW Team Study: Continuation of the Report on the Wisconsin Winnebago Project," 1965, HCN.

23. NOLP: Nancy Oestreich Lurie, "The Time Has Come for Us, Dear Friends, to Say Adieu (for Another Year, Anyway . . .)," Memorandum to Wisconsin Winnebago Business Committee, June 27, 1965, HCN.

24. NOLP: Lurie, "Time Has Come."

REFERENCES

Manuscripts and Archives

HMMP. Miller, Helen Miner. Papers. Newberry Library, Chicago.

NOLP. Lurie, Nancy Oestreich. Papers. Milwaukee Public Museum.

STP. Tax, Sol. Papers. Special Collections Research Center, Regenstein Library, University of Chicago.

Published Works

Arndt, Grant. 2019. "Rediscovering Nancy Oestreich Lurie's Activist Anthropology." *American Anthropologist* 121 (3): 725–28.

———. 2023. "Joining the Ongoing Struggle: Vine Deloria, Nancy Lurie, and the Quest for a Decolonial Anthropology." *Journal of Anthropological Research* 79 (4): 468–91.

Barron, Nicholas. 2023. "The Shop Floor Conditions of Anthropology's Past and Present." *American Anthropologist* 125 (1): 174–76.

Bashkow, Ira. 2019. "Introduction: History of Anthropology That Is Designed to Inspire." *American Anthropologist* 121 (3): 708–9.

———. 2023. "There's More to Anthropology's Past Than Most of Us Know." *American Anthropologist* 125 (1): 177–80.

Cobb, Daniel. 2019. "The Personal Politics of Action and Applied Anthropology." *Ethnohistory* 66 (3): 537–63.

Deloria, Vine, Jr. 1969. *Custer died for your sins: An Indian manifesto.* New York: Macmillan.

Dinwoodie, David. 2023. "Decolonization and the History of Anthropology: The Implications of New Deal Anthropology from the 1930s to the 1950s." *Journal of Anthropological Research* 79 (4): 439–67.

Ganteaume, Cecil R. 1989. "Nancy Oestreich Lurie (1924–)." In *Women Anthropologists: Selected Biographies,* edited by Ute Gacs, Aisha Khan, Jerrie McIntyre, and Ruth Weinberg, 238–45. Urbana: University of Illinois Press.

Gudinas, Ruth A. 1971. "Wisconsin Winnebago Political Organization Structure/Cultural Incompatibility and Organizational Effectiveness." PhD diss., University of Chicago.

Harkin, Michael E. 2010. "Ethnohistory's Ethnohistory: Creating a Discipline from the Ground Up." *Social Science History* 34 (2): 113–28.

Landman, Ruth H., and Katherine S. Halpern, eds. 1989. *Applied Anthropologist and Public Servant: The Life and Work of Philleo Nash.* NAPA Bulletin 7. Washington, DC: American Anthropological Association.

Leacock, Eleanor Burke, and Nancy Oestreich Lurie, eds. 1971. *North American Indians in Historical Perspective.* New York: Random House.

Lesser, Alexander. 1961. "Education and the Future of Tribalism in the United States: The Case of the American Indian." *Social Service Review* 35:1–9.

Levine, Stuart, and Nancy Oestreich Lurie (eds). 1965. *Midcontinent American Studies Journal* Vol. 6, No. 2, *The Indian Today*.

Lewis, Herbert. 2024. *Correcting the Record: Essays on the History of American Anthropology*. New York: Berghahn Books.

Lurie, Nancy Oestreich. 1944. "Cultural Change Among the Wisconsin Winnebago." *Wisconsin Archeologist* 25 (4): 119–25.

———. 1955. "Problems, Opportunities, and Recommendations." *Ethnohistory* 2 (4): 357–75.

———. 1956. A Reply To "The Land Claims Cases: Anthropologists in Conflict" *Ethnohistory* 3 (3): 256-279.

———. 1957. "The Indian Claims Commission Act." *Annals of the American Academy of Political and Social Science* 311 (May): 56–70.

———. 1961. "The Voice of the American Indian: A Report on the American Indian Chicago Conference." *Current Anthropology* 2 (5): 478–500.

———. 1964. "A More or Less Anthropological View of the General Council." *Wisconsin Winnebago* 1 (6): 4–5.

———. 1965. "An American Indian Renascence?" *Midcontinent American Studies Journal* 6 (2): 25–50.

———. 1968. "Variant Adaptations of Minority Groups to Encompassing Systems." In *Proceedings of the VIIIth International Congress of Anthropological and Ethnological Sciences*, vol. 2, *Ethnology*, 154–56. Tokyo: Congress of Anthropological and Ethnological Sciences.

———. 1971a. "An American Indian Tribal Renascence." In *Proceedings of the VIIth International Congress of Anthropological and Ethnological Sciences, Moscow (August 3–10, 1964)*, vol. 11, edited by S. P. Tolstov, 91–96. Moscow: Congress of Anthropological and Ethnological Sciences.

———. 1971b. "As Others See Us." *New University Thought* 7 (1): 2–7.

———. 1971c. "The Contemporary American Indian Scene." In *North American Indians in Historical Perspective*, edited by Eleanor Burke Leacock and Nancy Oestreich Lurie, 418–80. New York: Random House.

———. 1972a. "Menominee Termination: From Reservation to Colony." *Human Organization* 31 (3): 257–69.

———. 1972b. "Two Dollars." In *Crossing Cultural Boundaries: The Anthropological Experience*, edited by Solon T. Kimball and James B. Watson, 151–63. San Francisco: Chandler.

———. 1973. "Action Anthropology and the American Indian." In *Anthropology and the American Indian: Report of a Symposium*, edited by James Officer, 5–15. San Francisco: Indian Historian.

———. 1989. "Philleo Nash and American Indian People." In *Applied Anthropologist and Public Servant: The Life and Work of Philleo Nash,* edited by Ruth H. Landman and Katherine S. Halpern, 16–20. Washington DC: National Association for the Practice of Anthropology.

———. 1994. "Winnebago Veterans and the Warrior Tradition." *Ho-Chunk Wo-Lduk* 8 (17): 3–4.

———. 1998. "Selective Recollections on Anthropology and Indians." *Current Anthropology* 39 (4): 572–74.

———. 1999. "Sol Tax and Tribal Sovereignty." *Human Organization* 58 (1): 108–17.

Miller, Helen Miner, and Nancy Oestreich Lurie. 1963. *Report on Wisconsin Winnebago Project: Contribution of Community Development to the Prevention of Dependency.* Washington DC: U.S. Social Security Administration.

Nash, Philleo. 1937. "The Place of Religious Revivalism in the Formation of the Intercultural Community on the Klamath Reservation." In *The Social Anthropology of North American Tribes: Essays in Social Organization, Law and Religion,* edited by Fred Eggan, 377–442. Chicago: University of Chicago Press.

Peroff, Nicholas C. 1982. *Menominee Drums: Tribal Termination and Restoration, 1954–1974.* Norman: University of Oklahoma Press.

Peterson, Helen. 1962. "Mrs. Helen L. Peterson, Speaker at the Wisconsin Winnebago General Council Meeting, December 9, 1961." *Ho-Chunk Wazee ja cheer la: Published by the Wisconsin Winnebago Business Committee for Its Tribe,* April.

Provinse, John, and Ruth Useem. 1954. "Wenner-Gren Foundation Supper Conference: The American Indian in Transition." *American Anthropologist* 56 (3): 387–94.

Shames, Deborah, ed. 1972. *Freedom with Reservation: The Menominee Struggle to Save Their Land and People.* Madison, WI: National Committee to Save the Menominee People and Forests.

Smith, Joshua. 2015. "Standing with Sol: The Spirit and Intent of Action Anthropology." *Anthropologica* 57 (2): 445–56.

———. 2021. "Reckoning with Rietz: A Sketch of an Action Anthropologist." In *Centering the Margins of Anthropology's History,* edited by Regna Darnell, 37–52. Lincoln: University of Nebraska Press.

Stocking, George. 2000. "'Do Good, Young Man': Sol Tax and the World Mission of Liberal Democratic Anthropology." In *Excluded Ancestors, Inventible Traditions: Essays Toward a More Inclusive History of Anthropology,* edited by Richard Handler, 171–264. Madison: University of Wisconsin Press.

Tax, Sol. 1961. "What the Indians Want." *Chicago Sun-Times,* June 11, sec. 2, 1–2.

———. (1958) 1975. "Action Anthropology." *Current Anthropology* 16 (4): 514–17.

wwbc (Wisconsin Winnebago Business Committee). 1963a. "Announcement of Award for Research in Community Development Granted to the Wisconsin Winnebago Tribe by the Social Security Administration of the United States Department of Health, Education, and Welfare." *Wisconsin Winnebago* 1 (2): 3.

———. 1963b. [Final election results]. *Wisconsin Winnebago* 1 (2): 3.

———. 1964. *Historical Background of the Winnebago People.* [Black River Falls]: Wisconsin Winnebago Business Committee.

13

Unmasking "The Fallacy of Misplaced Concreteness"

Nancy Lurie, Jean Nicolet, and the Ho-Chunks

PATRICK J. JUNG

Nancy Oestreich Lurie's death on May 13, 2017, at the age of ninety-three deprived the anthropological profession of one of its most passionate advocates. Lurie's contributions to anthropology and the ideas that shaped the arc of her career will provide future researchers with a wealth of topics to explore. Only a limited number of biographical studies concerning Lurie currently exist (Ganteaume 1988; Arndt 2019). Nevertheless, these works, when augmented by her prolific scholarly output, illustrate clear patterns. She is, and likely will remain, most known for her commitment to action anthropology, a field largely developed by Sol Tax at the University of Chicago, where Lurie received her master's degree in 1947. Action anthropologists sought, in partnership with Native leaders and activists, to assist American Indian communities with seemingly chronic social and economic challenges. It was a radical break within American anthropology, the practitioners of which had previously remained somewhat aloof from the societies they studied. Lurie's entry into action anthropology at the American Indian Chicago Conference, organized by Tax in 1961, inspired her to assist the Wisconsin Ho-Chunks (then called the Winnebagos) with the creation of a tribal government in 1963. She also assisted the Menominees of Wisconsin with the restoration of their tribal status in 1973 after more than a decade of suffering under the federal government's ill-conceived termination policy (Stapp 2012; Ablon 2012).

Less well known is Lurie's abiding interest in historical documents as sources of cultural and ethnohistorical information. Franz Boas, the

"father of American anthropology," had developed historical particular-
ism, which asserted that every culture had its own unique path of development. Boas and his students generally eschewed historical documents
produced outside of a cultural system and preferred artifacts from within
a culture, particularly language and oral traditions, as sources of data (Darnell 1998, 2001). Lurie, who came of age intellectually during the 1940s and
early 1950s, when Boas's virtual monopoly over American anthropology
began to wane, never fully embraced this paradigm. Still, like Boas and
his students, she was keenly interested in cultural change. This led to her
interest in the writings of Ralph Linton, who developed the fundamental
ideas concerning acculturation along with Melville J. Herskovits (Lurie's
dissertation director at Northwestern University) and Robert Redfield.
The concept of acculturation as a mechanism to explain cultural change
over time informed Lurie's research (Lurie 1944, 1952, 1968; Kluckhohn
1958; Darnell 1998). Another formative influence was James S. Slotkin, who
directed Lurie's first fieldwork experience among the Ho-Chunks in 1944
while she was still an undergraduate at the University of Wisconsin. Tax
later wrote of Slotkin, "In historical-documentary research he was unex-
celled. . . . He spared no effort in tracking down accurate sources" (Tax
1959, 845; Hass and Danky 1996, 271). Both her published master's thesis
(1948), and her unpublished doctoral dissertation (1952) devote considerable space to Ho-Chunk history and acculturation based on primary
source documents. Thus Lurie's mentors inculcated in her a deep appreciation for diachronic analysis through historical methodology.

Equally important was the research she did for the Indian Claims Commission in the 1950s, a task that often required research into unpublished
manuscripts in the U.S. National Archives (Lurie 1978a). In a 1961 article
on ethnohistoric method, Lurie lauded the value of primary source documents for synchronic analysis when she noted that "while the basic methods of using documentary evidence have been learned from the historian,
the ethnohistorian has also developed techniques of his own and uses the
evidence for a variety of purposes beyond historical concerns with acculturation and diffusion" (79). A full account of Lurie's contributions to
history and ethnohistory awaits further inquiry. Nevertheless, her astute
insights and capacity for both historical and ethnohistorical research are
evidenced by her research on French explorer Jean Nicolet, the first Euro-

pean known to have visited the Ho-Chunks, likely in 1634 (Jung 2018, 72–73). She refuted many of the myths surrounding Nicolet, and her discoveries shed new light on the early history of the French in North America, as well as Ho-Chunk prehistory and protohistory.

The French called the Ho-Chunks the Puans, a rough translation of the Algonkian Ouinipegou (Winnebago in English), or "people of the stinking water," a reference to their residence at Green Bay of Lake Michigan. The French had learned of the Ho-Chunks' existence as early as 1615, about two decades before Nicolet made contact. Lurie discussed Nicolet's voyage only cursorily in her thesis (1948, 45) and dissertation (1952, 47). She delved more substantively into the topic in a 1960 essay on the protohistory of the Ho-Chunks. Even at this early stage, she expressed reservations about the accepted historical interpretation that Samuel de Champlain, the commander of the colony of New France, had sent Nicolet westward to find the elusive Northwest Passage, a waterway to the Pacific Ocean and the Far East. Lurie also expressed doubt regarding the claim Nicolet wore a Chinese robe in the expectation he might find an outpost or colony of settlers from Asia after traveling westward beyond Lake Huron. "Such, at least, is the explanation," she wrote, "for the Chinese robe donned by Nicolet when he was about to greet the Winnebago" (Lurie 1960, 793).

Lurie continued, over the next fifty years, to question this account, which originated when Benjamin Sulte speculated in 1876 that Nicolet had worn a Chinese robe during the course of his journey (428–30). Later writers repeated Sulte's assumption, artists immortalized it in paintings and statues that reinforced the idea in the public mind, and what had been speculation evolved into historical dogma. Lurie's initial skepticism served her well. She continued her research and discovered Sulte had committed an error that resulted in later researchers embellishing his already flawed narrative with additional misinterpretations and even outright fabrications, which had accumulated in the historical record. Lurie described this phenomenon of accrued error embraced as certainty as "the fallacy of misplaced concreteness," a term proffered by English mathematician Alfred North Whitehead (Lurie and Jung 2009, 9; Whitehead 1929, 7). Her key discovery was that Nicolet had donned a cape typical of those worn as outerwear in seventeenth-century Europe. The cape was made of *damas de la Chine*, or China damask: a type of silk cloth, not a style of robe. The word "China" had thrown off early Nicolet scholars, particularly Sulte, and others perpetuated the error (Lurie and Jung 2009, 9–16).

In 2005 Lurie commenced what was originally planned as an article on Nicolet's journey. I was honored that she invited me onto the project to assist with historical research, particularly a thorough examination of Champlain's writings and cartographic productions. After four years of research and writing, the article developed into a book titled *The Nicolet Corrigenda: New France Revisited*, published in 2009. Lurie had several goals with this work. The first was to provide corrections (or corrigenda) to the long list of errors that had plagued earlier studies of Nicolet. The second was to reexamine the prehistory and protohistory of the Ho-Chunk people in light of these corrections. In the first case, Lurie argued, under-standing the nature of Nicolet's journey would further elucidate the early history of the French in North America. This, in turn, would facilitate the second goal of better understanding the Ho-Chunks in the early seven-teenth century (Lurie and Jung 2009, 1–4).

Correcting Sulte's error by asserting Nicolet wore a cape typical of those worn by seventeenth-century European gentlemen may seem to be little more than overzealous antiquarianism. However, that single correction per-mitted Lurie to further rectify some of what had been assumed about the early French period in North America. Previous researchers had believed Champlain's interest in finding the Northwest Passage had been his prin-cipal reason, or at least a significant motivation, for ordering Nicolet on his voyage. However, this argument rested completely on the "fact" that Nicolet traveled with a Chinese robe in tow as he made his way westward (see, e.g., Butterfield 1881; Jouan 1888; Kellogg 1925), a Chinese robe that Lurie found to be nonexistent. This necessitated a closer examination of Champlain's writings, which revealed that he had abandoned the notion of the Great Lakes providing a direct passage to the Pacific Ocean as early as 1624. Instead, Nicolet's mission was purely diplomatic and sought to end the hostilities between the French-allied tribes of the Lake Huron region and the Ho-Chunks at Green Bay. The French sources that chronicled Nicolet's journey made this clear; the "myth of Nicolet's Chinese robe," as Lurie called it, had obscured, or at least distorted, this simple reality from the time of Sulte onward (Lurie and Jung 2009, 11; see also Jung 2018).

Champlain's purpose in sending Nicolet to the Ho-Chunks was a component of his larger project for the colony of New France and its principal trading post, Quebec. The English had conquered Quebec and controlled New France from 1629 to 1632. When Champlain returned to Quebec after France recovered the colony, his objective—in fact, his single-minded focus—was securing New France and the trade network he had painstakingly established during his two decades of leadership before the English conquest. He sought to prevent European rivals from again subjugating the colony; he also believed the Haudenosaunee (Five Nations League of the Iroquois) in present-day New York posed a grave threat to the Native peoples with whom the French traded. Champlain's written works offer copious evidence of these intentions. While they mention nothing about Nicolet, his mission, or the threat posed by the Ho-Chunks, *The Jesuit Relations*, published reports of the Jesuit missionaries, particularly the narrative of Barthélemy Vimont, provide the requisite evidence to conclude Champlain also saw the Ho-Chunks as a threat to the western end of the French trade network in the same manner as the Haudenosaunee imperiled New France's southern flank (Lurie and Jung 2009; see also Jung 2018).

Previous scholars had noted Champlain's waning interest in the search for the Northwest Passage in his later years but were reluctant to concede he might no longer have believed by the 1630s that the Great Lakes provided such a passage. Their reluctance stemmed solely from the mistaken notion that Champlain had sent Nicolet westward with a Chinese robe (see, e.g., Butterfield 1881; Kellogg 1925; Delanglez 1947; Heidenreich 1976). Once Lurie debunked this myth, Champlain's objectives on his return to Quebec became clear, as did the evolution of his geographic and cartographic thinking concerning North America during the span of his career. Nagging anomalies that had undermined an accurate understanding of Nicolet and Champlain for a century and a half turned to dust. Lurie proudly noted that "having pulled this thread," she could not resist unraveling "a whole tapestry of errors, inventions, sloppy scholarship, and passionately partisan defenses of conflicting conclusions" (Lurie and Jung 2009, 1).

Lurie also continually questioned the English translations of *The Jesuit Relations* produced by the editorial team under the direction of Reuben Gold Thwaites over a century earlier. Lurie was not the first researcher to discern that many of the translations of the seventeenth-century French were less than perfect.[1] For example, Thwaites's team had translated the term *grande robbe*, a description of Nicolet's apparel, as "grand robe," when a more accurate translation would have been "large cape" (Thwaites 1896–1901, 23:278–79; Lurie and Jung 2009, 10–20).

Another key term Lurie questioned was *au delà*, which Jesuit Paul LeJeune had used in describing the route Nicolet traveled. *Au delà* could denote either moving through or moving past a location. Thwaites's team had translated the phrase as "beyond" (Thwaites 1896–1901, 18:230–31). Later researchers took this to mean Nicolet went through the Sault Ste. Marie rapids and into Lake Superior rather than past the rapids and into Lake Michigan. Lurie correctly surmised LeJeune had used *au delà* in the latter context, particularly since he had employed the term in the same manner elsewhere in his narrative. A later passage by LeJeune unequivocally revealed that Nicolet had traveled past, not on, a "great river" that would have taken him to the "sea." I determined, along with Lurie, that the "great river" referred to the St. Marys River and the Sault Ste. Marie rapids, while the "sea" referred to Lake Superior (Lurie and Jung 2009, 51–57). Moreover, Conrad E. Heidenreich, a well-known historical geographer, had earlier arrived at the same conclusion (1997, 95). This discovery laid to rest the assertion that Nicolet had traveled to Lake Superior, a theory championed by historians whose arguments Lurie meticulously dismantled. Mistakenly locating Nicolet's landfall in the Lake Superior basin, Lurie argued, also forced these scholars to place the Ho-Chunks along the shores of Lake Superior despite an abundance of ethnohistorical and archaeological evidence, as well as Ho-Chunk oral traditions, that placed them at Green Bay (Lurie and Jung 2014).

Thus Lurie's discoveries allowed her to fill in some of the yawning gaps of information concerning the Ho-Chunks. For example, understanding that Nicolet's mission was purely diplomatic suggested the Ho-Chunks were a far more powerful society in the western Great Lakes than had previously been assumed. Champlain had organized similar embassies to the formidable Haudenosaunee (Iroquois); Nicolet's mission suggested the Ho-Chunks were an analogous power in the western Great Lakes and a potential threat to the French trade network (Lurie and Jung 2009, 99). The French sources concerning the Ho-Chunks, meager as they are, indicate a warlike society with an aggressive reputation among other Native groups farther east, such as the Odawas and Wendats (Hurons). This aggressiveness resulted in a deadly assault against an Odawa trade party that compelled Champlain to order Nicolet on his westward journey, a mission that likely occurred in 1634 but might have been undertaken in 1633 (Jung 2018, 110). Lurie summarized this novel interpretation of the Ho-Chunks when she noted they "were not only a serious barrier to the extension of French trade and empire to the West because of their war-like proclivities but also these proclivities betokened tribes and customs unfamiliar to the French, thereby requiring a special diplomatic overture" (Lurie and Jung 2009, 93). This conclusion paralleled evidence collected by earlier ethnographers such as Paul Radin. Lurie went on to write, "The fact that Nicolet was sent expressly to make peace with the Puan [Ho-Chunks] is consistent with a cultural focus on warfare that was elaborated beyond French experience with even the notoriously warlike Iroquois" (Lurie and Jung 2009, 99).

Lurie also understood the limitations all researchers faced, given the paucity of data concerning Nicolet and the Native peoples of the western Great Lakes during the early seventeenth century. Nicolet's landfall had been a contentious issue among scholars for over a century. While she had definitively dismissed his proposed landfalls along Lake Superior, various locations along Lake Michigan also had to be examined, such as Red Banks, on the western shore of Green Bay's Door Peninsula; present-day Neenah-Menasha in Wisconsin; and the Chicago area. Knowing that any conclusion was necessarily tentative, given the ambiguous nature of the narratives penned by Vimont and LeJeune, Lurie asserted, with a dose of caution, that Nicolet's likely destination was the Grand Village of the Menominee, now Marinette, Wisconsin, and a location that had never been proposed by any previous researcher. This site, more so than any other proposed landfall, best meshed with the available evidence, particularly the fact that upon his arrival, Nicolet was greeted with an unequivocally Menominee word, Manitouiriniou, or "the wonderful man or being" (Lurie and Jung 2009, 51, 114, 116).

Determining the location of his landfall had long been the domain of amateur researchers eager to claim Nicolet as the "first white man" to visit their respective localities. Lurie understood that a greater ethnohistorical question was at stake—specifically, the nature and composition of the

Ho-Chunk polity. French sources suggested it was an ethnically mixed entity that included Algonkian speakers such as the Menominees, who likely were a subordinate people of the predominant Chiwere Siouan–speaking Ho-Chunks. Lurie believed Nicolet conducted his diplomacy in the country of the Menominees because it was a neutral location, or at least a less perilous one. The Menominee country offered security that would have been compromised had he traveled into the heartland of the Ho-Chunks (Lurie and Jung 2009, 115–17).

While Lurie struggled with some questions related to Nicolet and the Ho-Chunks, her contributions provide an important foundation for further inquiry. Lurie used the name Ho-Chunk throughout *The Nicolet Corrigenda* even though she believed this moniker did not come into use until the early nineteenth century (pers. comm., August 16, 2012). I later discovered French records employing the term as early as 1721 (Jung 2018, 7; Charlevoix 1761, 62). Lurie also understood that the society the French called the Puans was very different from that of the historic Ho-Chunks of the postcontact era. The Ho-Chunks of the precontact period, Lurie argued, might have included other Chiwere Siouan speakers such as the emergent Otos, Iowas, and Missourias in addition to the ancestral Ho-Chunks. The Menominees appear to have been subordinate to the Ho-Chunks but, along with other Algonkian-speaking groups, might nevertheless have been an integral component of the Ho-Chunk polity. The Ho-Chunks became engaged in a war with the Inohka tribes (Illinois Confederacy) in the years after Nicolet's visit, probably about 1646, and this conflict resulted in a catastrophic population loss. The remnants of the Ho-Chunks later created a new society with a social organization that mirrored that of their Central Algonkian neighbors. What emerged from this ethnogenesis was the Chiwere Siouan–speaking Ho-Chunk Tribe of the historic period (Lurie and Jung 2009, 2, 72). Earlier, Lurie (1978b, 694–95) had speculated that the precontact Ho-Chunks were likely matrilineal, given the retention of certain matrilineal traits such as the inheritance of war bundles and clan affiliations through the female line in the absence of qualified male heirs. In my own research (Jung 2023), I have uncovered additional evidence that supports this conclusion.

Lurie also devoted a considerable portion of *The Nicolet Corrigenda* to Ho-Chunk prehistory and protohistory, including material from an unpublished paper she wrote in 1973. She argued that the Ho-Chunks had originally resided at Aztalan, a Mississippian site in southern Wisconsin and one of the northernmost outposts of the great civilization of Cahokia, east of present-day St. Louis. From there they migrated northward to the Door Peninsula in northeastern Wisconsin, where they resided at the time of Nicolet's visit and where their descendants later emerged as the historic Ho-Chunk people (Lurie 1973). However, a general consensus exists among archaeologists that the ancestors of the Ho-Chunks were the carriers of the archaeological complex known as Oneota. Thus Lurie's theory of Mississippian origins has garnered little support. Archaeological researchers still appreciate that Lurie sought to harmonize the extant archaeological evidence with Ho-Chunk oral traditions. She collected many of these oral traditions during her extensive fieldwork over the course of almost seventy years, and several point to the influence of Mississippian culture on Oneota societies, even if this was not the ultimate source of their ancestry. Archaeologist William Green writes, "This non-Oneota model is not widely accepted because no post-Aztalan Mississippian sites have been found in Wisconsin. However, [Lurie's] model has value because it exemplifies that scholars have had to think 'outside the box' when trying to reconcile HCC [Ho-Chunk-Chiwere] traditions of a past hierarchical organization [i.e., Mississippian] with the absence of such evidence in Oneota and Effigy Mound [archaeological complexes]" (Green 2014, 61).

Thus Nancy Lurie, throughout the span of her long career, made significant contributions to our understanding of history, ethnohistory, and archaeology that have controverted much of the commonly accepted wisdom in these fields. While scholars have not concurred with all her conclusions, they have nevertheless benefited from her insights. Her passion and talents, her seemingly limitless curiosity, and the power of her intellect across disciplinary boundaries were the wellsprings of her substantial scholarly oeuvre. Lurie's works in cultural anthropology, action anthropology, and applied anthropology stand as her greatest legacies and offer promising areas for future research. Her historical and ethnohistorical investigations are also worthy of investigation and should not be ignored. She keenly understood that even the smallest rectification to the historical record can have enormous implications for our conception of the human past and the societies it has encompassed.

NOTE

1. For an assessment of the translations in Thwaites's work, see Codignola (1996).

REFERENCES

Manuscripts and Archives

Lurie, Nancy Oestreich. 1973. "A Winnebago-Aztalan Hypothesis." Milwaukee Public Museum, Wisconsin.

Published Works

Ablon, Joan. 2012. "Sol Tax, Pioneer in Participatory Research." In *Action Anthropology and Sol Tax in 2012: The Final Word? Journal of Northwest Anthropology* Memoir 8, edited by Darby Stapp, 13–18. Richland WA: Northwest Anthropology.

Arndt, Grant. 2019. "Rediscovering Nancy Oestreich Lurie's Activist Anthropology." *American Anthropologist* 121 (3): 725–28.

Butterfield, Consul. 1881. *History of the Discovery of the Northwest by John Nicolet in 1634 with a Sketch of His Life.* Cincinnati: Robert Clarke.

Charlevoix, Pierre-François-Xavier de. 1761. *Journal of a Voyage to North-America.* Vol. 2. London: J. Dodsley.

Codignola, Luca. 1996. "The Battle Is Over: Campeau's *Monumenta* vs. Thwaites's *Jesuit Relations, 1602–1650.*" *European Review of Native American Studies* 10 (2): 3–10.

Darnell, Regna. 1998. *And Along Came Boas: Continuity and Revolution in Americanist Anthropology.* Philadelphia: John Benjamins.

———. 2001. *Invisible Genealogies: A History of American Anthropology.* Lincoln: University of Nebraska Press.

Delanglez, Jean. 1947. "A Mirage: The Sea of the West (Part I)." *Revue d'histoire de l'Amérique française* 1 (3): 346–81.

Ganteaume, Cecile R. 1988. "Nancy Oestreich Lurie." In *Women Anthropologists: A Biographical Dictionary,* edited by Ute Gacs, Aisha Khan, Jerrie McIntyre, and Ruth Weinberg, 238–45. New York: Greenwood.

Green, William. 2014. "Identity, Ideology, and the Effigy Mound–Oneota Transformation." *Wisconsin Archeologist* 95 (2): 44–72.

Hass, Paul H., and James P. Danky, eds. 1996. "The Society at One Hundred Fifty Years." *Wisconsin Magazine of History* 79 (4): 258–363.

Heidenreich, Conrad. 1976. *Explorations and Mapping of Samuel de Champlain, 1603–1632.* Toronto: University of Toronto Press.

———. 1997. "Early French Exploration in the North American Interior." In *North American Exploration*, vol. 2, *A Continent Defined*, edited by John Logan Allen, 65–148. Lincoln: University of Nebraska Press.

Jouan, Henri. 1888. "Jean Nicolet, Interpreter and Voyageur in Canada, 1618–1642." In *Collections of the State Historical Society of Wisconsin*, vol. 11, edited by Reuben Gold Thwaites, 1–22. Madison: State Historical Society of Wisconsin.

Jung, Patrick J. 2018. *The Misunderstood Mission of Jean Nicolet: Uncovering the Story of the 1634 Journey*. Madison: Wisconsin Historical Society Press.

———. 2023. "Traces of the Feminine: Matriculture in the Traditional Ho-Chunk Life World." *Matrix: A Journal for Matricultural Studies* 3 (1): 118–39.

Kellogg, Louise. 1925. *The French Régime in Wisconsin and the Northwest*. Madison: State Historical Society of Wisconsin.

Kluckhohn, Clyde. 1958. "Ralph Linton 1893–1953: A Biographical Memoir." In *Biographical Memoirs*, vol. 31, 236–53. Washington DC: National Academy of Sciences.

Lurie, Nancy Oestreich. 1944. "Cultural Change Among the Wisconsin Winnebago." *Wisconsin Archeologist* 25 (4): 119–25.

———. 1948. "Trends of Change in Patterns of Child Care and Training Among the Wisconsin Winnebago." *Wisconsin Archeologist* 29 (3–4): 39–140.

———. 1952. "The Winnebago Indians: A Study in Cultural Change." PhD diss., Northwestern University.

———. 1960. "Winnebago Protohistory." In *Culture in History: Essays in Honor of Paul Radin*, edited by Stanley Diamond, 790–808. New York: Columbia University Press.

———. 1961. "Ethnohistory: An Ethnological Point of View." *Ethnohistory* 8 (1): 78–92.

———. 1968. "Culture Change." In *Introduction to Cultural Anthropology: Essays in the Scope and Methods of the Science of Man*, edited by James A. Clifton, 274–303. New York: Houghton Mifflin.

———. 1978a. "The Indian Claims Commission." *Annals of the American Academy of Political and Social Science* 436 (1): 97–110.

———. 1978b. "Winnebago." In *Handbook of North American Indians*, vol. 15, *Northeast*, edited by Bruce Trigger, 690–707. Washington DC: Smithsonian Institution.

Lurie, Nancy Oestreich, and Patrick J. Jung. 2009. *The Nicolet Corrigenda: New France Revisited*. Long Grove IL: Waveland.

———. 2014. "Jean Nicolet (Again): Comment on Ronald J. Mason's 'Where Nicolet and the Winnebagoes First Met.'" *Wisconsin Archeologist* 95 (2): 303–7.

Stapp, Darby. 2012. Introduction to *Action Anthropology and Sol Tax in 2012: The Final Word? Journal of Northwest Anthropology* Memoir 8, edited by Darby Stapp, 1–10. Richland WA: Northwest Anthropology.

Sulte, Benjamin. 1876. *Mélanges D'Histoire et de Littérature*. Ottawa: Imprimerie Joseph Bureau.

Tax, Sol. 1959. "James Sydney Slotkin, 1913–1958." *American Anthropologist* 61 (5): 844–47.

Thwaites, Reuben Gold, ed. 1896–1901. *The Jesuit Relations and Allied Documents: Travels and Explorations of the Jesuit Missionaries in New France, 1610–1791*. 73 vols. Cleveland: Burrows Brothers.

Whitehead, Alfred North. 1929. *Process and Reality: An Essay in Cosmology*. New York: Macmillan.

14

Merging Worlds

Writing to Be Read, Hanging Out with Indian People

ALICE B. KEHOE AND DAWN SCHER THOMAE

Nancy Lurie advised, "Colleagues tell me to write more scholarly. I tell them, I prefer a thousand interested readers to writing for ten academics" (pers. comm.). The same ethos underlay her work at her beloved Milwaukee Public Museum. A series of remarkably innovative exhibits—most of them, alas, temporary—grew out of her broad collegiality with her city's residents and Wisconsin's First Nations. Many who took her classes at the University of Wisconsin–Milwaukee remember her decades later for her outstanding lectures, which were fascinating and so clear. Through books and articles, museum exhibits, lectures, and action anthropology, Lurie proselytized for an anthropological standpoint valuing diversity within our common humanity.

In this remembrance, we describe her corpus of books and some of the exhibits she designed. In either case, she sought to work within a team. Her eyes lit up as her collaborators set to their shared task.

LURIE'S PUBLICATIONS

Following is a list of Lurie's best-known authored or edited publications: *The Subsistence Economy of the Dogrib Indians of Lac la Martre in the MacKenzie District of the Northwest Territories* (1961), with June Helm; *Mountain Wolf Woman, Sister of Crashing Thunder: The Autobiography of a Winnebago Woman* (1961); *The Dogrib Hand Game* (1966), with Judith Helm and Gertrude Kurath; "Women in Early American Anthropology" (1966); *The American Indian Today* (1968), edited with Stuart Levine, which received the Anisfield-Wolf award, "the only American book prize focusing on works that address racism and diversity";[1] *Wisconsin Indians* (1969); *North Ameri-*

can Indians in Historical Perspective (1971), edited with Eleanor Burke Leacock; "Winnebago" (1979); *A Special Style: The Milwaukee Public Museum, 1882–1982* (1983); *North American Indian Lives* (1985); "Relations Between Indians and Anthropologists" (1989); *Women and the Invention of American Anthropology* (1999); *The Nicolet Corrigenda: New France Revisited* (2009), with Patrick Jung; and *Love and Other Letters* (2010). This last book is an edited collection of letters between her parents during her father's war service. Out of the eleven books, she only authored two alone: the popular handbook on the Indian peoples of her home state, and the centennial history of her museum.

Lurie sought out scholars who shared her active concern for setting records straight to strengthen her work by placing it in a body of comparable research and interpretation. She also wrote over one hundred editorials; articles published in popular magazines and other journals, including Milwaukee Public Museum's *Lore*; and chapters in other edited books. These and her many interviews carried her understanding of America's history and its First Nations to many sectors of the public.

Three of Lurie's books were published by Waveland Press. Its anthropology editor, Tom Curtin, is a Milwaukee native descended from pioneer American linguist Jeremiah Curtin, whose family settled in Milwaukee in the 1840s. Under Tom Curtin, Waveland specializes in inexpensive paperback ethnographies and other anthropological texts suitable for undergraduate courses. Curtin saw Lurie regularly at American Anthropological Association meetings and promotes writing, like hers, meant for the largest potential readership. At the same time, he values good scholarship. In addition to their shared Milwaukee gemütlichkeit, both editor and writer reflected their hometown tradition of good craftsmanship priced for ordinary citizens.

Of Lurie's books, *Mountain Wolf Woman* was the most challenging for her to write. Women's personal histories were ignored by most anthropologists of Lurie's and earlier generations. Paul Radin (1883–1959), a Franz Boas student, spent decades recording Winnebago/Ho-Chunk culture; his 1923 monograph, *The Winnebago Tribe*, remains available in paperback (1970). Lurie, always struggling against society's subordination of women, saw clearly that Radin, like most of his peers, interviewed mostly men and wrote of men's doings. Egregiously, to Nancy, he assisted a man,

Sam Blowsnake, in composing his autobiography and innocuously titled it *Autobiography of a Winnebago Indian* (1920), as if Sam Blowsnake were typical of all members of his nation. Six years later Radin reworked the book into *Crashing Thunder: The Autobiography of an American Indian*, using Blowsnake's elder brother's Winnebago name.[2] With the mythical-sounding name and uninhibited accounts of improper behavior, the book was a breakthrough in exhibiting an Indian with everyman's derelictions, neither a noble savage nor a vicious one. Blowsnake had worked as a performing Indian in Wild West shows, and his travels with the shows facilitated his shenanigans. He was far more an actor than a realistic representation of an Indian.

Lurie remained closely involved with Ho-Chunk communities throughout her adult life. She had a wigwam built for her in Black River Falls, the tribe's homeland, and stayed there for the two annual powwows and many other events. She spent more time with women in the communities, observing and participating in their homemaking and family maintenance tasks. Among her friends was Sam's sister Stella Blowsnake Stacy (1884–1960), whose Ho-Chunk name was Mountain Wolf Woman (Xéhachiwinga, pronounced "Hay-ah-cho-win-kah"). Stacy had adopted Lurie as her niece and stayed in Lurie's home in Milwaukee while the two worked to create a woman's autobiography. According to a book about women in frontier Wisconsin, "Although Radin visited Lurie while Mountain Wolf Woman was there, he remained uninterested in her experiences" (Jensen 2006, 483n20). Lurie's book is feminist and decolonizing to its core, although it was written before either of these viewpoints had figured in anthropological discourse. A spin-off, *Mountain Wolf Woman: A Ho-Chunk Girlhood* (2007), by Diane Holliday, extended these viewpoints to children in Wisconsin schools' middle grades.

Lurie's two coedited volumes, with Stuart Levine and with Eleanor Burke Leacock, also can be viewed as decolonizing. Published less than a decade after the 1961 Chicago Indian Congress, on which Lurie worked with its originator, Sol Tax, both books revealed American First Nations as societies with actual discoverable and documented histories continuing to today. They helped establish the discipline of ethnohistory.[3] Eric Wolf's *Europe and the People Without History* (1982) did not come out until a decade after the Lurie-Leacock volume.

"The Urban Habitat: The City and Beyond" was Lurie's first exhibit when she at last obtained her dream job as curator of anthropology for the Milwaukee Public Museum (MPM) in 1972. She never forgot that when she had initially applied for that position years earlier, museum director W. C. McKern had been startled, saying, "A woman curator? No, Nancy" (pers. comm., Nancy Lurie). Determined to bring a historical dimension to the museum's static presentations, Lurie engaged the museum's zoologist and botanist to integrate their environmental knowledge with her anthropological view of the longue durée development of urban habitats, specifically Milwaukee. Gifted MPM head of exhibits James Kelly made it strikingly real: As one walked up the gangplank to the replica *Godspeed*, bringing European urban dwellers to America, one felt it gently swinging above harbor waves. Reality hit hard near the end, where a nauseating section of a local streambed was filled with garbage. The message was only too clear: Cities do not signify unqualified progress. We who live here, take heed! Clean up!

In stark contrast to the Urban Habitat's mountain of trash and clogged streambed was the European Village section. Opened in 1979, it remains intact, whereas the Urban Habitat closed less than a decade after its 1981 installation. Although the two exhibits could have been placed for complementarity, their purposes were anything but complementary. European Village is adjacent to the Streets of Old Milwaukee, a nostalgic pseudo-memory to thousands of Milwaukeeans. Like the Streets, the Village is a walk-around section with not-quite-full-size buildings and artifacts displayed to be viewed through the windows. Everything is perfectly clean and neat, feeling timeless. Pretty as the Village is, it was a significant innovation, for it celebrates immigrants, ordinary people who nevertheless created beautiful objects and carried them to enrich Milwaukee. Immigrants' families and local ethnic societies donated a large proportion of the displayed artifacts, solicited by the curator of European history, Lazar Brkich. As a strategy of outreach to the general public, this concept for the exhibits fits with Lurie's aim for her publications to be enjoyed by thousands, not just by "ten academics" (pers. comm.).

The culmination of Lurie's passion for drawing a wide public into her anthropological perspective was "A Tribute to Survival," an exhibit that serves as the introductory area to the museum's North American Indians halls. For decades that space was dominated by a breathtaking bison hunt diorama in which a mounted Plains Indian was running down his massive prey. A rattlesnake in the corner threatened both, and all the children in Milwaukee knew to press a button to make the snake move. Opened in 1993, Lurie's "Tribute" replaced the Wild West scene. On a rotating platform, thirty-seven life-size figures cast from actual Wisconsin Indian residents, ages five to seventy-nine, re-create the Grand Entry to a powwow. They are dressed to the hilt in regalia crafted by themselves, their families, or other Wisconsin tribal members. A drumbeat sounds as they circle.

"A Tribute to Survival," which opened in 1993, is the visible outcome of Lurie's postcolonial understanding, fostered by her experience with Sol Tax's Chicago conference. Lurie may have been the first urban museum curator to work with an advisory committee of First Nations representatives, invited from the various Indian organizations in Milwaukee. During the turbulent 1980s, when repatriation was hotly debated and Indians staged protests against museums, the committee helped make Lurie aware of the range of opinions of citizens who were Indian, and she worked toward consensus regarding the museum's practices. Lurie drew on these years when she worked with anthropological and Native colleagues to draft the Native American Graves Protection and Repatriation Act, passed by Congress in 1990.

Those years of long discussions about MPM's many exhibits showing Indians and casting lifelike figures of committee members, their families, and associates all helped maintain goodwill toward the museum. Lurie enjoyed recounting one incident during this period, when a group of Chicago Indians came to demand that the museum remove from exhibit what was billed as the skeleton of an "Aztalan Princess" recovered by former MPM director Samuel Barrett from the site of Aztalan. To the surprise of the protestors, Lurie immediately agreed to remove the bones. She did not think it necessary to inform them that the bones were those of a white man whose skeleton had been prepared and sold by Ward's Natural Science supply company. The Aztalan burial's bones were too fragile, and too valuable for study, to leave the curated collections storage area.

LURIE AS A PERSONALITY

Lurie said she hated speaking engagements. Visiting one-on-one with emerging anthropologists, colleagues, and students from around the world was her pleasure. Her passion about anthropology, tribal relations, and museums was clear to everyone who met her, and she honored those around her by giving them copious amounts of her time. In particular, she was committed to seeing more female students go into the field. This feminist concern did not interfere in her relations with male students, whom she mentored into professional positions, or with male colleagues. Lurie taught us, her junior women colleagues, that adroitly avoiding confrontations is a good strategy, a womanly approach that usually makes people receptive to one's suggestions.

Many times, Lurie remarked that she was the only child of only children. Yet she enjoyed a rich family life, with three generations in her childhood home and many cousins nearby. Her work defined her life, and she chose that above all else, but her keen appreciation of others' goodness was reciprocated with strong affection and a desire to collaborate with her. Later in life, as she worked daily with me (Dawn Scher Thomae) as the MPM collections manager, I absorbed not only Lurie's knowledge and skills but also her attitude toward working at the Milwaukee Public Museum: "We are just the custodians or caretakers of the material housed at the MPM. We do not own it" (pers. comm.). In the same spirit, Lurie felt that her relationships with others should develop out of respect and goodwill. It is astounding how many people we meet who had brief experiences with Lurie, perhaps as a student in an undergraduate course years ago or at a museum event, eagerly describe her warmth and the impact she made on them.

Similarly, Lurie's scrupulous attention to experiences and opinions of First Nations people is the reason the museum has had such positive relationships with hundreds of Native peoples around the country. Precepts she taught me (Dawn Scher Thomae) include the following: "If there is a disagreement between Native peoples or tribes, never step in. If it's a disagreement between Native peoples and the government, always step in."

Another was that "we can't change the past [in relation to U.S. government actions, relationships with museums, and so on], but we can start from the here and now and move forward." That eminently sensible and positive tenet led her fellow anthropologists to elect her to our highest office, president of the American Anthropological Association, and then in 2006 to give her the treasured Franz Boas Award for Exemplary Service. The association notes, "Awardees have made many sacrifices, usually without personal reward, and sometimes against personal safety. They have all used anthropology for the benefit of others ... [making] outstanding applications of anthropological knowledge to improving the human condition."[4]

With this small tribute, we have endeavored to convey how Dr. Nancy O. Lurie, section head and curator of anthropology at the Milwaukee Public Museum, greatly influenced so many lives. We hope everyone who reads this takes to heart her message that the good life lies in serving and sharing with fellow humans. A Milwaukee neighbor of mine (Alice Kehoe), Doris Hildebrant Rank, the same age as Lurie, admonished one of our kids, "God gave you a good intellect so you can help other people." This Milwaukee sentiment was Lurie's mantra.

NOTES

1. Anisfield-Wolf Book Awards, "About: The Awards," accessed November 11, 2024, https://www.anisfield-wolf.org/about/.

2. Jasper Blowsnake was Sam's serious, hardworking elder brother, as Max Radin, a professor of law at the University of California–Berkeley, was to his maverick younger brother Paul.

3. In 1978 Houghton Mifflin asked me (Alice Kehoe) to write a textbook on North American Indians, and with a sabbatical coming up, I agreed on the condition that it would be my perspective. Influenced by Lurie and her work, I wanted it to present a seamless history for each region ("culture area") from the deepest time known, Terminal Pleistocene, to the present. And the book had to include a chapter on Mexico because, from a historical perspective, interactions between Mesoamerica and Anglo-America are necessary in a history of North American First Nations. Reviewers of the manuscript told the editorial staff, "We don't teach American Indians this way; we teach a classic ethnography example for each culture area, and we teach Mesoamerica in a separate course" (pers. comm., 1979). When my manuscript was nearly finished and half had been turned in,

Western Pacific Industries attempted a hostile takeover of Houghton Mifflin (Mitgang 1978). The editorial staff departed hurriedly, notifying me that my book would not be published. The representative for another publisher, Prentice-Hall, listened compassionately to my story and had me send the manuscript to his editor, and that man said he would take a gamble on this radical departure from standard texts depicting timeless primitives. When the book came out in 1981, it changed the model for textbooks on North American Indians. This new model reflected Lurie's pioneering realism regarding America's First Nations.

4. "Franz Boas Award for Exemplary Service to Anthropology," American Anthropological Association, accessed February 3, 2025, https://americananthro.org/prizes-and-awards/franz-boas-award.

REFERENCES

Helm, June, and Nancy Lurie. 1961. *The Subsistence Economy of the Dogrib Indians of Lac la Martre in the MacKenzie District of the Northwest Territories.* Ottawa: Northern Co-ordination and Research Centre, Department of Northern Affairs and National Resources.

Helm, June, Nancy Lurie, and Gertrude Kurath. 1966. *The Dogrib Hand Game.* National Museum of Canada Bulletin 205, Anthropological Series, no. 71. Ottawa: National Museum of Canada.

Holliday, Diane. 2007. *Mountain Wolf Woman: A Ho-Chunk Girlhood.* Madison: Wisconsin Historical Society.

Jensen, Joan M. 2006. *Calling This Place Home: Women on the Wisconsin Frontier, 1850–1925.* Minneapolis: Minnesota Historical Society.

Kehoe, Alice. 1981. *North American Indians: A Comprehensive Account.* Hoboken NJ: Prentice-Hall

Leacock, Eleanor Burke, and Nancy Oestreich Lurie, eds. 1971. *North American Indians in Historical Perspective.* New York: Random House.

Leslie, Stuart W. 1982. "Review of The Urban Habitat: The City and Beyond." *Technology and Culture* 23 (3): 417–29.

Levine, Stuart, and Nancy Lurie, eds. 1968. *The American Indian Today.* DeLand FL: Everett Edwards.

Lurie, Nancy Oestreich, ed. 1961. *Mountain Wolf Woman, Sister of Crashing Thunder: The Autobiography of a Winnebago Woman.* Ann Arbor: University of Michigan Press.

———. 1966. "Women in Early American Anthropology." In *Pioneers of American Anthropology: The Uses of Biography,* American Ethnological Society

Monograph 43, edited by June Helm, 29–81. Seattle: University of Washington Press.

———. 1969. *Wisconsin Indians*. Madison: Wisconsin Historical Society.

———. 1979. "Winnebago." In *Handbook of North American Indians*, vol. 15, edited by Bruce Trigger, 690–707. Washington DC: Smithsonian Institution.

———. 1983. *A Special Style: The Milwaukee Public Museum, 1882–1982*. Milwaukee: Milwaukee Public Museum.

———. 1985. *North American Indian Lives*. Milwaukee: Milwaukee Public Museum.

———. 1989. "Relations Between Indians and Anthropologists." In *History of Indian-White of Relations*, vol. 4, *History of Indian-White Relations*, edited by Wilcomb E. Washburn, 548–56. Washington DC: Smithsonian Institution.

———. 1999. *Women and the Invention of American Anthropology*. Long Grove IL: Waveland.

———, ed. 2010. *Love and Other Letters*. Milwaukee: Milwaukee County Historical Society.

Lurie, Nancy Oestreich, and Patrick Jung. 2009. *The Nicolet Corrigenda: New France Revisited*. Long Grove IL: Waveland.

Mitgang, Herbert. 1978. "Authors Protest Conglomerate Deal." *New York Times*, April 20.

Radin, Paul. 1920. *The Autobiography of a Winnebago Indian*. University of California Publications in American Archaeology and Ethnology, vol. 16, no. 7, 381–473.

———. (1923) 1970. *The Winnebago Tribe*. Lincoln: University of Nebraska Press.

———. 1926. *Crashing Thunder: The Autobiography of an American Indian*. Appleton MN: Appleton.

Wolf, Eric. 1982. *Europe and the People Without History*. Berkeley: University of California Press.

15

Introduction to Nancy Lurie's "Applied Anthropology"

JOSHUA SMITH

In addition to Nancy Lurie's enormous contributions to anthropology, ethnohistory, and museology, she served as an expert witness in federal court cases for many tribes, including the Menominee. Throughout her career, she carried on the action anthropology tradition in her tireless efforts with the Menominee, helping them fight termination while working on many action projects with them, as well as with the Wisconsin Winnebago and the United Indians of Milwaukee.[1] In 1971 Lurie drafted a paper as part of her preparation for providing testimony in support of the Menominee's claim seeking damages from termination.[2] The paper, simply titled "Applied Anthropology," has remained unpublished for more than half a century until now, yet it maintains extraordinary relevance to the history of anthropology today.

Lurie's discussion covers major developments and shifts in applied anthropology through examples of the Menominee's experiences in resisting colonialism and asserting control over their own affairs. Her analytical deconstruction of applied anthropology as it related to U.S. policy, colonialism, and Indigenous governance represents "three major steps of development": "overcoming ethnocentrism and theoretical inadequacy; overcoming political naivete; and overcoming anthropological egocentrism." Her purpose in drafting the paper was to point out the mistakes of undertaking planned community change, which for Lurie was doubly criminal in the case of termination. She provided a cogent review of the history of applied anthropology to show that there can be no excuses for the damages termination caused Indigenous peoples, nor is there an acceptable argument for destructive legislative intentions of termination policy, which for Lurie represented "vested ignorance."

The first section, titled "Overcoming Ethnocentrism and Theoretical Inadequacy," is a critical analysis of applied anthropology and government policy in the allotment era. Her main thesis is that "all of the errors made in the allotment policy of the 1880s, apply equally to the termination policy instituted in the 1950s and imposed on the Menominee between 1924 and 1961." Lurie emphatically underscored this thesis by making the comparison that the consequences of allotment were as disastrous as the consequences of termination in losses of self-determination, primarily because of the sudden requirement for experts to manage Menominee affairs. Such policies caused community disorganization, led to outsiders profiting at the expense of the Menominee, and created impediments to the Menominee's ability to control their future. Lurie punctuated her analysis with the stern indictment that the government ought to have known how devastatingly impractical termination would be for the Menominee because of the history of allotment policy and damages done to the tribe leading up to 1954.

The next section, "Overcoming Political Naivete," outlines step-by-step how colonialism vis-à-vis termination policy was mobilized. Lurie succinctly arrived at the premise that "no colonialism is preferable to even the most benevolent colonialism for most people," revealing the insidious irony (or "political naivete") of termination that "made the Menominee Reservation a colony of the state of Wisconsin as a matter of realpolitik by the federal government." Moreover, she described in precise terms how this worked.

First, termination established Menominee Enterprises, an entity that required non-Menominees to serve as corporate managers. Additionally, the state of Wisconsin set up a home office in the "colony" while another entity was created, the Menominee Indian Study Committee, which was actually "a legislative advisory committee looking to Menominee interests in terms of the state's interests." Second, the corporation required "a native leadership elite to be responsible to the mother country for collecting tribute, easing the way for private commercial exploitation, keeping the natives in line and cooperative." What this did to the community, Lurie noted, was that "it undercut and destroyed traditional structures of government and controls exercised by the people to make leadership answerable to the community by substituting a county form of government having virtually no control." The end result was that "the restricted choice of county status or division between several counties given the Menominee was a cruel and cynical device that forced the Menominee to appear to have committed themselves willingly to colonial status against the only other alternative of certain destruction as a people identified with their own land."

In the third section, "Overcoming Anthropological Egocentrism," Nancy articulated the shortcomings of both cultural evolutionist and functionalist theories of applied anthropology as it changed between World War I and the end of World War II, leading up to Menominee termination. In a direct challenge to cultural evolutionary thinking, Nancy pointed out how the Menominee remained Menominee despite enormous challenges. In short, change did not equal assimilation, as cultural evolutionists have argued (Pinkoski and Asch 2004). The Menominee never ceased to be Menominee. Instead, "they held fast to their land against a series of threats and became less beholden to the bureau and the bureau's version of indirect rule and the leadership structure it fostered."

The fourth section, "Damages to the Menominee Could Have Been Prevented," juxtaposes the knowledge contained in published accounts of applied anthropology with the development of the termination policy, documenting how policymakers had willfully ignored available anthropological knowledge. The paper concludes with a fifth section, "Principles of Planned Change," outlining four ways in which termination policy in general, and the termination of the Menominee in particular, violated the established principles of applied anthropology.

Throughout the paper, Lurie drew on her prior research into the history of anthropology and anthropological theory—in particular, her research into early women anthropologists, which led to her discovery of Alice Fletcher's role in the allotment policy (Lurie 1966a, 1966b), and her review of anthropological theories of culture change, with its account of the relationship between British functionalism and applied anthropology in the context of British colonialism (Lurie 1968). Lurie's "Applied Anthropology" thus provides a glimpse into how she synthesized her previous work to serve as a foundation for her contributions to the Menominee project. Although this paper was never published, elements of it appeared in a number of her publications during the period, including her 1972 article

"Menominee Termination: From Reservation to Colony," which appeared in *Human Organization*, the leading journal for applied anthropology in the United States. It was presented as part of her legal testimony for the Menominee case in 1971.

NOTES

1. Action anthropology is a theoretical and methodological response to both "scientistic" anthropology and assimilationist policy. Conceptualized by Sol Tax, it is a response to both cultural evolutionary theory and Indigenous peoples' struggles for decolonization. Action anthropology is explicitly distinct from the practices of applied anthropology. Contrary to much of the literature within anthropology, action anthropology is neither atheoretical social work nor merely characterized by the singular legacy of the University of Chicago's graduate student fieldwork with the Meskwaki Nation (1948–59), where it first came into practice. The two principles of action anthropology evident throughout Tax's work are nonassimilation and self-government (Smith 2010, 2015; see also Lurie 1999; Tax 1952, 1962; Polgar 1979; Stanley 1996).

2. David Wilkins and Heidi Stark define termination policy as federal Indian policy from approximately 1953 to the mid-1960s that legislatively severed federal benefits and support services to certain tribes, bands, and California rancherias and forced the dissolution of their reservations. This policy was exemplified by House Concurrent Resolution No. 108 in 1953, Public Law 280, which conferred on several designated states full criminal and some civil jurisdiction over Indian reservations, and by a federal policy focused on the relocation of Indians from rural and reservation areas to urban areas (Wilkins and Stark 2011, 312).

REFERENCES

Lurie, Nancy Oestreich. 1966a. "The Lady from Boston and the Omaha Indians." *American West* 3 (1): 31–33, 80–85.

———. 1966b. "Women in Early American Anthropology." In *Pioneers of American Anthropology: The Uses of Biography*, American Ethnological Society Monograph 43, edited by June Helm, 29–81. Seattle: University of Washington Press.

———. 1968. "Culture Change." In *Introduction to Cultural Anthropology: Essays in the Scope and Methods of the Science of Man*, edited by James A. Clifton, 274–303. Boston: Houghton Mifflin.

———. 1972. "Menominee Termination: From Reservation to Colony." *Human Organization* 31 (3): 257–69.

———. 1999. "Sol Tax and Tribal Sovereignty." *Human Organization* 58 (1): 108–17.

Pinkoski, Marc, and Michael Asch. 2004. "Anthropology and Indigenous Rights in Canada and the United States: Implications in Steward's Theoretical Project." In *Hunter-Gatherers in History, Archaeology and Anthropology*, edited by Alan Barnard, 187–200. Oxford: Berg.

Polgar, Steve. 1979. "Applied, Action, Radical, and Committed Anthropology." In *Current Anthropology: Essays in Honor of Sol Tax*, edited by Robert Hinshaw, 409–18. Paris: Mouton.

Smith, Joshua. 2010. "The Political Thought of Sol Tax: The Principles of Non-Assimilation and Self-Government in Action Anthropology." *Histories of Anthropology Annual* 6:129–70.

———. 2015. "Standing with Sol: The Spirit and Intent of Action Anthropology." *Anthropologica* 57 (2): 445–56.

Stanley, Sam. 1996. "Community, Action, and Continuity: A Narrative Vita of Sol Tax." *Current Anthropology* 37 (1): 131–37.

Tax, Sol. 1952. "Action Anthropology." *American Indigena* 12:103–9.

———. 1962. "Task Force on Indian Affairs: Implementing Change Through Government." *Human Organization* 21 (2): 125–36.

Wilkins, David E., and Heidi Kiiwetinepinesiik Stark. 2011. *American Indian Politics and the American Political System*. Lanham MD: Rowman and Littlefield.

16

Applied Anthropology

NANCY OESTREICH LURIE

Applied anthropology, like any field of endeavor, has had its false starts and faltering steps and has learned from its mistakes.[1] Naturally, constant striving for improvement continues, but applied anthropology reached the point of being a mature, recognized subdiscipline of anthropology well over twenty years ago. firmly based in well-developed and tested method and theory. For all that, the major mistakes in undertaking planned community change that applied anthropology recognized and publicized long ago were repeated in the formulation of termination policy and implementation. Well-known and validated principles to guide planning and carrying out of programs in the interest of social groups were violated or totally ignored in the formulation of termination policy and implementation. In order to make clear the enormity of the irresponsibility of termination in disregarding lessons as available from the study of recent history as the theoretical analyses of applied anthropology, a review is offered to show that there was no excuse for the damage done by termination or any argument that good legislative intentions were confounded by a lack of experience, precedent, or guiding principles. The termination policy represented nothing more than vested ignorance. Applied anthropology has concerned itself particularly with systematizing a body of useful knowledge in order to impart it effectively and make it as broadly known as possible to those who might have reason to use it. The history of applied anthropology can be seen as progressing through three major steps of development: overcoming ethnocentrism and theoretical inadequacy; overcoming political naivete; and overcoming anthropological egocentrism.

The potential for the practical use of anthropology was discerned initially in Britain early in the nineteenth century, but the enthusiasm of early advocates of applied anthropology faded in the face of still unresolved disputes about the origin and nature of man, racial differences, and other matters that purely academic anthropology as a whole had yet to thrash out (Reining 1962).

The first major systematic application of anthropology in the United States occurred in the 1880s, when the weight of anthropological theory of the time was left to the justification and design of the policy to allot the Indian reservations. The anthropologist Alice Fletcher subscribed to the premise shared by most educated people of her day that the general historical outline of man's cultural evolution from Stone Age hunting to Steel Age agriculture would unfold smoothly and inexorably for all mankind in the same way, not only in technological terms but along the same ideological course that had led to Euro-American culture as Fletcher knew it. This presumably natural course of events, she hypothesized, was unnaturally impeded by the reservation system, which perpetuated the institution of communally held tribal property. Early in her first fieldwork, she responded sympathetically to the Omaha's expression of fear about losing their land, as had recently happened to their Ponca neighbors, but did not understand that they wanted assurance of the strength of their treaty. She soon took on an important role in helping design and promote the Omaha Allotment Act of 1885, prototype of the General Indian Allotment Act of 1887. Her scientific rationale for allotment was a simplistic syllogism that, while convincingly logical, was unfortunately unsubstantiated: Indians were evolving to a "civilized" state represented by the United States of the 1880s; the hallmark of civilization is private property; by giving each Indian private property he would be able to protect fully for himself, he would become civilized, prosper, and be happy.

Fletcher's initial error lay in the assumption that her particular sociocultural system was the goal and envy of the rest of the world, and in her work with the Omaha, she gravitated immediately to those individuals who were highly deviant (one of them even became an anthropologist), whose attitudes and behavior reinforced her assumption—the mixed-blood La Flesche family and their small coterie of like-minded Omaha friends. Actually, a generation before Fletcher came to study the Omaha, the La Flesches had begun the process of phasing out of their Omaha identity and by the next generation were to be absorbed into the Euro-American population (La Flesche [1900] 1963). However, Fletcher considered the La Flesche–led minority as exemplary models and in the vanguard of a course the rest of the Omaha would naturally follow. The La Flesche family supported Fletcher's proposal that the Omaha reservation be allotted (the idea was not entirely original to her) in agreement with an ideological outlook they shared with her rather than with the rest of the Omaha. The latter neither understood nor were given the program but acquiesced largely because of Fletcher's obvious sincerity of concern for their welfare regarding their land and because their educated tribesmen who could communicate with the white people approved of it. Such support was depended on by proponents of allotment that the Indians desired the program and had even requested it.

Fletcher made other methodological errors that, thanks in part to her unhappy example, anthropologists were not to make in the future. In addition to relying on people like the La Flesche family for Indian support of her ideas, she relied on the inspiration and data supplied by Thomas Henry Tibbles, a white missionary whom Fletcher accepted as an expert and authority in Indian policy reform because he was genuinely fond of and concerned for the Omaha and other tribes, had spent many years among the Indians, and married an Omaha woman, the sister of Francis La Flesche cited above. Furthermore, Fletcher really did not understand her own culture as well as she might have in her plan to commit the Indians to diversified, largely subsistence family farming on limited acreage as the way to American plenty and evolutionary contemporaneity. Mechanization, large-scale agricultural enterprises, increasing availability of rail transport of surplus produce to distant markets, and growing urban industrialization were already squeezing experienced white farmers off the land and into the cities. Even if Indians had wanted to farm, allotment from the outset was a losing proposition (Lurie 1966a, 1968).

Not only was allotment impractical, it was disastrous. It left the people of allotted reservations worse off than ever, depriving them of much of their land and handicapping them in future efforts to improve their economic lot. Instead of helping Indian people achieve the economic and personal security and independence it promised, allotment contributed to progressive loss of their main capital resource; increasing poverty; discouragement and distrust about government promises to protect their rights as set forth in treaties [and] in other contractual agreements; opening the door to speculators and other land-hungry whites to profit at the Indians' expense; and distrust of any educated leadership, setting Indian against Indian, as shall be discussed later in more detail. However, instead of planning out the need for the Bureau of Indian Affairs, whose officious oppressiveness stimulated Fletcher to act in the Indians' behalf, allotment required ever-increasing personnel to administer the ongoing and ever-complicating effects of allotment and various, mostly subsidy programs necessitated by the effects of allotment.

Indian protest and the evidence of problems created by allotment led to a series of minor and inadequate revisions in the policy. As problems mounted, the government quietly shelved the program in regard to tribes it had not yet gotten around to or that had managed to resist the program. But the government, having made an enormous error, refused to rectify it by getting at the root cause of the problems of allotted reservations by stopping land loss or restoring Indian land. Acreage continued to slip out of Indian ownership at an alarming rate, while remaining Indian land rapidly devaluated for Indian use because of successive division and redistribution to heirs of original allottees. After 1900 the Indian population began increasing as the land base continued decreasing. It was not until 1934 that the government briefly accepted the fact that Indians were not phasing out and that adaptive cultural pluralism of communities was a more reasonable expectation then solving Indian problems by waiting for all the individuals to assimilate into the dominant population. An attempt was made to get at the basic problem in restoration and stronger protection of Indian land.

Indian people and anthropologists certainly learned quickly enough what should have been learned by anyone who wants to help people and has the power to do so. In general analytical terms, the lessons from allotment are that policy should not be based on ethnocentric assumptions no matter how well intentioned; people should be fully informed of the policymakers' objectives and intended methods before being asked to agree to a program; token, unrepresentative agreement to a program by the people to be affected should not be used as a substitute for careful first-hand study of what the people to be affected really see as their problem and what they would consider effective solutions upon being apprised of all the socioeconomic alternatives available from the cultural source of preferred assistance; simplistic general procedural fiats cannot solve complex problems but only create new ones in not anticipating the effect of overlooked variables; programs the people do not understand and cannot handle largely for themselves, but require experts and outsiders to implement and manage, succeed only in perpetuating themselves but are not successful; programs should be undertaken not only after careful study of the nature of the local group to be affected but with full consideration as well of the nature of surrounding demographic, economic, and socio-cultural conditions that impinge on the local group.

All the errors made in the allotment policy of the 1880s, as set forth in the above generalizations, apply equally well to the termination policy instituted in the 1950s and imposed on the Menominee between 1934 and 1961. The resulting consequences of termination are proving as disastrous as the consequences of allotment in progressive land loss; impoverishment; loss of self-determination as experts are required to manage Menominee affairs; community disorganization and demoralization; exploitation of Menominee resources to profit outsiders at the expense of the Menominee; and handicapping the Menominee in regard to future efforts to improve their lot. They were worse off in 1961 than they were in 1951, and they are worse off in 1971 than they were in 1961.

The direct lesson of history should have given the government pause when it embarked on the termination policy, apart from the warnings of scholarly criticism and Indian opposition. By 1961, when Menominee termination was declared final, its own developmental history since 1954 should have been sufficient warning not to go through with a clearly impractical plan, already damaging the Menominee.

OVERCOMING POLITICAL NAIVETE

The highly speculative foundation of cultural evolutionary theory was a matter of academic concern in anthropological circles even while Fletcher was working with the Omaha. For the next several decades, beginning with the 1880s, American anthropologists steered clear of practical concerns in the interest of collecting accurate data on which to eventually build reliable theory. Their zeal extended to resenting any interference in Native life, benevolent or otherwise, as destroying precious survival of precontact data before anthropologists could get on the scene to record them. This self-serving attitude came through to many Indian people as a kind of benign neglect, since anthropologists were genuinely interested in the things Indians knew best and cherished, accepted Indians for who they were without trying to change them, lived with Indian people on their terms, and shared, albeit for reasons of their own, the Indians' resentment of governmental and missionary meddlers. At the level of direct interpersonal relationships, anthropologists extended assistance as a matter of friendship and rapport on a reciprocal basis that was appreciated and not demeaning to Indians. In retrospect, we realize that Indian people put up with a lot of inconvenience and annoyance from visiting anthropologists until anthropologists developed more finesse and delicacy in cross-cultural relationships. Such tolerance came partly from the novelty value and secret amusement anthropologists afforded the Indians, and partly out of the hope that these curious people who were at least sincerely eager to be informed might in some way be of real help to the Indians (Lurie 1966b, 1971).

Although theoretical orientations remained implicitly evolutionary with the fatalistic acceptance that Indian culture and the Indian population would inevitably phase out of existence, sensitivity was beginning to develop in regard to processes and rates of cultural change. However, anthropologists of this period were most interested in studying continuing embroideries of traditional styles, tastes, and customs on innovations to the virtual neglect of the fact that the innovations were thus being made part of Indian culture and serving to perpetuate distinctive Indian societies. Anthropologists could appreciate this process in regard to acquisition of the horse but not in seeing Indians going from here to there for their own reasons by railroad.

Interest in practical applications of anthropology revived in the 1920s with the rise of British functionalist theory, as opposed to cultural evolutionary theory, and developed in field studies in areas not yet seriously challenged or changed by European contact. Many British anthropologists began their careers as colonial officers, and it was through their efforts to communicate more effectively with those whom they administered that the policy of "indirect rule" was developed. Meanwhile, professional anthropologists who came out of an academic background were unwilling to overlook the welfare of those they studied in the pure pursuit of data. They added rationalization and systematization to the applied anthropology underlying indirect rule (Malinowski 1929; Radcliffe-Brown 1930).

The functionalists argued that administration should avoid interference in, conform to, respect, and utilize as much as possible of the native sociocultural system. The primary theoretical interest of functionalism was to discern, analyze, and understand the principles underlying the interrelationship and interaction of the parts of a culture to make up the dynamic, operating whole. They scorned the evolutionists' interest in survivals and their objectives to reconstruct cultural history from bits and pieces of the past. The functionalists concentrated on noting how modifications in one part of a culture can have ramifications and repercussions throughout. They observed that colonial administration often imposed gratuitous modifications that not only disorganized native life but defeated administrative goals. However, the functionalists as applied anthropologists made some assumptions that, if less obvious, were as untenable as the earlier evolutionary assumptions that all cultures evolve predictably along the course that had been followed by Euro-American civilization. The functionalists assumed that the forms of native sociocultural systems and the meanings invested in them had remained virtually static prior to European contact, without the occurrence of dysfunctions and functional reorganization as innovations were processed into the systems to account for such things as agriculture and complex institutional structures. They further assumed that with anthropological study, colonial contact influences could be made to fit the existing culture, and once smooth working relationships were established, matters would go on indefinitely to everyone's satisfaction and mutual benefit.

American anthropologists in particular were quick to accuse the functionalists of being hired hands of empire, scientific prostitutes, unprincipled culture mongers, and a number of really insulting things besides. They pointed out that Natives could be left to their own devices only to the extent that they still fulfilled their quotas of goods and services to the mother country. Abuse and exploitation occurred even under the most benevolently intended indirect rule because fundamentally it was merely a Machiavellian contrivance to let a few powerful Natives do most of the mother country's dirty work of keeping the rest of the Natives in line.

More temperate analyses pointed out exactly and objectively how indirect rule preserved, protected, and reinforced traditional roles and institutions of leadership and social control, while undercutting traditional checks and controls to make leadership directly responsible to the interests of the people. Ruling elites, even operating in accordance with traditional forms and garbed in traditional trappings, were answerable not to their people but to the colonial officers. Such elites were encouraged to develop increasingly greater financial interest and ego involvement in maintaining the colonial status quo to stay in office. Indirect rule only selected those traditional features that could serve colonialism or would not interfere with it and did not fulfill the claim made by the applied anthropologists that colonialism was made to fit the native culture and interests. It prevented the natural course of functional integration and change in which leaders are answerable to the people and innovations are incorporated to satisfy the interest of the society as the society defines it.

Native peoples became increasingly dissatisfied with their land being appropriated for settlers to take economic pressures off the mother country and the exploitation of their persons and resources by private, foreign commercial interests (which also played the game of indirect rule) that limited their opportunities to obtain things enjoyed by the Europeans in their midst and committed them to the lowest socioeconomic stratum in the social hierarchy in their own land. Their resistance to their frustration and powerlessness was expressed in delinquency, uncooperativeness, apathy, sabotage, and whatever other weapons and psychological outlets were at hand. Such behavior was deplored by Native elite and colonial administrator alike, who agreed on the necessity of putting down the troublemakers who did not understand the situation and were trying to destroy all the good, traditional things they had worked so hard to preserve in the Natives' interest.

The sad thing was that Native leaders were not necessarily venal or vicious by nature, but the system made them that way. They were impressed by the power controlled by the Europeans and, being increasingly estranged from and repudiated by their own people, underestimated the strength of useful knowledge their people were gathering, in spite of indirect rule, from observation and association with the outsiders in their midst. Potential leadership from the Native ranks was firmly repressed. Some elitist traditional leaders endeavored to bring concessions and compromises from colonial overlords in the Native interest, but they were increasingly resented for what they could not do rather than appreciated for what they tried to do under the circumstances. Anthropologists able to analyze the situation recoiled from the idea of leading insurgency but were in no position—or thought they were in no position—to try to change the entire power relationship. Some chose to continue work as applied anthropologists within the system by trying to soften and alleviate problems of health, nutrition, sanitation, and vocational education that had been created largely by the fact of colonialism. Others disdained the whole idea of applied anthropology on ethical grounds and would only conduct pure research, which by the beginning of the 1930s was beginning to be directed toward understanding the dynamics of culture contact situations under the rubric of acculturation studies. If such objectivity did not help people, it was argued, at least it did them no harm.

However, in Africa, at least, even such "pure" anthropology paid the price of being deprecated by the growing but powerless cadre of Native intellectuals and their expanding number of followers as the "science of savages." Even if anthropologists had no truck with applications to quiet discontent with colonialism, they were, it was alleged, still actively contributing to counterinsurgency insofar as their assiduous study of "the Natives" might well be used by others in the manipulative practices of colonialism (Macquet 1964; Fanon 1966). When the "third world" began to erupt in the 1950s, colonial powers accepted with more or less good grace what a few Cassandras, among them anthropologists, had been trying to tell them for a long time: No colonialism is preferable to even the most benevolent colonialism for most people.

It is useful to review the elements of colonial policy in general. A territory is acquired by conquest, coercion, persuasion, or the game of realpolitik among mighty powers who decide who shall have jurisdiction over what areas; whether or not a new mother country was keen about having the colony, it must be held for at least enough gain that it is not a burden, and preferably it should be managed to the positive benefit of the mother country in providing tribute in cash, goods, labor, opportunities for commercial exploitation by private interests of the mother country, and a place to send settlers. The easiest way to govern a territory is to operate by indirect rule with a show of Native leadership and institutions. The leaders' power is shored up and their cooperation ensured by giving them a financial stake in the colonial status quo or, if they are conscientious about the fate of their people, by convincing them of the complexity and might of the colonial power and that they are the people's only hope. Systemic estrangement of leaders from the people is necessary to avoid any contrary input of information. The leaders are answerable to the colonial power for the flow of tribute, and the mother country conveniently lets them bear the brunt of the people's discontent.

The Native subjects do express discontent because they can see that they are losing out. They are not really self-determining with their "own" leaders and institutions, and the system does not ensure the continuation of their own culture and identity but merely freezes them at a certain point in their history that may not have been one of the best ones to begin with from their point of view. They are prevented socially and economically from changing along their own lines and incorporating innovations in their own way to their full and direct benefit. Outsiders exploit their resources to help them meet tribute levies but not to benefit them as a society. Settlers may move in and expropriate more resources, relegating the mass of the people to the lowest socioeconomic rungs in the hierarchy of class in their own society. The alien society points to the few exceptions who have been supported to get the system going and maintain it as evidence that the others are hewers of wood and drawers of water because they are incompetent, lacking abilities, and think because they gave up a little land for which they were paid, the world owes them a living.

When the Natives protest, their intellectuals and nascent leadership are put down rigorously as a lesson to the others by the combined force of the colonial power and the captive Native leadership. The troublemakers are accused of trying to destroy all the things the colonial administration and leadership have so carefully designed and have worked so hard to maintain in the interests of preserving the Native society. Efforts may also be made to absorb the new Native intellectuals into the colonial leadership clique, but this is a dangerous measure promoted by desperation to keep the system going, because if the new intellectuals have powerful friends in the mother country who disapprove of colonialism, they are bound to cause trouble.

Termination made the Menominee Reservation a colony of the state of Wisconsin as a matter of realpolitik by the federal government. The state did not want this responsibility but once saddle with it was obliged, "in the greater interest," to operate as a colonial power to see that its new territory would not be a burden and preferably would benefit the mother country by providing it annual quota of tribute, being exploitable by private commercial interests from powerful segments of the society of the mother country, and even provide for settlers clamoring for land, in this case more recreational areas. The state inherited a ready-made colonial administration with the provision of "district officers" from the mother country to make the important decisions in the interests of the mother country.

The termination plan, in setting up Menominee Enterprises, Inc., requires that a certain number of the corporation managers shall be non-Menominees. The state in turn set up its "home office" to the colony, the Menominee Indian Study Committee, which is really a legislative advisory committee looking to Menominee interests in terms of the state's interests. The termination plan regarding the corporation provides for a Native leadership elite to be responsible to the mother country for collecting tribute, easing the way for private commercial exploitation, keeping the Natives in line and cooperative, and bearing the brunt of the Natives' wrathful discontent. It undercut and destroyed traditional structures of government and controls exercised by the people to make leadership answerable to the community by substituting a county form of government having virtually no control regarding disposition of resources on which the well-being of the community depends and by taking away most of the vote from the people in matters regarding their resources in setting up an Assistance Trust to handle minor and so-called incompetent votes and a Voting Trust to control land and elect corporation directors. The restricted choice of county status or division between several counties given the Menominee was a cruel and cynical device that forced the Menominee to appear to have committed themselves willingly to colonial status against the only other alternative of certain destruction as a people identified with their own land.

It is instructive to note that during the period 1954–61 and immediately after termination became final, there were still people actively opposing the termination plan who argued that if the government was absolutely and unchangeably bent on abolishing the reservation, it would be better to sell the reservation entirely to the state to manage the forest and mill and maintain the rest as parkland as a memorial to the Menominee to proclaim their continued identity. The Menominee people would get the proceeds and make their way at least with a decent economic foundation. The neighboring Wisconsin Winnebago, for example, never had a reservation and, while nominally under the Indian Bureau, in fact got neither much help nor meddlesome administration from it up to 1962, and the Winnebago had kept their identity and a good deal more of their traditional culture going that suddenly became more precious to the Menominee when faced with what they considered a genocidal policy against them.

This view was vehemently opposed by those who were outraged at the thought of selling the land and promoted willingness to go along with termination as a better alternative, since the Menominee who worked on the plan had striven to get safeguards for the land in such provisions as the Voting Trust and keeping shares nonnegotiable. The so-called sellouts retorted that the land would eventually be broken up and sold anyway, with no prospect of ever getting it back should there be a shift in the wind from Washington. The Menominee people as individuals who were supposed to be "freed" by termination to manage for themselves would realize no profit to help them make the transition out of protected reservation life. The "sell-out" faction pointed to the allotted reservations in the state and the fact that just *planning* termination had led to loss of services and facilities the Menominee had enjoyed prior to 1954. They predicted with chilling accuracy what would happen if termination became final. But nobody listened. If anyone had listened and heeded, the seeming "factionalism" (used to justify outsiders' taking control of Menominee affairs to save the Menominee from themselves) would have vanished in general agreement to keep federal trust over the land and merely lift the unnecessary administrative restrictions exercised by the Indian Bureau.

Because the Menominee people were not isolated "bush" Natives at the beginning of their colonial experience, young intellectuals were already coming up from the ranks, and dissatisfaction erupted in less than a decade when it became apparent that the state and commercial interests had developed a real stake in maintain the colonial status quo. The corporation management officially criticized efforts by Menominee to avail themselves of the opportunity presented in 1971 to abolish the Voting Trust and be enabled to elect corporation managers directly who would be responsible to a Menominee constituency and expected to work to establish different relationships with the dominant powers the Menominee recognize as vital to their best interests and survival as a people.

On April 3, 1971, the First Wisconsin Trust Company, in charge of the Menominee Assistance Trust, cast its block of votes against the majority of the Menominee, who wanted to abolish the Voting Trust. The First Wisconsin Trust Company's information input on which it based its decision was not from the Menominee people but the colonial administration in charge that designated opposition as evidence that the Menominee clearly need a firm hand to manage for them. The colonial administration and local elite joined forces to suppress troublemakers who continued to protest against company policies in regard to land sales. Thus exemplary, sober, self-supporting Menominee with no criminal records have now served time in jail for the courage of their principles in the tradition of Gandhi and Kenyatta.

When the proxy fight to abolish the Voting Trust began to raise a serious threat, the corporation tried the desperate measure of offering to expand the number of Native leadership jobs to win possible malcontents from the ranks of the opposition. The effort was only partially successful, since two of the young intellectuals who are expected to cause trouble on the now-expanded Voting Trust were elected by the vote of the people in spite of the colonial power's effort to defeat them. The First Wisconsin Trust Company did *not* cast its vote for these two college-educated people.

Finally, and fortunately, the Menominee leadership elite were not simple bush chiefs, dazzled and flattered beyond reason by the responsibilities they were called to take on. Forced by circumstances into an unhappy colonial situation, they still reflect the experience and habits of leadership under the Indian Bureau, which will be discussed more fully in the next section. Their estrangement from the community pains and disheartens them too. They are aware of the damage done by termination and seek restitution for the Menominee as parties to the present litigation. This discussion is intended not to criticize them, but to point out how termination has victimized *all* the Menominee by placing them in roles not of their own making that bring about certain behaviors and attitudes to paralyze healthy community life: an appearance of venality and viciousness on the one hand and an appearance of irresponsible rabble rousing on the other. Experienced leaders, young intellectuals with new ideas, potential leaders with experiences outside the colonial situation that could be put to good use, and the Menominee people as a whole are prevented from getting together. The social damage done to the Menominee by termination is fully as great as or greater than the substantial quantifiable material damage.

Significantly, the state of Wisconsin did try to avail itself of some anthropological expertise, but by 1953 no American anthropologist, particularly one whose specialty and field experiences centered in Africa, could in conscience approve the kind of data the state might use in a manipulatory scheme of indirect rule.

OVERCOMING ANTHROPOLOGICAL EGOCENTRISM

Despite the taint of colonialism, by the 1930s functionalism and acculturation studies had developed around anthropological premises as a basis for practical solutions to problems in situations where anthropologists felt they could take part without compromising their ethical principles. Assistance agencies without ulterior motives and groups desiring what these agencies had to offer were both interested in overcoming blocks to communication and cooperation that confounded the carrying out of presumably mutually agreed-upon objectives. But old suspicions were not easily dispelled. When John Collier Sr. added an anthropological staff to the Bureau of Indian Affairs, many American anthropologists were critical of colleagues who participated in the work as being no better than the British, Belgians, French, and Dutch.

However, there were important differences. In the first place, American anthropologists were highly sensitive to the ethical and methodological questions raised in the colonial examples. In the second place, there were significant demographic and historical differences in the formal and informal relationships between Euro-Americans and Indian tribes compared with European colonial relationship to Native peoples. Where colonial administrations were established to expedite exploitation of foreign territory, the Indian Bureau—whatever its faults in fact—in principle represented the government's promise to protect Indians' lands and rights. The Indians had bargained for their reservations in the aftermath of American colonial expansion that simply appropriated most of the land. American anthropologists defined their practical role not as colonial officers or advisers to colonial administrations on how to manipulate local cultures and peoples but as liaison personnel, helping make Indians' problems and needs comprehensible to administrators and acting as buffer and neutralizer to those forces hindering Indians' efforts or attempting to impose things Indians did not want.

The purely academic arguments between cultural evolutionists and functionalists had provided anthropology as a whole with some tested perspectives on which all could agree in general. Constant change was recognized as implicit to the nature of culture. As men's primary survival mechanism, culture must be adaptable to meet new threats and take advantage of new opportunities to prompt the survival of the society sharing a particular cultural system. However, a culture does not exist apart from the people who share it, even though for comparative purposes it can be treated in the abstract as an "extrasomatic" or "superorganic" phenomenon governed by its own scientific laws. There must be continuity of culture for people to live together and carry out activities with maximum mutual understanding and minimum conflict and confusion. Functionalist studies had helped indicate with reliable precision how innovations are made to fit existing institutions, tastes, skills, and value systems to be acceptable and useful. New ways are found to do old things; old things are put to new uses.

Initially, American applied anthropologists were quite confident that given their expert knowledge of a culture, they could predict whether an innovation would be rejected out of hand, readily accepted, or accepted only if certain possible and agreeable modifications were made in the innovation, the receiving culture, or both. They became very adept at pinpointing why a particular program had failed or succeeded. They proved to be useful troubleshooters to restore working relationships over cultural boundaries once resistance to a program occurred and cooperation had broken down between an agency and client community. But where such analysis is possible after all the significant facts are in, the best-informed expert, in practice, cannot possibly know every significant thing about a culture in advance, and from day to day the outside expert's data grow slightly out of date. Useful experience showed that the very subtle variables or most recent ones that are most easily overlooked often turn out to be of greatest significance in determining how an innovation is to be tested.

Many American applied anthropologists learned and perfected their trade in the Collier administration, working in a liaison and troubleshooter capacity between Indian communities and the Indian Bureau. However, the major contribution to applied anthropology lay in the philosophy underlying the Collier program, which anticipated what in time came to be known as an action anthropology approach in applied work to guard against errors in expert judgment. Collier sought the direct participation of Indian people in program planning, decision-making, and implementation of work. No outside expert, no matter how well informed, and no single member of a community could anticipate all the variables and problems particular proposals might involve. Self-determining communities, given the opportunity to review all that resource experts might offer and knowing themselves, in the final analysis were the best experts on what they wanted and could use. The anthropologist could help make their preferences and decisions analytically comprehensible across cultural barriers to communication.

However, Collier inherited a bureaucracy that was used to giving the orders and had never shown much patience for sitting through Indians' preferred procedures of decision-making—long, seemingly irrelevant discussions and arguments to air all issues and assess all facts from the viewpoint of the various interest groups in the community in order to hammer out consensus and agree on objectives and procedures. Furthermore, many old bureau hands were offended at the implication that they did not operate in cooperation with community. As a matter of fact, a modified form of indirect rule had obtained for a long time in reservation administration. From the beginning, the bureau had shown a marked preference for dealing with Indian people who appeared most like themselves. This was understandable insofar as the bureau was supposed to be phasing Indians out of their distinctiveness. Like Alice Fletcher, bureau people tended to view such exceptional Indians as beacons in a course others were expected to follow. However, some of these so-called acculturated people did not choose to phase out completely and become assimilated into the dominant society but maintained ties of kinship, friendship, and common interests to greater or lesser degree with their communities. It was from their ranks on many innovations that a kind of traditional leadership elite was drawn.

Some developed a personal stake in the status quo akin to that of many bureau administrators who worked to stamp out Indian culture but were not determined to get the Indians phased out before they retired. These leaders were not as easily perceived, compared with indirect rule in Africa, because they did not act like "chiefs" or wear traditional trappings. Quite the contrary, the "traditional" badge of office was to be least Indian in manner and appearance of anyone in the community. Because the bureau was not a true colonial administration in the official business of exploiting foreign land and peoples for the other country, it did not have official sanction to shore up the power of such leaders or pay them off. The main job was to get on with the business of administering the complicated heirship and welfare affairs with the greatest efficiency and fewest complaints to higher-ups from disgruntled Indians.

Indians took ready advantage of the fact that they had far easier access to the home office than Natives in far-flung posts of empire had to the mother country. But it was still expedient and time-saving for a superintendent to work through the elite to keep the tribe in line and get what he wanted done by making judicious concessions negotiated by the elite in the tribal behalf. Although bribery was not unknown, ordinarily it was hard for the local elite to be terribly venal, given the bureau's resources. But it was also hard for the community to get much done on its terms even when leaders the bureau was willing to deal with were also fully in tune with and sympathetic to the interests of their communities. If leaders were too obviously Indian oriented, they lost credibility and effectiveness with the bureau as proper spokesmen for the Indian interest as the bureau defined it. If they were too obviously tools of the bureau or simply ineffectual, the community made trouble to discredit their usefulness to the superintendent and then backed other leaders with the right credentials as negotiators but, it was hoped, more scruples or skill. Such "factionalism," the result of having to manipulate power rather than exercise it directly, was then used to justify the bureau's presence and officiousness in community affairs, since the people obviously were not ready or able to manage for themselves. Generally, the less economically dependent a reservation was on the bureau, the more the Indian community could exercise self-determination; develop responsible, stable leadership; and utilize what benefits the bureau might be able to offer.

Collier saw useful models in such obviously Indian communities as the Pueblos, with whom he had been long familiar prior to becoming Indian commissioner. There was little estrangement between leadership and the people as a whole, and leaders derived their authority from traditional sources. Some of the eastern Pueblos had even developed a dual political organization in response to conquest, with truly traditional leaders for internal affairs and another new set of functionaries for neutralizing demands and negotiating in the communities' behalf with the succession of Spanish, Mexican, and American administrations. Collier was also quite aware that they had not lost land like the allotted tribes. He instituted measures to finally halt the process of land loss set in motion by the allotment program and began an Indian land restoration program. Collier recognized that the Pueblos were exceptional in their conservatism of Native governing arrangements and endeavored to develop responsible tribal government elsewhere by giving the reservation communities the power, if they wished, to organize under their own constitutions and charters to handle their own affairs and enter into contracts for purposes of community development.

Although Collier's administration made errors—Collier was criticized for being both an unregenerate bureaucrat trying to impose alien structures on still viable tribal organizations and an impractical romantic trying to turn back the clock and bring back the buffalo—the wonder is not that it failed in its ultimate purpose to make the reservations self-respecting, self-determining communities, but that it succeeded at all. The program was really in effective operation only seven years, from the passage of the Indian Reorganization Act (IRA) of 1934 to the outbreak of World War II in 1941, although Collier did not tender his resignation until the end of the war. In that short space of time, Collier's message struck a responsive chord among Indian people, and a great majority of the tribes under federal jurisdiction availed themselves of the provisions of IRA despite entrenched suspicion and a wait-and-see attitude about anything the bureau might propose.

One of the major shortcomings of IRA was the great power still held by reservation superintendents whom Collier had expected to respond with understanding and cooperation. Both Collier and his anthropological team overlooked the importance of dealing with administrative culture with the same objective patience with which they dealt with Indian culture in promoting understanding and cooperation. (Applied anthropologists are still subject to this criticism, their distaste for bureaucracy founded in part on the cozy relationships of British anthropologists and colonial administrations that led to outcries concerning professional ethics.) On some reservations IRA helped systematize the form of indirect rule already in effect, and the difficulty could not be rectified by the time Collier left office.

When the war began, domestic programs were cut back, including those of the Indian Bureau, but even before 1941 Congress had grown suspicious of Collier's idealism and notions that assimilation was not the final solution to the Indian problem. As long as there were Indians, the government would be in the Indian business, at least to the extent of protecting land as promised in treaties and other agreements. Collier's program had even attempted to firm up those old obligations. Collier tried to keep his program alive in the face of growing opposition, in preparation for meeting problems that would occur after the war, but Congress was not impressed. Wartime prosperity had temporarily alleviated many of the critical problems of poverty on the reservations, as people left for the armed services and to work in defense factories. Those left at home benefited from income from such outside sources. The war had been a tremendous mass educational experience, and people returned with new skills, goals, and ideas they could use in connection with the provisions of IRA. They just needed capital to get started and begin building decent community life.

Congress was besieged by Indian clamor for help and complaints about the heavy hand of the bureaucracy at the local level. Furthermore, there was an even bigger "Indian problem," because the Indian population had risen markedly during the war to further strain inadequate land bases and undeveloped resources. Collier was conveniently blamed for the Indian problem by throwing out the baby instead of the old Indian Bureau bathwater. In the words of Senator Arthur V. Watkins, the old assimilationist policy underlying the new termination program was to designed to "free" the Indians. "Unfortunately, the major and continuing Congressional movement toward full freedom was delayed for a time by the Indian Reorganization Act of 1934, the Wheeler-Howard Act. Amid the deep social concern of the depression years, Congress deviated from its accustomed policy under the concept of promoting the general Indian welfare. In the post-depression years Congress—realizing this change of policy—sought to return to the historic principles of much earlier decades" (Watkins 1957, 48).

The procedure whereby the Menominee were terminated—"freed" into the handicaps of a colonial administrative structure, as has been shown—first reduced them to the kind of impoverished powerlessness characteristic of the worst administrative conditions of reservations of the pre-Collier era by depriving them of effective governing organization and capital to cope in their own interests.

Even in Collier's time, the Menominee represented a "success story" as impressive as the Pueblos. Significantly, the Menominee, like a number of the Pueblos, saw no need for adopting the provisions of IRA organization in 1934, having achieved what IRA was designed to provide for other tribes. Developing out of a Woodland tradition that placed a premium on flexibility and opportunism, in contrast to the Pueblos' traditional emphasis on conservativism, they remained as "Indian" as the Pueblos by their own lights. Aware and even regretful that they had given up or had been forced to give up many ancestral traits under the pressure of white encroachment, bureau policies, and missionary zeal, the Menominee had taken on new things and made them their own, investing them with their own meanings, functions, and uses, and used old means to gain new ends to survive and continue to be recognized as the Menominee people. After all, the Menominee had not always had gardens either but in late pre-Columbian times had taken on this innovation from neighbors whom archaeology indicates differed markedly from them in culture and probably language as well. As far as anyone knows, they had become no less Menominee Indian for being less critically dependent on wild food and acquiring new subsistence skills. They had always borrowed decorative motifs, songs, ceremonials, dances, and crafts from their Indian neighbors and borrowed new items and skills from non-Indians since the beginning of European contact in the seventeenth century.

By the twentieth century they were experienced not only in judicious borrowing but judicious rejection as well, deciding by their own methods on the basis of their own values what would and would not serve their interests. Thereby they held fast to their land against a series of threats and became less beholden to the bureau and the bureau's version of indirect rule and the leadership structure it fostered in comparison with the allotted tribes dependent on the bureau to manage their complicated heirship affairs and administer vast amounts of welfare aid. In fact, by 1951 they had succeeded in challenging the bureau's administrative competence and accountability to net a judgment of $7,600,000 without even having the benefit of the Indian Claims Commission Act, which was designed to assist litigation of tribal claims.

The Menominee intended to use their judgment to improve the mill, improve community services and employment opportunities, and pay $1,500 per capita. Although it was their money, it was held in the federal treasury and needed official approval for release. While the Menominee had prospered relative to most other tribes, they were not wealthy as individuals, and the bureau kept a tight rein on management of their corporate and personal affairs. This rankled. A certain amount of negotiating by tribal leaders, as described earlier, was called for to forward the community interest, and there were dissatisfactions that were expressed in a certain amount of "irresponsible" fiscal and personal behavior. As early as 1928 the Menominee were deemed soon able to handle most of their internal affairs, and yet the bureau had made no effort to phase Menominee into higher-echelon managerial positions and continued to exercise oppressively paternalistic control over individuals' affairs, demanding accountings of intended use of income from the tribe's income-bearing funds before releasing it—like a stern father doling out his children's allowances. But the Menominee knew what was going on, even if they often could not take as much action as they wished. They understood the forest and the mill; they understood that it was their money that provided community services that many other tribes had to get from the bureau, and then not of such quality; and they understood contracts in their support of medical and educational services provided by the Catholic mission.

In the period of 1951–53 the Menominee offered about as ideal a situation as could be imagined for creative, positive, long-range community improvement to become a truly self-determining community well on the way to total self-sufficiency. Instead, release of their funds was held up while they were submitted to a combination of carrot-and-stick permission to agree to termination, just the principle of termination, to get their per capitas. Confusion, suspicion, loss of faith in leadership unable to negotiate for them as they wished, and fear entered their lives. Some people simply withdrew from any discussion of termination, hoping the idea would blow over; others though the idea should be met head-on by vigorous opposition; and others thought they ought to cooperate in order to have some control and say in the matter.

Whatever differences existed and exist as to strategies for coping with the problems posed by and later resulting from termination, there are two points on which all Menominee agree. Termination was not their idea. There was no protermination faction. And they were told that they had better agree to termination and help direct its course, or Congress would contrive to terminate them in one way or another. It was on this threat that unity was broken. Some people actively opposed to termination or so confused as to the right course for the most part began avoiding gatherings for fear of being stampeded or coerced into agreement. Others, concerned about their per capitas, saw the opposition to termination by the more educated and informed as evidence of bureau and elite playing hand in glove to deprive them of what was rightly theirs, and the "principle of termination" they were asked to agree to set no deadlines or procedures. It was, they thought, just a term they could manipulate once they got their money.

For all that, a vote that was not officially recognized or accepted indicated that nearly 200 people, with none opposing, were willing to forgo per capitas if the price had to be agreement to all the riders that involved termination to get the money released. The officially accepted vote of 169 in favor of termination and 5 opposed was obtained under circumstances of inadequate notice; continued use of a reduced quorum set up during the war, when so many people were away and it was difficult to conduct tribal business; and, according to people who were there, so much legalistic discussion that they were confused. Other people who were present and voted for termination did so reluctantly but out of sincere conviction that a show of cooperation was their only hope of getting termination on any of their conditions as opposed to the likely prospect of the government running roughshod over the Menominee. These people included leaders who understood and were experienced in the necessary techniques of wheeling, dealing, negotiating, and conciliating to get concessions out of the bureau in the community's behalf.

One of the five people who voted against termination is now close to ninety years old and is still actively opposing the leadership who took the path of conciliation and compromise and have been among those considered reasonable enough to serve in offices managing Menominee corporation affairs since termination. He joined the proxy fight to abolish the Voting Trust and came all the way down to Milwaukee to join the picketing at the first Wisconsin Trust Company in protest against its block vote being cast to keep the Voting Trust in effect. It was people like Ernest Neconish, whose knowledge and experience told them when compromise was indicated and when to stand fast, who kept Menominee leadership responsible to the people for so many years and allowed for effective exercise of the talents of the educated bilinguals in dealings with the bureau.

But the atmosphere of haste, confusion, uncertainty, and imminent threat posed by the efforts to get the Menominee to agree to termination disregarded traditional techniques of decision-making that called for thorough, careful review and understanding of all the facts and their implications. Not only were the Menominee not informed of what was in store to make a considered decision, they could not be informed because it was only after the government got its token approval of termination that work began on planning how it would be carried out. The bureau neglected its responsibilities, apparently in realization it would be closing up shop on the reservation, and the people could get little satisfaction from that quarter of community affairs. Work on the termination plan was carried out at a distance by experts, and Congress decreed that much of it should be paid for out of the tribal treasury. The treasury was depleted for the per capitas. Furthermore, it turned out the tribe did not have as much capital at the beginning for efforts to terminate them as had been assumed because the bureau erred in its bookkeeping and had underpaid annual interest payments to the Menominee that had to be rectified. The tribe could no longer maintain its utilities, and they had to be sold; the hospital could no longer be maintained and had to be closed; the mill could no longer support a significant proportion of the population.

As a depression settled on the reservation, many Menominee left out of economic necessity to find work in the urban areas, where they were even less able to keep up with events and the plans regarding termination. The disorganization, demoralization, and depopulation all suggested to those working on the termination plan that the Menominee were not to be trusted to manage many of their own affairs for fear they would dissipate the tribal estate out of profligacy, lack of understanding of the complexities of stocks and bonds, and relocation in the cities where they were expected to remain and lose their loyalty to Menominee ties, since this was the objective of the relocation program. Menominee involved in developing the termination plan stalled for time and concessions, concerned primarily with keeping the land intact for Menominee who would remain there. The safeguards against dangers presumed to be posed by the Menominee themselves ironically placed ultimate power in a few hands to dispose of the land over which the Menominee had no voice or control when those in charge decided it was necessary to sell land to keep the corporation and county in business. By this time, all the factors encouraging the maintaining of the colonial status quo had set in. Arguments from the dissatisfied Menominee that their leadership should seek reversal of termination were met with the same disdain as the cries of African and Asian colonies for independence. The termination plan even took control over the annual timber harvest out of experienced Menominee hands, and the state of Wisconsin proved its fallibility of judgment in grossly overestimating the cut for a sustained yield operation.

The results of termination to date have included the worst effects of allotment in the loss of individuals' holdings to taxation, checkerboarding the land into white and Indian holdings, loss of great sections to private development getting the lion's share of the profit and taking away any future opportunity for the Menominee to develop the land along lines they would prefer to their direct benefit, and an invasion of affluent non-Menominees to make the majority of the Menominee the laboring and servant class if they are to derive any economic benefit from the summer residents. If only a quarter of the new proposed lots are sold to retired persons who will vote in the county, the Menominee will have lost control over county government, with dismal prospects for school millage assessments and other taxes to benefit the Menominee. The results of termination to date have also resulted in the worst effects of colonialism in depriving the people of real self-determination and providing for the exploitation of their persons and property to benefit the state of Wisconsin and non-Menominee residents of the state of Wisconsin. Finally, termination also resulted in reducing a strong, self-reliant reservation community with prospects, potential, and optimism for significant self-improvement to the despair, dependency, and demoralization characteristic of the worst reservation conditions Collier had tried to alleviate.

DAMAGES TO THE MENOMINEE COULD
HAVE BEEN PREVENTED

The proponents of termination willfully disregarded any guidance with a Collier taint, as the quotation from Senator Watkins makes evident, including anthropological knowledge—perhaps particularly including anthropological knowledge. Yet during the war, the government had sought and relied on the work of applied anthropologists to prepare survival manuals for American servicemen who might be shot down or washed ashore on strange terrain, dependent on help from Native peoples; had based strategy on anthropological studies of cultural imperatives underlying enemy behavior; and had employed anthropologists to teach conversation skills in a variety of languages. By the end of the war, the government was supporting a great deal of anthropological research in the newly acquired Trust Territory of the Pacific and established an anthropological staff on the model pioneered by Collier in the Indian Bureau. American and United Nations assistance programs overseas employed applied anthropologists. By the 1950s the congressional proponents of termination should have been aware of a source of advice from anthropologists.

The Society for Applied Anthropology was founded in 1941 and instituted a journal, now called *Human Organization*, in order to facilitate exchanges of information and discussions of method and theory among the increasing number of anthropologists and other social scientists who, in the words of the society's constitution, are concerned with "the promotion of scientific investigation of the principles controlling relations of human beings to one another, and the encouragement of the wide application of these principles to practical problems" (regularly reprinted in the inside front cover of *Human Organization*). Articles and monographs even antedating the founding of the Society for Applied Anthropology had begun to show consistent agreement in orientation and validation of basic practical premises in regard to relations of human beings to each other.

Long before House Concurrent Resolution 108 was passed, there was a popular access to knowledge not only of anthropology in general but applied anthropology in particular. As early as 1949 Clyde Kluckhohn's popular survey of anthropology, *Mirror for Man*, devoted an entire chapter to applied anthropology, titled "Anthropologists at Work" (168–95). This widely read, prizewinning book, which is still being reprinted, begins with Kluckhohn's statement "This book is intended for the layman" (ix).

As more and more universities introduced courses in applied anthropology immediately after the war, the need for a full-length text was ably met in 1952 by a casebook edited by Edward Spicer, *Human Problems in Technological Change*. Spicer's book remains required reading in the training of applied anthropologists and, like Kluckhohn's book, is widely recommended for specialists in such fields as education, government, health, agriculture, and the like whose work involves them in cross-cultural programs.

That applied anthropology had become an integral and recognized part of the field of anthropology as a whole is reflected in the landmark volume of 1953 edited by Alfred L. Kroeber, *Anthropology Today*, which had an entire section designated "Problems of Application" (731–894). Discussion of the essays in this section appear in a companion volume edited by Sol Tax et al., *An Appraisal of Anthropology Today* (1953).

Shortly after the Menominee Termination Act was passed, and while the termination plan was being drawn up, a number of other publications appeared on the practical value of anthropology. These include the UNESCO-sponsored volume edited by Margaret Mead, *Cultural Patterns and Technical Change* (1955), which provided discussion of method and theory for use of the layman and gave instructive case studies from a number of different areas.

Another publication that appeared in 1955 was *Health, Culture, and Community*, edited by Benjamin D. Paul. It narrowed its substantive case material to assist technicians in cross-cultural health and medical programs while also enunciating basic principles applicable in programs of planned change in general. The following year, Homer G. Barnett published *Anthropology in Administration* (1956), detailing principles and actual problems and experiences in regard primarily to the Trust Territory of the Pacific but with implications far broader than that geographic area. By 1957 the British had come a long way from their naive forays into applied anthropology of the 1920s, as seen in the textbook published by Lucy Mair, *Studies in Applied Anthropology*, which showed congruence with generalizations developed in applied anthropology in the United States.

The year 1957 also saw the publication of two articles, somewhat in the form of a debate, in the *Annals of the American Academy of Political and Social Science* (vol. 311, May) that gave dramatic evidence of the gap between scholarly and congressional thinking on termination. Oliver La Farge, a writer with intimate knowledge of Indian peoples and cultures who enjoyed the status of colleague among the ranks of professional anthropologists, wrote an article titled "Termination of Federal Supervision: Disintegration and The American Indians." La Farge took explicit notice of Menominee expressions of dissatisfaction with termination and deplored the "atmosphere of haste, of jamming through, of bad drafting, misrepresentation, and pressure" surrounding legislation concerning termination (45–46). This was followed by an article by Senator Watkins promoting termination as "freeing" the Indians and making some special self-congratulatory references to the Menominee. Watkins ends his article in a burst of spread-eagle rhetoric— "THESE PEOPLE SHALL BE FREE!"—and modestly likens himself, as the main proponent of termination, to the Great Emancipator (54–55). This is not a simple case of the truth lying somewhere between wide differences of opinion. Watkins's statements misrepresent facts as they existed at the time and dismiss opposition summarily with ridicule rather than reason. History has proved La Farge the true prophet in foreseeing a course of socioeconomic disintegration in what was meant by "termination" as officially proposed in 1953 and subsequently implemented for the Menominee.

Between 1949 and 1959 two major projects provided extensive and systematic tests of principles of applied anthropology and exemplified the growing general trend toward what is known as an "action anthropology" approach in applied work. Rather than concentrating on achieving specified programmatic ends of isolated innovations by anthropological means that would maximize cooperation and minimize resistance, such as introducing techniques to reduce infection in traditional midwifery practices, an action approach involves the community in defining its problems, choosing among and adapting from all the alternative solutions that might be available, and carrying out programs. Action anthropology distrusts the idea that the outside expert is omniscient about what is appropriate for a community but sees the people who must live with a program after the experts leave as the best judges of what will serve their purposes. Knowing the community, the anthropologist can make an input of knowledge and alternatives and his best judgment as to risks and consequences of various courses in terms the community can understand, and he can act as liaison between the community and resources they need when they cannot perform this function for themselves. The objective is to provide knowledge, training, resources, and experience to enable a community seeking help to not only solve its immediate problems but be better able to cope with new ones that may arise.

The Fox Indian Project of the University of Chicago Anthropology Department (1949–59) and the Cornell University Anthropology Department Project at Vicos, Peru (1952–57), dealt with very different kinds of communities and problems with quite similar action methods. Sol Tax, who coordinated the Fox project, coined the term "action anthropology" to describe what, indeed, many anthropologists had been doing independently for some time in various parts of the world. An extensive bibliography exists in regard to the Fox and Vicos projects, as well as other action projects and the concept of action anthropology itself, but a representative selection would include the following: Tax (1952, 1958, 1959); Gearing et al. (1960); and Holmberg (1958, 1965).

As this list indicates, there was no dearth of cautionary information, much of it written as much for use by nonanthropologists as by anthropologists, for the government to have developed a better policy than the idea of termination as it was propounded in general and implemented specifically for the Menominee. The remarkable thing is how the government managed to replicate every bad step in history in the administration of Indigenous peoples and systemically violated every basic principle of responsible planned change derived from scientific study and analysis of tested experience.

PRINCIPLES OF PLANNED CHANGE

Although many of the principles of applied anthropology have been adverted to in the foregoing, it is instructive to review certain basic concepts and indicate how they were violated specifically in regard to the termination of the Menominee. Principles will be discussed under Roman numerals plus A, and the Menominee instances under Roman numerals plus B.

I. A. George Foster opens his textbook in applied anthropology with an oriental fable to underscore a first principle: "Once upon a time a monkey and a fish were caught up in a great flood. The monkey, agile and experienced, had the good fortune to scramble up a tree to safety. As he looked down into the raging waters, he saw a fish struggling against the swift current. Filled with a humanitarian desire to help his less fortunate fellow, he reached down and scooped the fish from the water. To the monkey's surprise, the fish was not very grateful for this aid" (1962, 1).

Every text in applied anthropology expresses the principle and its corollary embodied in the ancient wisdom cited above; one should know the needs and habits of others and not judge by one's own needs and habits before taking action in the other's behalf; precipitous action, however well intentioned, is likely to do more harm than not dealing at all with the apparent problem that evoked the action. All the succeeding principles to be discussed are really only expansions and detailed features of this basic theme.

I. B. Congress, like the monkey in the fable, scooped up the struggling Menominee with the ill-advised rescue operation of termination. Like the fish, the Menominee are not very grateful for this aid, as witness the present litigation.

II. A. There must be mutual understanding and agreement between an assisting agency and client community on wants and needs—that is, on definition of problem and proposed solutions. If full understanding is not achieved at the outset, it follows that proposed solutions are likely to fall short of their intent be irrelevant to the community's needs, to fail completely, to even do more harm than good. Spicer points out:

> Understanding that change is a process which people are undergoing all
> the time, gives us a vantage point from which to view conscious efforts

to alter culture. We begin to see resistance as a symptom of something wrong in the cross-cultural situation, perhaps of the real impracticality of the imposed change, perhaps of unsatisfactory relations between the worker and the people. Once resistance is seen as a symptom of special conditions rather than a constant element, it becomes possible, through the study of cases in which resistance appears, to discover causes of success and failure. (1952, 18)

One of the often cited cases from the Spicer volume concerns an agricultural agent working in a Hispanic community in the American Southwest. The problem for which the community needed help was the low yield of their corn, their primary subsistence crop. Responding sympathetically, but seeing the problem entirely in his terms, the agent studied alternatives to come up with a high-yield hybrid variety that was appropriate to the soil, climate, and local farming technology. Because the agent was an agreeable person who made every effort to respect local etiquette, the Hispanic farmers were receptive to his innovation as a friendly gesture. Yet most of the people abandoned the new corn after one season, and by the third season all had gone back to using their old, low-yield corn. The new corn did not store well according to the methods used in the areas, its consistency and other properties made it nearly impossible to use with their traditional methods of cooking, and furthermore, it tasted awful (1952, 35–40).

When so many cultural variables are involved in defining a problem to find a solution to meet all needs in such a simple case as seed corn, the potential for error in proposing massive, far-reaching innovations should have given pause to the proponents of termination. The Hispanic farmers were able to resist an inappropriate innovation by polite noncooperation and at least go on living with their old problem rather than being stuck with a lot of new ones.

II. B. Both Congress and the Menominee deplored the Menominee's lack of "freedom" to manage their own affairs, but they did not define the problem in the same way. The government defined the problem as the very thing the Menominee thought was a guarantee and protection of their freedom to continue developing as an increasingly self-sufficient community—federal trusteeship over their land and such other features of the federal-Indian relationship as were spelled out by treaty. The Menominee defined the problem as the crescive bureaucratic arrogation of functions and power in their personal, municipal, and financial affairs that were never mutually agreed upon and that restricted and hampered Menominee efforts to operate and develop freely as a community and even as individuals. When the Menominee sought cooperation, understanding, and assistance to expedite release of what was really their money from their judgment of 1951 to carry out programs they had decided on as appropriate to their needs and wants, the government, following its definition of the problem, promoted its solution of termination. Menominee resistance—in terms of complaints, withdrawal from discussions of termination, foot-dragging, and diversionary actions—was not recognized for what it was: evidence that there was something wrong in the cross-cultural situation, that the proposed change was impractical and relations between proponents of termination and the Menominee were unsatisfactory. The government disregarded such reactions, evidently in the belief that something was wrong with the Menominee, who would have to live with the government's solution to their problem.

III. A. Anthropology students, whether or not they intend to go into the applied field, are trained in methods of reliable objective cultural description and analysis. Among many other things, they are taught to prepare for the possibility of experiencing "culture shock"—that is, psychic difficulty in strange situations where one's customary expectations and operational responses to other people and the social environment prove inadequate, inappropriate, and unavailing. Yet most anthropologists would agree that it is generally easier to discern and describe the nature of highly exotic cultures in reliable detail, simply because of the obvious contrast they afford to the familiar, than it is to study people who appear to have much in common with oneself. Many anthropologists have found that culture shock is apt to come in situations that are not particularly strange, or in initially very strange communities, after the big cultural hurdles one is prepared for have been crossed and one is beginning to feel at home. Some seemingly small thing in perception and attitude can suddenly open enormous gaps in one's comprehension and general peace of mind, as well as one's working relationships in the community.

A similar concept in psychology, "cognitive dissonance," refers to the sense of discomfort and disbelief when the presumably familiar somehow gets out of focus. Anthropologists, if they want to carry out their work, are obliged to come to rational grips with the fact of culture shock and not indulge themselves in petulance or the notion that all the rest of the community is wrong. They must understand the underlying local logic and function of traits and behaviors that at first blush seem irrational, inexplicable, or bad. Many programs of planned change, however, have foundered because technicians and administrators react to fundamental cultural differences between themselves and the community as behavior that in their culture would be tactless, delinquent, stupid, eccentric, or wrong-handed. They expect people to shape up to their expectations and go ahead with the plans, trying to force people to shape up. A basic principle underlying this discussion is that the more the outsider finds the local culture similar to his own, the more likely he is to underestimate or overlook the strength of subtle cultural differences that have stood the test of time and contact to give identity, continuity, and meaning to the local culture. Such subtle differences will be the source of emphatic resistance and hostility if challenged or threatened. As Kluckhohn observed in his chapter on applied anthropology: "The applied anthropologist continually draws attention to the fact that what to a foreigner may appear to be simple and trivial habits that may be ignored are often so related to the deepest feelings as to invite serious conflict if they should be scorned" (1949, 181).

Such themes, foci, orientations of culture, cultural cores, or value systems, as they have been variously approached and termed by anthropologists, evoke resistance for the very understandable reason that while a people may have made massive concessions and adaptations to survive, once those essentials go, the people lose a vital, cherished part of their identity and self-worth as individuals and a necessary integrating force as a society.

III. B. One of the primary reasons for singling out the Menominee for termination was that they appeared "ready," presumably lacking only a simple, legalistic step to become socioculturally indistinguishable as Indians. Because the Menominee had achieved greater economic security and well-being than the majority of other Indian groups, they seemed less Indian to the proponents of termination, who, as products of Euro-American society and culture, found an important symbolic explosion of their self-worth in economic competitiveness and material possessions. Concern about what would become of the Menominee as a people as a result of termination was brushed aside with specious analogies to this Euro-American experience. Indians, too, could retain their "heritage" by harking back, like Euro-Americans, to their ancestral nationalities in a few sentimental mementos of surnames, material family heirlooms, and even putting on the "old" costumes and dancing the "old" dances for gala occasions. The late Robert Rietz, long the director of the Chicago Indian Center, remarked on this kind of attitude toward Indians: "Yes, they can be just like us, only different." Senator Watkins revealed his total lack of understanding of the Menominee's fears when he observed complacently, "Now, doing away with restrictive federal supervision over Indians, as such, does *not* affect the retention of those cultural and racial qualities which people of Indian descent would wish to retain; many of us are proud of our ancestral heritage." (1957, 48).

Watkins's analogy lost sight of the fact that the Menominee were an established contemporary community in their own land, maintaining and utilizing basic Menominee core values to survive and prosper at least modestly by making judicious selections and adaptations in interaction as a community with the larger, Euro-American–dominated society. The Menominee relied on the federal government to protect their rights, to exist as a peaceful minority, from threats by more powerful neighbors in the dominant society. Termination, defined implicitly as assimilation, and its actual implementation with the Menominee struck at the very core of Menominee existence. This can be seen in the sense of threat, outrage, and despair evoked by the official closing of the tribal roll as symbolizing a policy of genocide, quite apart from the bitterness it evoked in regard to its implications and effects in handling the tribal estate.

Termination also struck at a whole series of interrelated concepts, attitudes, and traditions in regard to land and its resources. Whatever differences the Menominee had and are having in trying to agree on effective strategies to survive as a people, land remains the rallying force and arguing point. It was concern for the land that led to some of the restrictions in the termination plan, albeit they failed of their intent. It was sale of land that finally sparked open rebellion and organized protest. It was the Menominee's ineffable relation to their land that had guided their decisions not to be moved to Minnesota, to turn down immediate gain in the long-range interest when besieged by the lumber barons in the nineteenth century, to resist allotment, and to vote for separate county status as the better of the restricted alternatives given them.

Finally, termination destroyed a basic integrating force in replacing the traditional organization structure with a county government, whereby they are expected to act like rural whites, and a complex corporation, whereby they are expected to act like big-time investors—of which not many are found even among rural whites. The new structures leave a number of functions unattended to, a primary one being communication. The Menominee could make judicious decisions because everyone knew what was going on or could find out. It was the sense of community achievement that gave meaning to Menominee life, of being able to say "our telephone company," "our hospital," "our mill" that gave the Menominee distinctiveness. These were the things that had come out of the Menominee heritage of adaptive coping.

It is interesting to note that when economic development funds were obtained for the Menominee in an effort to lessen the economic crisis posed by termination, well-meaning outsiders conceived of the idea of a Visitors' Destination Center that includes plans for a museum, Menominee guiding on nature trails, and the like. The Menominee's self-appointed friends are puzzled that the Menominee promptly named it the VD Center in derision, have made little effort to stop vandalism in the breaking of windows and destruction of signs, and are much more interested in the place as meeting space for community affairs than any other purpose. They opposed plans for a commercial tourist development, with a convention center where Menominee could serve traditional food and generally play Indian—the outsiders' idea of the "Menominee heritage." Unlike so many tribes deprived of the opportunity to operate as self-aware, effective communities, the Menominee did not have to exploit their ethnicity to proclaim their "Indianness" and Menominee identity. Expressions of traditionalism and contemporary achievements were integrated as simply Menominee society and culture.

IV. A. Although basic principles of applied anthropology could be expanded on and detailed, this discussion will limit itself to the more glaring errors involved in termination. Thus a final principle discusses the basic action anthropology dicta: that the people who must live with a program are the best judges of what will suit them; program proposals and implementation must provide for honest and full assessment by the people involved; and outside expertise should be used to inform, advise, and if necessary, carry out some of the work at the community's behest but should not be in a position to make fundamental decisions for the community. In a small community, the less the need for elaborate structures and the easier it is for information to be communicated and for decision-making to involve all interested members.

IV. B. When the general principle of termination was developed, it evoked opposition from informed Indian people generally that should have given pause to the proponents of termination. Indian people made efforts to study the idea and offer their views, but these were disregarded. Thus the National Congress of American Indians convened an emergency conference after passage of House Concurrent Resolution 108 and passed a resolution exposing the dangers of termination and the need for full knowledge and approval of tribes concerned for any legislation to terminate them. Similar reactions were expressed by the Association on American Indian Affairs, the American Friends Service Committee, and other Indian interest groups that endeavor to keep abreast of Indian opinion and provide a platform for expression of Indian views. Indian students who attended the Workshop on American Indian Affairs sponsored by the University of Chicago Anthropology Department and held at Colorado College at Colorado Springs in the summer of 1956 dealt with federal Indian legislation and policies and devoted important attention to termination, publishing a workbook to further communication of information. The Menominee were certainly engaging in behavior that indicated they were opposed to termination. Yet the main proponents of termination persisted in contending that opposition came only from a vocal minority of Indians and those non-Indians who, out of misguided sentiment, were opposed to "freeing" the Indians (see Watkins 1957, 48).

However, the widespread complaints about termination and the entire Indian policy of the 1950s alerted both candidates in the 1960 presidential campaign to make public statements promising reappraisal and reform of policy. Encouraged by this development, Sol Tax conceived the idea of an action anthropology project that would provide as broad a survey as possible of informed Indian opinion reached according to methods Indians themselves would plan and manage. Tax hoped that such agreement by a representative sample of Indian people would be useful to and a meaningful influence on whichever candidate won the presidency.

The American Indian Chicago Conference of 1961 got underway at the local level across the country in January and culminated in a weeklong conference in Chicago in June, by which time mailings, regional conferences, and distribution of informational material had contributed to growing consensus and ironing out of "factional" differences between reservation and nonreservation tribes, city Indians and country Indians, and Indians from all parts of the country. The effort resulted in the *Declaration of Indian Purpose*, which was printed and widely distributed after the conference and, during the summer of 1961, presented by a special delegation from the conference to President Kennedy at the White House. The *Declaration* begins, after acknowledgments and other preliminaries, with proposals and recommendation in regard to specific topics of Indian concern, opening with "Legislative and Regulatory Proposals," in which the first recommendation is to "abandon the so-called termination policy of the last administration by revoking Housing Concurrent Resolution 108 of the 83rd Congress" (5). Under the proposals regarding "Law and Jurisdiction" (13–16), the first recommendation is the "Return of Indian Lands: . . . . Restore all Indian lands that were consumed by termination policy" (15).

Appendix 2 of the *Declaration* provides a chronological history of developments in Menominee termination from 1953 to 1961 that was prepared at the Indians' request by a legal resource person and ends with this paragraph added as a result of discussions at the Conference itself:

[It was the recommendation of] members of the Menominee Tribe, should any tribe ever consider accepting termination, they conduct a thorough survey of all the results, costs and legal implications of this program. They pointed out that only the favorable side was told to members of their tribe and that the cost of setting up a county government, the taking of land for highway right of way without remuneration, the cost of maintaining county services formerly paid for by the government were all either not mentioned or only slightly touched upon. The prospect of getting a per capita payment of $1500 looked big to the Indians, many of whom were in poor circumstances, but the losses which they incurred in taxes, and cost of county operation far exceeded any benefits that may have resulted from the termination program. They asserted that they had even had to purchase the land upon which their homes were located from the holding corporation which was set up in conjunction with termination. They therefore wished to go on record as warning all Indians and Indian tribes to beware of termination and not be misled by rosy promises. (35)

Shortly before the above was published, termination had become final for the Menominee but had already done damage from a Menominee point of view that is substantiated in hard fiscal data, to say nothing of the social and psychological price the tribe has paid. Yet despite protest and expressions of grievance from the largest representative example of Indian opinion ever achieved, the government has only provided emergency stopgap measures, has forced the Menominee to part with valuable land assets, and has required that new programs that have come out of Washington be used not for long-range benefits but, like other measures, simply to keep the county and corporation going to maintain the basic mistake of termination (Lurie 1961).

NOTE

1. Lurie prepared this essay in June 1971 as the basis of her testimony in support of the Menominee in their case, scheduled for December 1971 in the U.S. Court of Claims, seeking damages from termination.

REFERENCES

American Indian Chicago Conference. 1961. *Declaration of Indian Purpose: The Voice of the American Indian*. Chicago.

Barnett, Homer G. 1956. *Anthropology in Administration*. Evanston IL: Row Peterson.

Fanon, Frantz. 1966. *The Wretched of the Earth*. New York: Grove.

Foster, George. 1962. *Traditional Cultures: The Impact of Technical Change*. New York: Harper and Row.

Gearing, Fred, Robert McC. Netting, and Lisa R. Peattie, eds. 1960. *Documentary History of the Fox Project, 1949–1959: A Program in Action Anthropology*. Chicago: University of Chicago.

Holmberg, Allan R. 1958. "The Research and Development Approach to the Study of Change." *Human Organization* 17:12–16.

——. 1965. "The Changing Values and Institutions of Vicos in the Context of National Development." *American Behavioral Scientist* 7 (7): 17–19.

Kluckhohn, Clyde. 1949. *Mirror for Man*. New York: McGraw Hill.

Kroeber, Alfred L., ed. 1953. *Anthropology Today*. Chicago: University of Chicago Press.

La Farge, Oliver. 1957. "Termination of Federal Supervision: Disintegration and the American Indians." *Annals of the American Academy of Political and Social Science* 311:41–46.

La Flesche, Francis. (1900) 1963. *The Middle Five*. Madison: University of Wisconsin Press.

Lurie, Nancy Oestreich. 1961. "The Voice of the American Indian: A Report on the American Indian Chicago Conference." *Current Anthropology* 2 (5): 478–500.

——. 1966a. "The Lady from Boston and the Omaha Indians." *American West* 3 (4): 31–33, 80–85.

——. 1966b. "Women in Early American Anthropology." In *Pioneers of American Anthropology: The Uses of Biography*, American Ethnological Society Monograph 43, edited by June Helm, 29–81. Seattle: University of Washington Press.

——. 1968. "Alice Cunningham Fletcher." In *International Encyclopedia of the Social Sciences*, vol. 5, 491–94. New York: Macmillan and Free Press.

——. 1971. "As Others See Us." *New University Thought* 7 (1): 2–7.

Macquet, Jacques. 1964. "Objectivity in Anthropology." *Current Anthropology* 5:47–55.

Mair, Lucy. 1957. *Studies in Applied Anthropology*. London: Athlone Press.

Malinowski, Bronislaw. 1929. "Practical Anthropology." *Africa* 2:23–38.

Mead, Margaret. 1955. *Cultural Patterns and Technical Change*. Dublin: Mentor Books.

Paul, Benjamin D., ed. 1955. *Health, Culture, and Community*. New York: Russell Sage Foundation.

Radcliffe-Brown, Alfred R. 1930. "Applied Anthropology." *Report of the Australian and New Zealand Association for the Advancement of Science*, 1–14.

Reining, Conrad C. 1962. "A Lost Period of Applied Anthropology." *American Anthropologist* 64:593–600

Spicer, Edward. 1952. *Human Problems in Technological Change*. New York: Russell Sage Foundation.

Tax, Sol. 1952. "Action Anthropology." *American Indigena* 12:103–9.

——. 1958. "The Fox Project." *Human Organization* 17:17–19.

——. 1959. "Action Anthropology." *Journal of Social Research* 2:1–9.

Tax, Sol, Loren Eiseley, Irving Rouse, and Carl Voegelin, eds. 1953. *An Appraisal of Anthropology Today*. Chicago: University of Chicago Press.

Watkins, Arthur V. 1957. "Termination of Federal Property and Person." *Annals of the American Academy of Political and Social Science* 311:47–55.

17

Nancy Oestreich Lurie

Bibliography

PATRICK J. JUNG

Nancy Oestreich Lurie (1924–2017) produced a significant body of written works spanning the disciplines of cultural anthropology, applied anthropology, action anthropology, archaeology, history, and ethnohistory. Lurie wrote for a wide variety of audiences. She authored articles for top academic journals and books for prestigious university presses but was equally comfortable writing for the general public and penned newspaper editorials, essays for local historical society newsletters, and even a book for adolescents. She wrote on many topics regarding North American Indians, and while most of her research and writing focused on the Ho-Chunk people of Wisconsin, she also worked with other Wisconsin tribes, particularly the Menominee Indians during their battle against federal termination in the late 1960s and early 1970s. As a university anthropologist, she conducted fieldwork among the Dogrib Indians of Canada in 1959, 1962, and 1967, and these research experiences resulted in several important publications.

Lurie spent many years as an anthropology professor at the University of Michigan and the University of Wisconsin–Milwaukee, but museums were always her passion. She was born in Milwaukee and fell in love with the Milwaukee Public Museum as a child. She achieved her girlhood dream of receiving an appointment at the institution in 1972, and she went on to spend the remainder of her professional career there. Even after she retired in 1992, she maintained a museum office that she occupied until the end of her life. She filled this space with books, papers, articles, and artifacts; filing cabinets contained the notes that chronicled her seven decades of fieldwork. Lurie fervently believed that museums fulfill an important educational role, and both her service to the Milwaukee Public Museum and her rich corpus of written works reflect her abiding interest in sharing the wisdom she accumulated throughout her career.

This bibliography is presented as the most complete catalog of Lurie's oeuvre to date and includes publications written and edited by Lurie and those in which she is listed as a contributor. The references section consists of the original first editions of her various writings as well as works that were substantially revised and republished, with the differences between the editions explained in the notes. Those that were later translated or reprinted are cited in the notes with their complete bibliographic information. In one case, a work frequently attributed to Lurie was actually written by another author, and this error is also explained in a note. Finally, this bibliography does not include the many reviews of books and exhibitions that Lurie penned over the course of her career.

1943. "Butterflies and the American Indian." *Wisconsin Archeologist* 24 (1): 1–6.

1944. "Cultural Change Among the Wisconsin Winnebago." *Wisconsin Archeologist* 25 (4): 119–25.

1948. "Trends of Change in Patterns of Child Care and Training among the Wisconsin Winnebago." *Wisconsin Archeologist* 29 (3–4): 39–140.

1950. "Winnebago Folklore." *Badger Folklore* 2 (3): 3–9.

1951. "Esau Was an Indian." *Badger Folklore* 3 (1): 9–11.[1]

1952. "Dog Children Among the Winnebago Indians." *Lore* 2 (2): 54–56.

1952. "The Horibul Speling of Collidge Stewdints." *Milwaukee Journal*, December 10, pt. 1, 24.

1952. "Tragedy of the American Indian Is Repeated in African Colony." *Milwaukee Journal*, November 2, pt. 5, 1, 3.

1952. "The Winnebago Indians: A Study in Cultural Change." PhD diss., Northwestern University.

1953. "Where Black Hawk Met Defeat." *Milwaukee Journal*, January 17, pt. 1, 7.

1953. "Winnebago Berdache." *American Anthropologist* 55 (5): 708–12.

1954. With Verne F. Ray. "The Contributions of Lewis and Clark to Ethnography." *Journal of the Washington Academy of Sciences* 44 (11): 358–70.

1954. With John W. M. Whiting. "A Technique for Teaching Ethnology." *American Anthropologist* 56 (3): 442–45.

1955. "Problems, Opportunities, and Recommendations." *Ethnohistory* 2 (4): 357–75.[2]

1956. "A Reply to 'The Land Claims Cases: Anthropologists in Conflict.'" *Ethnohistory* 3 (3): 256–79.

1957. "The Indian Claims Commission Act." *Annals of the American Academy of Political and Social Science* 311 (May): 56–70.

1959. "Indian Cultural Adjustments to European Civilization." In *Seventeenth-Century America: Essays in Colonial History*, edited by James Morton Smith, 33–60. Chapel Hill: University of North Carolina Press.[3]

1960. "Winnebago Protohistory." In *Culture in History: Essays in Honor of Paul Radin*, edited by Stanley Diamond, 791–808. New York: Columbia University Press.

1961. "Dogrib Indians of Canada." *Lore* 11 (2): 60–67.

1961. "Ethnohistory: An Ethnological Point of View." *Ethnohistory* 8 (1): 78–92.

1961. *Mountain Wolf Woman, Sister of Crashing Thunder: The Autobiography of a Winnebago Woman.* Ann Arbor: University of Michigan Press.[4]

1961. "The Voice of the American Indian: A Report on the American Indian Chicago Conference." *Current Anthropology* 2 (5): 478–500.

1961. With June Helm. *The Subsistence Economy of the Dogrib Indians of Lac la Martre in the MacKenzie District of the Northwest Territories.* Ottawa: Northern Co-ordination and Research Centre, Department of Northern Affairs and National Resources.

1962. "Comments on Bernard J. James's Analysis of Ojibwa Acculturation." *American Anthropologist* 64 (4): 826–33.

1962. "The Wisconsin Winnebago: Tribe-Minority Group-Tribe." Paper presented at the symposium Ethnic Minorities Around the World, American Association for the Advancement of Science, Philadelphia, December 27, 1962. Helen Miner Miller Papers, box 8, folder 85, Newberry Library, Chicago.[5]

1963. "Introduction to Roy F. Barton." *Autobiographies of Three Pagans in the Philippines.* New Hyde Park NY: University Books.[6]

1963. With Helen Miner Miller. *Report on Wisconsin Winnebago Project: Contribution of Community Development to the Prevention of Dependency.* Washington DC: U.S. Social Security Administration.

1964. *Historical Background of the Winnebago People.* Black River Falls: Wisconsin Winnebago Business Committee.

1964. "A More or Less Anthropological View of the General Council." *Wisconsin Winnebago* 1 (6): 4–5.

1964. "Seneca Tribe in Trouble." *Milwaukee Journal*, February 29, pt. 1, 12.

1965. "An American Indian Renascence?" *Midcontinent American Studies Journal* 6 (2): 25–50.[7]

1965. "Anvendt Etnologi i U.S.A." *Jordens Folk* 1 (4): 134.

1966. "A Checklist of Treaty Signers by Clan Affiliation." *Journal of the Wisconsin Indians Research Institute* 2 (1): 50–73.

1966. "The Enduring Indian." *Natural History* 75 (9): 10, 12–13, 18, 20–22.[8]

1966. "The Lady from Boston and the Omaha Indians." *American West* 3 (4): 31–33, 80–85.

1966. "Women in Early American Anthropology." In *Pioneers of American Anthropology: The Uses of Biography*, American Ethnological Society Monograph 43, edited by June Helm, 29–81. Seattle: University of Washington Press.[9]

1966. With Nadine Day Sieber and the Wisconsin Winnebago Research Team. *Continuation of Report on Wisconsin Winnebago Project: Contribution of Community Development to the Prevention of Dependency*. Washington DC: U.S. Social Security Administration.

1966. With June Helm and Gertrude Kurath. *The Dogrib Hand Game*. National Museum of Canada Bulletin 205, Anthropological Series, no. 71. Ottawa: National Museum of Canada.

1967. "President's Comments." *Central States Anthropology Society Bulletin* 2 (1): 1–2.

1968. "Alice Cunningham Fletcher." In *International Encyclopedia of the Social Sciences*, vol. 5, 491–94. New York: Macmillan and Free Press.

1968. "Angry US Indians Refuse to Vanish: Insist on Own Paths to Progress." *Milwaukee Journal*, August 4, pt. 5, 3.

1968. "Cradle from Lapland." *Lore* 18 (3): 92–99.

1968. "Culture Change." In *Introduction to Cultural Anthropology: Essays in the Scope and Methods of the Science of Man*, edited by James A. Clifton, 274–303. Boston: Houghton Mifflin.

1968. "Elsie Clews Parsons." In *International Encyclopedia of the Social Sciences*, vol. 11, 426–28. New York: Macmillan and Free Press.

1968. "Historical Background." In *The American Indian Today*, edited by Stuart Levine and Nancy Oestreich Lurie, 25–45. DeLand FL: Everett Edwards.

1968. "The University of Wisconsin–Milwaukee." *Central States Anthropology Society Bulletin* 2 (2): 1–3.

1968. "Variant Adaptations of Minority Groups to Encompassing Systems." In *Proceedings VIIIth International Congress of Anthropological and Ethnological Sciences*, vol. 2, *Ethnology*, 154–56. Tokyo: Congress of Anthropological and Ethnological Sciences.

1968. "Winnebago History and Culture." Unpublished paper. Wisconsin Historical Society, Madison. Excerpted and edited from two lectures presented at the Seminar in Winnebago Culture and Acculturation for Community Leaders, Black River Falls, Wisconsin, March 22, 1968. Duplicated and distributed by the Division of Children and Youth, Wisconsin Department of Health and Social Services, La Crosse.

1968. With Stuart Levine, eds. *The American Indian Today*. DeLand FL: Everett Edwards.

1969. "What the Red Man Wants in the Land That Was His." *Saturday Review*, October 4, 39–41, 80–81.

1969. *Wisconsin Indians*. Madison: Wisconsin Historical Society.[10]

1969. "Wisconsin: A Natural Laboratory for North American Indian Studies." *Wisconsin Magazine of History* 53 (1): 3–20.[11]

1970. "Ads Tell One Story, Indians Another." *Milwaukee Journal*, September 6, pt. 1, 10.

1970. *Anthropologists in the United States and the Indian Claims Commission*. Toronto: Canadian Association in Support of the Native Peoples.

1970. "Comments on Bernard J. James's 'Continuity and Emergence in Indian Poverty Culture.'" *Current Anthropology* 11 (4–5): 449–50.

1970. "Stephan Francis Borhegyi, 1921–1969." *American Anthropologist* 72 (6): 1398–1408.

1971. "An American Indian Tribal Renascence." In *VIIth International Congress of Anthropological and Ethnological Sciences, Moscow (August 3–10, 1964)*, vol. 11, edited by S. P. Tolstov, 91–96. Moscow: Congress of Anthropological and Ethnological Sciences.

1971. "As Others See Us." *New University Thought* 7 (1): 2–7.[12]

1971. "The Contemporary American Indian Scene." In *North American Indians in Historical Perspective*, edited by Eleanor Burke Leacock and Nancy Oestreich Lurie, 418–80. New York: Random House.

1971. "Erminnie Adele Platt Smith." In *Notable American Women, 1607–1950: A Biographical Dictionary*, vol. 3, edited by Edward T. James, Janet Wilson James, and Paul Boyer, 312–13. Cambridge MA: Belknap Press of Harvard University Press.

1971. "The Menominee Indians: Introduction." *Indian Historian* 4 (4): 32.

1971. "Menominee Termination, or Can the White Man Ever Overcome a Cultural Lag and Learn to Progress with the Indians?" *Indian Historian* 4 (4): 33–43.[13]

1971. "The World's Oldest On-Going Protest Demonstration: North American Indian Drinking Patterns." *Pacific Historical Review* 40 (3): 311–32.[14]

1971. With Eleanor Burke Leacock, eds. *North American Indians in Historical Perspective*. New York: Random House.[15]

1972. "Indian Drinking Patterns." *American Journal of Orthopsychiatry* 42 (4): 554.

1972. "Indians Purchase Land in Manitowoc County in 1856." *Manitowoc County Historical Society Newsletter* 8 (2): 5–6.

1972. "Indian Women: A Legacy of Freedom." In *Look to the Mountain Top*, edited by Robert Iacopi, Bernard L. Fontana, and Charles Jones, 29–36. San Jose: Gousha.[16]

1972. "Menominee Termination: From Reservation to Colony." *Human Organization* 31 (3): 257–69.[17]

1972. "Two Dollars." In *Crossing Cultural Boundaries: The Anthropological Experience*, edited by Solon T. Kimball and James B. Watson, 151–63. San Francisco: Chandler.

1973. "Action Anthropology and the American Indian." In *Anthropology and the American Indian: Report of a Symposium*, edited by James Officer, 4–15. San Francisco: Indian Historian.

1973. "An Aztalan-Winnebago Hypothesis." Unpublished paper. Milwaukee Public Museum.

1973. "Need Justice." *Milwaukee Sentinel*, May 21, pt. 1, 18.

1974. "Comments on Karl H. Schlesier's 'Action Anthropology and the Southern Cheyenne,' and Robert A. White's 'Value Themes of the Native American Tribalistic Movement Among the South Dakota Sioux.'" *Current Anthropology* 15 (3): 294.

1974. "Forked Tongue in Cheek or Life Among the Noble Civilages." *Indian Historian* 7 (2): 28–40, 52, 54.

1975. "Menominee-reservatets ophor og genoprettelse." *Jordens Folk* 11 (3): 97–105.

1975. With Phillip Sidoff. "Mexican Kickapoo Collection." *Lore* 25 (3): 24–29.

1976. "American Indians and Museums: A Love-Hate Relationship." *Old Northwest* 2 (3): 235–51.

1976. "Comments on J. Anthony Paredes's 'New Uses for Old Ethnography.'" *Human Organization* 35 (3): 320–21.

1976. "Laundered Colonial Linen." *Reviews in American History* 4 (3): 365–71.

1976. "Not Built in a Day." *Lore* 26 (3): 3–37.[18]

1976. "The Will-o'-the-Wisp of Indian Unity." *Indian Historian* 9 (3): 19–24.[19]

1978. Foreword to *Keepers of the Game: Indian-Animal Relationships and the Fur Trade*, edited by Calvin Martin, ix–x. Berkeley: University of California Press.

1978. "The Indian Claims Commission." *Annals of the American Academy of Political and Social Science* 436 (1): 97–110.

1978. "Our Most Shameful Passion—Eating." *Milwaukee Journal*, January 8, Sunday Features, 12.

1978. "Winnebago." In *Handbook of North American Indians*, vol. 15, *Northeast*, edited by Bruce G. Trigger, 690–707. Washington DC: Smithsonian Institution.

1979. "Elsie Clews Parsons." In *The World Book Encyclopedia*, vol. 15, 162. Chicago: World Book–Childcraft International.

1979. "The Good, Bad, but Never Indifferent Indian." *Reviews in American History* 7 (2): 163–69.

1980. "How to Take Down a Totem Pole and Have It Too." *Milwaukee Indian News*, June, 3.

1980. "A Papago Woman and a Woman Anthropologist." *Reviews in Anthropology* 7 (1): 119–29.

1980. "Publications of Robert E. Ritzenthaler in *The Wisconsin Archeologist.*" *Wisconsin Archeologist* 61 (4): 497–99.

1980. "Robert E. Ritzenthaler." *Wisconsin Archeologist* 61 (2): 292–97.

1981. "Museumland Revisited." *Human Organization* 40 (2): 180–87.

1981. "Robert Eugene Ritzenthaler, 1911–1980." *American Anthropologist* 83 (3): 607–11.

1981. "Scientist Responds to Creationists' Theories." *Milwaukee Churchman* 91 (4): 6.

1981. "Social Sciences Will Suffer." *Milwaukee Journal*, March 27, pt. 1, 10.

1981. "The Winnebago People." In *First Annual Hochunkgra Days*, 40–43. Tomah WI.

1982. "Indian People." *Wisconsin Academy Review* 28 (2): 3–6.

1982. "Quality Film for TV." *Milwaukee Sentinel*, November 24, pt. 1, 10.

1982. "To Save the Menominee People and Forests." In *Approaches to Algonquian Archaeology: Proceedings of the Thirteenth Annual Conference*, edited by Margaret G. Hanna and Brian Kooyman, 243–52. Calgary: University of Calgary Archaeological Association.

1983. "A Lesson for Curators." *African Arts* 16 (2): 90.

1983. "President-Elect Asks Department Chairs for Help in Promoting Understanding." *Anthropology Newsletter* 24 (2): 16.

1983. "President Lurie Responds." *Anthropology Newsletter* 24 (9): 2.

1983. *A Special Style: The Milwaukee Public Museum, 1882–1982*. Milwaukee: Milwaukee Public Museum.[20]

1984. "A Message from the President." *Anthropology Newsletter* 25 (7): 1.

1985. "Arts Funding: 2 Sides to Coin." *Milwaukee Journal*, November 9, pt. 1, 10.

1985. "Bingo Offers Indians Low-Cost Development." *Milwaukee Journal*, August 11, pt. 4, 7.

1985. "Epilogue." In *Irredeemable America: The Indians' Estate and Land Claims*, edited by Imre Sutton, 363–82. Albuquerque: University of New Mexico Press.

1985. *North American Indian Lives*. Milwaukee: Milwaukee Public Museum.

1985. "Turning 84 and More Vigorous Than Ever." *Anthropology Newsletter* 26 (1): 1, 5.

1985. With Judith A. Gray and Dorothy Sara Lee, eds. *The Federal Cylinder Project: A Guide to Field Cylinder Collections in Federal Agencies.* Vol. 2, *Northeastern Indian Catalog, Southeastern Indian Catalog.* Washington DC: American Folklife Center, Library of Congress.[21]

1985. With June Helm, Sidney Mintz, and Eric Wolf. "American Anthropological Association." In *A Report to the Congress of the United States on the State of the Humanities and the Reauthorization of the National Endowment for the Humanities,* 17–25. New York: American Council for Learned Societies.

1986. "Beaded Twined Bags of the Great Lakes Indians." *Bulletin of the Detroit Institute of Arts* 62 (1): 38–45.

1986. "Money, Semantics, and Indian Leadership." *American Indian Quarterly* 10 (1): 47–63.

1986. With William H. Hodge. "James Henri Howard (1925–1982)." *American Anthropologist* 88 (3): 692–94.

1987. "Collecting Contemporary American Indian Art." *Museum Anthropology* 11 (4): 3–7.

1987. "Getting Facts Straight." *Milwaukee Sentinel,* February 17, pt. 1, 12.

1987. "Han Ola og Han Per: Peter J. Rosendahl's Norwegian-American Comic Strip." *Lore* 37 (1): 26–28.

1987. "Menominee Termination and Restoration." In *An Anthology of Western Great Lakes Indian History,* edited by Donald L. Fixico, 439–78. Milwaukee: American Indian Studies, University of Wisconsin–Milwaukee.

1987. "The Reorganization of AAA and the Nature of the *American Anthropologist.*" *Anthropology Newsletter* 28 (4): 1–16.

1988. "Facts of Indian History Need Repeating." *Milwaukee Journal,* May 11, pt. 1, 13A.

1988. "In Search of Chaetar: New Findings on Black Hawk's Surrender." *Wisconsin Magazine of History* 71 (3): 162–83.

1988. "Recollections of an Urban Indian Community: The Oneidas of Milwaukee." In *The Oneida Indian Experience: Two Perspectives,* edited by Jack Campisi and Laurence M. Hauptman, 101–7. Syracuse NY: Syracuse University Press.

1988. "Relations Between Indians and Anthropologists." In *Handbook of North American Indians,* vol. 4, *History of Indian-White Relations,* edited by Wilcomb E. Washburn, 548–56. Washington DC: Smithsonian Institution.

1989. "Collecting Contemporary Native American Art." *Native Arts Studies Association Newsletter* 6:2–3, 6.

1989. "8,000 Indians Can Call Milwaukee Home." *Milwaukee Sentinel*, April 4, pt. 1, 8.

1989. "Federal Policies Shaped Destinies of State's Tribes." *Milwaukee Sentinel*, April 4, pt. 1, 5, 8.

1989. "Philleo Nash and American Indian People." *Annals of Anthropological Practice* 7 (1): 16–20.[22]

1989. "Readers' Views." *Milwaukee Journal*, May 11, pt. 1, 18A.

1990. "Interim Report, AAA Commission on Native American Remains." *Anthropology Newsletter* 31 (4): 1, 16–18.

1991. "Milwaukee Public Museum: Show Them We're Still Here and Plan to Stay." *Winds of Change* 6 (4): 114–18.

1991. "Reburial Commission Report." *Anthropology Newsletter* 32 (5): 3.

1992. "Major Gift from Potawatomi Bingo to Milwaukee Public Museum." *Anthropology News* 33 (8): 32.

1994. "Winnebago Veterans and the Warrior Tradition." *Ho-Chunk Wo-Lduk* 8 (17): 3–4.

1996. "Milwaukee's Native American Presence in the Period of White Contact." *Milwaukee History* 19 (3): 70–84.

1996. With Paul H. Hass and James P. Danky, eds. "The Society at One Hundred Fifty Years." *Wisconsin Magazine of History* 79 (4): 258–363.[23]

1998. "Fletcher, Alice Cunningham." In *Encyclopedia of World Biography*, vol. 5, 486–87. Detroit: Gale Research.

1998. "Selective Recollections on Anthropology and Indians." *Current Anthropology* 39 (4): 572–74.

1998. With Duane Anderson. "A Lost Art Form: A Case Study of 19th Century Feathered Capes Produced by American Indians in the Great Lakes Region." *Museum Anthropology* 22 (2): 3–16.

1999. "Comments on Douglas E. Foley's 'The Fox Project: A Reappraisal.'" *Current Anthropology* 40 (2): 187–88.

1999. "Sol Tax and Tribal Sovereignty." *Human Organization* 58 (1): 108–17.

1999. *Women and the Invention of American Anthropology*. Long Grove IL: Waveland.

2000. "Black Hawk (1767–03 October 1838)." *American National Biography*. Oxford University Press. https://doi.org/10.1093/anb/9780198606697.article.2000074.

2000. Contributions to *The People of Denendeh: Ethnohistory of the Indians of Canada's Northwest Territories*, by June Helm. Iowa City: University of Iowa Press.[24]

2001. "Ada Deer, Champion of Tribal Sovereignty." In *Sifters: Native American Women's Lives*, edited by Theda Purdue, 223–41. New York: Oxford University Press.

2003. "Fabulous Footwear?" *Science* 301 (5637): 1184.

2004. "June Helm (1924–2004)." *American Anthropologist* 106 (4): 792–94.

2004. "Will C. McKern, Personal Recollections." *Wisconsin Archeologist* 85 (2): 12–16.

2005. Introduction to "That Uniquely Human Pleasure," by June Helm. *Anthropology News* 46 (1): 4–6.

2007. "Making of a Museum Anthropologist." *Anthropology News* 48 (5): 32.

2007. With Ross Hunt. "The Hunt Family's Trip to West Germany to Attend the Bundesgarten Show." *Anthropology News* 48 (2): 20–21.

2009. With Patrick J. Jung. *The Nicolet Corrigenda: New France Revisited*. Long Grove IL: Waveland.

2010. *Love and Other Letters*. Milwaukee: Milwaukee County Historical Society.

2012. "Programmed History." *General Anthropology* 19 (1): 1, 7–9.

2014. With Patrick J. Jung. "Jean Nicolet (Again): Comment on Ronald J. Mason's 'Where Nicolet and the Winnebagoes First Met.'" *Wisconsin Archeologist* 95 (2): 303–7.

NOTES

1. A similar article titled "The Story of Esau and Jacob, Reinterpretation Based on a Peyote-Vision Experience" was listed as forthcoming in the curriculum vitae at the end of Lurie's unpublished doctoral dissertation. It was supposed to have been published in volume 4 of *Badger Folklore* (1952), but this volume was never published, as the journal apparently ceased publication with volume 3.

2. This essay was reprinted under the alternate title "Anthropology and Indian Claims Litigation: Problems, Opportunities, and Recommendations," in *Applied Anthropology: Readings in the Uses of the Science of Man*, ed. James A. Clifton (Boston: Houghton Mifflin, 1970), 199–212.

3. This essay was reprinted with citations in James M. Banner Jr., Sheldon Hackney, and Barton J. Bernstein, eds., *Understanding the American Experience: Recent Interpretations*, vol. 1 (New York: Harcourt, Brace, Jovanovich, 1973), 41–65. It was reprinted without citations in James Kirby Martin, ed., *Interpreting Colonial America: Selected Readings* (New York: Harper and Row, 1973), 36–52.

4. This is arguably Lurie's most famous work, and it was reissued as a paperback edition by the University of Michigan Press in 1966. It was translated

into Italian by P. d'Oro and published by Rusconi Libri in Milan under the title *Donna Lupo di Montagna: Autobiografia di un'indiana Winnebago* in 1989 and 1996. Fabbri, another Milanese publishing house, reprinted this translation in 2006 as part of the series Voci di donne, no. 74. The book was also translated into Polish by Aleksander Sudak and published by Tipi in Warsaw under the title *Górska Wilczyca, siostra Grzmiącego Pioruna: autobiografia Indianki z plemienia Winnebago* in 2012 as part of the series Biblioteka Tawacinu, no. 38.

5. This unpublished paper was the basis for the pamphlet published in 1964 for the Wisconsin Winnebago Educational Conference in La Crosse, under the title *Historical Background of the Winnebago People*, reprints of which were issued in 1965 and 1967. (The 1967 edition appears under the alternate title *The Wisconsin Winnebago People*.) Helen Miner Miller is listed as a coauthor for the 1964, 1965, and 1967 editions, while Nadine Day Sieber is listed as a coauthor only for the 1967 edition. All three editions appear to have been published in Black River Falls by the Wisconsin Winnebago Business Committee.

6. This book was originally published as Roy F. Barton, *Philippine Pagans: The Autobiographies of Three Ifugaos* (London: Routledge, 1938). The 1963 reprint includes a new introduction by Lurie.

7. The original 1965 article listed here was subsequently reprinted in an anthology titled *The American Indian Today*, which is listed under its publication date of 1968. This anthology includes the articles published in the 1965 issue of the *Midcontinent American Studies Journal*, as well as the essay "Historical Background," which was an original contribution to the 1968 anthology and is also listed separately. Lurie served as the editor of the anthology along with Stuart Levine. In 1969 this book received the Anisfield-Wolf Book Award from the *Saturday Review* magazine for its contributions to promoting diversity and racial harmony. The anthology was republished by Penguin Books under the same title in 1970.

8. This article was reprinted for public distribution in Madison, Wisconsin, by the Governor's Commission on Human Rights and in Augusta, Maine, by the State Department of Indian Affairs. Several authors have mistakenly attributed another essay in a later issue of this periodical to Lurie, an article supposedly titled "How Many Americans Are Part of the American Scene?" in vol. 76, no. 2 (February 1967). However, Lurie wrote no essays for *Natural History* other than the article listed here. The article that has mistakenly been credited to her is likely that by Robert L. Bennett titled "New Era for the American Indian," *Natural History* 76, no. 2 (February 1967): 6–11.

9. This 1966 essay was revised and republished in 1999 by Waveland Press as a book, which is also listed separately in this bibliography. The book includes a preface by Lurie that is not found in the 1966 essay.

10. The Wisconsin Historical Society published revised editions of this work in 1978, 1980, and 2002.

11. This article received the William B. Hesseltine Award from the State Historical Society of Wisconsin for the best article published in the *Wisconsin Magazine of History* for 1968–69. It was reprinted as a booklet in 1970 under the alternate title *Wisconsin Indians: Lives and Lands* (Madison: State Historical Society of Wisconsin).

12. This article was reprinted in Morton H. Fried, ed., *Explorations in Anthropology: Readings in Culture, Man, and Nature* (New York: Thomas Y. Cromwell, 1973), 443–48, and later in Jeanne Guillemin, ed., *Anthropological Realities: Readings in the Science of Culture* (New Brunswick NJ: Transaction Books, 1981), 493–99.

13. This article was reprinted as a booklet with the alternate title *Menominee Termination: A Monograph* (San Francisco: Indian Historian, 1971).

14. This article was reprinted in Norris Hundley Jr., ed., *The American Indian: Essays from the Pacific Historical Review* (Santa Barbara CA: American Bibliographical Center–CLIO, 1974), 55–76.

15. This is an anthology that includes an essay written by Lurie, which is also listed separately. The book was reprinted in 1988 by Waveland Press in Long Grove IL, with a new foreword by Lurie.

16. This essay originally appeared as an article in the April 1972 issue of *American Way*, the magazine of American Airlines.

17. An updated, expanded, and revised version of this article was published in 1987 as an essay in *An Anthology of Western Great Lakes Indian History*. Given the substantial differences between these two works, both versions are included in this bibliography.

18. This article was reprinted as a separate work titled *Not Built in a Day*, Publications in Museology, no. 6 (Milwaukee: Milwaukee Public Museum, 1979).

19. This article was reprinted in Robert Hinshaw, ed., *Currents in Anthropology: Essays in Honor of Sol Tax* (The Hague: Mouton, 1979), 325–35.

20. The chapters of this book were originally published as a series of ten articles in *Lore*, the quarterly journal of the Milwaukee Public Museum. The series began in vol. 32, no. 3 (Fall 1982) and continued until vol. 34, no. 1 (Spring 1984), with several issues including two of the articles. The museum published the articles and book as part of its centennial celebra-

tion. The book includes a preface by Lurie and a foreword by Kenneth Starr, the museum's director at the time of publication, which were not part of the original journal series. In the interest of space, the individual articles published in *Lore* are not included in this bibliography. This book received the Gambrinus Award for the best book on Milwaukee history from the Milwaukee County Historical Society, the Publication Excellence Award from the American Association of Museums, and the Book of Merit Award from the State Historical Society of Wisconsin. It was reprinted by the Milwaukee Public Museum in 1992.

21. This volume is one in a set of catalogs that list audio recordings of American Indian music and oral traditions in the possession of federal repositories, such as the National Archives, Smithsonian Institution, and Library of Congress. It also includes information concerning audio recordings in the possession of the Milwaukee Public Museum. Lurie provided information about audio recordings of the Ho-Chunk people, particularly those in the museum's Huron H. Smith Collection. While neither she nor any other contributor was listed as author of any part of the volume, she was especially instrumental in providing information for two sections: "Winnebago Indian Music and Spoken Word: The Paul Radin Collection" (310–22) and "Winnebago Indian Music: The Huron H. Smith Collection" (323–24).

22. This volume of *Annals of Anthropological Practice* was reprinted in its entirety as a separate bulletin with the original pagination found in the journal issue. For Lurie's essay in this bulletin, see Ruth H. Landman and Katherine Spencer Halpern, eds., *Applied Anthropologist and Public Servant: The Life and Work of Philleo Nash*, National Association for the Practice of Anthropology Bulletin, no. 7 (Washington DC: National Association for the Practice of Anthropology, 1989), 16–20.

23. Lurie was one of seventy-three authors who provided essays for this collection celebrating the sesquicentennial of the State Historical Society of Wisconsin. Her essay is found on pages 268–71. It was reprinted in Marlin F. Hawley, *Embracing the Antiquities: Archaeology at the State Historical Society of Wisconsin, A History to 1976* (Madison: Wisconsin Historical Society, 2019), 88–89.

24. This book was subsequently republished under the same title and with the same pagination by McGill-Queens University Press in 2002 and 2009.

CONTRIBUTORS

Grant Arndt, Anthropology Program, Department of World Languages and Cultures, Iowa State University. Email: gparndt@iastate.edu

Dmitry V. Arzyutov, Department of Slavic and East European Languages and Cultures, the Ohio State University. Email: darzyutov@gmail.com

Regna Darnell, Department of Anthropology, University of Western Ontario. Email: rdarnell@uwo.ca, rddrhizome@gmail.com

Judy Daubenmier, American Studies, University of Michigan. Email: jdaubenm@gmail.com

Lena Dávila, Institute of Anthropological Sciences, University of Buenos Aires. Email: davila.lena@gmail.com

Anna Engelking, Institute of Slavic Studies, Polish Academy of Sciences. Email: engelking@ispan.waw.pl

Frederic W. Gleach, Department of Anthropology, Cornell University. Email: fwg1@cornell.edu

Patrick J. Jung, Department of Humanities, Social Science, and Communication, Milwaukee School of Engineering. Email: jung@msoe.edu

Alice B. Kehoe, Professor Emeritus of Anthropology, Marquette University. Email: akehoe@uwm.edu

Nancy Oestreich Lurie, Curator Emerita, Milwaukee Public Museum. Deceased.

Patrícia Ferraz de Matos, Institute of Social Sciences, University of Lisbon. Email: patricia.ferraz.matos@gmail.com

Leila Monaghan, Department of Anthropology, Northern Arizona University. Deceased.

Larry Nesper, Department of Anthropology, University of Wisconsin-Madison. Email: lnesper@wisc.edu

James M. Nyce, Department of Anthropology, Ball State University. Email: jnyce@rocketmail.com

Richard J. Preston, Professor Emeritus of Anthropology, McMaster University. Email: prestonr@mcmaster.ca

Vilma Santiago-Irizarry (translation), Department of Anthropology, Cornell University. Email: vs23@cornell.edu

John David Smith, Department of History, University of North Carolina at Charlotte. Email: jdsmith4@uncc.edu

Sylvia Angelica Smith. Email: jdsmith4@uncc.edu

Joshua Smith, Shuasmi Research. Email: actionanth@gmail.com

Dawn Scher Thomae, Curator of Collections/Senior Collection Manager, Milwaukee Public Museum. Email: thomae@mpm.edu

Sandra Tolosa, Institute of Anthropological Sciences, University of Buenos Aires. Email: cahsandra@gmail.com

www.ingramcontent.com/pod-product-compliance
Lightning Source LLC
Chambersburg PA
CBHW022259280326
41932CB00010B/915